Imperial Heights

For Mark Mazower,

with best wishes and the
remotest of echoes from Salonica
(by way of Héhard),

Eric J___r

FROM INDOCHINA TO VIETNAM: REVOLUTION
AND WAR IN A GLOBAL PERSPECTIVE
Edited by Fredrik Logevall and Christopher E. Goscha

Imperial Heights

Dalat and the Making and Undoing of French Indochina

—

Eric T. Jennings

UNIVERSITY OF CALIFORNIA PRESS

Berkeley   Los Angeles   London

Parts of chapters 7, 8, and 13 appeared in previous form in *Historical Reflection/Réflexions historiques, Modern Asian Studies,* and *The Journal of Vietnamese Studies,* respectively.

University of California Press, one of the most distinguished university presses in the United States, enriches lives around the world by advancing scholarship in the humanities, social sciences, and natural sciences. Its activities are supported by the UC Press Foundation and by philanthropic contributions from individuals and institutions. For more information, visit www.ucpress.edu.

University of California Press
Berkeley and Los Angeles, California

University of California Press, Ltd.
London, England

Library of Congress Cataloging-in-Publication Data

Jennings, Eric Thomas.
    Imperial heights : Dalat and the making and undoing of French Indochina / Eric T. Jennings.
        p.   cm.—(From Indochina to Vietnam : revolution and war in a global perspective ; 4)
    Includes bibliographical references and index.
    ISBN 978-0-520-26659-9 (cloth : alk. paper)
    1. Đà Lat (Vietnam)—History.   2. Đà Lat (Vietnam)—Colonial influence.   3. France—Colonies—Asia—History.   I. Title.
    DS559.93.D3J46   2011
    959.7'6—dc22   2010042773

Manufactured in the United States of America

19   18   17   16   15   14   13   12   11
10   9   8   7   6   5   4   3   2   1

This book is printed on Cascades Enviro 100, a 100% postconsumer waste, recycled, de-inked fiber. FSC recycled certified and processed chlorine free. It is acid free, Ecologo certified, and manufactured by BioGas energy.

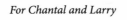

For Chantal and Larry

CONTENTS

ILLUSTRATIONS

FIGURES

MAPS

Cities have received relatively little attention in the history of the French empire in general and that of colonial Indochina in particular. True, Philippe Papin and William Logan have provided us with excellent overviews of Hanoi, and Vietnamese scholars such as Tran Huy Lieu, Tran Van Giau, and Dang Phong have penned engaging accounts of Hanoi and Saigon through the centuries. However, one searches in vain for an account of the colonial city—its social, political, cultural, and economic dynamics, as well as its postcolonial transformations.

With *Imperial Heights: Dalat and the Making and Undoing of French Indochina*, Eric Jennings provides just such a study. Rather than focusing on Saigon or Hanoi, Jennings gives us the first detailed account of the city of Dalat from its colonial conception in the late nineteenth century to its national promotion as a major tourist destination today. This city, located in the cool highlands of lower central Vietnam, was home to the first French hill stations, where colonizers came to seek relief from the stifling tropical heat. Such stations existed in various parts of the colonial world, and scholars (including Jennings himself) have written widely on their sociopolitical significance.* *Imperial Heights* is the first examination of the French equivalent in Indochina. And a remarkably rich history it is, including in the later years. Dalat was the city Vichy wanted to turn into the political capital of Indochina, the place where Governor General Jean Decoux lived during World War II. During the Indochina conflict, Bao Dai ran the Associated State of Vietnam from there, and the city

---

* Eric T. Jennings, *Curing the Colonizers: Hydrotherapy, Climatology, and French Colonial Spas*, Durham, N.C.: Duke University Press, 2006.

was affected in important ways by both the French war and the American war that followed. Yet, as Jennings shows, it was well after the fighting ended that Dalat experienced some of its most important socioeconomic and cultural changes. Over the past two decades, as Vietnam has moved from a communist command economy to a remarkably vibrant market-oriented one, Dalat has adjusted accordingly, to the point that national authorities now celebrate its colonial and royalist past as part of their strategy of attracting tourists to this city's beautiful hotels and hill stations. Although Jennings uses Dalat to demonstrate the "making and undoing of French Indochina," he concludes by showing how colonial nostalgia remains an important part of the making of Dalat today.

By focusing on a city and adopting a *longue durée* approach, Eric Jennings provides a new and powerful take on French colonial history and that of Vietnam. He has written an exciting and original book, expertly researched and beautifully crafted, one certain to appeal to general readers and specialists alike. We are proud to have it in our series.

Fredrik Logevall, Cornell University
Christopher Goscha, Université du Québec à Montréal
17 September 2010

ACKNOWLEDGMENTS

This project could never have been realized without the Social Science and Humanities Research Council of Canada. SSHRC supported multiple research trips to Vietnam and France, and provided time off to write. The Canadian Institute for Health Research funded essential research for chapters 1 and 3. A Victoria College Senate Research Grant and a Spooner Fellowship made possible further research at the French colonial archives and in Vietnam. A JIGES research award took me to sources in Zürich.

A special thank-you goes out to my research assistants, Nick Bentley, Chi Thuc Ha, Katie Edwards, Mairi MacDonald and Thuy Linh Nguyen. Thuy Linh Nguyen sifted through Vietnamese periodicals, newspapers, and poetry, as well as Vietnamese-language secondary sources, translating Dalat-related material into English.

Over the years, a community of colleagues has guided me towards sources on Dalat. Fruitful leads were provided by Hazel Hahn, Christopher Goscha, Agathe Larcher-Goscha, Laurence Monnais, Hy Van Luong, Nhung Tran, Christina Firpo, Penny Edwards, David Del Testa, Robert Aldrich, Gilles de Gantès, Pascal Bourdeaux, Patricia Lorcin, Stein Tønnesson, David Biggs, Sébastien Verney, Caroline Herbelin, Philippe De Villers, Erica Peters, Pierre Brocheux, Alain Ruscio, Aline Demay, Rebecca Rogers, Ellen Furlough, Mathieu Guérin, Mitch Aso, Charles Keith, Jean Michaud, and Mike Vann. Mr. Jacques Veysseyre opened his father's papers to me. J. P. Daughton, Tina Freris, Christopher Goscha, Peter Zinoman, Raphaëlle Branche, David Marr, Owen White, Emmanuelle Saada, Panivong Norindr, Alice Conklin, Elspeth Brown, Paul Cohen, Chantal Bertrand-Jennings, Larry Jennings, and an anonymous reader all provided valuable feedback on chapter drafts or presentations that later turned into chapters. Librarians and archivists on several continents have helped along the way: I wish to extend my thanks to Toronto's Interlibrary Loan Services, and to the staff at Cornell's Kroch Library, perched atop a pine-covered hill overlooking a lake that calls to mind Dalat. *Merci* as well to Olivia Pelletier, Lucette Vachier, and Jacques Dion at the ANOM, to Stéphane Kraxner at the Institut Pasteur, Sister Sieffert at the Congrégation Notre-Dame, to Bernard Mouraz at the Gendarmerie Archives, and to Daniel Weiss at the GTA in Zürich. Finally, thank you to Professor Phan Huy Le for his assistance with libraries and archives in Vietnam.

At UC Press, I would like to thank Niels Hooper, Eric Schmidt, Suzanne Knott, and Caroline Knapp for seeing this project through to fruition, and William Nelson for map production. My gratitude also goes to Celia Braves for the index.

Parts of chapters 7, 8, and 13 appeared in previous form in *Historical Reflections / Réflexions historiques, Modern Asian Studies,* and *The Journal of Vietnamese Studies,* respectively. I thank all three journals for their permission to reprint parts of these articles.

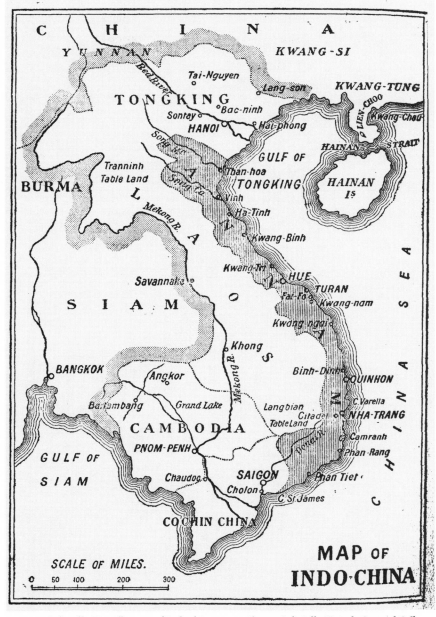

MAP 1. Gabrielle Vassal's map of Indochina, 1910. From Gabrielle Vassal, *On and Off Duty in Annam* (London: Heinemann, 1910).

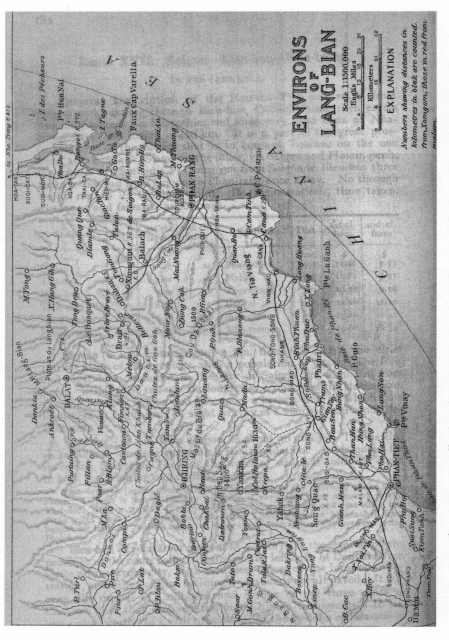

MAP 2. Environs of Lang-Bian, *An Official Guide to Eastern Asia*, vol. 5 (Tokyo: 1920). Courtesy of Kroch Library, Cornell University.

Introduction

Dalat is a singular, unexpected, almost incoherent place. Imagine Davos, Aspen, or Chamonix in Vietnam. Nestled high in Vietnam's rugged interior, 150 miles northeast of Ho Chi Minh City (formerly Saigon), this colonial-era mountain resort features hundreds of quaint French regional villas, the golf course of Vietnam's former emperor, a grand luxury hotel, colonial-era boarding schools, pagodas, and monasteries—all set against tall pine trees and artificial lakes. Neither the surroundings, nor the architecture, nor the climate square with what most tourists expect to find in Vietnam.

Yet Dalat has its followers. Before my second trip there, a Vietnamese-Canadian travel agent expressed envy at my destination. "Ah, Dalat, my first kiss," he sighed. The sentiment is widely shared, as droves of Vietnamese newlyweds have ascended to Dalat in recent years, earning it a reputation as "Vietnam's wedding and honeymoon capital" and "Vietnam's romantic getaway."[1] The resort elicits similar reactions among many French settlers, officials, and even their descendents. Websites reunite long-lost classmates from Dalat's Lycée Yersin. A large percentage of Indochina's French population either was born in Dalat, vacationed in Dalat, or was at some point schooled in Dalat, a site long considered the colony's nursery. To this day, Dalat cultivates nostalgia and breeds a sort of wistfulness.

For a city of some 160,000 inhabitants, Dalat today has achieved an almost mythical and remarkably varied reputation: it is at once a site of romance, education, privilege, leisure, pilgrimage, and science—the latter thanks to its U.S.-built experimental nuclear reactor. Why this fascination, and how do colonial and postcolonial perceptions of the place differ? There can be no doubt that Dalat's tourist office is counting on colonial villas and an almost-Swiss pastoral landscape to draw tourists. How can this be in Communist Vietnam? Dalat, I would argue, is so enigmatic in large part because it almost uniquely encapsulates the colonial era, and its contested legacy and memories. Indeed, Dalat captures the colonial era, and exudes a colonial aura, precisely for the reasons listed above: it seemed and still seems out of place in Vietnam, its ratio of colonial to postcolonial architecture is probably the highest in Vietnam, and its climate and décor run contrary to tropical expectations.

Dalat's colonial founders had intended it to serve as a clone of France. So remarked British traveler Norman Lewis in 1951, as the colonial era entered its twilight: "Here," he noted with obvious contempt, "a forlorn attempt has been made to create a sub-alpine atmosphere, but it remains nothing more than an uninspired imitation. . . . It looked like a drab little resort in Haute-Savoie."[2] This is a recurring theme. The 1998 edition of a popular French guidebook series *(Le guide du routard)* considered Dalat the equivalent of "Barbotan-les-Thermes in Indochina, Aix-les-Bains in a rice bowl, and Bagnoles-de-l'Orne in a conic hat"—in other words, a local Vietnamese riff on a French spa-town. However, in the 2006 edition of the same guidebook, the verdict had inexplicably changed: "No, Dalat is not Barbotan-les-Thermes in Indochina nor Bagnoles-de-l'Orne in a conic hat. But it is a *ville paysage* designed in the colonial era by the French in Cochinchina, who suffocated of Saigon's damp tropical heat."[3] Perhaps irate Barbotanian and Bagnolian readers had written in between the two editions, to complain, like Lewis, that Dalat did not pass muster as a replica of their hometown. To heap scorn on the inexactitude of the copy is of course to miss the point entirely. Dalat at once created, blurred, and confounded boundaries. The hill station's role as an ambiguous piece of France in Southeast Asia would be crisply encapsulated by a French officer during the First Indochina War: Dalat, he remarked, felt "so close, yet so far away."[4]

This "French replica" was not created in a whim of fancy or as some curio. Rather, its establishment—and the cloning exercise it implied—was considered an absolute necessity. Through Dalat, colonialism could be made possible, precisely by carving out an oasis in the tropics, a respite from disease, a separate and new center of power in a minority nonethnic Vietnamese region, a site of French bourgeois domesticity, in short a colonial tabula rasa.

This book offers a historian's equivalent of a thick description of colonial-era Dalat, before considering some of the site's postcolonial legacies.[5] The hill station was as critical to the creation of Governor Paul Doumer's modern Indochinese federation in 1897, as it was to colonialism's last gasp—the Dalat conferences of 1946. Because the site was at once paradigmatic of, and central to French colonialism in Indochina, because it played a crucial role in the emergence, course, and demise of French colonial Indochina, I consider its many facets. These range from the vast—Dalat's role as a pyrrhic capital of the colony—to the seemingly minute—disease, sanitation, urban plans, colonial comforts.

Some of the issues tackled in this work are strikingly current: climate fears, colonial violence, mosquito-transmitted tropical epidemics, attempts to control an eth-nically diverse territory from a safe zone, the periodic repatriation of imperial troops, colonial divide and rule strategies, and colonial tourism, to mention only a few. Yet this book remains an attempt to understand a specific place, time, and process, which is to say the apogee of European imperialism. Dalat reveals as much about colonial priorities as it does about colonial anxieties, divisions and fractions, sensibilities, and strategies. It affords us an incomparable window onto the actual workings of empire. It shows how a "healthy" and "safe" space was transformed into a site of power, and how that site of power, in turn, bent and morphed from its initial conception into something quite different. Through Dalat, one can compare grand imperial schemes against results on the ground, imperialist rhetoric against local practices.

Though it was halted in its tracks in 1954, French colonialism in Indochina remains hotly debated to this day. In North America, the historical field was long distorted by the centrality of the Vietnam War, often seen as marking either the inexorable rise of Vietnamese communism, or the equally preprogrammed collapse of French "hegemony." This is beginning to change, as a new generation of historians gain access to archives and challenge both teleological and hegemonic interpretations. In France, the fiftieth anniversary of the battle of Dien Bien Phu (1954–2004), and rancorous debates over how to teach and remember empire have left a deep imprint on the field of colonial studies.[6] In a recent opinion piece on Indochina in *Le Monde,* writer Antoine Audouard pleaded for a middle ground between "hypocritical contrition" and "glorifying the civilizing mission."[7] Indeed, recent public debates over empire are notable mostly for their polarization and their superficiality. Caricatures prevail. On one side, colonial lobby groups imbued with nostalgia insist on rehabilitating colonialism, through an emphasis on schooling, road construction, or hospitals. On the other side, a second camp systematically conflates colonialism and genocide, or presents colonialism as unchanging and monolithic.[8]

The story of Dalat exposes the limitations of these perspectives. Dalat was not a product of French hegemony, so much as an admission of vulnerability. It was certainly a meticulously planned site and a controlled environment—yet one shaped more by internecine conflict, competition, and even chaos, than by any single vision. And what original visions one can discern, predicated on lingering climatic determinism, appeared already to some at the time to be deeply flawed. Moreover, events and practices at Dalat often ran at odds with early, lofty blueprints for a highland colonial utopia. Terrifying violence accompanied the hunt for Indochina's hill and rest station. Yet, Dalat subsequently emerged as a playground for French and Vietnamese elites alike. Far from faltering in the 1940s and 1950s, its importance rose steadily on the eve of, and following the French defeat. The hill station in fact emerged as the Indochinese federal capital in 1946, and served as an unofficial seat of power until 1955. It represented a potent symbol of domination and control, yet already by the 1930s, its weaknesses were exposed. Apologia focused on hospitals or roads does not hold water either: Dalat's hospitals were strictly segregated, its roads the bitter fruits of forced labor. Dalat was literally built on the backs of Vietnamese and indigenous minority laborers and peasants. This site of leisure and power exposes at once fault lines, practices, contradictions, ironies, and legacies of empire.

Without aspiring to total history, I do hope to restore the texture of French colonial Indochina and postcolonial Vietnam by telling quite different stories through a single site. This is at once a local and a global history: Dalat's founders drew inspiration in Brazilian, Swiss, Dutch, British, and American colonial models, and from previous experiments in Japan. German, French, and British scientists exchanged insights on colonial altitudes. Nonetheless, Dalat tells a different story from most other hill stations and mountain resorts the world over; far from being reduced to some imperial "curio" immediately following decolonization, it retained critical significance well into the 1960s. Its capacity for reinvention is especially noteworthy: Dalat served at once or alternatively as a military site, a Eurasian space, an educational center, a safe zone enabling European domesticity, an elite Vietnamese ideal, a religious refuge, and a critical point of contact with Indochina's ethnic minorities.

Mentalities and epistemologies are central to the first chapters of this book: I wish to shed light on sensibilities, anxieties, institutions, and networks that both gave rise to and drove Dalat—in short to the context in which Dalat was founded and grew. They remain, it seems to me, the keys to understanding colonialism in all of its complexity. Practices, accommodations, and compromises are the focus of the book's central chapters, as this controlled product of French colonialism came unraveled shortly after reaching its zenith during the Second World War. Finally, colonialism's afterlife—the ways in which colonial-era schemes colored postwar Southeast Asia and were recycled, abandoned, or reconditioned after and during colonialism's gradual demise (far more gradual than analyses centered on Dien Bien Phu suggest)—will be considered in the book's final chapters.

Previous generations of historians were often hamstrung not just by deterministic frameworks, but also by sources. When I first began working on this project, few outside Vietnam knew what had become of the Résidence supérieure d'Annam (RSA) archives—miles of documents concerning the region of Central and Southern Vietnam where Dalat is located. With the help of colleagues, I uncovered them in Ho Chi Minh City. Since the research for this book was completed, the RSA archive has come full circle, and has been moved to Dalat itself. This book is thus the fruit of detective work in Hanoi, Ho Chi Minh City, Dalat, France, Switzerland, Canada, and the United States. Some of these archives had until very recently been completely closed.

Most important, Dalat makes for a compelling and evocative story, one that does not require a neocolonialist fresco, a Manichean agenda, or a single overarching theory, to tell. Some of the characters I bring to the page are the stuff of novels: the Swiss scientist who cracked the bubonic plague's secret and "founded" Dalat, and a deranged officer who went on a murderous rampage to beat him to the prize; an Italian elephant hunter called upon to scout the site; a British adventuress cum tiger hunter; the Vietnamese laborers who went on strike while toiling on the Lang-Bian road; the Paris municipal councilor who later became Dalat's first mayor; the world-renowned architect who displayed his sketches of Dalat at Le Corbusier's Congrès international d'architecture moderne in 1933; the last emperor of Vietnam, who made Dalat his sanctuary; or the Viet-Minh daughter of Dalat's head school inspector. All left an imprint on this protean marker of empire in Southeast Asia, which today gathers throngs of Vietnamese honeymooners, victims of nostalgia, and Ho Chi Minh City middle class on weekend getaways.

Escaping Death in the Tropics

DISEASE AND CLIMATE

At the turn of the twentieth century, a French soldier noted in awe and consternation that the cemetery adjoining Saigon's military hospital was "more populous than a large European city." This was all the more troubling, wrote the infantryman, since Saigon had only been French since 1859, and the city's garrison certainly never surpassed two thousand men at any given time.[1]

The health of French soldiers, officials, and settlers had been of paramount concern to the colonial administration in Indochina since the earliest days of conquest. As this soldier's testimony suggests, there was reason to worry. During the first phase of invasion, French naval medics passed harsh judgment on the climate of Cochinchina—the southernmost part of modern-day Vietnam—a region France conquered between 1858 and 1862. After having spent a total of four years there, in 1876 Dr. Auguste-Pascal-Marie Danguy des Déserts declared Cochinchina's climate so vile that he doubted Europeans could ever acclimatize to it.[2] The more modestly named Dr. A. Léon concurred. He had participated in the conquest of Cochinchina in 1858 and 1859. Léon described the climate around Saigon as nothing short of "murderous" and pronounced its soil "unhealthy." The region around Tourane (modern-day Da-Nang) elicited a similar, if not harsher, verdict. Léon recalled of his time there: "the climate is tough, the region unhealthy, the temperature excessive and the food lacking in variety."[3]

Dr. François-Eugène Bernard, who served in the same campaign, eventually dedicated a dissertation to determining how Cochinchina's climate impacted European troops. His findings likewise gave cause for alarm. He observed that troops hailing from Northern France survived only a matter of days in these climes before needing to be repatriated. Algerian units fared no better, victims of a humid climate un-like that of their homeland, but also of fatal nostalgia, which purportedly hindered recovery from the inevitable fevers. It was fevers, Bernard acknowledged, that felled most servicemen. Europeans in the advanced "anemic" stages of malaria could count on a single, slim, hope: repatriation. "One cannot cure anemics here in Cochin-china," Bernard affirmed. "These wretches will all perish unless a prompt return to France can wrench them from certain death."[4]

To be sure, Bernard, Danguy des Déserts, and Léon were unaware of the root cause of these fevers. The clouds of mosquitoes Bernard describes as tormenting French sailors were not even considered prime suspects. One of the great ironies behind Dalat is that this sanatorium founded on climatic determinism was estab-lished the very year—1897—in which the British scientist Ronald Ross, then work-ing in India, debunked climatic determinism by establishing malaria's mosquito vec-tor. Doctors like Bernard, Léon, and Danguy des Déserts were certainly mistaken to think of Cochinchina's climate, soil, or even latitude as the cause of death. Yet they grappled with the pathogen, whatever it might be, recognizing that it was both "very powerful" and "very rapid in its effects." Fundamentally, they were not far off the mark on one central point: Casualty rates were unspeakably high. Bernard tells of a unit of 319 artillerymen that arrived in Cochinchina in 1862; four years later, only fifty remained.[5] Bernard and Léon's esteemed colleague, Dr. Mondot, argued that Europeans could in no case hope to survive more than four and a half years in Cochinchina.[6] Bernard considered this optimistic. In his experience, Europeans died after on average two years in the region. He consequently recommended two years as the absolute maximum duration for a military posting to the area.

Disease—and not just malaria—actively shaped French priorities in Southeast Asia from the outset. The ravages of dysentery, in particular, prompted the French military to abandon Tourane in 1860, and to fall back on Cochinchina.[7] Yet the South offered little respite from disease. In 1861, two years after Saigon had fallen to the French, 11.5 percent of military personnel perished from illness in Cochin-china.[8] That same year, Saigon's main clinic alone registered 2,774 patients, out of whom 170 perished and 371 were urgently repatriated. In the words of Dr. Fontaine, Cochinchina's terrifyingly high figures established "[its] deserved reputation for unhealthiness."[9] Cholera, too, was ravaging the South. In northern Cochinchina (at Baria) and southern Annam (Qui Nhon) in 1882, a cholera outbreak claimed sev-eral European lives and stirred fear as high as the governor general's office.[10]

Doctors continued to battle high death rates well into the late nineteenth century. Between 1861 and 1888, the mortality rate among military personnel in Cochin-china only dipped below those of troops in British India for six out of twenty-seven years (in 1869, then again between 1873 and 1877).[11] More anecdotally, Dr. Fon-taine, a *médecin principal des colonies,* perished from tropical disease between the time he submitted his article on death rates in Cochinchina for consideration, and its publication—a bad omen even for those familiar with journal backlogs.[12] His own untimely demise, coupled with the statistics he presents, belie his claim that the "progress of hygiene" was rendering Indochina hospitable to colonial troops. To be sure, mortality levels in the early 1880s had dropped to 2 percent of French naval troops stationed there. Yet they crept once again above the 2 percent bar in 1896. What is more, the 2 percent mortality rate from disease amongst colonial troops in Indochina between 1883 and 1888 compared unfavorably with 0.97 percent for Algiers, 1.1 percent for Tunis, and 1.5 percent for Oran in 1895. France's Southeast Asian territories remained twice as murderous as its nontropical North African ones.[13]

If anything, colonial administrators chose some of the grimmest points of reference in tropical health to describe Indochina. Thus, an 1892 report by Prosper Odend'hal on the valleys of Khanh-Hoa and Kinh-Dinh, in the hinterland of Nha-Trang (Annam) reads: "The soil is excellent, the water abundant year round. Unfortunately, here one can apply the proverb we learned in Guyana: 'One could become rich in a year, were it not for the fact that one dies in six months.'"[14]

Death was only part of the story. According to an 1888 account, no European left Cochinchina completely unscathed. After a few weeks, Frenchmen reportedly took on a "yellowish hue"—likely a symptom of hepatitis. As their health decayed, they reportedly grew increasingly irritable.[15] Comportments and civilities too fell victim to the climate. Cochinchina "survivors" pondered the degenerative and debilitative cost of their time in the colony.

REPATRIATION

According to Dr. Fontaine, a significant number of fatalities occurred in the process of transporting patients. Within Indochina, many perished en route to the main hospitals. Fontaine attributed this to cost-cutting measures that had eliminated express river vessels, leaving patients with only slow, multipurpose steamers. These made frequent stops before reaching Saigon's hospital.[16] Repatriation to France constituted the preferred option for the seriously ill. This preference stemmed almost entirely from the prevailing notion that a change of "air" could cure disease. Simply put, the method of choice for overcoming tropical afflictions was to escape the tropics as quickly as possible. An 1853 French guide to tropical hygiene and medicine already advocated two possible routes: latitudinal movement, also known as repatriation; or the simpler, cheaper alternative of altitudinal movement within the colony, in other words, seeking higher ground on location.[17] In Indochina over the course of the 1890s, governors, military leaders, and doctors would debate the merits and drawbacks of these two types of escapes from the tropics.

Baron Albert d'Anthouard de Wasservas has left a vivid account of a return trip aboard a medical evacuation vessel. In 1885, the baron departed Saigon after the standard three-year posting of the era. He was not rushed home early, despite having lost twenty-seven kilos (sixty pounds) to the notorious "Cochinchina diarrhea," one of the banes of the colonizers. His fellow passengers aboard the medical transport ship *Bien Hoa* included 250 seriously sick, bed-bound patients—soldiers and administrators for the most part—as well as numerous convalescents, and 150 Vietnamese prisoners, resistors to colonialism, bound for a penal colony in distant Guyana. The long voyage to France via the Suez Canal was punctuated by the death of a naval infantryman, buried at sea. D'Anthouard, conversely, saw his health improve during the crossing. He invoked the reasoning of the time to explain this turn of events: "one says of colonial diseases that while they worsen in their land of origin, they improve when one changes airs or climes."[18]

However, the repatriation policy fast proved problematic both practically and financially. Already in 1876, a medic noted that the ship-voyage home took a terrible toll on seriously ill patients. As a result, he asked, "After this arduous crossing, how many [Cochinchinese administrators and settlers] will see only Toulon's Saint-Mandrier hospital as their last piece of France?"[19] Contrary to d'Anthouard's received wisdom, death often struck upon reaching French shores, although as Gilles de Gantès observes, these "deferred deaths" are hard to tabulate.[20] The toll was also terrifying on board the evacuation ships themselves, even with teams of doctors on hand. Alexandre Kermorgant reports that casualties on repatriation vessels from Cochinchina soared at thirty to forty deaths per transport in the 1860s, before gradually tapering off to some six to eight deaths per voyage.[21]

In 1886, the Breton naval doctor Lazare-Gabriel-Marie Palud defended his thesis on the *Vinh-Long*, a medical transport ship serving Indochina exclusively. Palud provided vivid details about conditions on board: two live milk-cows were along for every voyage, and bore responsibility for providing fresh milk to sick children; elsewhere on board, a chamber containing seven to eight barrels of ice kept perishables cool until Saigon, where an ice plant resupplied the ship.[22] Palud observed that at least twelve fits of malarial fevers occurred on each westward crossing. Malarial patients were immediately wrapped in blankets and served *thé punché*, tea spiked with rum. In dire cases, they were injected with quinine sulfate.[23] Palud witnessed radically different mortality rates on his three crossings. In the winter of 1884 he observed nine fatalities on board, which translated into 2 percent of all passengers; in the summer of 1885 the mortality rate had spiked to thirty-three people, or 6 percent of passengers, twenty-two of whom had succumbed to "chronic diarrhea"; on his third trip, 1885–86, it dropped to three dead or 0.5 percent of passengers.[24]

The scale of repatriation operations was remarkable for the era, the costs involved daunting. In 1894, 19.6 percent of naval infantrymen, and 37.6 percent of naval artillerymen were repatriated for health reasons—a total of 290 men from those branches of the navy alone. Two years later, 19 percent of naval infantrymen, and 40 percent of naval artillerymen posted in Indochina were repatriated to France—

340 men in all. Between 1890 and 1896, dysentery had been responsible for a third of all such repatriations, and malaria for a quarter.[25] These figures account only for naval personnel rushed home outside of the regular rotation table. Administrators too were being repatriated in droves, though they are not reflected in Dr. Fontaine's statistics. Although admittedly risky, in the absence of an Indochinese sanatorium, repatriation was still considered one of the few alternatives to certain death.

Until the late 1890s, the state contracted out transport to and from Indochina to two companies, the Messageries maritimes and the Compagnie nationale de navigation. Hoping to both save on the tremendous costs of this operation and improve hygienic conditions on board, in 1895 the Ministry of the Colonies studied the possibility of creating a new Indochina line, under direct state control. In their discussions with steamship companies, the Ministry of the Colonies insisted that every ship include a hospital equipped with 150 beds. Here was another sign that horizontal repatriation continued to account for a large part of all returns.[26]

Yet like Kermorgant, Palud was convinced that the trips had become on average less murderous than twenty-five years prior, when it had been common for fifty or sixty patients to perish per ship. Palud imputed these earlier rates to an unspoken policy of repatriating the seriously ill from their deathbeds, so as to lower Indochina's already horrifying morbidity rates and reassure the public (casualties at sea were registered in a separate column).[27] Thereafter, doctors successfully lobbied to send home only those likely actually to survive the passage.[28] Among those favoring such a reform was the hygienist Georges Treille, who insisted on counting all those who died on return voyages in the colony's own death column.[29] Palud could see only one alternative to the repatriation system, which condemned the seriously ill to perish in Indochina or on the way home: a highland sanatorium in Indochina itself.[30] In the words of historian Robert Aiken, who has studied the hill stations of British Malaya: "one rationale for the development of hill stations was that they obviated the necessity of a long and costly journey home by providing more accessible places with a benign, home-like climate that promised physical and emotional renewal."[31] This option appeared increasingly appealing in light of the physical and financial costs of repatriation.

DR. MÈCRE'S YOKOHAMA SANATORIUM

Already in 1876, Dr. Danguy des Déserts bemoaned that Cochinchina possessed no sanatorium. Unlike Guadeloupe or Réunion islands, whose hill stations and spas allowed colonials to reinvigorate on location, Cochinchina offered no such site where "exhausted personnel . . . can regain strength so as to confront new hardships."[32] In most of France's overseas territories, wrote Danguy des Déserts, colonial life was marked by a cycle of sufferings and reprieves. At present, Cochinchina offered only suffering. The French naval, colonial, and medical establishments would soon set their sights on reprieves from "murderous" Cochinchina, which in Danguy des Déserts' words, "[presents] only swampy flatlands where we find the same insalubrity."[33]

Dr. Kermorgant, an authority in tropical medicine with special expertise in the field of colonial sanatoria, claimed that "from the very beginning" French officials had sought an appropriate site for a convalescence center in Cochinchina—in other words a salubrious, cooler site bearing some resemblance to a European climate. Unfortunately, he wrote, the mountains of Cochinchina itself had proven too low— Ba-Dinh stood at a mere 884 meters (3,000 feet), and Chua-Chang a paltry 600 meters (2,000 feet). In the absence of readily accessible, local, cool microclimates, those whom Kermorgant termed "fatigued functionaries deemed insufficiently ill to be repatriated to France, and who seemed likely to return to their posts after a short while" were routinely steered to Yokohama, Japan.[34] Kermorgant had been careful to identify a very specific category. The severely ill were still to be sent to France without question. However, the "fatigued" or anemic could be reinvigorated in short order through treatment in Japan—indeed, to some extent, simply through osmosis of Japan's temperate climate.

The French sanatorium in Yokohama had its origins in the Sino-French war of 1883–85. At the time, Admiral Amédée Courbet had ordered wounded and sick soldiers evacuated to Yokohama, where the doctor of the French legation, Louis Mècre, treated them at his small hospital on the French concession.[35] In 1886, the Ministry of the Colonies took interest in Mècre's achievements, noting that the remarkable recovery of soldiers should be attributed to "his fine care, and to Japan's favorable climate."[36] With most of Courbet's fleet reassigned to other operations in 1886, both the Ministry of the Colonies and the French authorities in Indochina saw an opportunity. In 1887, Louis Mècre founded a sanatorium in Yokohama, financed by the government of Cochinchina, which provided an annual subsidy. Soon, the contract with Cochinchina was folded into Mècre's previous deal with the French navy, with both agreeing to share the sanatorium's annual subsidy of 10,000 francs. In 1893, the governor general of Indochina, Jean-Marie de Lanessan, renewed the contract, increasing the annual subvention. De Lanessan's sympathies for Mècre's endeavor are hardly surprising, given that the governor had previously served as naval doctor himself.[37] The new sum of 15,000 francs was absorbed by Indochina's various parts, with Cochinchina paying six-thirteenths, Annam and Tonkin three-thirteenths each, and Cambodia one-thirteenth (the Indochinese Union was founded in 1887, but Laos would only be incorporated into it in 1898). Presumably, this formula was intended to reflect the relative degree of actual use of the sanatorium.[38]

How had French authorities in Indochina been persuaded to outsource healthcare to Japan?[39] For one thing, local budgets actually stood to save by sending patients 4,338 kilometers (2,700 miles) from Saigon to Yokohama, rather than ten thousand kilometers (6,271 miles) to France. More significantly, Yokohama was considered a healthy, proto-European environment. In 1897, the Minister of Foreign Affairs drew the following portrait of the Yokohama site: "situated on a hill dominating the sea, exposed to sea breezes, under a temperate clime, this land is particularly salubrious."[40] The French ambassador to Japan extolled the location's marine "saline emanations." Yokohama lent itself admirably, he explained "to a rest center where soldiers and functionaries of all ranks, weakened by Indochina's climate, could regain their strength and rebuild their fragile health." Yokohama would spare colonial troops and functionaries "the tribulations of the long and painful crossing of the Indian Ocean and the Red Sea." How many might have been saved, asked the ambassador, "had they benefited earlier from a temperate clime, rather than perish on the voyage home?"[41] The ambassador betrayed an ulterior motive when he expressed hope that the sanatorium would also foster deeper ties between Japan and French Indochina. Still, the sanatorium's main asset was its potential as a panacea, one capable of saving numerous lives. How? Reimmersion in temperate climes and exposure to maritime breezes constituted the two chief remedies. Underpinning this scheme was the prevalent logic of the sanatorium and of "changing air"—immortalized by Thomas Mann and Marcel Proust, and practiced from Cabourg to Coney Island.

To be sure, the Ministry of the Colonies had emphasized both Japan's climate, and Mècre's "fine care." Mècre had indeed proven himself during the Sino-French conflict. Of the ninety-seven patients he received at that time, he boasted that only three had succumbed. He claimed to have cured all the gravest manifestations of "diseases from hot climes," including dysentery, anemia, and malarial fevers.[42] His sanatorium offered hydrotherapy—then a French method of choice in the war against tropical disease—as well as leisure, thanks to its billiard room and comfortable living quarters.[43]

Dr. Mècre's relations with the government of Indochina soured overnight in December 1897, when Indochina's new governor, Paul Doumer, refused to honor his end of the contract. The Mècre files reveal the doctor's understandable outrage. They also shed light on the reasons for this 1897 volte-face. The Minister of the Colonies presented the chief motive for this abrupt decision as follows. He explained to one of Mècre's powerful defenders, Senator Gauthier that "the new sanatorium which is to be constructed in Indochina proper will render unnecessary the sending of [sick] officials to Japan."[44] The Yokohama scheme, a compromise between repatriation to France and a sanatorium in Indochina proper, had run its course.

A SANATORIUM IN INDOCHINA

Unbeknownst to Mècre, plans for an Indochinese sanatorium had been brewing for at least a decade, though years of debate remained ahead to decide on specific locales. In 1887, Indochina's Conseil supérieur de santé had reported to the governor general on the need for local convalescence centers, dedicated to treating "our Indochina functionaries." The recommendation was solidly buttressed by several rationales, which the Conseil supérieur de santé de la Marine echoed in January 1888. For one thing, the "possibility for our officials to recover locally would bring notable savings, avoiding us costly repatriations."[45] This must have been music to a governor's ears. Indochina's fiscal deficit had begun to soar in the 1880s.[46] Then too, humanitarian principles dictated that the sick be treated locally, given how many perished on the return trip through the Gulf of Aden and the Red Sea.[47] Yokohama could only provide an unsatisfactory semisolution, since patients still faced at best a twelve-day ocean crossing to reach it.[48] As a result, those too sick could not be sent there, and those not sick enough avoided undertaking the voyage altogether. Finally, emulation of a colonial rival undoubtedly constituted the main driving force for this project. In the words of the Conseil supérieur de santé de la Marine: "France in Indochina owes its officers, soldiers, functionaries, and sailors what England has so successfully achieved in India for its army and its local administration."[49] Throughout its existence, Dalat would be compared to hill stations the world over, but especially to those of the British Raj.

The pendulum had begun to swing towards an Indochinese hill station in 1887. However, the choice of its future site remained hotly contested, and would remain so well into the early years of the twentieth century. Indochina's Conseil supérieur de santé contented itself with recommending that a technical subcommittee determine multiple sites of convalescence based "upon the rules of hygiene."[50]

Alexandre Kermorgant provides hints of a failed experiment on a hill near Baria, southeast of Saigon, which unraveled abruptly because of high casualty rates in 1887.[51] The Baria failure showed that high altitude did not suffice, argued Kermorgant. According to him, "admittedly altitude is beneficial to some patients. But one must, first and foremost, remove trees and cultivate the lands. Otherwise, one runs the risk of placing a future convalescence site on a hotbed of malaria, one all the more intense because the virgin tropical ground will have to be stirred up [by construction]."[52]

Kermorgant's article appeared in the *Annales d'hygiène et de médecine coloniales* in 1899, just over a year after the same journal had reported Ronald Ross's conclusive demonstration (1897) that the *Anopheles* mosquito constituted malaria's sole vector of transmission. What is more, mosquito transmission had been suspected for some time before Ross, with the French doctor Alphonse Laveran first advancing a mosquito hypothesis in 1884, after having uncovered malaria's parasitic nature in 1880.[53] Yet Kermorgant remained frozen in the miasmic mold; malarial emanations, he feared, could be stirred from the fertile, virgin soil of the tropics after it had been disturbed. At Baria, but even more so at Dalat, French colonial doctors would negotiate and shift between miasmic and modern paradigms, between accumulated climatic knowledge and the new realities of bacteriology and microbiology. In these contests over Indochina's sanatoria, climatic determinist, telluric, and miasmatic models would prove remarkably resilient.

YERSIN'S TRAVELS AND THE SEARCH
FOR INDOCHINA'S SWITZERLAND

In July 1897 Governor Paul Doumer ordered his subordinates to compile information on possible locations for a "mountain sanatorium where functionaries and settlers alike will be able to rebuild their strength, whereas today they are obliged to return to France to the greatest detriment of our budget and their business." Doumer recognized the nefarious reputation of Indochina's highlands, but he attributed it to "the state of abandonment in which the natives have left them." Echoing Kermorgant, Doumer advocated a "preliminary deforestation" of the chosen location, "so that one will be able to find in the mountains of this land the vivifying air which one finds the world over at high altitudes." Most of the Résidents supérieurs and other high-ranking officials responded with lists of possible seaside resorts. Only in Annam did authorities read Doumer's memo closely enough—or perhaps only there did they dare brave the interior's terrible reputation—to investigate several highland options, across Annam.[54]

The scientist cum explorer Alexandre Yersin responded promptly to Doumer's request for information on a mountain sanatorium. The Swiss-born doctor's legendary reputation stems largely from his discovery of the bacillus of the bubonic plague in 1894—immortalized as *Pesta yersinia* in his honor. He was a dedicated Pasteurian, having worked as assistant to Louis Pasteur and Emile Roux in 1886, and later founded a laboratory in Nha-Trang that would become a Pasteur Institute in its own right in 1905. Trained in Switzerland, Germany, and France by the likes of Pasteur and Robert Koch, Yersin's scientific credentials and achievements have made him a household name in France, Switzerland, and Vietnam: founder of Hanoi's medical school, introducer of the Brazilian rubber tree variety to Indochina, and of course breaker of the plague's secret. Yersin's curiosity led him not only to touch on all fields from botany to biology and medicine, but also to achieve breakthroughs in each of these areas. So tell us, quite convincingly, the various hagiographies of Yersin, one of the few colonials in whom French and Vietnamese seem to find common admiration, since his name and likeness survived the many street-name and statuary purges in Vietnam since 1945.[55]

In addition to Yersin's logs and copious notes, the Pasteur Institute in Paris was recently entrusted with his voluminous correspondence with his Swiss mother. Through this source, a more nuanced portrait of the scientist emerges—perhaps simply a more human one. It reveals that in 1893, after having clashed with escaped Vietnamese political prisoners on his descent from the Lang-Bian to the coast, Yersin attended the execution of their rebel leader with morbid wonder. He insisted on photographing the condemned leader, named Thouk. He later noted that the rebel's head was only severed on the fifth saber blow.[56] In 1895, in an altogether different setting, Yersin quipped of Réunion island's population: "the creoles are lazy . . . the negroes and mulattos try to take on European airs—how unoriginal and un-picturesque."[57] The scientist's filial devotion led him to collect "curious objects" for his mother on his trips amongst Indochina's highland minority peoples.[58] In 1894, in the midst of his travels through the Indochinese highlands, he reported with disappointment that he would have to hand over this bounty to the Museum d'histoire naturelle in Paris. The museum's director, he explained, served on the dreaded mission commission, and would certainly not approve of artifacts collected on official business being handed out as family presents.[59] Finally, Yersin was no colonial liberal, or advocate of reform. He complained privately, in correspondence with a fellow explorer, of Governor de Lanessan's purportedly naïve policy of "Annamitophilie."[60] None of these snapshots detract from Yersin's achievements in the field of plague studies. They do, however, remind us that Yersin served not simply the Pasteur Institute, the Messageries maritimes, and science; he was also deeply implicated in French imperialism, even in its most extractive and oppressive dimensions.

This inquisitive, brilliant scientist took considerable interest in Doumer's project. He responded to the governor on July 19, 1897, presenting material on Annam's highlands that he had collected on his three treks through the region in 1892, 1893, and 1894.[61] The diaries contained hints of an idyllic site for Doumer's sanatorium. Interestingly, Yersin's missions of 1892 through 1894 had not actually been aimed at finding a suitable locale for a health station. Rather, he subsequently recalled that his goals had involved "reporting on the [interior's] resources, on the possibility of raising animals, studying forest resources, and seeking exploitable metals in the mountains."[62] Yet Doumer would subsequently mine the journals of these expeditions for a sanatorium site. Fortunately for the governor general, Yersin had recorded nearly everything that caught his eye.

"A vast, barren plateau featuring rounded hills."[63] So reads Yersin's journal entry for June 21, 1893. Yersin had stumbled upon the expansive Lang-Bian plateau. Three days earlier, Yersin had caught his first close glimpse of the Lang-Bian summit, overlooking the plateau by the same name, where Dalat would later rise.[64] He put pencil to paper, faithfully capturing its contours in the margins of his text.

On his return to the Lang-Bian in February 1894, Yersin recorded other useful details. Two days' walk from Lang-Bian, he already registered morning temperatures of 2 degrees Celsius. No doubt the imposing mountains, and these temperature readings, reminded Yersin more of his native Switzerland than of the Vietnamese coast where he had lived since 1891. On the Lang-Bian plateau he observed graceful deer or elk that roamed freely. He remarked that they were "the true kings of this strange land."[65] The map Yersin drew of his itinerary shows that he crossed much of the Lang-Bian plateau, from south to north.

At Dankia, a village on the edge of the Lang-Bian plateau, Yersin noted that he stood at an effective border. Beyond here, he commented, indigenous minorities no longer paid a tax to Annam. In fact, the chief at Dankia purportedly refused to lead Yersin any further; villages beyond were considered "independent." Here Yersin touched on one of the unstated objectives of his three voyages. "Governor Lanessan," he writes, "had given me license to assure the Ma Moï that the Protectorate would care for them, that one day a Frenchman would come to protect them." He deemed his second trip a success because "the Moïs now know that we exist, that we must protect them, and they would not understand any indifference on our part."[66]

Why this insistence on protecting the diverse, ethnolinguistically distinct minorities of Annam's mountainous interior, pejoratively termed "Moï"—meaning "savage" in Vietnamese? And from whom did they supposedly need to be protected? The answer, as it happens, was from the very auxiliaries Yersin had brought with him. In 1894 Yersin had traveled with fifteen *linh*, Vietnamese militiamen, and countless "coolies." On his 1892 mission, Yersin had recruited some forty porters and two Vietnamese servants.[67] On his 1894 mission, no fewer than fifty-four porters accompanied him.[68] It was ethnic Vietnamese like them, Yersin believed, who had long oppressed highland minorities, save for a few stubbornly independent peoples beyond Dankia. Yersin claims to have seen this dynamic of oppression at work within the columns of his own exploration missions. He relates: "I witnessed unbelievable events: simple coolies having ascended the [Lang-Bian] plateau, passed for [Annamese] district chiefs, sent by mandarins. They then proceeded to collect 'tax' by means of lashings."[69] Time and again, Yersin asserted that the Lang-Bian lay beyond Vietnamese civilization. He later recalled: "there are no relations between the inhabitants of this region and the Annamese. A few Cambodians, elephant and rhinoceros hunters for the most part, sometimes pass through to trade. But even they are rare. Most Moïs have never even seen a gun."[70] Several principles had been coined. The mountainous interior lay beyond Vietnamese control, and hence offered unique advantages to the colonizer. Highland minorities required protection, indeed liberation, and could easily be swayed to support the French cause. Here was an ethnopolitical opportunity, alongside the averred climatic one.

Had Doumer and his staff read Yersin's reports more critically, they might have spotted clouds on the horizon. For one thing, Yersin's diaries are replete with cases of indigenous minorities resisting the scientist and his schemes. Indeed, for his third mission (1894), Yersin requested and obtained the support of a small unit of militiamen, fifteen in all, so as to avert the confrontations he had encountered on his two previous trips. On the cusp of this third trip, Yersin confided to his mother, "I am starting to know these nasty savages, the Bihs and the Radés, who have already caused me so many miseries."[71] As for the healthfulness of central Annam's mountains, careful investigation would have revealed it too to be dubious. In February 1893, at the tail end of his second expedition, a desperate Yersin had wired Hanoi. He reported suffering from "violent pernicious fevers, resulting from [his] last trip through the mountains."[72] The description is entirely compatible with malaria. On his expedition the following year, Yersin did not place his faith blindly in the cool nights at higher altitude. He wrote his worried mother that he still weighed his regular 60 kilos (132 pounds) and was in perfect health, thanks to "a daily dose of quinine."[73]

In 1897, after carefully reading the scientist's diaries, Doumer responded enthusiastically, even though the Lang-Bian remained only one of several possible locations at this point. He once again called upon Yersin, entrusting him with a mission to the Lang-Bian plateau. This time, he had a single, clear objective: "study the location of a sanatorium that the governor general would like to establish in the mountains."[74] Two months later, Yersin boasted to his mother that he had persuaded the governor to "create a sanatorium in the Lang-Bian." This was certainly accurate, although Doumer reserved the right to establish other hill stations, and had yet to determine which would serve as Indochina's chief sanatorium.

In the Lang-Bian mountain range, Yersin explained to his mother, "there is a vast, barren plateau of some four hundred square kilometers in the middle of which rises a mountain. The plateau's average elevation is of 1,500 meters [5,000 feet] above sea level; the mountain surpasses 2,000 meters. I believe the region to be healthy because it is barren." Then Yersin betrayed his secret hope: "[The Governor has ordered] the construction of a road and railroad that will lead to the plateau directly from Nha-Trang. All of this will increase Nha-Trang's importance!"[75] Revealed here are not only Yersin's miasmic theories (in the miasmic model, decaying organic material played an important role in transmitting malaria, and the more barren an area, the better), but also a hidden agenda: that the scientist's beloved town of Nha-Trang, home to his laboratory, would grow in importance thanks to the future Lang-Bian sanatorium.

LANG-SA

If Yersin emerged as Doumer's most trusted local health advisor, Alexandre Kermorgant remained the sanatorium expert. In June 1898, Kermorgant was asked to assess Yersin and Doumer's plans for transforming the Lang-Bian plateau into a hill station. He began by bemoaning that no local Simla or Darjeeling—the famed hill stations of British India—had been found in the previous decades. This had led wealthy French settlers in Cochinchina to seek reinvigoration in the British colony of Singapore, and French officials and troops to find treatment at Yokohama, at great cost to the administration. At last, the Lang-Bian plateau promised to remedy this situation. Thanks to the Lang-Bian, wrote Kermorgant, "the sanatoria problem in the Orient has been resolved, which will ease the burden on state funds." All stood to gain according to the optimistic Kermorgant: the soldiers, settlers, and administrators who could sojourn there, and the administration whose coffers would benefit in equal measure.[76]

Doumer, the future president of France, had strongly endorsed the sanatorium project—though he still remained vague about its precise location. In April 1898, he had stressed to the Minister of the Colonies the "high importance" that he ascribed to the project, given the "significance of this enterprise for French colonialism in Indochina." He reiterated his goals: finding a salubrious plateau on which Europeans could enjoy "vivifying air, a temperate climate, analogous to some extent to Southern Europe's, and capable consequently of restoring their health and vigor, altered by the humidity and heat of the lowlands."

A host of sites were considered, based on recent expeditions and consultations with explorers. Bavi, near Hanoi, was ruled out because "woodland fever" seemed to overcome all who stayed there. Doumer considered the Tonkin's natural sanatorium solution to lie in China, in the Yunnan, which would soon be connected to Indochina by rail, but which presented the disadvantage of lying outside French borders. Instead, Doumer focused on Annam, where several sites seemed propitious. Certainly, the Lang-Bian had much to offer. The Lang-Bian, he opined, combined all of the necessary conditions: sufficient altitude, water supply, fresh air, and breezes.[77] Other regions within Annam still held promise, including the hinterland of Tourane (Da-Nang), where explorations for a hill station were about to begin.

To convince the Minister of the Colonies, Doumer cited outside opinions. Indochina's inspector of agriculture, Jacquet, who had been sent to examine the Lang-Bian's potential for sustaining European fruits and vegetables, declared: "I can barely contain my enthusiasm at the sight of this wonderful region." Proof of the land's healthfulness, insisted Jacquet, could be found in the highland minorities indigenous to the plateau. "They are robust and strong," he wrote, "next to the emaciated peoples of the valleys." Enter another witness. Jacques de Montfort, a world traveler and legendary marksman who had visited the Lang-Bian as a tourist, reported: "It is impossible to find a more pleasant temperature than on this plateau; the air is very dry, and a gentle breeze blows day and night."[78] Doumer concluded with a flourish. Not only could the Lang-Bian become "a site of rest and comfort for tired settlers and administrators," it could one day become an administrative hub or even a de facto capital, and a military base where troops could be kept fresh and ready for combat.

Doumer dubbed the Lang-Bian's future sanatorium "Lang-Sa," which he understood to denote "French town" in Vietnamese (from Phu Lang Sa).[79] Here, in other words, stood not only an ideal sanatorium site, but also a future French administrative hub. Its advantages were many: buffered from Vietnamese centers of power, nestled in healthy mountains, offering a vast expanse for future constructions, climatically akin to Southern France, and surrounded by minority peoples allegedly seeking French intervention.

Doumer's fascination with the Lang-Bian plateau was anything but incidental. He hoped to exploit Indochina's handful of "temperate and healthy regions." "May they be populated with settlers," implored Doumer, "and we will indestructibly establish both civilization and French sovereignty over this part of the Far-East."[80] Thus, hills stations held the key to perpetuating the French presence in, and domination over, Indochina. Such was the grand vision of Paul Doumer.[81]

The general principle of associating altitude, power, and health, had been firmly established. Details, however, had yet to be ironed out. Doumer kept his options open, realizing that Indochina's vast distances might call for several hill stations, spread out between Tonkin and Southern Annam. His 1897 memo to administrators had urged them to consider all healthy highland sites for a possible sanatorium. In this process, Doumer came to rely upon some of the intrepid travelers who had trekked the mountains in the 1890s.

INDOCHINESE CONTEXT: 1897

Starting in July 1897, Doumer positioned teams of explorers in their starting blocks. Their finish line was Indochina's highland sanatorium. So far, we have followed only one of their itineraries, Alexandre Yersin's; in the following chapter, we will turn to his chief competitor, Victor Adrien Debay. Clearly, Doumer assigned a high priority to this race, since he initiated it within months of taking office.

The year 1897 proved fateful for the colony, or rather the Indochinese union, as it had been known for a decade. Paul Doumer's nomination to the post of governor general that year marked a sea change. One of his predecessors, de Lanessan, had advocated the respect of Indochina's many cultures, had championed a form of indirect rule, and even considered reversing the division of Annam and Tonkin— a partition that had torn Northern Vietnam away from the Nguyen dynasty in Hué. He had guaranteed the rights of the protectorates. In contrast, Doumer's mandate involved creating a strong central government—the Gouvernement général de l'Indochine. Accordingly, in 1897, Doumer founded Indochina's direction of finance, as well as its *régies*, or state monopolies. He stripped the Nguyen as well as the Cambodian monarchy of much of their power. Mostly, Doumer set into motion a massive increase in the size of the colonial administration. By 1900, Indochina's ratio of European officials to total population already dwarfed that of British India and the Dutch East Indies.[82] Soon the number of European functionaries across Indochina would soar from 2,860 in the year Doumer took office, to 5,683 in 1911.[83] According to one source, Doumer ushered in "a great era of bureaucracy."[84]

Most of Doumer's objectives depended on the success of a sanatorium or hill station. With Europeans already perishing from disease at high rates, doubling the size of the European administration could only be justified by creating a site for periodic "cures."

As for carving out a French space in the Annamese interior, this decision was either tributary to Doumer's 1897 reforms, or vice versa. Under de Lanessan, only Cochinchina—a colony rather than a protectorate—could have even been considered for such a project. We have seen that Cochinchina's highest altitudes were deemed inadequate for a sanatorium. In fact, de Lanessan had favored the Yokohama option, a sanatorium that lay on a clearly defined French concession. The new plan to create a French convalescence site in the protectorate of Annam signaled a clear shift in the French relationship with the Nguyen dynasty. Such were the broader geostrategic stakes that Doumer pondered in 1897 as he dispatched columns of explorers into Annam's rugged interior.

Conceding a manifest fragility, French colonial doctors in nineteenth-century Indochina resorted to desperate and costly measures: repatriation and term limits on the length of stay in the colony. Colonial officials were acutely aware of the high morbidity rates Europeans suffered—rates so high that medics could barely write a paper on the topic and hope to see it published in their lifetime; so high that the administration tried to distort them by shipping the dying back to France so as to have them count as lost at sea. Desperation and a firm belief in the toxicity of Indochina's climate drove the costly and bizarre attempt to evacuate sick administrators to distant yet clement Japan. With the advent of Paul Doumer, and the French government's commitment to create an unusually strong administrative presence in Indochina, new, more practical and economic solutions needed to be found. Advocates of colonial sanatoria adroitly channeled a web of fears—of the climate, of mysterious fevers and emaciating digestive disorders, and even of indigenous peoples themselves—to justify a seemingly utopian project: the creation *ex nihilo* of a European health center, or even a French city, high atop the "uncharted" mountains of Annam.

Murder on the Race for Altitude

THE MISSION

The utopian project of finding and establishing a colonial mountain refuge had a dark side. It also did not focus solely on the Lang-Bian; rather colonial authorities scoured all of Indochina searching for the ideal site for Indochina's main hill station, and later mandated a network of ancillary hill stations. Though situated further north in Annam, the saga of Victor Debay's hill station mission constitutes a key to understanding the mentalities that went into making Dalat, because it sheds light on some of the brutal methods, the competition, and the urgency, even madness, associated with the search for a colonial highland sanctuary.

At this story's core is the relationship between empire, health, violence, and labor. In 1900 and 1901, Victor Adrien Debay, a captain with years of experience in the Annam highlands, cut a swath of destruction and death as he carried out Governor Doumer's orders to find a second suitable site for an Indochinese hill station, this one within reach of Tourane (modern-day Da-Nang) and Hué. Depending on the captain's findings, the site might one day rival or supplant the Lang-Bian as Indochina's prime sanatorium. How did this hill station imperative shape or condition the murderous bedlam wrought on Vietnamese and highland minorities alike? Through the perpetrator's trial, we will ponder the rampage both in its possible uniqueness and in the broader context of colonial power relations, and ultimately, contemplate some of its root causes.

Colonial sources evoke two competing columns set in motion by Governor Paul Doumer to find the optimal site for an Indochinese hill station. One was dispatched to southern Annam, the other to central Annam. The two-pronged effort was nothing short of a race to uncover French colonial Indochina's salvation: healthy places where Doumer's dream of a large administration and flourishing settler colony could take root. The first column was led by the scientist Alexandre Yersin, the second by a captain, Victor Adrien Debay. As they prepared to set out on their respective missions, few clues hinted which of the two sites would ultimately become Indochina's prime rest center, its nexus of leisure and power.

Indeed Yersin and his competitor departed on relatively even footing, although the famed Swiss scientist admittedly got off the mark several years earlier. As a result, buzz about the Lang-Sa / Lang-Bian site had reached the halls of the Ministry of the Colonies in Paris before Debay's expedition had even been gathered. The colonial press reported in April 1901 that a mission had set out in January of that year to sleuth for a hill station site in Central Annam.[1] The reality was somewhat more complex. Governor Doumer in person had apparently named Debay to head an exploratory mission in February 1900. No doubt Doumer was drawn to the fact that, like Yersin, Debay had conducted long treks through the Annamese and Laotian interior in the 1890s. The captain had spent some 750 days hiking through the mountainous terrain, in 1894, 1895, 1896, and 1897.[2] For this February 1900 expedition, Debay was accompanied by a number of other officers, each placed in charge of prospecting in different areas of the Annamese interior. Their instructions were as clear as they were specific. The future hill station ought to be located within a 150 km radius of Tourane.[3] The site needed to surpass 1,200 meters in altitude, to feature a southeastern exposure and dry, swamp-free ground, yet possess water reserves. It had to be situated "in the middle of pine forests in a pleasant locale," and be easily accessed from Tourane and Hué.[4]

In December 1900, Governor Doumer, frustrated at finding so few other sites besides the Lang-Bian, bade Debay to lead a new mission in search of a hill station. This time, Lieutenants Becker, Decherf, and Venet joined Captain Debay. As with the previous mission, they relied heavily on those they termed indigenous porters, translators, coolies, laborers, and servants. This motley crew left for the mountains for this second mission in February 1901.[5]

The spirit of competition between hill station explorers remained strong, their sense of purpose intense. Reflecting on the massif in Central Annam, Debay declared it "perhaps even better than the [upper] Donnaï," where Yersin had been conducting his own reconnaissance.[6] Like Yersin, Debay was naturally convinced of his mission's importance. "Acclimatization," he wrote in a 1904 article about his assignment, "is never perfect." White people, he argued, gradually succumb to the heat and humidity of the tropics. Their character, he wrote ominously, "becomes more nervous, their emotions more extreme and less pleasant." To this climatic shock, there was "but one remedy: flee its causes." Hence, he explained, the necessity for colonial hill stations, although he added pointedly, "a complete cure would also require the action of moral factors that no sanatorium can provide, and that can only be found in one's homeland." Indeed, he noted, no matter how useful the sanatorium, it could only forestall an eventual repatriation to the metropole.[7] In a sense, these passages contain little by way of original insight: Debay repeated the received, and generally pessimistic, wisdom of his time with respect to the acclimation of Europeans in so-called tropical zones. Yet the author's inflections also suggest a deeply personal experience of the colony's deleterious effects, and of possible courses for salvation.

THE PERPETRATOR

Kurtz's character in Joseph Conrad's *Heart of Darkness* was not just the stuff of fiction. After Parisian investigators tried to elucidate the mass death wrought by two rogue officers, Voulet and Chanoine, in their rampage across Central Africa only two years prior to Debay's mission (1898), they ultimately concluded that the men had gone insane because of the African heat.[8] Debay seems to have implied something similar in his 1904 article, to explain his spate of crimes, which were admittedly on a smaller scale than Voulet and Chanoine's. Yet the mercurial Debay's files suggest that demons haunted him long before he reached the tropics.

Victor Adrien Debay was born on August 28, 1861 in the village of Serzy-et-Prin, near Reims. The son of Jean-Marie Adrien Debay and Louise Clotilde Eilisa Delamarck, he was not born into wealth. He joined the army as an entry-level soldier in 1882, at age 21. The French military of the 1880s was both reeling from defeat at the hand of Prussia in 1870, and deeply involved in a quest for redemption overseas, in Africa, Southeast Asia, and the Indian Ocean. Debay finished his training with a good ranking, placing 144th out of 406 cadets. Thereafter, he rose steadily through the ranks: he entered the Saint-Cyr officer school in 1886, and achieved the rank of lieutenant in the *infanterie de marine* in 1891, before ascending to captain in 1898. At some point in this process, no doubt before serving in the military, he earned a university degree.[9]

Despite these promotions, certain stains marred Debay's file. His dossier reveals that in 1884 he waited for a fellow soldier to fall sick, before pouncing on him and throwing him to the ground repeatedly for having allegedly disrespected him some time before.[10] Debay reached Indochina in May 1890, and was first posted in Cochinchina. By October 1890, he was transferred to Tonkin, which was in a state of war. In April 1891, his superior drew a balance sheet of Debay's qualities and faults: "This officer was given a poor grade in Cochinchina. He has been full of zeal and energy since arriving in Tonkin, especially on campaign, where he has shown remarkable bravery; he is almost fearless. . . . He is moreover well educated, with a university degree in arts and sciences. However, he is compulsively active, and his character exceedingly nervous, not well adjusted."[11] A portrait emerges of a fearless fighter, possessing a hair-trigger temper, and increasingly prone to fits of rage.

In 1894, Debay shows up once again in colonial records, this time pestering the administration of Annam and of Indochina to fund his travels to the mountainous interior of Annam. A lettter from the interim governor of Indochina, Léon Chavassieux, to the Résident supérieur d'Annam, dated September 14, 1894, hints that Debay concocted these explorations himself. It certainly concludes that the lieutenant should not receive financial support for them from the colonial administration. Indeed, the correspondence reveals that both ex-Governor de Lanessan and the Minister of the Colonies had decided on previous occasions not to support Lieutenant Debay's adventures. If he wished to pursue them, he could, but they underscored the ruinous expenses necessary for such an expedition. Among these the governor listed the costs of feeding and paying the column of porters, the escort and the interpreter Debay had requested.[12] This further fleshes out Debay's character: in addition to his temper, the lieutenant had an established reputation as something of a loose cannon, intent on quixotic adventure on his own terms.

THE CRIMES

When investigators in Tourane got hold of the Debay case in late 1901, they were flooded with literally hundreds of testimonies from ethnic Vietnamese and highland minorities alike, attesting to the captain's pattern of brutal, murderous behavior, and his terrifying, impulsive ways. In a letter to the head prosecutor in Hanoi, the *juge de la paix*, Tricon, drew up a list of some of the captain's worst offenses: the death by beating of a "coolie," Nguyen-Van-Chieu, in 1897; the death by beating of another "coolie," Nguyen-Van-Nieu that same year; the death by beating of a farmer, Le-Van-Si, in 1901 during the expedition to find a hill station in the Bana area; the death by beating of the highland minority man, Dinh-Vi, during that same mission; the death by beating some years earlier of Nam-Au, another farmer; arson leading to death, committed on a host of houses and one pagoda in Quan-Nam province; the severe beating between 1897 and 1901 of at least seventy-one other "coolies."[13]

The forms that this violence took—Debay had for instance dragged one of his victims by the hair down a mountain, while simultaneously beating him—led Tricon to term the acts especially "barbarous."[14] In almost every case, the cause of Debay's outbursts was either unknown, or altogether trivial—mostly annoyances and misunderstandings.[15] Debay, for instance, appears to have expected all of his interlocutors to speak French, and became enraged when they did not. Thus, on the Bana hill station expedition, he beat a highland minority man on the head for not understanding a French-language question.[16] His irritation did not stop there. On a separate occasion, when a porter on the route to Bana moved too slowly for his taste, Debay punched him violently in the nose, causing major bleeding. Furious that this did not help pick up the pace, Debay ordered two minority men to beat the porter with sticks, while he kicked the forlorn man. The 26-year-old victim would require a month's bed rest, and still bore the scars at the time of his testimony.[17]

The case against the captain could have been stronger still but for the fact that witnesses fled, and that Tricon's jurisdiction did not extend beyond Annam. Among other reports that could not be confirmed were the summary shooting of highland minorities who had disturbed Debay during a nap, and the torture of a village chief so as to obtain information. Countless crimes could not be corroborated or catalogued. When investigators reached the hill station site around Bana to collect testimonies, villagers fled upon hearing the name Debay.[18]

A "Debay method" emerges from these reports. Again, it bears some resemblance to the famous Voulet-Chanoine episode, insofar as forced recruitment, pillage, terror, and abductions were central to Debay's modus operandi. Those termed "coolies" in the written transcripts and reports were so only in Debay's mind. Most of them were in reality torn from their fields or houses, and forced to work for Debay for no remuneration. The official translator recorded this as "requisitioning" in the record of evidence.[19] One witness, a highland minority village chief named Huynh So, attested: "I am very old [the colonial scribe noted that the witness looked "in his 60s"]. When the Captain came, he stayed four days in my village, in the 6th month of the Vietnamese calendar of this year. He asked me to take him into the mountains myself. I told him I was too old, but would do so anyways. . . . After telling me to go faster, he took a stick and hit me repeatedly. I turned to avoid the blows, so he threw me on the ground and kicked me."[20] This typical incident took place during Debay's hill station expedition, in 1901. Debay no doubt deliberately targeted a village elder and chief, in a bid to send a hierarchical and terrifying message about coolie recruitment. Debay also insisted, in this instance as in others, that indigenous people of his choosing guide him on his expedition. Geographical information gathering had a long history in colonial contexts, and traditionally involved either an exchange of goods or money; European cartographers in particular had for centuries relied on indigenous informants to collect local knowledge.[21] Yet although Debay's mission lay at the intersection of reconnaissance and cartography, his approach was far more direct: he commandeered those he deemed influential to literally lead him to his goal, against their will.

Similarly, Debay's notions of hospitality and shopping would be equally foreign to most of us. Nguyen Van Deo, a 39-year-old farmer in Pho-Nam, testified that Debay ordered him to receive him at home. Debay quickly lost patience at not having been brought a lamp, and proceeded to lash his involuntary host forty-eight times with rattan.[22] On another occasion, during the expedition to lay a path to the Bana hill station, Debay relentlessly beat conscripts, burned their homes, shot their livestock, destroyed their rice supplies, and imposed penalties to be paid in pork, poultry, rice, and tobacco, without ever giving laborers a salary.[23] When later pressed on his motivations for this conduct, Debay would rest his argument on the scarcity and reticence of labor, and on the sacrosanct nature of his mission.

THE HILL STATION IMPERATIVE, LABOR, AND MADNESS

In his own writings, Debay constantly invoked his missions, his zeal, bravery, and devotion to a higher cause—in this case the Bana hill station as a panacea for Indochina. In his rebuttal to Tricon's accusations, sent from France in May 1902, Debay explained first that the laziness and ill will of Vietnamese auxiliaries accounted in part for the reports of abuse against him. Between long passages railing against his own enemies in the colonial administration and in the army, Debay betrayed some of the choices he faced in his hill station expeditions. Less concerned than Yersin about triangulations of power between highlanders and ethnic Vietnamese, Debay dispensed beatings indiscriminately. Yet, he explains, he was especially compelled to use force and coercion when it came to finding ethnic Vietnamese porters and coolies to accompany him into the mountains. He elaborated, "I frequently had to requisition coolies to conduct work or to ensure transport in the mountains. Annamese dislike being requisitioned in general; they are even more hostile to it in the mountains where fever strikes them often. It was thus more or less impossible to recruit volunteers, despite the high salaries I offered them."[24] Like Yersin, Debay encountered stiff resistance to mountain expeditions. And like the Swiss scientist, he never once deduced that the highlands' enduring reputation for ill-health might bode poorly for the French colonial health station that was to be constructed there.

Most of Debay's crimes were connected in some way to the recruitment of laborers. In a 1904 book on the colonization of Annam, Debay lamented that existing dispositions for recruiting laborers in Annam fell well short of what might be expected. The current system, of either relying on local chiefs or of negotiating directly with individuals was, in his words, "very poor, and upsetting for all involved: the settler, who only receives irregular and mediocre work from natives, . . . the coolies, who prefer to remain in their rice fields and villages, . . . the village notables who are stripped of laborers, and the *résident de province,* who is flooded with complaints."[25]

As he set out on the two hill station expeditions (1900 and 1901), Debay confronted the labor question head-on, in his own impulsive way, by hijacking Vietnamese and highland minorities alike, leaving behind him a swath of devastation. The method had probably been honed during his earlier travels in 1894, undertaken despite the administration's refusal to fund his mission.

Roughly half of Debay's many recorded crimes occurred on the Bana expeditions. Debay appears to hint at the reasons for his increasing recourse to violence, recognizing at one point his "needless violence and regrettable brutality."[26] The heavy price paid by his own entourage was, according to Debay, taking a toll on his mental health. Several lower-ranking officers on his second hill station mission had to abandon course. Lieutenant Vennet fell sick with fevers, and was urgently repatriated to France, as a dire case. The same fate awaited Lieutenant Becker, while Lieutenant Decherf actually perished, not from the fevers that were in fact tormenting him, but from a timber mishap during bridge construction on the path to the site of the future hill station.[27]

It was precisely at Decherf's funeral that Debay gave a speech so bitter and bizarre that many officials and military colleagues present chided him for it. Amongst other things, Debay apparently named himself and the deceased as some of the few soldiers on risky missions whose higher goal was nonmonetary. In a remarkable self-diagnosis in his 1902 letter, Debay deduced that neurasthenia (an ill commonly attributed to the colonies), as well as hypochondria, dysentery, insomnia, and the "struggle against everyone and everything" all conspired to render this public speech so off-color.[28] The colony, in other words, had gotten to both him and his men.

Far be it for the historian to judge whether this explanation holds water. Debay's mental health issues seem certain; his 1902 letter certainly smacks of paranoia, and in it he repeatedly hints at his "peculiar state of mind."[29] What matters here is how certain Debay was that Indochina itself was responsible for ruining his health, eroding his manners, and deteriorating his conduct. The terrible irony was that the final straw came on a mission that was supposed to find a respite from the colony, a lofty peak for perpetuating European rule, a haven for colonizers, a fountain of health. Instead, the quest had plunged Debay into an abyss of mental illness.

LEGAL PROCEEDINGS AND SENTENCING

From the outset, the legal proceedings against Debay took a peculiar turn. For one thing, Tricon's findings were released only after Debay had returned to France (he set sail on November 30, 1901). Then too, it was unclear initially whether Debay would face justice in France or in Indochina. The Ministry of War opted for justice in Indochina, or rather by Indochinese authorities, on the revealing grounds that, "given the conditions in which the events took place, and the nature of the testimony, matters can only be appreciated in their proper context in Indochina, where they took place."[30] Only in Indochina could Debay's actions be understood.

The case against Debay would be decided by military justice, although the charges had initially been brought forward by a civilian prosecutor. In an army still reeling from the scandal of the Dreyfus Affair, and from the extraordinary stories of brutality in Congo and in the Voulet-Chanoine expedition, the obvious temptation was to sweep this new story of gratuitous colonial brutality under the carpet. Still, despite ultimately opting for a cover-up, the army brass initially agreed that Debay needed to be punished in some way, so deleterious was his behavior to French empire.

Proceedings against Debay had been launched by a lead prosecutor in Indochina, Simon Georges Edgard Assaud, and not by Tricon, as Debay assumed. In
his justification for pursuing the case, Assaud asserted that the body of evidence
against Debay was irrefutable, the accusations against him, "alas, established." Assaud added his political analysis of the situation, deeming that Debay's murderous
rampages could undercut "France's good name" in Indochina.[31] Debay's crimes, in
other words, had profoundly harmed France's position in Indochina.

As in the Dreyfus trial, military justice would prove a sham in the Debay case.
Debay's fate was simply decided by the Minister of War, on the advice of the Franco-
Sénégalese métis General Alfred Dodds, then posted in Indochina. The latter
seems to have weighed the evidence against Debay, seeking advice from colleagues
in Paris and Hanoi. Surprisingly given his African parentage, Dodds conceded Debay's point that natives were generally prone to exaggeration, and that their good
faith was in many cases dubious. Considerable discussion seems to have taken place
around this point. The Direction des troupes coloniales had honed the argument
in a series of drafts, adding in marginalia near the mention that the testimonies were
"exaggerated," the critical point that "they come exclusively from natives."[32]

Dodds also decided that homicide charges were unwarranted, because it could
not be ascertained after the fact that these deaths had directly resulted from Debay's beatings. Only the charge of "numerous cases of violence" against natives stuck.
On this point, Dodds did not once refer to the hundreds of recorded testimonies.
In the General's opinion, the reaction of indigenous people to hearing Debay's name
was enough to confirm the captain's guilt. In so doing, Dodds maintained his car-
dinal principle of discounting native testimonies, even on matters in which he ruled
in their favor.

Next, Dodds considered Debay's responsibility. He depicted Debay as mentally
strained "from the action of climate, and the isolation in which he was forced to
live." Consequently, Dodds evinced, Debay's "responsibility is very limited, but he
cannot be considered entirely irresponsible of the violence that he inflicted." Dodds
recommended that Debay be placed on "military inactivity"—that he keep his rank,
but be suspended indefinitely and without pay from the army.[33]

The Ministry of War then considered whether to take the matter further, and
bring Debay's crimes before the Conseil de guerre. The matter was weighed in the
military justice wing of the Ministry of War. A certain Taupin noted that it was ultimately up to General Dodds to decide whether Debay should face the Conseil de
guerre. Since Dodds' opinion on the matter was already known, there was in Taupin's
opinion, no point in pursuing the matter. Here Taupin read between the lines, de-
tecting an additional reason why Dodds would like to see the Debay case disappear: "no doubt [Dodds thinks] without saying so explicitly, that it would be inop-
portune to fan the flames of discontent in Indochina through a judicial debate over
assaults that were, after all, undertaken in all cases in the service of [Debay's] mis-

sion." Thus, the Ministry of War contended, Debay's violence was not gratuitous; it had been conducted in the line of duty. Furthermore, spreading the details of this case would only serve to further erode French prestige in Southeast Asia. The Ministry of War agreed with General Dodds: Debay would be placed on the army's "inactive" list.[34] This took place on March 13, 1902, based on a presidential decision of March 7.

Under the circumstances, one might have expected Debay to consider himself fortunate. Instead, on July 23, 1902 the captain petitioned for a full inquiry, certain that he was the victim of intrigues by rivals in Indochina. The army remained firm, an inquiry being precisely the result it wanted to avoid.

September 1902 correspondence also shows that the Ministry of War was not credulous about Debay's culpability. It pointed out that Debay's lengthy response to Tricon's accusations never challenged the countless beatings of which he was accused. The captain merely sought to excuse them.[35] Thus, for hundreds of cases of violence and at least ten confirmed murders, Debay was sentenced to being temporarily laid off, while keeping his army rank.

REHABILITATION

Less than two years later, Debay's pestering paid off. In January 1904, a report reached the Minister of War pleading for clemency. Debay had apparently expressed contrition for the violence he inflicted, and had pledged "to be motivated by better intentions in the future." The report also vaunted Debay's valor, as well as his family status, his three children, and lack of personal fortune.[36] The arguments carried the day: Debay was recalled to duty and reinstated at full pay and rank on March 30, 1904.

Debay was then assigned to the fourth Régiment d'infanterie coloniale, before being quickly shifted to the fourth Régiment de tirailleurs tonkinois on October 22, 1904. This spelled a return to Indochina. Unsurprisingly, Debay was back to his old ways in little time. A 1908 report on Debay confirms that the captain continued his vicious abuse of Vietnamese. Now under somewhat closer watch as the leader of Indochinese tirailleurs, he proved utterly unrehabilitated. His superior noted in 1908, "I am convinced that this officer has been guilty of acts of violence on our colonial soldiers (punches, slaps to the face), and that he does not even spare native officers. . . . [Debay] is intelligent and active, but bitter and brutal. He is absolutely inept at commanding native troops."[37]

Unable to inflict his reign of terror over innocent villagers in the countryside, Debay now brutalized French colonial troops serving under the tricolor flag, much closer to the spotlights of his superiors. If anything, he had grown more brazen. Following this report, Debay retired in 1908, only to come out of retirement in 1914 to fight in the First World War, when he was placed at the command of West African troops. The Ministry of War seems to have remained deaf to the countless warnings about Debay's penchant for violence against the colonized.

ACCOLADES

In his May 26, 1902 response to the crimes of which he was accused, Debay relied on multiple strategies. One involved discrediting indigenous witnesses. Another was to list the important missions that had been assigned to him, including the 1900 and 1901 quest for a hill station. Finally, Debay enumerated the honors that had been bestowed upon him. Among them were three separate nominations he had received for France's highest distinction, the Legion of Honor.[38]

By decree of July 12, 1906, Debay was successfully named Chevalier de la Légion d'honneur. This was no small reward, especially in an institution that fetichized the Napoleonic ribbon. The title of Chevalier came with fringe benefits, including an allowance of 250 francs per year.

How had a repeat offender, whose file was replete with reports of unwarranted violence and unprovoked, brutal murder, been chosen for such an honor? Had Debay received protection from further investigation? Certainly, Debay was well enough connected to publish several articles and a book, even in his two-year period of unemployment. Were the accusations against him so much as considered during the nomination process? Debay's Legion of Honor file is silent on these scores. It merely extracts elements of praise from the captain's personnel file: his bravery in April 1891 in an operation against "pirates" in Indochina, his tireless efforts at exploring Annam's interior in 1900. No injuries are recorded, despite Debay's persistent claim that he had lost partial sight in one eye. And Debay's crime wave of 1900 is magically transformed into exemplary service.

In 1918, Debay ascended the Legion of Honor's echelons to the status of Officier de la Légion d'honneur, which he still occupies posthumously to this day (Debay died in 1921).[39] A quick overview of current Legion rules suggests that Debay, having never been convicted of a crime, runs no risk of being struck from the order. One might expect Debay's legacy in Vietnam to be more tarnished. And yet a bridge to Bana hill station—perhaps the very one where Decherf perished—still bears Debay's name.[40]

COLONIAL VIOLENCE IN CONTEXT

The main contours of the Debay story are not as unique as they may sound—leaving aside the Legion of Honor. Voulet and Chanoine had also turned into "bloodthirsty pillagers" in their quest to secure laborers and supplies. Two other officers deeply implicated in that wholesale slaughter later rose to the ranks of general. And in another infamous scandal of the same era, Gaud and Toqué's sadistic torture and massacres in the Congo, were treated just as lightly by French justice in 1903. The two were freed long before serving their five-year prison sentence. In an army shaken by the Dreyfus Affair, these crimes, like Debay's, were especially unwelcome.[41]

Were these crimes the direct result of colonial power relations, or of the permissiveness of the colonial realm? Certainly Debay's file contains few cases of violence against fellow Europeans, notwithstanding his early outburst against a sick comrade. Debay seems to have refrained from beating innocent bystanders during his years in Marseille. In her detailed analysis of torture during the Algerian War, Raphaëlle Branche sees the practice of colonialism itself profoundly shaping forms of violence, repression, and counterinsurgency.[42] This squares well with the Debay saga, insofar as the captain's mission, his deeply colonial conception of labor relations, his reading of indigenous responses, all conditioned when and how he deployed violence.

Sven Lindqvist and Olivier le Cour Grandmaison take cases like this one— interestingly, no historian to date has stumbled upon the Debay story—as indicative of colonialism's murderous impulses. Both draw direct lines between colonial massacres and the Holocaust. Both equate empire and genocide explicitly.[43] Debay's crimes cannot be bent to fit this line of thought. For one thing, Debay's crime spree was decidedly low-tech, explicitly and no doubt deliberately unmodern. He used his old Winchester rifle sparingly; instead Debay favored his fists and feet as weapons. Moreover, Debay's actions stand out in the archival record. Prosecutors in Tourane and Hanoi, the Minister of War, and the highest ranking general in Indochina all pondered Debay's deeds, agreeing that they were out of the ordinary, reprehensible, and mostly, counterproductive. That Debay was granted the Legion of Honor is more illustrative of an army stubbornly unwilling to recognize its initial error in judgment than of an institution rewarding serial murder and abuse as a modus operandi.

In her book *Absolute Destruction,* Isabel Hull has taken an intriguing revisionist position to the study of colonial violence. Examining tragic events in southwest Africa around the same time as the Debay, Chanoine and Voulet, and Gaud and Toqué scandals, she interprets imperial Germany's indiscriminant massacre of Herrero combatants and civilians as resulting from "institutional extremism." Rather than racism or even ideology, Hull posits that German military culture itself led to the bloodbaths in southwest Africa. She rules out racism as the prime mover of this slaughter, because, in her words: "The ubiquity of racialist thinking in Europe and the West before 1914 makes it hard to see how racism could tell us why Europeans went to extremes in some situations and not in others."[44] Whereas Hull's argument is premised on the homogeneity of military culture, our case hinges on the colonial crucible and on individual agency, though the two certainly meet, insofar as the ends appear to have justified the means in the colonies (even here, Hull seems to suggest that for imperial Germany, the ends justified the means in Europe as well).

Although these different incidents all took place in close chronological proximity, they also occurred in quite different contexts. German violence in southwest Africa was undertaken to repress an uprising. Voulet and Chanoine were, for their part, on a mission of conquest, reminiscent of French colonial violence during the conquest of Algeria, or American colonial massacres in the Philippines.[45] Debay, in contrast, was charting inland zones whose inhabitants displayed no particular defensiveness, let alone hostility to him. Indeed, most of his victims had agreed to assist the captain in some way, be it by hosting him in their house or by agreeing to guide him through the mountains. In this sense, Debay deployed degrees of violence common in Indochina during the conquest phase, some decades earlier. Yet he did so utterly gratuitously, after having obtained subordination and submission. Even the colonial prosecutors in Hanoi and Tourane were bewildered by the senselessness of Debay's terror.

However senseless, the precise form of Victor Adrien Debay's actions was clearly informed by his current environment. He deliberately picked on village chiefs and elders, he strategically terrorized villagers into paying a variety of arbitrary levies, he willfully used the language of requisitions, corvées, and forced labor, and he intentionally turned victims on each other, ordering coolies to beat other coolies. He subsequently pointed to the inadequacy of rules governing labor recruitment to justify his use of force.

In turn, Debay's invoking of the hill station objective speaks to his full adherence to Doumer's vision for Indochina. Debay was hell-bent on recruiting mountain guides and scouting a path to a climatic panacea, even when local populations expressed terror at the prospects of zones they knew to be unhealthy.

There can be little doubt, as well, that Debay targeted only indigenous people for violent treatment. Ambient racism was manifestly a factor here. Even Debay's choice of weapons suggests colonial emulation. Most testimonies reveal that Debay beat, kicked, and lashed his victims, reserving his rifle for shooting at farm animals. Here Debay took to extreme ends a practice—slapping or kicking Indochinese— that was widespread as a way of "correcting" servants or employees in the colonies. In another colonial context, the Belgian Congo, it was the whip that became metonymic with colonial rule.[46]

Even Debay's acquittal was sadly in line with colonial practice and seems perfectly in keeping with the following observation by historian Pierre Brocheux: "Indochinese news chronicles are riddled with everyday incidents marked by brutality, humiliation and injustice. In spite of Albert Sarraut's warning against 'racial verdicts,' French people guilty of murder were acquitted, or condemned with parole, or fined token amounts."[47] In this sense, both Debay and his verdict were products of a colonial system.

A full explanation is far from complete. It would be impossible to overlook the perpetrator's mental issues, or for that matter, to deny his measure of accountability—

TARIF MILITAIRE

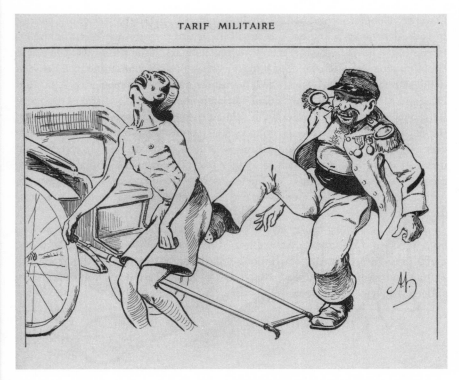

FIGURE 1. "Military rate" for a rickshaw in French Indochina. From A. Joyeux, *La Vie large des Colonies* (Paris: Maurice Bauche, 1912).

even though the two may seem in contraposition. Whether psychopathic or paranoid, Debay evidently suffered from severe mental disorders. He and his superiors recognized this without hesitation, without ever discounting his responsibility. However, when confronting Debay's mental health, they imputed his disorders to Indochina and to the colony, much as I have just traced Debay's forms of violence to the colonial context, and to the paramount importance of the hill station mission he undertook.

A WEB OF HILL STATIONS

·Bana, the hill station "discovered" by Debay, would grow into one of many small sanatoria that later served to complement Dalat. These ancillary hill stations rose to some prominence after Dalat had definitively emerged as Indochina's prime hill station, by the time of the First World War. Bana was only developed in 1919, after

Governor General Sarraut had decided to privilege Dalat over all other hill stations in 1917, describing it as the resort for all Indochina.[48] The Great War, and the interruption of naval traffic that it engendered, had taught the administration not to count on repatriation for soldiers and civil servants alike. Consequently a network of hill stations sprouted all over the Indochinese union: others included Sapa, Tam Dao, and Mau-Son in Tonkin; Bokor in Cambodia; Tranninh in Laos.[49] By 1930, Bana was described as follows by the *Bulletin de l'Agence économique de l'Indochine:* "the hill station's wooden cottages line its hills; a modest hotel fills up with every tourist season. One of the reasons why Bana seems destined to grow, is that it caters to Central Annam much better than Dalat."[50] Like British India, with its impressive range of hill stations catering to different urban centers, be they Calcutta, Madras, or Delhi, Indochina now boasted a gamut of highland sanatoria of varying stature.

Although Doumer had opted for Dalat over Bana as Indochina's main resort, both Yersin and Debay ultimately founded hill stations, displaying very different methods in the process. To the symbolic violence of colonial domination from atop a mountain bastion, was added, in the case of Bana, the humiliation of arbitrary and horrifying colonial violence.

Health, Altitude, and Climate

AN OASIS IN THE TROPICS

At the turn of the century, the head of French military forces in Indochina, General Théophile Pennequin sought to convince Paris of the need to fund the Lang-Bian sanatorium. Born in 1849, Pennequin had served in the Franco-Prussian War and the Madagascar campaign of 1883–85; he had risen rapidly in the ranks of the naval infantry and participated in several missions in Indochina (1877 to 1882, 1888, 1889).[1] The general did not mince words: "One [simply] cannot acclimatize to the colonies: each day brings a further diminution of strength. . . . Cochinchina is a terrible man-eater."[2] Pennequin tapped into acclimatization anxieties, as had each of the hill station's champions.

Finding a viable escape from malaria and other tropical maladies was no trivial matter. Mortality for European soldiers and officials in Indochina remained on the order of 2 to 3 percent at the turn of the twentieth century. Though he kept his options open in Central Annam, Doumer had decided to create a hill station on the Lang-Bian in 1897, the very year Ronald Ross confirmed malaria's transmission by mosquitoes. The French scientist Alphonse Laveran, who trained some of the staunchest supporters of the Lang-Bian hill station, had first hypothesized about a possible mosquito vector after discovering the plasmodia in a malarial victim's blood in 1880.[3] The rationales used for selecting the Lang-Bian reveal as much about the slow application of scientific breakthroughs in the colonies as they do about the dialectic between power and the physical vulnerability of whites in the tropics.

In his 1899 article on colonial sanatoria, Alexandre Kermorgant relied on a popular trope of late-nineteenth-century science. In his words, "Unfortunately, we forget too often that man[kind] is like a plant; no care should be spared when transporting him [sic] beyond his place of origin, to acclimatize him to a new land."[4]

Throughout the nineteenth century, ethnographers, doctors, and biologists alike increasingly called into question the cosmopolitanism of humankind.[5] By the 1870s in France, a countercurrent, comprised in large part of colonial hygienists and doctors, tried to stem the hard-line view that Europeans risked degeneration within a single generation when transported to the tropics. These hygienists did not contest the climatic paradigm; they simply envisioned some opportunity for colonial settlement without instant degeneration.[6] Such hygienists maintained that a "colonial catechism" of their own making could achieve "small acclimatization," which is to say the ability to adapt, to withstand disease, and indeed to survive as whites in the tropics.[7] Hill stations played a central role in this process. It is in this context that one must understand Kermorgant's conclusions. In his words: "If hill stations are beneficial to weak people in our own climes, imagine how much more precious they are to victims of anemia in our overseas possessions."[8] Colonials required prescriptive codes, periodic reseasoning in familiar climes, and perhaps most important, coddling. The Lang-Bian, Kermorgant and his colleagues hoped, could provide all of the above. Hygienists and administrators alike soon imagined it as an enabler of settlement and empire in Indochina.

MINIMUM REQUIREMENTS

In July 1897, Doumer recited what his health advisers had listed as the ideal requirements for a hill station: "The conditions which hygienists lay out for a highland health station are the following: an altitude of at least 1,200 meters, abundant water, a fertile land, the possibility of establishing communication lines."[9] The clinching factor in favor of the Lang-Bian plateau was without a doubt its climate. Yersin had vaunted to Doumer the breezes and low temperatures which prevailed on the vast plateau.[10] He had described its climate as similar to the Mediterranean's in springtime.[11] Having recommended the Lang-Bian, he then proceeded to outline the goals of a colonial sanatorium: "We can only hope for the prompt realization of [Governor] Doumer's project. Giving the colony a highland sanatorium is a humanitarian deed. Europeans will find—within hours by train from Saigon—a climate close to that of France. They will be able to spend the warmest months in the Lang-Bian, when the heat in the lowlands is debilitating. They will regain strength there, and will return to their posts without loss of time or resources for the colony."[12] Here, Yersin synthesized the myriad rationales for a colonial hill station: reducing expenses by cutting down on furloughs to France; saving lives; improving productivity by making short reinvigoration stints possible; creating a cool oasis for Europeans sweltering in Cochinchina; and carving out a piece of France in Indochina.

Yersin's 1898 report on the future site of Dalat begins with the following *évidence*: "the utility of a highland sanatorium in regions like Cochinchina and Cambodia, which have a debilitating effect on Europeans, this utility cannot be questioned."[13]

Within a year, French meteorologists had conducted a battery of tests on the Lang-Bian plateau, to determine how closely the region matched the resorts of the Raj. Average temperature statistics (in Celsius) taken between 1899 and 1901 reveal the following comparisons:[14]

	AVERAGE TEMPERATURE	LOWEST TEMPERATURE RECORDED
Lang-Bian	18.3	2
Nuwara Eliya (Ceylon)	16.7	4.5
Darjeeling (India)	12.2	3.5
Simla (India)	12.8	6.4
Ootacamund (India)	12.8	4

The Lang-Bian was clearly seen as France's answer to the British hill stations in India, which acted as de facto summer capitals and "pinnacles of power."[15] In fact, Yersin implied more subtly, the Lang-Bian's climate reflected that of France, while Simla and Darjeeling's chilly 12-degree averages mirrored that of Britain.

The Lang-Bian was widely believed to enable periodic reacclimation, thereby guaranteeing the survival of the French "race." In his 1902 report, General Pennequin broached the question of a future military camp on the Lang-Bian in explicitly racialized terms: "Our race will never be able to settle or prosper in Indochina, and is withering away from the deleterious climate. If a few families can enjoy the same health in the Lang-Bian as they had in France, then perhaps Europeans will be able to exert themselves, to work, prosper and perpetuate their presence here."[16]

If permanent settlement itself depended on hill stations, then the Lang-Bian's critical importance could not be doubted. For Pennequin much more was at stake on the Lang-Bian than rest and relaxation: the very survival of the French "race" in the tropics depended on escaping the nefarious climes of the lowlands. If the Lang-Bian could provide an escape from this pathological tropical environment, he argued, then it could become the focal point of colonial power in Indochina, and perhaps a breeding center for the French "race" in the tropics.

Very early on, colonial doctors countenanced the notion that the Lang-Bian could not only allow weary colonials to reinvigorate and avoid malaria, but could also provide a tranquil and disease-free space for European domestic life. Climate conditioned not only disease, but also quality of life. Thus Captain Bigaud reported in 1900, "once a railway, comfortable buildings, and paved roads have been established, the Lang-Bian will become a passable 'little piece of France,' and will be considered a good colonial sanatorium."[17] Bigaud's words reveal the utopianism, or dystopianism, underlying French colonial Dalat. On an inaccessible, high altitude plateau, this officer already envisioned stately buildings and a railroad. He also betrayed the paradox of Dalat's nascent sociocultural function: Dalat's objective was to recreate France overseas. However, by Bigaud's own account, even the finest replica could only be deemed "passable" next to the real thing.[18] Bigaud pined for the actual metropole, but grudgingly accepted Dalat as an adequate substitute.[19]

AN EARLY SKEPTIC

For all the optimism of Yersin, Bigaud, and Pennequin, serious doubts emerged about the Lang-Bian's purported healthfulness almost immediately after the sanatorium's foundation in 1898. The Jewish French naval artilleryman, topography specialist, brother of Bernard Lazare (of Dreyfus Affair fame), future rubber expert, and funder of the French Resistance, Captain Fernand Bernard leveled no doubt the strongest critique of the hill station.[20] Bernard knew the topic well, as he had been assigned to draw up the earliest feasibility assessment of a road or railroad to the Lang-Bian in 1898. Upon reaching the Lang-Bian in late November 1898, he wrote to his parents of the misery, grey skies, and rain he encountered there.[21] He was instantly "disillusioned" with the future sanatorium, in no small part because of the toll the place was taking on his entourage.[22] A few days later, he related to his parents that "all the Vietnamese have fallen sick here. The most optimistic will tell you that they are unused to the cold and lack moral vigor, but I see this instead as a sign that the climate is not so wonderful, and could be harmful to European convalescents."[23]

Bernard remarked that he must have been only the eighth or ninth European to set foot on what he sarcastically termed this "earthly paradise," adding that all were hardened explorers, in no way comparable to the convalescents Doumer wished to bring atop the plateau. He struggled to explain to his parents how and why an entire administration could have gone so wrong in choosing a health station: "Dr. Yersin whose name will no doubt ring a bell . . . is the one who invented this sanatorium. He simply got carried away by the fact that it is cooler than Saigon." The prescient captain quipped that climate and health need not be connected.[24]

Bernard's first impressions stuck. He soon emerged as the most steadfast and vocal opponent to the hill station, even while being assigned on missions to develop it.[25] In 1901 Bernard launched a salvo in the widely circulated Revue de Paris, taking much broader aim than just the Lang-Bian. Bernard's self-described "alarm bell" essay began by positing the strength and unity of the Annamese nation, predicting that one day the Annamese would oust the French in much the same way as they had expelled the Chinese or the Mongols. Among allegations of misspending, among analyses of misguided assimilation attempts, among tales of lavish opera houses erected at huge cost while elementary sanitary infrastructures were left terribly wanting, one finds a solidly mounted case against the Lang-Bian sanatorium.[26]

Firstly, Bernard contended, Doumer's plan to link the Lang-Bian to the rest of the colony by rail constituted a monumental waste of funds—tax monies wrenched from Vietnamese peasants, he might have added. He predicted that this white elephant of a rail line would run virtually empty; after all, he could count only sixty-eight planters in all of Tonkin and Annam. Creating a sanatorium for such a miniscule European elite, he implied, verged on madness. Secondly and even more seriously, Bernard called into question the Lang-Bian's healthfulness. He noted the extreme caution taken by the Dutch in Indonesia in selecting their hill station. He added that it was not enough to take temperature readings. Here was a frontal assault on Yersin. He continued, "The new theories demonstrated by the recent work of Laveran and Blanchard in France, Grassi and Celli in Italy, Ross in England, and Koch in Germany, lend us specific investigative tools when it comes to malaria. [And yet] no mosquito study has been undertaken on the Lang-Bian, no analysis has been conducted on the blood of natives, or on that of animals. Nothing, in short, leads us to affirm the Lang-Bian's appropriateness as a sanatorium."[27]

Bernard's analysis would ultimately prove scientifically flawless. But did it have any impact at the time? It arguably contributed to stalling development.[28] The Lang-Bian rail line would be delayed time and again before it finally wound its way near the plateau in the 1920s. Still, despite his comparative evidence from Burma and Indonesia, his own firsthand data from the Lang-Bian, and his knowledge of medical breakthroughs from London to Rome, Bernard was unable to debunk climatic logic or scuttle the Lang-Bian sanatorium altogether.

OVERLAPPING PARADIGMS

General Pennequin's grandiloquent narrative of racial survival did not, of course, square with the viral, parasitical, and bacteoriological realities on the ground, the threat so keenly articulated by Captain Bernard. Soon, some of the very doctors who had so strongly endorsed the creation of a sanatorium on the Lang-Bian were forced to recognize that the plateau was anything but disease-free. Early construction on the road connecting Phan Rang to the Lang-Bian plateau proved so murderous to indigenous laborers that it was temporarily suspended. Doctors debated whether these high mortality rates "proved anything against the Lang-Bian" or whether they simply confirmed the unhealthfulness of the forests the road crossed.[29] Bernard, not surprisingly, took the former position. He invoked an April 1900 mission to the Lang-Bian, comprised of twenty Europeans and a hundred Vietnamese. Three months later, four Europeans had perished and eight lay in hospital. Bernard was less specific about "Annamese" losses, mentioning only that eighty of the hundred Vietnamese involved in the expedition had "died or been lost."[30]

Dr. Etienne Tardif, the twenty-three-year-old Bordeaux naval medical school graduate accompanying Paul Guynet's 1899 road-building mission to the Lang-Bian, adopted a much rosier outlook, and offered another explanation for casualties.[31]

He had not recommended nor personally taken preventative doses of quinine while on the mission, convinced that such a prophylaxis was unnecessary.[32] Admittedly, he remarked, some had contracted "fevers": a few Vietnamese "boys" or servants, and other Vietnamese workers who had been assigned to deforestation en route to Lang-Bian from the coast. Mainly, Tardif leaned on race to dismiss what could have been a clear warning sign: "[these fevers among Annamese] are hardly surprising," he wrote, "given the Annamese race's meager resistance to disease."[33] Yet Tardif could not ignore the loss of Sergeant Osman, who perished from "pernicious fevers" on January 13, 1900 during the fourth phase of road construction.[34] What is more, Osman succumbed at a time when Tardif himself was "sick as a horse from fevers."[35] Indeed, four Europeans, including the wife of expedition leader Paul Guynet, were bedridden for four days, "felled by an intense and unrelenting fever."[36]

Most alarmingly, Tardif observed daily cases of malaria among Vietnamese workers even on the Lang-Bian plateau. Two Europeans also fell ill on the plateau itself. Tardif, whose 1902 book was actually aimed at countering critics like Bernard, dismissed these cases on the grounds that each of the European victims had spent fifteen years apiece in the colonies.[37] Even so, the association of the Lang-Bian with health was potentially tarnished.

The health rationales for selecting the Lang-Bian were modeled uncritically upon British hill stations. Dane Kennedy has demonstrated how pervasive climatic determinism was in the British scramble for altitude in India. Nineteenth-century popular wisdom held that "like meat, Europeans keep better in the hills."[38] But tropical medicine had been transformed between the establishment of Simla in the mid-nineteenth century, and the fin de siècle. Simply put, the rationales that had buttressed the creation of Simla—or for that matter the French hill stations in the Caribbean, which Kermorgant considered the world's oldest—had crumbled by the turn of the twentieth century, especially in the etiology of malaria.[39]

The case of the Lang-Bian demonstrates that residual geoclimatic determinism and germ theory overlapped and in fact coexisted in French colonial medicine, and this well into the first part of the twentieth century. This coexistence can be traced to the nearly two decades following Laveran's 1880 hypothesis, during which mosquitoes were already suspected as a vector, but never recognized as the sole source of the disease.[40] Harish Naraindas has analyzed the same phenomenon at work in British tropical medicine. The mid-nineteenth-century framework, which had given rise to "the sanatorium, the hill station, the voyage and the furlough (back to good old England!)," proved deeply imbedded in scientific consciousness.[41] Nor was the endurance of geoclimatism limited to France or England. Warwick Anderson and Wolfgang Eckart note its tenacity in Germany, where it found expression in the specialized field of "geomedicine." "However repressed," Anderson acknowledges, forms of nineteenth-century climatic determinism resurfaced periodically in the twentieth century.[42] If this was true for fields closely allied to medicine, then the endurance proved all the greater in the realm of mentalities and comportments. The language of moral contempt for the tropics lingered into the second half of the twentieth century.[43] Mark Bradley has demonstrated how profoundly twentieth-century U.S. views of Vietnam were steeped in climatic determinism.[44]

In the case that concerns us, the persistence of the climatic mold is striking, insofar as the mainstream medical establishment clung to it. It is not so much that French doctors in the 1910s or 1920s questioned malaria's mosquito transmission, but rather that they maintained climate's primacy in conditioning the disease. Climate still lay at the center of its explanatory terrain, and sometimes even constituted the remedy. Thus, Prosper Joseph Emile Borel, the malaria specialist at Saigon's Pasteur Institute, still argued emphatically in 1927 that reimmersion into the Lang-Bian's mild climes served to reduce symptoms of malaria almost immediately.[45]

HOW HIGH IS SAFE?

To doctors, the first signs of trouble arose around the minimum elevation required for malaria immunity. Dr. Henri Haueur's 1903 report on the Lang-Bian stated matter-of-factly that malaria rarely struck over 800 meters (2,600 feet), a pre-Rossian altitude that needed to be raised significantly if one were to avoid *Anopheles* mosquitoes, rather than merely tropical heat.[46]

Claims of the Lang-Bian's malaria-free status were quickly put to the test. In 1905, Dr. Joseph Vassal, a collaborator of Yersin's at the Institut Pasteur, issued a report to the governor general on malaria on the Lang-Bian.[47] Vassal had been trained by Alphonse Laveran, André Calmette, and other deans of French medicine. He drew from a vast international network, including doctors in England and Germany, among them the later-to-be-notorious Claus Schilling.[48] Vassal devoted his life to tropical medicine, working in Réunion, Indochina, and equatorial Africa, as well as in the Philippines.[49]

Vassal's 1905 report reads: "Malaria is the main factor to be considered when judging healthfulness in the tropics. Here, it is the only factor. What is more, it was the only reproach against [the Lang-Bian] that ever carried any weight." Because Vassal explicitly set about counting the *Anopheles* mosquitoes, known to transmit malaria, one is tempted to see his 1905 mission as an effort firstly to address Bernard's criticisms, and secondly to endow the Lang-Bian with Rossian legitimacy.[50] Indeed, Vassal redefined the sanatorium as "a sufficiently elevated mountain in the tropics, one cold enough to avoid infection through mosquitoes." Here again, Vassal married pre- and postmosquito paradigms. He added that temperate microclimates in the tropics served many purposes, including revivifying people "of the white race."[51]

Vassal began by acknowledging that moderate altitude was in itself insufficient to deter the stubborn *Anopheles* species. Hence, he noted anachronistically, the English had placed their hill stations in India near the peaks, rather than the slopes of the Himalayas. Vassal's description of his fieldwork is also revealing. He stressed the hostility of highland minorities towards the collection of blood—a theme that has attracted considerable attention in recent historical work on medicine and empire.[52] He wrote: "many natives feel repugnance at giving a drop of blood, and outright hostility at the idea of me taking blood from their children." So frightened were Lat children of this practice, he noted, that he had to entice them with knick-knacks in exchange for blood samples. Soon, Vassal added vaccination to his interventions in minority villages. By giving marbles to each child he vaccinated, and collecting mosquito samples from each of their homes by the same stroke, Vassal came to think of his marbles as abacus counting units.[53] Ultimately, Vassal concluded from both blood samples and mosquito collection (tricky business, since the *Anopheles* strike at dusk or at night) that the Lang-Bian's *Anopheles* mosquitoes were simply too dazed by the cold to spread malaria. Hence, deduced Vassal, the "vigorous and healthy appearance" of Europeans living on the Lang-Bian.[54]

Vassal relented somewhat in a 1907 article in the *Quinzaine coloniale*. Here, he enthusiastically supported the adoption of antimosquito measures in Indochina, similar to those undertaken in Algeria. However, Vassal introduced new evidence to suggest that the Lang-Bian's 1,500 meters would amply suffice to avoid malaria. He cited extensively from Italian, British, and American studies, showing a scarcity of *Anopheles* at such heights. And in the handful of *Anopheles* one might encounter, Vassal questioned whether the malarial parasite could properly evolve through its host under chilly conditions. *Anopheles,* Vassal concluded, "acclimated with difficulty" to the cold, in much the same way as humans acclimated with difficulty to the tropics. Still, Vassal raised one disturbing possibility. Mankind, he wrote, "sometimes manages to create what [Robert] Koch has called an artificial climate." In that case, Vassal cautioned, *Anopheles* might be able to survive in the dwellings of a sanatorium, after having been introduced by train or other transportation from lowland areas.[55] The Lang-Bian risked backfiring.

When asked in 1914 by the government general to reassess on location the Lang-Bian's role as a sanatorium, Vassal did not fundamentally change his verdict. He attributed the malaria he witnessed amongst ethnic Vietnamese on the Lang-Bian to migration, rather than any endemic outbreak. If anything, Vassal was more insistent than ever. He observed that children who had never left the plateau appeared healthy, while those who had traveled beyond it were sapped by malaria. This led him to deduce unconditionally, "the [offending] mosquito does not exist on the Lang-Bian." Lastly, he entered into evidence the fact that he had seen no quinine depositories en route to the Lang-Bian—a curious indicator to say the least, since it could equally well signal the medical system's shortcomings as the region's healthfulness. In sum, asserted Vassal, "it is now confirmed beyond the shadow of a doubt that we have an incomparable hill station within easy reach of Cochinchina, only two days away from Saigon."[56]

DANKIA, LANG-SA, OR DALAT?

The Lang-Bian was a vast, grassy plateau; where exactly would the future health center rise? On Yersin and Doumer's initiative, a model farm, a meteorological station, and a small military outpost had been established in the vicinity of the minority village of Dankia, on the northern extremity of the plateau as early as October 1897.[57] This was the proposed site for the creation of Lang-Sa—the future sanatorium Doumer had envisioned.

Meanwhile, thirteen kilometers to the southeast, on the least densely populated part of the plateau, a single house had been erected that same year at a locality named Dalat—meaning "river of the Lat," the highland minority inhabiting the area.[58] In addition to the stream, the site was characterized by its beautiful clusters of pine trees. By 1899, Captain Guynet, leader of the Lang-Bian road construction team, reported that Dalat and Lang-Sa (Dankia) had been connected by a proper path. He asked the governor for monies with which to improve Dalat's single dwelling, so that the governor could soon visit the place in person. Guynet had fallen under the site's charm, and implicitly asked whether the governor was certain that he wished to "maintain Lang-Sa as the site of the sanatorium."[59] Indeed, one member of Guynet's team, Dr. Tardif, staked his medical reputation on the fact that Dalat stood at a higher elevation, and benefited from better breezes and hygiene than Dankia. In making this argument—for which he would later take ample credit—Tardif was conscious of challenging the legendary Yersin.[60] And because of Yersin's prestige, it took a personal visit by the governor general to the Lang-Bian in 1900 to finally overrule the Pasteurian giant on this point.[61]

That very year, Indochina's director of agriculture and commerce, Guillaume Capus, followed Guynet and Tardif's lead in recommending Dalat and not Dankia as the final site for Indochina's main sanatorium. The agricultural expert deemed Dalat perfectly ventilated, and found its views magnificent—noting that the site dominated the plateau. Capus added that Dalat stood fifty meters above Dankia. Finally, Capus invoked Dalat's handsome pine forests as powerful reminders of home.[62] Dalat was outpacing its rivals.

In November 1900, Governor Doumer informed local officials that he intended to make a prolonged stay with his family at Dalat. He ordered the immediate construction of a number of wooden structures: four cottages, a two-storey house expressly for his projected early 1901 visit, and a large, 52-meter-long building that could serve as a makeshift hotel.[63] He wrote the Ministry of the Colonies on January 24, 1901: "Dalat, which enjoys unrivalled climate and healthfulness, has been definitively chosen for the future health station."[64]

The sanatorium's location change was accompanied by a semantic shift: gone was Doumer's pretension of sending a power signal to the Vietnamese—in their tongue—with the term "Lang-Sa." "Dalat" alluded instead to the local minority people. Ultimately, the final decision had been couched in medical, not linguistic terms. Drs. Haueur and Tardif had determined that Dalat was healthier, higher, and better suited in its immensity to allow for a future military camp to adjoin the city. As final proof, Haueur pointed to the acclimatization guinea pigs posted there for the past four years. Of these early settlers, Haueur wrote "The few Europeans families settled [in Dalat] struck us as enjoying as good a health as French peasants. Their hue is pink, even reddish; they display vigor and embonpoint." Finally, Haueur observed, not a single *Anopheles* mosquito had been found in Dalat, and the outpost showed no sign of fever outbreaks.[65] This verdict would prove premature.

FOREIGN MODELS

We have seen that both the promoters and the critics of Lang-Bian consistently compared Indochina's prime hill station to those of other colonial powers. In 1899, for example, Doumer dispatched Yersin to inspect the upland stations of Dutch Indonesia. Much the same emulation was at work in other realms, as orientalist societies relentlessly appropriated and reappropriated methods and models across Southeast Asia.[66] Among the many points of reference for Dalat's developers were Simla in India (founded circa 1831), Petropolis in Brazil (founded in 1843), and Baguio in the Philippines (established in the late nineteenth century).

Fernand Bernard's arguments against the Lang-Bian were buttressed, as we have seen, by solid evidence relating to hill stations of other colonial powers. Ironically, Bernard had accumulated this knowledge after being dispatched in 1900 by the governor general of Indochina to investigate Dutch hill station plans in Jakarta. In his private correspondence, Bernard held even fewer punches than in his *Revue de Paris* article. Bernard bemoaned that "while the Dutch have decided that they do not have the luxury of creating another hill station whose outcome is uncertain and which would cost six million [francs], Mr. Doumer has fallen for the Lang-Bian, and projects to sink twenty million [francs] into it."[67]

While Bernard drew from foreign models to try to kill the Lang-Bian in its tracks, in a 1908 article Joseph Vassal used Baguio in the Philippines as a shining example for the Lang-Bian. Vassal began by observing that Spanish colonizers had preferred the Philippines' mineral water spas to upland stations. Baguio, he contended, was only developed after the American conquest. Vassal wrote in wonder about every aspect of Baguio: the luxurious sleeping cars used to reach it, the well-paid Japanese workers who toiled on the site, its quaint villas and cottages, its hospital and military base, even its pine trees. Numerous parallels emerge with the Lang-Bian. Vassal commented on the vastness of the two plateaus, their nearly identical average temperatures, their common altitude, as well as on the wave of skepticism to-wards developing Baguio—an implicit allusion to Bernard's campaign against Dalat. That the American authorities "were not shaken" by this opposition was, in Vassal's opinion, an important lesson for Indochina's leaders. Vassal concluded that Baguio's legacies, especially the massive American investment in the site, should exert a positive impact on planning for the Lang-Bian.[68]

Baguio remained a guiding light for years to come. In 1916, Indochina's Gov-ernor Ernest Roume dispatched an information-gathering mission there, to tap American hill station knowledge. The ensuing report was once again overwhelm-ingly positive, at a time when Dalat itself was reaching a fork in the road: "During the hot season in 1908, the local land registry office sent a number of its European [read 'white'] and Philippino agents to Baguio. . . . The expenses involved were lim-ited, and largely paid off, given the efficiency of this cure on the mental and phys-ical well-being of these officials, whose productivity increased thanks to Baguio."[69] The report noted every detail with wonder: "There are in Baguio several private res-idences, many surrounded by gardens, where American roses and violets grow pro-fusely. Here one has the complete illusion of the motherland."[70]

As new hill stations were born, the government general of Indochina took stock of the latest methods and trends. Thus in 1923, the French consulate general in Sin-gapore kept Hanoi abreast of the development of the new Dutch hill station of Brastagi in Sumatra, and its success at drawing British colonials from Malaya and Singapore. Antiquated though hill station logic may have been in medical terms, in practical terms Dalat's development had involved considerable comparative re-search and international scientific dialogue.[71]

FROM DENIAL TO BLAME

The debate between Vassal and Bernard over the Lang-Bian soon dragged in other parties. It speaks to a fundamental tension both between cautious and quixotic col-onization visions, and between modern and premodern medical models. In 1913, a military doctor, Dourne, bluntly questioned Vassal's methodologies. It was pre-posterous, argued Dourne, to deduce much of anything from reports that a few Eu-ropeans supposedly enjoyed "perfect health" on the Lang-Bian. Dourne attributed the unwavering faith in Dalat to more than medical obstinacy: careful inquiry, he wrote, "might show that [Dalat's] enthusiasts are after personal gain."[72] Here was a serious allegation. Reliable medical data would soon vindicate Dalat's detractors, but not before the hill station emerged as central to the operation and perpetua-tion of empire in Indochina.

Dourne and Bernard had established that Dalat was far less salubrious than utopian colonial planners had argued. Compounding this irony is the fact that the hill station's era of accrued development (starting at the time of the First World War)

came on the heels of a marked improvement in European survival rates in the Indochinese lowlands.[73] In other words, the search for a colonial panacea was rooted
not only in outdated fears, but also in antiquated public health imperatives.

By the 1920s, British colonial studies were seriously undercutting the notion that
Anopheles mosquitoes entered a state of shock at 5,000 feet (1,500 meters)—the exact altitude of Dalat. In a 1924 article on the northern Indian hill station of Shillong in the *Indian Journal of Medical Research,* Henry Shortt warned, "The height
of Shillong (5,000 ft or 1,500 meters) is in itself no bar to the presence of malaria
which is known to exist up to an altitude of 9,000 ft (2,743 meters)—Quito on the
equator—and while at such altitudes the periodic exacerbations of the disease are
unlikely ever to assume alarming proportions, yet they may be sufficiently severe
to make well worthwhile the adoption of personal if not of municipal precaution-
ary measures."[74]

More vexing for French medicine, Shortt actually attributed the increase in
malaria at Shillong to the creation of a Pasteur Institute there in 1917. This in turn,
had brought more patients "from the plain . . . chiefly from Bengal and Assam, both
notoriously malarial provinces."[75] Vassal's worst fears about a possible "artificial environment" for *Anopheles* seemed realized.

Also in 1924, Dr. Marcel Terrisse, Dalat's medic-in-chief, was beginning to take
stock of the hill station's vulnerability to disease. He wrote ominously of smallpox
outbreaks in Upper Donnaï province that killed "several hundred" people, of cases
of plague nearby, and, distressingly, of malaria. "It is presently established," Terrisse
wrote, "that malaria afflicts Dalat's native population." Here was a disavowal of Vassal and Yersin's rosy prognosis. Worse still, Terrisse observed, "Mosquitoes are numerous both in Dalat and in the Annamese village." Around the Lang-Bian Palace
Hotel, he noted, visitors were bothered by swarms of the insects.[76]

As a response, Terrisse sketched a bold plan to stem disease. One part involved
having prisoners drain some of the most stagnant lakes, like the one closest to his
own residence. Yet by January 1925, Dalat's municipal hygiene council expressed
concerns about some of Terrisse's more draconian proposals, especially article nine
of a projected decree, which stipulated that "all Asian outsiders to Dalat" should be
subjected to a forced medical visit. The hotel owner Mr. Desanti spoke out strongly
against the measure, which he said would discourage "wealthy Asians" from visiting Dalat. Elie Cunhac condemned the measure as impractical, adding that the
movement of highland minorities would be nearly impossible to control. In the end,
the wording was changed to "all Asian outsiders to Dalat from milieus likely to constitute a medical threat." Milieu, which could stand in for both place and social standing, once again came to the fore. Dalat's hygienists were scrambling to contain the
news that the sanatorium offered no respite from illness; they did so with some of
their instruments of choice, including segregation and isolation.[77]

A worrisome 1927 article by Borel specifically called into question Dalat's malarial resistance—thereby interrogating its raison d'être. Borel showed that a stunning 29.83 percent of patients at Dalat's hospital in 1925–26 had checked in for malaria-related treatment.[78] Even if one accepts Borel's argument that most were vacationers who had contracted malaria in the lowlands, these findings must have added to the concerns identified by Terrisse. Yet Borel remained unflappably upbeat, insisting, "this terrible disease has not yet acclimatized to Dalat." He added: "[French] children enjoy remarkable health in Dalat."

Borel nevertheless advocated aggressive measures against the mosquitoes. These, he suggested, had managed to infiltrate Dalat because of new industry, and, ironically, because of modern urban planning. According to Borel, the new artificial lakes and the brick works had certainly drawn the mosquito to Dalat. Furthermore, Borel invoked a reliance on coastal laborers for Dalat's many building projects—some of whom were infected with malaria and constituted contagion threats.[79] In short, these industries and new urban plans had "created multiple new sites . . . conducive to the development of Anopheles larvae."[80] The scientist drafted a map showing some fifteen sites needing to be drained or filled within Dalat proper. A quick glance at the map suggests that significantly more Anopheles had turned up in the European administrative quarter immediately northwest of the Lang-Bian Palace Hotel, and in the European villa clusters around the lake, than in either the "current Annamese village" (village annamite actuel) or the "Annamese village under construction" (quartier annamite en construction").[81]

High-ranking colonial officials had already been warned in 1924 that the proliferation of artificial lakes increased the risk of malaria propagation. None other than the Résident supérieur of Annam had written the governor general of Indochina to this effect in June 1924. At that time, local engineers had countered that the risks of malaria were overblown, and that in any event lakes were being positioned where greater-risk swamps previously stood.[82]

A year after Borel's article, an anonymous contributor to the Bulletin économique de l'Indochine reported that most of his suggestions had been carried out: vegetation had been removed in the shallows of Dalat's lake, which had been redirected to maximize sunshine and minimize shade. The brand-new Annamese quarter had been completed, featuring major improvements. These were summarized as "better hygienic conditions, improved aesthetics, and heightened sanitary surveillance." Control, beautification, and hygiene went hand in hand. More needed to be done, including cementing household floors.[83] This of course, demonstrates how colonial racism hijacked medical priorities—Borel's map had identified the central French quarter, rather than any Vietnamese district, as a breeding ground for mosquitoes.

Interestingly, a thorough 1934 collection campaign conducted by Treillard would turn up no Anopheles in either French or Annamese houses at Dalat, whether "in comfortable villas or in huts"—read in neither European nor in Vietnamese dwellings. Conversely, concluded the study, the cattle pens belonging to the local

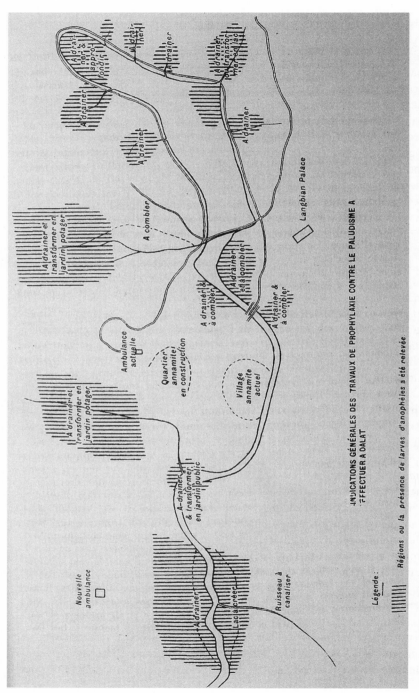

FIGURE 2. "Prophylactic works against malaria to be undertaken at Dalat." From Prosper Joseph Emile Borel, "Dalat et le paludisme," *Bulletin économique de l'Indochine* 187 (1927): p. 397. Areas in hash marks denote "those in which *Anopheles* larvae have been detected." "A drainer" signifies "to be drained."

indigenous highland minority, the Lat, had "become a refuge for numerous adults of this mosquito species, which certainly gorge on the blood of the buffaloes."[84] In the racialized urban geometry of colonial disease prevention, blame had finally shifted to the displaced, water-buffalo-raising Lat people, whose hunting, cattle grazing, and cultivation grounds had been seized to build Dankia and Dalat after 1898. This logic was of course eminently suspect even by its own standards, since many French explorers had previously romanticized the Lat as the hardy, "primitive" guardians of the pristine and disease-free plateau "discovered" by Yersin in 1893.

By 1937, Shortt's scenario, in which outsiders introduced malaria to a hill station, came to pass in Dalat. Annam's director of health informed the Résident supérieur of a malaria epidemic in the nearby Djiring and Dran regions. What caught the director's attention was not so much this outbreak in itself, but the consequences for Dalat. In his words, "The hospitalization in Dalat of patients [from Dran and Djiring] presents the danger of spreading malaria [to Dalat], since there are already anopheles mosquitoes . . . on location in Dalat." The director therefore deemed it "illogical to send carriers of this disease to Dalat, especially since patients could just as readily be rerouted to Phanrang or Phan Thiet"—in other words onto coastal areas.[85]

One should of course bear in mind that colonial schemes of containment and segregation were out of step with a much messier reality on the ground, even in Dalat's highly controlled environment. In 1928, Dalat's municipal council had chastised the town's hospital for putting into proximity "mandarins, coolies, prisoners, rich natives and moïs" within its indigenous quarters. As for the hospital's European building, it was deemed plainly "insufficient."[86] And yet, neither the relative inadequacy of the European wing, nor the lack of class segregation of the indigenous hospital were rapidly redressed. Colonial fantasies of control and segregation were sometimes just that.

In the case of the 1937 malaria outbreak, two imperatives clashed: the colonial hospital's role as a propaganda tool and carefully crafted symbol of colonial munificence, and Dalat's function as guarantor and protector of European health.[87] Lucien Auger, the Résident of Dalat's region of Haut-Donnaï, put forward the compromise solutions of creating a *lazaret*, or quarantine station elsewhere in the highlands, or of expanding Phanrang's hospital. The ideas fell on deaf ears. "We have no money for this" reads the Résident supérieur's observation in the margins.[88]

Fortunately for all colonial institutions involved, Phan Thiet was soon able to take on more patients from Dran and Djiring, thanks to the coincidental opening of its new maternity ward, which created spaces in its regular wards. Still, Dalat's medical authorities had stood firm. Auger even wrote in January 1938 that in future, malarial patients from Dran and Djiring would be turned away from Dalat. He suggested hardening the 1924 policy of checking Asian visitors, and establishing "sanitary checkpoints" to enforce this decision.[89] Ironically, Dalat had strayed

FIGURE 3. Dalat's hospital, circa 1930. Private postcard, author's collection.

from its original vocation as a site for malaria treatment, to one that turned away victims of the disease.

GEOMEDICINE AND RACE

Climatic determinism, as we have seen, proved remarkably resilient in the case of Dalat. In fact, in some instances it actually gained momentum in the first half of the twentieth century. In a 1939 article published in the highly respected *Archives des Instituts Pasteur d'Indochine,* meteorologist Paul-Antoine Carton set out to determine the "average climatic conditions appropriate for different ethnic categories within the white race." Here, Carton returned to a point already suggested by Yersin: British, Dutch, and French people might require subtly different conditions for their respective hill stations in the tropics. But Carton was not a product of the 1880s; he represented a major break with Vassal, Yersin, and their cohort. Carton recognized an intellectual debt to the French eugenicist Alexis Carrel, as well as to the influential Italian agricultural geographer Girolamo Azzi, whose "average climatogram for the white man"—elaborated under Mussolini—served as Carton's chief indexing tool.[90] Unsurprisingly, Paris' climate matched almost identically the "ideal climate for the white man."[91] Admittedly, like nineteenth-century racialists before him, Carton delineated the necessary conditions "required by the white man" in the tropics. However, he achieved this through new, complicated formulae involving temperature differentials and humidity levels. Here, malaria and other specific diseases and their vectors were in effect tributary of wellness and racial integrity. Carton assessed each of Indochina's hill stations in turn, from the most famous, Dalat, to the Tam-Dao near Hanoi, and a host of more obscure sites.

Carton's evaluation of Dalat is intriguing. On the one hand, he deemed the resort's fine reputation to be deserved. Dalat, he opined, "is currently the best hill station for Europeans in French Indochina." On the other hand, he bemoaned that Dalat fell short of duplicating France's climate exactly. Its temperature was characteristic of "intermediate climes, between the tropical and the equatorial types." Carton elaborated that "the climatogram of Dalat is to Saigon's roughly what the climatogram of the average white man is to Hanoi's."[92] All things being relative in this scheme, Dalat was ideally suited to racially regenerate settlers in Hanoi, but lacked the tonic punch to guarantee racial redemption for their brethren in much warmer Saigon. Carton's approach represented an intriguing resurgence of climatology, under a new guise.

DURAS ON CLIMATE

Long after Vassal's dubious victory over Bernard, Dalat remained enduringly synonymous with health, reinvigoration, and whiteness. This belief was not restricted to the medical profession. None other than famed novelist Marguerite Duras enlisted the trope of Dalat as a racial reinvigorator. In her Indochina trilogy, Duras contrasts the narrator's Chinese lover with Hélène Lagonelle, one of the narrator's companions at boarding school and "her other love." The two are rivals, antithetical.[93] The lover is associated with trysts in Cholon, the bustling Chinese suburb of Saigon; Lagonelle hails from quiet, French Dalat.

The Chinese lover is not Lagonelle's only opposite. Duras herself had grown up in Sadec, Vinh Long, Hanoi, and Saigon, all in the Indochinese lowlands. The novelist also identified more closely with the Vietnamese than with chic colonial society.[94] Lagonelle, in stark contrast, epitomized unacclimated highland whiteness. The actual Lagonelle eventually left Indochina for the metropole, after marrying a Frenchman in Dalat.[95] Although attracted to Lagonelle, the acutely class-conscious narrator of *L'Amant* never identifies with Dalat, nor with the hill station's social universe—even though she likely envies it. Revealingly, Duras chooses to introduce Lagonelle as follows in *The Lover*: "Hélène Lagonelle comes from the high plateaus of Dalat. . . . She has the pink and brown hues of the mountain, Hélène Lagonelle, she stands out [at the boarding school] from all the children bearing the greenish stain of anemia, of torrid heat."[96] In the final installment of her Indochina trilogy, *The North China Lover,* Lagonelle becomes simply *"Hélène Lagonelle, dite de Dalat."*[97] In this later novel, Lagonelle blames her fatigue in Saigon on the need to "acclimat[e] . . . after Dalat."[98]

Dalat not only spared Lagonelle the greenish hue of her young compatriots in Saigon, it also caused the climatic equivalent of the bends when she returned to the sweltering colonial metropolis. Far be it for me to suggest that the radical change of temperature between Dalat and Saigon went without consequences on one's wellness, regardless of race. Rather, I wish to show that Dalat's pristine, healthful, French reputation was, and long continued to be, articulated in climatic terms.

By the 1930s, the era in which Duras's Indochina novels are set, Dalat had emerged as the colony's premier site of European schooling, as well as a predominantly white female space where French families could thrive in the absence of fathers and husbands, who worked in the deltas, in Saigon, or in Cambodia. In other words, Dalat had become a place to nurture the most supposedly fragile European constitutions, like Lagonelle's, precisely on the basis of Pennequin's conceptions. The general, after all, had held that racial perpetuation could be facilitated by the Lang-Bian's temperate microclimate. In Duras's universe, like Pennequin's or Carton's, Dalat preserved health and averted, even cured, disease on the basis of climate.

REST CAMP OR BOOT CAMP?

Duras provides one window onto medical practices, perceptions, and uses of Dalat. However, nowhere is the actual application of colonial medical knowledge at Dalat more clearly evident than in the question of troop health and bureaucratic furloughs. At the dawn of the twentieth century, a soldier by the name of Silbermann reached Cochinchina as his final assignment, bringing to a close fifteen years of military service. The veteran of Algeria, Madagascar, China, and Tonkin had never before seen soldiers coddled as they were in Cochinchina. "They are treated here as delicate objects, fragile organisms," he observed, jarred. The seasoned soldier elaborated, "they are only sent outside their bases in dire cases."[99] Paradoxically, the discourse of European frailness was deployed most insistently in the military.

In 1903, Dr. Maurice Cognacq posited that the Lang-Bian would "fortify" weakened colonial troops, and remedy their malaria, anemia, and dyspepsia. Besides, the plateau's size would make it a wonderful shooting range. Cognacq showed little patience for skeptics who claimed that the region would leave troops bored, idle, and nostalgic. Like Dr. Haueur before him, Cognacq predicted that prostitutes and bars would soon follow the troops onto the mountain. In short, Cognacq believed that virtually all of Cochinchina's troops should be stationed on the Lang-Bian plateau, save for a small unit posted at Saigon and Cap Saint-Jacques.[100] General Pennequin shared this outlook, writing in 1904 that Dalat outshone every other hill station and sanatorium in the French empire, certainly those in the "old colonies": the resorts of Camp Jacob and Balata in the Caribbean, and the spa of Salazie in Réunion.[101]

Questions about the Lang-Bian's actual efficacy as a thermal panacea, and delays in constructing the rail line conspired to stall the creation of a "vast military camp" on the Lang-Bian. A 1906 article posed the chicken-or-egg question of whether the military camp should come before or after the rail connection. The article concluded the latter, since the narrow road from Phan Rang was not yet suitable for automobiles, let alone the rapid deployment of massed troops.[102] General Emile Voyron disagreed. The enemy, whomever that might be, might not show the courtesy of waiting ten years for the railroad to be completed. Voyron was intent on using Dalat for keeping troops fresh, literally and figuratively. He instructed that fifty soldiers be sent there immediately, so as to pave the way for five hundred more.[103] Voyron's order kept Dalat relevant at a time when several factors, including labor shortages and serious doubts about healthfulness, threatened to undermine the hill station. In August 1906, the military requested funds to raise hygienic standards at Dalat, with an eye to posting Voyron's fifty soldiers there.[104]

Governor General Paul Beau strove to balance civilian and military interests. He remarked in 1904 that Dalat's emerging military role should not infringe upon its other functions. He insisted on reserving spaces for "the civil population, both European and indigenous, comprised of not only vacationers and convalescents, but also suppliers, settlers, and industrialists."[105] At its core, this tension revolved around colonial priorities; it also mediated and reflected competing claims of vulnerability. The issue came to a head in the late 1920s. Governor General Pierre Pasquier considered Dalat's central role to be as "a rest station dedicated to women and children."[106] He deemed this primary identity incompatible with Dalat's function as a garrison town, and therefore halted construction on barracks within town limits. Other problems were surfacing. In 1931, for example, the govenor general's office in Hanoi requested that military personnel hold their fire on the wild deer roaming in Dalat's parks, and cease using them for target practice, since they constituted one of the town's attractions.[107] Sensing it was unwelcome in the center of town, in 1930 the military agreed to housing a maximum of 150 military personnel in Dalat proper. The military opted for a number of properties on the outlying plateau, including Camp Saint-Benoît, opened in 1939.[108] A delicate balance was struck, in which soldiers and sailors occupied positions on the outskirts of town.

SAILORS IN THE HILLS

That the French navy lobbied for a convalescence center at Dalat, 150 miles inland from the port of Saigon, speaks to Dalat's aura. Like their colleagues in the army, naval personnel in Indochina pined for fresh mountain breezes. The principle of a navy rest center in Dalat was established in 1917, as the hill station blossomed. At that point, discussion involved only one or two villas for officers.[109]

By 1928, new imperatives gave a sense of urgency to the project and expanded its scope, in spite of reservations on the part of civilian authorities about Dalat's gradual militarization. On June 18, 1928, the Minister of the Navy wrote to his subordinates in Indochina, approving the creation of villas for officers and a large barrack for enlisted sailors. The establishment of the first French submarine unit in Indochina had precipitated this turn of events. Naval officers explained that cramped conditions on board these tiny submarines amply justified that their occupants rest at Dalat between voyages.[110]

In 1931, the navy drew up strict rules on the use of Dalat's officer villas and sailor barracks. The officer villas would require a fee, but transportation expenses would be reimbursed if a medical certificate could be produced. Sailors convalescing in the barracks could do so free of charge, and have their transport reimbursed. When conditions permitted, sailors' families could be housed in the officers' villas. Everything was done to smooth civilian-military relations. On the touchy subject of firearms and illegal urban hunting, the head of the navy in Indochina insisted that hunting was strictly prohibited in Dalat proper, and that any violations of this rule would be prosecuted.[111]

The Centre de repos de la marine de Dalat (CRM), as the naval villa and barracks became known, would continue to be used into the 1950s. The establishment's requisite coat of arms speaks to its functions. It displays a French sailor wearing his typical pompom hat, reading in the hills, the imposing Lang-Bian peaks looming in the background. The sailor's pose is relaxed. The entire crest could evoke the simple incongruity of a sailor in the Alps, but for a panther atop the crest, which adds a degree of complexity by situating the scene in Indochina.

LEGISLATING REST AND REINVIGORATION

The very year the naval instructions on Dalat were issued (1931), General Gaston Billotte established a rotation of rest leaves for army personnel at Dalat. He reasoned that if furloughs were properly managed, every year a third of all military personnel in Indochina could take a six-month leave at Dalat.[112]

The military and navy were not alone in rationalizing rest on the Lang-Bian. The civilian administration and even private firms built such leaves into their schedules, in an early colonialist version of welfare policy. Much as the military decided upon rotations at Dalat for various units—naval, artillery, infantry—so did the civil administration divvy the calendar and a set of Dalat villas between regions—Cochinchina, Cambodia, Tonkin, Laos, and Annam—as well as branches: agricultural services, tax services, the Ecole française d'Extrême-Orient, the Bank of Indochina, to name only a few.

This system sprang out of Dalat's original raison d'être. We have seen that in the 1880s, French soldiers and civil servants were allowed trips to France every three

FIGURE 4. Coat of arms of Dalat's Centre de Repos de la Marine. Author's collection.

years. By the turn of the twentieth century, military personnel were permitted to return every two years to the metropole, where they could spend an additional four months of convalescence leave.[113] Between 1910 and 1913, civil authorities in Indochina formulated similar demands, requesting that like their colleagues in the armed forces, they be allowed to return to the motherland every two years, rather than every three.[114] As Doumer had imagined, Dalat was soon introduced into this highly structured schedule, making available vertical, altitudinal furloughs in addition to the costlier horizontal alternative of repatriation.

Already in September 1904, Governor General Beau issued instructions to administrators in different parts of Indochina. He explained that Dalat would soon become a large military and civilian resort, a de facto summer capital for the government general of Indochina, as well as for the administrations of Cochinchina, Annam, and Cambodia. Accordingly, he asked for a complete list of personnel that could be sent to Dalat on furlough, and for the number of buildings each region would require. Cambodia's colonial administration responded with a proposal for individual dwellings for the *chef de cabinet,* as well as for different functionaries and their spouses.[115]

Colonial functionaries benefited from subsidized accommodation at Dalat. Their health care was covered as well. After all, Dalat's purportedly regenerative influence rendered it a prime site to receive medical attention before returning to the sweltering, unhealthy lowlands. Legislation from 1916 distinguished between officials on medical leave in Dalat, whose medical care was free, and vacationers, who had to pay.[116] By 1917, colonial inspector Saurin calculated that even vacationing officials and their families could count on an indemnity of three piastres per day, and the cost of their trip to and from Dalat, which did leave some costs to pay (a hotel, including room and board was estimated at five piastres a day).[117] As this colonial social net fell in place, more and more officials were able to afford a stay at Dalat. Meanwhile, nonfunctionaries could "croak." At least so bemoaned a leading Indochinese economic journal in 1923, speaking on behalf of planters, industrialists, and other nongovernment figures.[118]

By 1931, new legislation allowed any colonial official armed with a physician's note to spend a twenty-day medical leave at one of Indochina's accredited hill stations, complete with a spending allowance and per diem.[119] Little wonder that many a colonial administrator wound up in Dalat by way of a doctor's office. The welfare state that was still in its infancy in the metropole seems to have been advancing at great strides for a small minority—that is to say, European administrators—in Indochina.

DALAT AS PRETEXT?

This construction of a colonial social net reminds us that Dalat's original raison d'être had to do with the vulnerability of colonials in Indochina. Late nineteenth-century colonial doctors grappled with ways of reducing catastrophic death tolls in the army and beyond. They did so with the methods and mindsets of their time, but just as important, they did so rather fractiously. There was little consensus on necessary altitudes to avoid malaria in the early part of the twentieth century. Dalat attracted scientific scorn from some quarters—from the likes of Bernard and Dourne at the very time that it was being created. Is it therefore fair to deduce that Dalat was but a pretext, hiding other goals having to do with power, leisure and control?[120]

With the exception of a handful of vocal skeptics, it is remarkable how pervasively Dalat's healthfulness became rooted in colonial consciousness after the Rossian turn. Doctors, geographers, administrators, travelers, generals, and novelists alike shared this common conviction of salubrity. If anything, then, the kind of social engineering assumed in a "pretext theory" needs to take into account the very real fears of the tropics—manifested by a virtual worship of Dalat's clement climes. Place and health remained enduringly connected, with Dalat the "France substitute" compressing the massive distance between metropole and colony. The notion of changing air remained strong well beyond Dalat or the French colonial world—revealing a deep and wide-ranging link between physical health, climate, and environment.[121] But Dalat was not simply conceived as a change of air; it was coded as a racial necessity, even a lifesaver. Dalat emerged as a panacea largely because it matched European mappings of hygiene and wellness. It did so even as mountains of evidence conspired against it. One reason for this stubbornness has to do with the ways colonial society handled the question of fragility. As Dane Kennedy has observed in the case of British India, "the climatic preoccupations of the medical fraternity were a kind of shorthand, comprehensible to all Europeans, for identifying . . . concerns about the precariousness of the European presence in colonial India."[122] Medical discourses about Dalat, in other words, spoke broadly, and not just within medical circles, to a series of colonial anxieties to be examined in turn in the coming chapters.

4

Early Dalat, 1898–1918

In 1901, Prosper Odend'hal depicted Dalat as *"une ville en espérance"*—a city in one's mind, more than any sort of reality.[1] Three years later, Pierre Dru, an official in the Garde indigène, described the place as follows:

> We arrived . . . at Dalat: open terrain with short grass, a bit like a well-tended park, low hills; on each hill, a wooden house, each more comfortable than my own. On one hill lived the Inspector of the Garde indigène [Joseph-Jules Canivey] married to a European woman much younger than he—a kind and welcoming couple . . . ; on another, the unwed postal official who spends part of his days looking at his European neighbors through binoculars, not out of any maliciousness, but just out of curiosity and to kill time; on a third hill, the . . . house of the Résident supérieur d'Annam [Jean Auvergne], with windows, furnished no doubt at great expense with a piano, a billiard table . . . china, laundry and so on, even a European gendarme's outpost to look over it; on a fourth hill, the administrator of the European Center [Paul Champoudry], sinecure in all of its splendor.[2]

In this almost caricatured setting, colonial officials bearing grand titles spent their days peering at each other, or hunting the region's tigers, while other administrators tried to manage the headache of bringing them supplies.

And yet, even though Indochina's future sanatorium consisted of only a handful of impractical homes on isolated hills, and some aligned spikes forming the outlines of future public buildings, the Lang-Bian figured prominently in Paul Doumer's 1902 report on the state of the colony.[3] More than a simple reacclimation chamber, Dalat emerged as a potential nerve center for the colony. Doumer mentioned troops on several occasions. Of all the agents of colonial power, surely their health and readiness for combat was most critical for perpetuating French domination over

Indochina. But Doumer envisioned the vast Lang-Bian plateau as more than a military base. Of this tabula rasa he wrote, "administrators and settlers will easily find rest, will send their families, and will have their children educated there." In a single phrase, Doumer anticipated each of Dalat's future colonial functions: a nursery for the French "race" in Indochina, a convalescence site, and a site of European domesticity where French women and children could enter the picture at last. Once connected to Saigon by a railroad, Dalat would quite simply permit the perpetuation of the French presence in Indochina.[4]

This chapter explores early Dalat. It considers a range of aspects, from Dalat's first European settlers to its transportation routes to agricultural experiments intended to make possible a wholesale cloning of French life, culture, and diet in Indochina. It also sheds light on some of the brutal methods employed to create this "utopia," most notably corvées and requisitions. In short, it considers how the idea of Indochina's sanatorium became reality.

THE THOUARD AND WOLFF MISSIONS

Doumer wasted no time in carrying out his designs for the Lang-Bian plateau. The governor believed that a rail and road link needed to be established before any major development of the hill station.[5] Accordingly, on New Year's Eve 1898, a mission set off for the plateau under the leadership of Captain Thouard and Lieutenant H. Wolff. The goals of this expedition were several: Thouard and Wolff were to chart the topography of both the plateau and its access routes, in view of establishing a future rail line, Louis Jacquet, Indochina's director of agriculture, was instructed to test the plateau's agricultural potential, specifically with an eye to introducing European varietals.[6] The Lang-Bian's role of panacea and rest station was already interwoven with its function as a breadbasket for the colony.

While Jacquet proclaimed his side of the mission an unmitigated success, the topographers expressed concerns. Thouard bemoaned to Dr. Yersin on March 29, 1898 that he had entirely exhausted his budget on coolie salaries. Savvy highland minorities, he lamented, no longer accepted knickknacks for payment as they once had for the Swiss doctor. More seriously, this expedition was discovering the hard way the fallacy of altitudinal immunity from disease. Thouard's words must have shaken Yersin: "The Europeans on my team are rather sick, and I am too, since I run around in wet grasses in the morning, I cross swamps, and I ford rivers. All of this has landed me a case of rheumatism that is acting up at present. Mr. Wolff is more or less all right. As for the [Annamese] coolies, they are all croaking of fevers. . . . If I had to do this again, I would think twice about undertaking such a mission for the reward of twelve francs a day."[7] Yet another source had cast doubts on the Lang-Bian's healthfulness.

Equally alarming was the finding that "there is no direct route between Nha-

Trang and the Lang-Bian."[8] Instead, Wolff and Thouard recommended that the future Lang-Bian railway line link up with the coast at Phan Rang, further to the south. Thouard and Wolff drafted a detailed topographical map as their final achievement. It revealed some of the dead ends and wild goose chases they faced in linking Dalat to the coast.[9] Dalat, it was becoming apparent, would require gargantuan human and financial commitments in order to become a reality.

ODDÉRA

The Italian elephant hunter Honoré Oddéra (sometimes spelled Odéra in reports) was certainly one of the most colorful early European visitors to Dalat. When asked by Doumer in July 1898 to find the optimal route for a rail line between Saigon and Dalat, Alphonse Chesne, the administrator in Bien Hoa deferred to Oddéra. Very few Europeans and even fewer Vietnamese, he explained, had dared to brave the leeches, flooded riverbeds, rapids, and "terrible woodland fevers" separating Northern Cochinchina from the Lang-Bian plateau.[10] Oddéra was an exception. Fernand Bernard depicted him in 1898 as the hunter prepared to show the captain possible paths to the hill station: "a singular character . . . who for the last several years has been roaming deep in the woods, living off his reputation as a tiger and elephant hunter."[11]

The hunter claimed to know both the forest and its inhabitants. He had sketched cursory ethnomoral portraits of the peoples one encountered along the route: the Cho Mas were "most peaceful and fearful," while the "Chou Rou" people between Rion and the Lang-Bian conversely were "much less sociable in mood."[12] The Italian adventurer, as we shall see, even drew up a Ma-French lexicon for use by engineers and military personnel working on the Dalat line.

In September 1898, the pachyderm enthusiast reported on his voyage from Bien Hoa to the Lang-Bian. He had hired teams of coolies at each stop. They cleared the bush, hauled the baggage, and provided passage across rivers like the Da Mi. Oddéra did not reveal whether or not they carried him as well, as was typical colonial practice. In any event, the team accomplished the grueling voyage in record time, leaving Bien Hoa on August 21, and arriving at Khong, on the southernmost tip of the Lang-Bian plateau, on September 4.

Once atop the plateau, Oddéra found the scenery bewitching. The big-game hunter described the setting as "magical." He waxed: "Here stand rounded mountains, like waves on a stormy sea frozen by a magician's wand." He was equally impressed by Jacquet's agricultural experiments. Indeed, Oddéra wholeheartedly embraced Doumer's grand scheme, predicting that "one day—if we can find an easy access road to this plateau—the [colonial] exile will find a land reminiscent of the motherland. . . . In the dry season they have recorded readings of four degrees Celsius here: this might as well be Siberia for the Cochinchinese!" Yet Oddéra recognized that two steep climbs at Dam-Mi and Balach likely precluded a rail line along the route he had taken. In due course, Saigon would be linked to Dalat by road along this route, while the rail line (along with another road) would run along the coast, before ascending to Dalat via Phan Rang, along the itinerary first recommended by Thouard and Wolff.[13]

GARNIER AND GUYNET

Alexandre Yersin's interest in the Lang-Bian had not waned. In May 1898 he visited the first installations at Dankia. He wrote Doumer from atop the plateau, urging the governor general to visit.[14] The governor would eventually take up the invitation, ascending the Lang-Bian on horseback in 1900.[15] The scientist counseled the head of the colony to bring at least two warm blankets for himself and each member of his entourage.[16] Yersin remained convinced of the sanatorium's merits, although his own designs had been thwarted. The Swiss researcher had just learned from Doumer that the future rail line would meet the ocean at Phan Rang, and not at his beloved Nha-Trang. Captain Garnier, with whom he was about to liaise, was entrusted with tracing a direct road link between the Lang-Bian and Saigon, as well as tracing the route of a paved road to Phan Rang.

Captain Léon Garnier appears to have borne no connection to the early explorer Francis Garnier. The former had completed officer training at Saint-Cyr before joining a commission charged with demarcating the border between China and French Indochina. He soon fell ill, and was repatriated to France in 1894.[17] On this his second stint in Indochina, in 1898–99, the young Garnier led teams of workers on road exploration around the Lang-Bian—a site dedicated to reducing precisely such repatriations to France. Garnier also scouted itineraries that could run directly from Saigon to the Lang-Bian.[18] By the 1920s, Garnier would become the Commissaire général du Lang-Bian, the governor general's representative in the region.[19]

Captain Paul Guynet's 1899 expedition involved implementing the actual paving of roads between Phan Rang and Dalat, and on to Dankia. Thanks to the labor of thousands of indigenous workers, major results were achieved. Doumer boasted that the road from Phan Rang to the Lang-Bian was virtually completed over the course of 1899.[20] In September of that year, Guynet indeed reported to Doumer that paving was being undertaken at a brisk pace—although the stretch between Balach and Som-Gon presented some difficulties because of swamps.[21] The cavalry captain from the Gard even considered the future of "his" sacred path to highland reinvigoration.[22] In an effort to dedicate the Dalat passage to European modes of transportation, he urged the governor to ban the use of cattle-driven carriages— read, indigenous modes of transport—whose uneven, almost square, wheels would eventually ruin the road.[23]

Guynet never lost sight of the prize, which is to say Dalat. Interspersed in his report on roads and laborers, one finds hints of early colonial activities at Dalat. The captain marveled, "I stayed at Dalat, and can tell you that the weather was delicious. We hunted the entire day without experiencing the slightest fatigue, and did so under better circumstances even than hunters in France this time of year."[24] Guynet manifestly favored wooded Dalat over Yersin's initial settlement at windswept Dankia.

By March 1900, the road from Phan Rang to Daban was complete. From Daban to Dalat and Dankia, a mule and porter path was already in place.[25] Only the Balach bridge and the mule-path stretch still needed significant upgrades. Indigenous laborers had accomplished nothing short of a titanic undertaking, in conditions ranging from convict labor to wage labor.

INDIGENOUS LABORERS

In his famous early work *French Colonialism on Trial* (1925), Ho Chi Minh pointed to the Dalat road-building expeditions as some of the most egregious examples of colonial abuses in all of Indochina. According to the budding revolutionary, "Requisitions [of labor] are nothing more than ill-disguised deportations. . . . Very few laborers return to their village, and in fact, the administration does nothing to ensure such a return. En route to the Lang-Bian, en route to the mountain where death awaited, underfed, going in fact days without food, the requisitioned or those serving the corvées either revolted or fled, provoking a terrible repression on the part of guards, and dotting the road with their corpses."[26]

The Dalat road and railway were indeed the bitter fruits of forced, coerced, requisitioned, wage, and corvée labor. A 1908 colonial source estimated that some twenty thousand indigenous "coolies" had perished trying to develop and build access routes to the Lang-Bian.[27] Colonial reports are sometimes vague about the type of labor used: forced or paid (sometimes the line separating the two was blurry), ethnic Vietnamese or highland minority. Still, by reading the colonial archives against the grain, certain patterns emerge.

HIGHLAND MINORITY LABORERS AND PORTERS

As early as 1898, Oddéra hinted that the highland minority "Ma" (a broad ethnolinguistic umbrella term, sometimes spelled Maa) could provide at least two thousand laborers to work on the road to the Lang-Bian. The elephant hunter argued that colonial officials were mistaken to dismiss such "Moïs"—the pejorative term for all highland minorities. Admittedly, he deemed them "intellectually inferior" to the Annamese. However, he suggested that if they could be introduced to consumer society, they would acquire a taste for labor and become fine workers.[28]

In 1899, Colonel Blim elaborated on these ideas. The typical Ma, he wrote, "is

solid, often athletic, and an excellent lumberjack and porter." Blim added the following caveat: "he still needs to be educated about remunerated labor." The leader
of this expedition aimed at establishing remote outposts to support road construction to the Lang-Bian noted that the Mas sometimes furnished him with some five
hundred porters at once. Yet he was keenly aware that the Ma considered this work
"to be a requisition," since "they do not count on remuneration for their work, and
they undertake transport from village to village without any enthusiasm." Blim's perhaps surprising solution was to extend French influence over the entire area so as
to tap into Ma labor in the future.[29] Here the civilizing mission and the language of
development or *mise en valeur,* were both tributary to labor demands in the service of a highland European utopia in Indochina.

Concretely, thousands of highland minorities were made to toil on the Lang-
Bian's infrastructures and roads. In his 1899 Cho-Ma-French dictionary, which he
drafted on the administration's instructions, Oddéra included such revealing
phrases as "How many coolies can this village provide?" and "I don't want children,
I need vigorous men."[30] A report from the Résident of Upper Donnaï province in
July 1900 revealed that "from Tanh-Linh to the Lang-Bian . . . almost every village
has been forcibly recruited. The number of porters requisitioned to date is superior
to thirteen thousand, and I estimate at six to seven thousand the number of coolies
used daily on different sites. Such are the needs for the Lang-Bian sanatorium, for
studies on the future rail line, and the placing of a telegraph line."[31]

A year later, the next Résident called for additional laborers from beyond the
highlands. Minority villages, he reported were literally being depleted through requisitions.[32] Indeed, the bimonthly reports hint, highland minorities subjected to this
intensive and sudden spate of unremunerated forced labor fled in large numbers
towards neighboring Laos.[33] Not only were people enrolled by force: often their carts
were commandeered as well.[34]

Through oral history, anthropologist Gerald Hickey has recovered some of the
voices of highland minority laborers. He relates the following Chru song—the Chru
being an ethnic group settled in the area between Phan Rang and Dalat:

I wept under the heavy burden I carried
I removed my head cloth to wipe my tears
After I passed three stations
My heart perspired
I used my garment to wipe my heart.[35]

The stations in the song may allude to the different posts scattered between Phan
Rang and Dalat when the road was being built in 1899.

However, it is equally possible that these "stations" might refer to the extensive
porter work practiced by highland minorities between Dalat's founding and the time

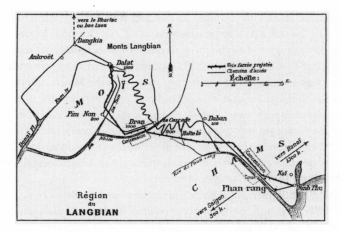

MAP 3. The sinuous porter and mule path to Dalat and the
projected rail line, 1905. From "Une visite au Sanatorium du
Langbian," *Revue de géographie* (February 1905).

that it was fully connected to the coast by road and rail in 1932.[36] In 1905, one such
station was described by an anonymous early French traveler, as a stop on the sinuous mule and porter path to the sanatorium.[37] Portering was relied on to keep the
Lang-Bian fed. Huge numbers of laborers were involved. Léon Garnier recalled how
in the hill station's earliest days, convoys of 250 coolies per week were necessary to
bring up supplies: sixty-kilogram sacks of rice were carried by four coolies each
(though by the time Gabrielle Vassal got to the hill station she recalled that the "maximum load" for minority porters was thirty kilos each).[38] In his 1901 report on the
hill station, Prosper Odend'hal admitted that bringing supplies to the few Europeans at Dalat had meant "exhausting the country with requisitions."[39] Passengers
too, mobilized hundreds of porters. On her voyage to the Lang-Bian circa 1907,
Gabrielle Eberhardt recalls some fifty porters carrying her and her small party of
whites to the hill station. She noted the "amusing, strident whistle" they made when
they grew tired.[40]

If anything, over the course of the first two decades of the twentieth century, the
administration came to privilege human over mule portering for the most challenging and winding part of the ascent. A 1916 study noted that the mule network
established en route to the Lang-Bian in 1902 had ceased to exist—"transport now
takes place on human backs."[41] The official transportation timetable for 1917 shows
that highland minority porters carried European travelers from Xomgon to Bellevue, where automobiles took them on to Dalat. They left Xomgon at 7 A.M., and
arrived at Dalat, in theory, at 1 P.M.[42]

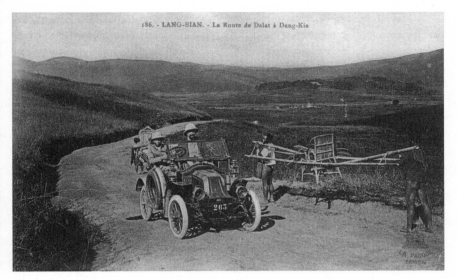

FIGURE 5. Overlapping modes of transport: an automobile chauffeured by a Vietnamese man crosses highland minority porters carrying an empty sedan chair, between Dankia and Dalat. Postcard, date unknown, author's collection.

ETHNIC VIETNAMESE LABORERS

Despite this significant reliance on highland minority labor, the majority of workers building the roads and railway leading to the Lang-Bian plateau were ethnic Vietnamese. In 1898, Garnier wrote Governor Doumer informing him of his plan to "take a certain number of needy families" from the more populated regions of Annam. These workers would, he wrote euphemistically, "permit the construction of the road from Phan Rang to the base of the plateau." Later Garnier specified that the families would be drawn from the north and center of Annam, and would be organized into villages along the path of the future road.[43] Mass resettlement and coerced migration were underway.

Different skill sets were sought. Levelers and stone-breakers represented a large proportion of the "coolies." A complex hierarchy emerged on the works project. Since Guynet's team counted only twenty Europeans, stretched out over the 117 kilometers from Phan Rang to Dankia, Vietnamese supervisors and translators were placed in positions of control over certain sites and tasks. Guynet tried to draw equivalencies between French and Vietnamese ranks: the *doïs* as sergeants, the *caïs* as corporals, the *beps* as first classmen. He relied heavily upon translators, since only one European member of his team (a forestry official named Paul Clerc) spoke much Vietnamese.[44]

In May 1899 as his team set off, Guynet provided revealing details about colonial labor practices. He drew up a complete list of bases, and assigned both overseers and a specific numbers of "coolies" to each station. Thus, 216 laborers from Cap Saint-Jacques in Cochinchina were charged with infrastructure support at Balach. "The less numerous coolies who could be found in the region"—likely *corvée* laborers—were assigned to improve the surface between Dongmé and Balach. Two hundred and eighty "coolies" from Phan Thiet province were posted at Mai Nuong, where they were to commence paving. Two hundred laborers from Tonkin, many of them skilled workers, were assigned to Dongmé. Guynet hoped to allocate another 1,500 to 2,000 "coolies" to the Phan Rang and Som Gon areas. Yet he complained that these numbers were insufficient, deeming it urgent to "call upon labor from other regions." Too many workers were being assigned to food and materiel convoys to the Lang-Bian, he complained.[45] Eight months later, Guynet lamented that laborers were being drawn away by the rice harvest and by Têt festivities.[46] He might have added, as had Wolff and his own medic Tardif, that workers were dying in droves, and escaping by any means possible.

Disease was decimating the ranks of workers. After remarking that his expedition's nineteen surviving Europeans would need to monitor aftereffects of malaria, Dr. Tardif added: "The workers have shrunk in numbers: they are being repatriated every single week."[47] Over the course of the fourteen-month Guynet expedition, Tardif observed that worker morbidity, which in his telluric model should logically have been dropping as excavation made way to leveling, was in fact increasing. Under these circumstances, laborers voted with their feet. After each pay, masses of emaciated, fever-ridden workers simply left.[48]

Desperation and discontent spilled over in September 1899, when workers toiling on the 200-meter Balach suspension bridge went on strike. Paul Clerc, the sole Vietnamese speaker among the French team, relayed the message that workers had not expected their recruitment advance (paid via their Chinese recruiter in their town of Quin-Hon in Binh-Dinh province) to be withdrawn from their second payment. A French member of the expedition, a *maréchal des logis* named Ely Cunhac, apparently attempted to defuse the situation with humor, whispering to Guynet that the strike bore an uncanny resemblance to social unrest in France.[49] Guynet retorted sharply that in France, dragoons would have mopped up the strike—much as he was about to do then and there. Dr. Tardif, who related these events, had been reading Emile Zola's *La faute de l'abbé Mouret*. As the alleged Balach strike leaders were ushered away at bayonet point, the doctor must surely have called to mind the strikers of Zola's great novel *Germinal*.[50]

Exploitative, indeed murderous labor practices endured on the Lang-Bian trail long after the route's near-completion in 1900 (part of it remained a mule-path, and the Balach suspension bridge had yet to be replaced by an Eiffel bridge). In a calculation that encapsulates colonial labor logic, the Résident in Phan Rang lamented

FIGURE 6. Som Gon, on the Lang-Bian road, 1899. A group of Vietnamese workers conduct leveling by hauling a massive tree trunk. From Dr. Etienne Tardif, *Un Sanatorium en Annam* (Vienne: Ogeret-Martin, 1902).

in 1901 that requisitioned indigenous minorities had barely been able to supply the Lang-Bian in food, let alone assist in construction tasks. Nor had the two hundred prisoners assigned to carrying sick patients up to the plateau sufficed. As a result, Prosper Marie Odend'hal complained, "we had to resort to beasts of burden."[51] To this administrator at least, two- and four-legged donkeywork seem to have been easily confused. Léon Garnier, for his part, subsequently told a journalist of the hardships of Dalat's first European patient-pilgrims. He cited the fact that supplies had to be carried up on "human backs"—neglecting to add whose backs were doing the hauling.[52] European rest-seekers carried up the mountain still groused about their own conditions.

In 1902 and 1903 an entrepreneur by the name of Charléty signed contracts with the colonial administration. They governed the transportation of passengers, and covered the eventual paving of the final stretches, from Daban to Dalat. Once again, prisoners came into play. The administration was to provide and feed three hundred convicts to pave the road, in order to make it fully accessible to automobiles.[53] Here Charléty and Odend'hal drew from the widespread practice of utilizing outsourced inmates for construction projects.[54]

On the roads leading to the Lang-Bian, columns of impoverished Vietnamese migrant families sweated and perished for miserable salaries, under abominable conditions (a 1905 source claimed that Lang-Bian railroad workers earned between

40 centimes and 1.50 francs a day, adding that this was far lower than the wages of workers on the Yunnan line).[55] By the standards of the day, they were the lucky ones insofar as they were remunerated at all. Alongside them toiled scores of convicts, minority highlanders enlisted under coercion, and local Chru, Cham, and other minorities enrolled by force into backbreaking portering. The very site destined to cure Europeans was exacting a terrible toll on indigenous laborers, whose sufferings the colonial administration mostly recorded in the column of economic waste.[56]

RAIL

Since 1898, the colonial administration had dreamt of creating a rail line to the Lang-Bian.[57] That very year, Yersin presaged: "On the Lang-Bian, Europeans will find a climate reminding them of France, mere hours by train from Saigon."[58] An 1898 law mandated the creation of the line. Initial leveling work was accomplished that year and the following one.[59] In 1903, a metallic bridge was erected at Balach (or Balat), some thirty kilometers west of Phan Rang.[60] Again, the cost proved daunting: numerous Vietnamese and minority workers, as well as French overseers, succumbed to disease while working on the bridge. Laborers fled, and the administration resorted to quadrupling salaries so as to complete the project.[61]

Disease continued to ravage columns of workers. Colonial officials seemed dumbfounded. In 1906, Garnier predicted that the rail line would take at least another ten years to complete because of labor recruitment challenges. Even "medically supervised and well paid workers" were found in very poor health. Some laborers from the Saigon region only lasted a matter of days before perishing or being evacuated from the area between Phan Rang and Dan-Him.[62]

In his 1898 report, Captain Fernand Bernard, the outspoken critic of Dalat, grudgingly recommended applying recent breakthroughs in rail adherence to connect the hill station to the coast. He invoked the Darjeeling rail line in India, as well as a recent line in Lebanon. Both used cog *(crémaillère)* technology. In his 1900 report, Captain Wolf likewise cited the Darjeeling Himalayan Hill line, and included photos and extensive data on the feat of engineering that it represented. As was so often the case, Dalat's creators, engineers, and planners emulated the hill stations of the Raj. In this case, that emulation put Dalat's rail line on the cutting edge of modern engineering.

The Dalat rail link took far longer to materialize than colonial planners had hoped.[63] Disease was not the only factor that accounted for the delay. The line had also proven ruinous for the colony: an initial two hundred million piastres had been raised for the project in 1898, yet in 1910, the line was abruptly stopped for lack of funds. Work would only resume two years later.[64] At the cost of many indigenous lives, and after several such delays, the steel track crept towards Dalat—reaching

Xomgon (still 83 kilometers from Dalat) in 1912, Sông Pha (40 kilometers from Dalat) in 1926, then Bellevue in 1927, and Arbre Broyé (within 10 kilometers of Dalat) by 1930.[65] The *Petit provençal* presaged in 1927: "This rail line will provide rest for all Europeans in Cochinchina and Annam." The newspaper added that ballooning expenses would be easily offset by the ensuing reduction in the high construction, materiel, and labor costs that had once been the norm in Dalat.[66] The distinctive *chef de gare* whistle would only be heard within Dalat proper at the end of 1932.[67] The effect on Dalat's popularity would prove prodigious.

IMAGINING DALAT

To imagine a summer capital of Indochina on the Lang-Bian plateau in the first decade of the twentieth century required a leap of faith. Governors Doumer and Beau and their associates had commissioned many a study in view of creating Indochina's main hill station ex nihilo. Meteorologists had painstakingly measured rainfall and temperatures on the Lang-Bian plateau. Specialists had studied future lines of communication. Others had experimented with a wide range of crops and livestock on the plateau. Still others compared Dalat's location with summer capitals and hill stations in tropical lands the world over.

Yet initial tests of the Lang-Bian by actual French settlers proved inconclusive at best. Dalat's very first mayor provides a case in point.[68] Before taking on the utopian project of founding a European city in highland Annam, Paul Champoudry had served as a Radical-Socialist municipal councilor in Paris, where he had overseen such matters as the creation of the subway and the international exhibition of 1900. The former geometry expert had earned a reputation on the capital's main elected body as a progressive force, a firm believer in social justice.[69] However, electoral failure had led the long-mustached sexagenarian, with his growing family, to seek adventure in Indochina.[70] In Dalat, he meticulously laid out the sites of future public buildings, and carved out individual leisure properties in what seemed to many French observers to be a "vast desert" of tall grasses and pine trees.[71]

In 1901, all told, Dalat counted the following buildings, many of which were still under construction: three cottages for administrators, a large building known as the Sala that doubled as a hotel, a cottage for the Résident supérieure d'Annam, another for the local administrator, another yet for the accountant, a house for guards and gendarmes, one customs office, a post office, a cottage for the public works department, a house for subaltern staff, and seven huts for soldiers or storage.[72] The largest edifice in early Dalat, the Sala, speaks to some of the varied influences already present at the hill station. A Khmer term, *sala* denotes a Cambodian shelter that served both as "a way-station for travelers and a communal meeting hall."[73] As Penny Edwards has shown, by the turn of the twentieth century, the term had infiltrated local colonial parlance to signify a "guest house or hotel."[74] Its presence in early Dalat attests not so much to the site's inherent hybridity, since the resort was meant to conjure up the motherland in its institutions, landscape, and architecture, but rather to the circulation of French personnel from all of Indochina through the hill station, even in its early days.

Dalat was no Paris, and Champoudry no Haussmann. After all, Champoudry's town was in a large measure virtual rather than real, much like his municipal budget. Any parallel might therefore seem strained were it not, some implied, for the fact that as the baron had in Paris, Champoudry was consumed with the idea of bringing sewers, symmetry, and a master plan to Dalat.[75]

The mayor's health and morale soon eroded in the miniscule, secluded European center on the Lang-Bian plateau. The only marriage he was ever in a position to officiate in Dalat turned out to be that of Berthe, one of his many daughters.[76] Since presiding over the wedding of one's offspring contravened French law, a temporary replacement mayor had to be called up to the plateau to perform the ceremony.[77] Soon Champoudry complained of more vexing and chronic problems: boredom, and worse still, poor health. The Lang-Bian's humidity and cool temperatures were sapping his health, he insisted. In 1901, he even petitioned the central administration in Hanoi to be relieved of his functions, enclosing a doctor's note attesting to pneumonia. By 1904 Champoudry implored Governor Beau to post him somewhere else, or at the very least to increase his budget and role.[78] If Dalat were at once a paradise and a remedy for Indochina's ills, Champoudry was either ungrateful or uniquely fragile.

THE TURNING POINT

As a result of some of these mixed health outcomes, but also because of chronic delays with the rail link, and serious debate over the financial cost of the Lang-Bian sanatorium, Dalat began to languish in 1909. Explorer Henri Maitre related the state of disrepair in which he found both Dalat and Dankia in December of that year: "Nothing is left of the prosperity of yesteryear, only pathetic ruins." Emblematic of this abandonment was a final bulletin on the wall at the residence of Dankia's inspector, giving the exchange rate of the piastre in March 1909, and after that nothing. It was as if time had stopped there and then, wrote Maitre. Dalat itself fared only slightly better. Maitre depicted it as physically unchanged since his last visit, yet eerily abandoned; only the small Vietnamese quarter, he wrote, offered much sign of life. It was a pity, concluded Maitre, to mothball the hill station after so many millions had been poured into it.[79] Indeed, the administration had borrowed vast sums to fund the Lang-Bian project: two hundred million francs in 1898 simply for the railroad. By 1909–10, funds were drying up.[80]

Only during the First World War did Dalat rebound, and emerge as a large-scale site of colonial tourism and leisure. In 1913, the hill station still numbered a dozen cottages. The Sala bungalow continued to operate as a hotel until its destruction in 1923.[81] Following Governor Albert Sarraut's call to better utilize the hill station in 1913, Dalat began to attract more European vacationers. The reason was simple. The Great War, and soon the U-boat menace, essentially severed the colony from the metropole in 1914. Gone was the ritual of periodic paid repatriation back to France; at last Dalat was able to fully fulfill its function of Indochina's "little France."

In 1917, with repatriations all but eliminated due to the Great War, and on the recommendation of colonial inspector Pherivong, Dalat was earmarked to become the main hill station for all of Indochina.[82] In the inspector's words: "The length of the world war has changed the duration of our service; many officials now stay six years or more in the colony. It has therefore become necessary to create a site where they and their families can restore their health in healthy and revivifying air."[83] Governor Albert Sarraut concurred, noting, "We have reason to hope that Dalat is destined to become the hill station for all of Indochina, and even for some of our neighbors in the Far-East."[84]

Colonial Expectations, Pastimes, Comestibles, Comforts, and Discomforts

"I thought that in the colonies chickens were skeletal, peas came in cans, and butter from a box . . . "

"No, no: at Dalat, there are papayas . . . but mostly strawberries, oranges, clementines, real lemons, just like in France. . . . Vegetables are not canned, but rather fresh, beautiful, and cheap. It's largely for this reason that vitamin-deprived colonials recover their good health. . . . While at Saigon at 11 A.M. all [European] women are at home, except perhaps for the most avid swimming pool faithful, in Dalat one sees them congregating at the Grenouillère, near the lake."

"And do they gossip, as in French resorts?"

"Indeed, and they do so all day, be it while golfing, hunting or fishing. What else do you want women to do?"

"And what about the men?"

"Hmm, they may be even worse."

"DALAT," *LA NOUVELLE DÉPÊCHE*, OCTOBER 12, 1935

This conversation printed by *La Nouvelle dépêche* in 1935 depicts Dalat as the quintessential anticolony. The hill station made European social life possible, allowing European women in particular, to live as in Europe. Gossip, banter, sporting, and cuisine all sprang up naturally, while they had been stifled in Saigon and the deltas. The highlands liberated the European body. Jean le Pichon went further still in 1943, turning his attention to Dalat's masculine transformative powers: "Dalat . . . has become a large resort, where colonials can be themselves again, where anemic children, can, under temperate climes, prepare to become men."[1] Sheltered as it was from the Indochinese sun, only Dalat's microclimate could recompose European masculinity, domesticity, and social life.

SETTING

Many a commentator marveled at the passage from the lowlands to Dalat—a veritable pilgrimage back to Europe. A 1908 account described the ascension of early settlers to the plateau: "After the suffocating climb through the forests of fevers and death, the air becomes lighter, we find a pine-covered mountainous region. It is as if one were inhaling France itself."[2] Similarly, in 1923, the widely circulated French magazine *L'Illustration* described the climb to Dalat as a nostalgic reintroduction into France: "Below, you saw coconut trees and rubber plantations, . . . giant bamboo, and now you are progressively climbing into Europe. . . . The Indochinese countryside makes way for that of the Alps."[3]

Visitors to Dalat were reminded of different French landscapes. For some, the Lang-Bian's distinctive pine forest stirred memories of the Landes. To others, the topography evoked the Vosges, the Alps, the Massif Central, or even the Pyrenees.[4] To others still, it conjured up the Riviera.[5] Léon Garnier observed in September 1898 that "the gentle hills on this plateau would not seem out of place around Bourbonne or Plombières."[6] In this instance, the Lang-Bian's rolling hills called to mind the Champagne, Ardennes, and Lorraine regions. Around 1940, one witness likened Dalat to a Scottish village.[7] This propensity for reminding colonials of home, or at least of Europe, legitimized Dalat's role as a cure: a cure for homesickness, for anemia, malaria—in short, for Indochina itself.[8]

HARDSHIPS OF EMPIRE

In 1897, the Lang-Bian had been touted as a potential lifesaver for colonials. From the very beginning, however, concerns over death and degeneration were linked to seemingly more mundane desires for comfort, a carefree existence, and improved quality of life. Michael Vann has summarized this link: "in order to preserve themselves, whites [in Indochina] had to be pampered."[9] Pampering was definitely part of the story at Dalat, although colonial doctors also counseled reinvigorating hikes and other sporting activities. By 1925, a colonial ministry directive placed the emphasis on Dalat's ability to "give Europeans the physical and moral rest they require periodically, in conditions of comfort and climate that are most appropriate for such relaxation."[10] Leisure, tourism, *bien-être*, reinvigoration, and sport found themselves inextricably connected.

Strange though it may seem to those familiar with the colonial dolce vita—the retinues of servants or scores of indigenous lovers—insouciance and comfort seldom ranked at the top of colonial expectations. French settlers, officials, and soldiers all braced for the colony long before reaching it. They were versed in missionary and literary tales of suffering and self-abnegation. They pored over manuals, and learned the colonial catechism. Maintaining racial standing, warding off disease, avoiding excesses such as drink that were believed to exacerbate the colonial malaise, such were the averred concerns of would-be colonizers. Settlers, administrators, and even doctors left for the colony with a heavy heart. As the newlywed couple prepared to set sail for Annam circa 1900, Gabrielle Vassal, bride of Joseph Vassal, born Gabrielle Maud Candler in the United Kingdom in 1880, was surprised to note that "even the doctors of the Paris Pasteur Institute . . . took leave [of us] as if they might never see us again."[11] Such farewells hardly inspired confidence.

The many prescriptive guides aimed at prospective settlers to Indochina must have only stoked such misgivings. In 1900, Drs. Kermorgant and Reynaud counseled colonials both to take cover under mosquito nets, and to avoid stirring the soil (a provision which also relegated all agricultural labor to natives). This dual recommendation reveals the coexistence of telluric and mosquito-vector etiologies. It also surely reinforced the discomforting sense of ubiquitous danger.[12] Like diet fads, some recommendations changed over time. The cruelly warm flannel belt, deemed indispensable for nighttime use by colonial troops in Indochina in 1886 "regardless of heat," was downgraded by 1900 to "useful in some cases."[13] What was a colonial to believe?

There was in any event no shortage of advice. Anthropologist Paul d'Enjoy's 1901 colonial health manual covered foreboding topics as diverse as spiders, sleep, and sex in the tropics. Close on their heels came seasickness, asphyxia, anemia, hepatitis, cholera, and malaria. As this range suggests, d'Enjoy was a man with broad interests: he had campaigned for a railroad into the Vietnamese interior, emerged as an expert in Vietnamese law, published on highland minority and Vietnamese cultures alike, and studied kissing and its practice in Europe and China.[14] This renaissance man's colonial handbook advocated slow eating and thorough chewing in the colonies. He stipulated that one should drink only with meals and always in moderation, and "never, rigorously never" go outside without a hat lest one be exposed to "mortal danger." Even those lucky enough to escape physical danger remained vulnerable to moral perils. D'Enjoy warned against nostalgia and spleen. "A sad man in the colonies," he stated plainly, "is condemned to rapid death."[15] Some suggestions have stood the test of time. D'Enjoy presciently warned of links between smoking and cancer.[16] Overall, however, the net effect of such advice literature, couched as it was in canonical, encyclopedic, and authoritative tones, was almost certainly to augment anguish, rather than alleviate it. A novel set in Indochina captures this prevailing colonial attitude at the turn of the century: "everyone here is frightened of everything: the sun, the moon, even of words [the novelist refers here to invented disease names like "Cochinchinite"]."[17]

In a 1910 speech to future Indochina administrators at Paris' colonial school, Edmond Nordemann listed some of the challenges facing colonials. Nordemann knew the matter firsthand, having served for twenty-four years in Indochina and learned Vietnamese sufficiently well to teach it at the Ecole des langues orientales. The professor kept his advice practical: he urged his students to learn the local languages. He also recommended that once in Indochina they hunt down mosquitoes in their rooms, and rely on mosquito netting as backup. Yet like Kermorgant and Reynaud, he also warned of the dangers of the earth itself. He counseled not to sleep on the ground floor so as to avoid "telluric emanations that rise from the soil under the moon's rays." Naturally, the white colonial helmet was de rigueur, as were two-story houses, steering away from the temptation of indigenous lovers, patience towards Indochinese servants, proper diet, and exercise. All of this was necessary if a Frenchman "wished to conserve good health, intelligence, and energy." Still, no matter how many precautions were followed, Indochina could not be considered a land of settlement. One must recognize, Nordemann explained to a future generation of colonial administrators, that "Indochina is not a settlement colony where Europeans can take root and multiply under normal conditions."[18] Dalat, in this sense, constituted the ultimate precaution—an artificial environment capable of making Indochina livable for the French.

DOUCEUR DE VIVRE

From the beginning, Dalat provided a space in which colonial anxieties could be allayed. Dr. Tardif recalled of one of his first nights on the Lang-Bian in 1899: "How well one sleeps when it is cold! I had not felt so relieved in four months. A light fog veils the landscape. Am I really in the colonies, or in France, enveloped by the Rhône's fog?"[19] Further on, the doctor took pleasure in small details, like chopping wood for a fire. He noted: "[These are] new, exquisite sensations: no helmet, no heat, no need for ice cubes, no mosquito net. God bless Dalat!"[20] Thanks to the hill station, all of Indochina's nuisances and sufferings were lifted at once.

Little wonder then, that Dalat's colonial motto reads "*Dat Aliis Laetitiam Aliis Temperiem.*" In addition to cleverly forming the acronym DALAT, the Latin conveys, "Offering joy to some, and temperate climes to others." It crisply encapsulates the relationship between vital racial regeneration, on the one hand, and leisure and tourism on the other.[21] The inscription adorned Dalat's colonial crest. The coat of arms features the Lang-Bian mountain and a tiger—the region's greatest hunting trophy along with the gaur and elephant. An ethnic minority man and woman, respectively hunting in a loincloth and standing topless, stand on either side of the coat of arms.[22] The ensemble captures a tension or at least a contrast: Dalat the familiar, the Europe-substitute on the one hand; and the exoticized and eroticized highland minority Lat and hunting site on the other.

Dalat served as the foil for the rest of Indochina. In a 1942 account tracing his heroic escape from Vichy-controlled Indochina, an anonymous Free French volunteer, almost certainly André Jubelin (a future admiral), began by describing Dalat,

FIGURE 7. Dalat's coat of arms, as seen on the cover of the *Petit guide illustré de Dalat* (Dalat, 1930).

his adventure's starting point: "For the first time in two years [in Southeast Asia], I am cold."[23] He added for his European readers, "those who have not known tropical lands will never understand the sensual pleasure of having cold air run down naked skin. I kept my window open all night." An inversion was at work. Whereas the tropics had been eroticized for time immemorial, in this instance Dalat's cool nights, rather than the more typical trope of tropical heat, was responsible for awaking the senses. What is more, implied Jubelin, those unfamiliar with the tropics could not even begin to fathom Dalat's importance. The Free French fighter continued: "The silence tonight [at Dalat] is prodigious. It had been so long since I had heard blood beating in my temples. Nights in Saigon, Hué, or Cholon are always noisy: songs of drinking sailors, some Chinese feast ruckus . . . and later . . . the noise of rickshaw drivers slapping the ground with their naked feat on the pavement. Tonight, none of that."[24] Again, Dalat was contrasted with Cholon's din, with the sounds and smells of Saigon's bustling Chinese suburb, immortalized by Marguerite Duras.

The young Dominique Mourey, who attended school in Dalat between 1937 and 1945, remembers a 1938 trip to Saigon, where he went to take a scholarship exam: "[On the train trip to the coast] the heat was stifling. . . . My mother, who was particularly sensitive, turned bright crimson. The boys [Vietnamese servants] themselves wiped their brows with towels. . . . Saigon was as hot as a steam bath. But it was a big city, lively and noisy. Dalat's provincial calm had made us unused to this setting."[25] Dalat's quiet and its coolness contrasted so much with the rest of the colony that they harkened back not just to Europe, but to provincial France. Like so many other colonials, Mourey vividly recalls that "remarkably . . . one required one or even two blankets at night in Dalat."[26]

In another context, Gregg Mitman has demonstrated the usefulness of health-seekers' memoirs and correspondence. His investigation into how "environment and place were mapped onto particular illness narratives" bears some parallel to our case.[27] So too does Janet Hoskins's contention that French colonial postcards need to be read as dialogical artifacts, whose messages, in relation to the card's image, render visible the "interiority of the colonizer."[28] Postcards sent from Dalat dwell on the region's temperateness and on the shock of finding a piece of France in such an unlikely site. In a January 5, 1928 postcard to Paris, a vacationer conveyed only two points: the remarkable temperatures on the Lang-Bian (12 to 18 degrees Celsius) and the author's impending return to sweltering Mytho in the Mekong Delta. In a June 1931 postcard, a woman wrote home to France: "I am writing this card from Dalat . . . since for health reasons I needed to flee the Saigonese climate and seek the hospitality of more temperate areas." On a December 1937 postcard depicting the villa in which the author was staying, a certain William wrote to Levallois-Perret (near Paris) that Dalat's nighttime low of 18 degrees Celsius made him bundle into "double blankets." Lest his Parisian interlocutor interpret this as a complaint, William added: "this land is truly marvelous." Yet another card, this one imprecisely dated, but clearly from the interwar years, contrasted Dalat's calm with "the agitation and heat of Saigon." "Ginette," explained the sender, "already has a clearer hue to her skin."[29] Dalat worked, if these postcards are to be believed.

This, in turn, speaks to the internalization of Dalat's medical rationales. In her 1943 diaries, a young Claudie Beaucarnot vacationing at l'Arbre Broyé near Dalat, remarked: "They say that one needs five days to acclimate. After this length of time, one's red blood cells replenish, and one feels healthy."[30] For his part, Mourey recalls the official justification for the low-income Cité Decoux in Dalat being "to replenish the red blood cells of colonial officials drained by an unusually long stay in the colony."[31] Visitors to Dalat actively described the beneficial effects that the climate, the site, the altitude, and the elements were having on their bodies. At Dalat, colonials were transformed, or rewhitened. If anything, they needed to reacclimate to being themselves.

THE PRODUCE OF HOME

Dalat revolutionized how the colonizers faced the tropics: it not only provided periodic reimmersion in clement climes, it also enabled the introduction and subsequent propagation of French foodstuffs throughout Indochina. Alongside his apocalyptic predictions of degeneration for the French in the Mekong Delta, General Pennequin observed with wonder in his 1904 report that one could grow European fruits and vegetables on the Lang-Bian plateau.[32] To Pennequin, both France's climate and its diet could be reproduced in Dalat.

Certainly, the promise of eating French was immensely attractive to homesick colonials. Between 1890 and the founding of Dalat, colonials throughout Indochina had relied heavily on imported canned goods so as to maintain Frenchness. Even colonial doctors recognized this practice to be problematic, as it triggered a new set of dietary deficiencies.[33] Saigonese high society so pined for French fruit and vegetables that one source recommended offering fresh artichokes as the ultimate dinner-party gift. The same turn-of-the-century source implied that Europeans were willing to pay a fortune, and literally queue on the docks, for the arrival of artichokes, melons, pears, and grapes from the metropole.[34] Félix Dioque, a customs official posted in Annam, wrote to his mother in 1907 about his futile and desperate attempts to grow a French vegetable garden. "It seems I am condemned to not eating vegetables this year," he bemoaned at one point.[35]

The archives register similar cravings for French meats. Several experiments were made at raising sheep on Phu Quoc island between 1870 and 1903: each time tigers and leeches conspired to doom the project.[36] The Lang-Bian's agricultural post would answer what had become urgent colonial demands. In 1904, the head of the Dankia experimental farm brimmed with optimism about his sheep herd, which thrived where sheep in other parts of Indochina struggled with the elements, predators, and pathogens. While advocating cross-breading between indigenous and French sheep, he deemed the future of sheep-raising at Dalat to be "exceptionally bright."[37] Subsequent results did not always match early expectations: Dankia's sheep would eventually prove vulnerable not only to tigers, but also to parasites.[38]

In 1898 Paul Doumer entrusted Jacquet, the head of agricultural services in Annam, with ascertaining the Lang-Bian plateau's potential as Indochina's French kitchen garden. Jacquet led the first of a series of expeditions intended to transform Dalat into Indochina's nursery and breadbasket. The farm he established at Dankia across the plateau from Dalat would later be directed by agricultural agent Paul Domerc, and after 1900, by Sous-inspecteur de l'Agriculture Auguste-Félix-Marie d'André. The latter's contract explicitly stipulated that he was responsible for "conducting experiments in agriculture and animal raising destined for feeding Europeans."[39]

Human relations proved more delicate than agricultural yields. Dankia's managers soon expressed concerns about the farm's viability. In 1899 Domerc deemed the barter system practiced at the farm to be both "defective and insufficient." It involved providing food to highland minorities in exchange for their work as farmhands. Like Oddéra and Blim before him, Domerc wished to transform highland minorities into avid consumers. In Domerc's words, "since these active and vigorous workers cannot leave their mountains, we must bring them goods and merchandise that will entice them." If this were accomplished, Domerc predicted, his farm could thrive with "all the coolies necessary."[40] The remarkable travel account left by Gabrielle Vassal suggests that "barter" was something of a euphemism to describe labor practices at Dankia. According to this firsthand witness and guest of d'André: "The [Moï's] agility and dexterity in driving or securing the fierce Breton bull . . . is most surprising. . . . [Yet] the Moïs never work for themselves unless it is absolutely necessary. . . . Unless requisition were in force, a European would never be able to hire a coolie."[41] Forced labor, more than barter, appears to have made the Dankia operation run.

Despite a tense labor context, Dankia soon yielded a cornucopia of European produce. After visiting the experimental farm, Garnier recalled in 1898: "During my stay I gorged myself on red lettuce, Brussels sprouts, radishes, green beans, tomatoes, carrots, . . . beats, sorrel, my dishes being garnished with a touch of parsley or chervil, all of which grow easily."[42] In 1901, Jacquet reported outstanding results with potatoes (a yield comparable to the metropole's), grapes, and strawberries. A few of the Breton cows introduced to the plateau in 1899 had perished, but not before bearing calves. Dankia's farm already counted sixty head of cattle.[43] By 1903, green beans, strawberries, potatoes, flagolet beans, carrots, celery, beets, parsley, sorrel, tomatoes, turnips, and onions were all thriving at Dankia. Hundreds of cattle, twenty-eight of them Breton milk cows, had acclimated to the plateau.[44] In 1906, following d'André's recommendations, sheep were introduced from the Berry region of France.[45] In 1907 Joseph Vassal took culinary stock of Dankia's possibilities: "It would be one of the Lang-Bian's great benefits to allow Europeans to eat as they do in France."[46]

The Lang-Bian's strawberries, especially, captured the attention of homesick Europeans. In a single sentence Gabrielle Vassal underscored at once how out of place they seemed in Indochina, and Dalat's pivotal role as the enabler of such wonders: "Strawberries, unknown anywhere else in this hot, insect-infested Annam, flourish here [at Dalat]."[47] In the freshness and Frenchness of its foodstuffs, at least, Dankia scored an unmitigated success.[48] If the Lang-Bian was a laboratory, it was first and foremost a bioagricultural one: turn-of-the-century colonial agro-specialists introduced everything from French herbs to sheep, flowers to multiple potato varietals.

EXPORTING DALAT

According to d'André, Dalat was sufficiently remarkable to actually attract new settlers from France to Indochina.[49] But would it be able to exert an influence even over settlers who could not afford frequent climbs to the hill station? Unlike its salutary climate, Dalat's fruits, vegetables, and meats could be exported to the rest of Indochina and beyond. Even colonials between leaves, or those of lesser means, could enjoy Dalat's green beans, strawberries, and other typically French fruits and vegetables, as networks of transporters and Vietnamese middlemen brought these products to Saigon, Hué, Tourane (Da-Nang), and Hanoi. This democratization of Dalat's horn of plenty was gradual and uneven, to be sure. By 1931, one voice complained that transport fees conspired to place Dalat's vegetables, fruits, cheeses and milk out of reach for many. Yet the article held out hope that soon large numbers of Vietnamese and Chinese would be able to enjoy Dalat's produce.[50] In the ensuing decade, Dalat's fruit and vegetables especially did slowly become more accessible; a 1936 Saigon ad for fresh Dalat artichokes insisted on the vendor's "moderate prices."[51]

Along the way, Vietnamese cuisine gradually appropriated several Dalat crops. The present-day visitor to Ho Chi Minh City can expect to find savory Dalat strawberry ice cream or *kem;* artichoke tea remains a Dalat specialty; and Dalat today produces red and white wine. These examples reflect a culinary hybridity at the very opposite of Dalat's initial purpose: catering to the colonial population with French foodstuffs.

HIKING AND SPORT

Un voyage à Dalat: quelle bonne
    aventure!
	A trip to Dalat: what
	    a fine adventure!

Déjà depuis longtemps on étouffe
    à Saigon.
	For some time, Saigon
	    has been suffocating.

Avez-vous entendu? "Voyageurs en voiture!"	Did you hear? "Passengers aboard!"

La machine a sifflé: montons vite
    en wagon.
	The engine has whistled:
	    let us climb in.

On arrive à Dalat—Ah—quels
    beaux paysages!
	We reach Dalat: ah, what beautiful
	    scenery!

Comme on respire ici l'air pur
    et frais du ciel!
	One breathes the clean, pure air
	    of the heavens!

Sautons vite du train, emportons
    nos bagages,
	Let's quickly exit the train,
	    take our bags,

Allons nous installer tout de suite à l'hôtel.	Settle right away in the hotel.

Sortons nous promener sur
    les hautes montagnes;
	Out we go for walks on the high
	    mountains;

Prenez tous votre élan: je grimpe le premier.	Get set: I'll climb first.

De là nous descendrons dans
    les vastes campagnes,
	From there let's descend into
	    vast plains,

Marchant à la queue leu leu, suivant bien le sentier.	Walking in line, following the path.

Par le même chemin retournons
    au Palace;
	By the same path, let's return
	    to the Palace;

Aujourd'hui c'est assez: allons nous reposer.	For today that's enough; let's go rest.
Venez donc vous asseoir sur la haute terrasse:	Come and sit on the high terrace:

De là-haut d'un coup d'oeil on peut
    tout observer.
	From there one can see everything
	    in a single glance.

Qu'aperçoit-on là-bas? Que la nature
    est belle!
	What is that over there? How
	    beautiful nature is!

C'est le pic du Langbian: quel énorme rocher!	It's Mount Lang-Bian: what a huge rock!
Ici tout à côté vous voyez la Chapelle,	Here next to us behold the chapel,
La petite Chapelle et son petit Clocher.[52]	The small chapel and its small steeple.

Father Soullard, who penned these lines in 1930, had taken two months' leave at Dalat on doctor's orders. These opening verses of a longer poem reveal Soullard's sublime vision of the seemingly mundane. They also explain some of Dalat's allure: revivifying walks, tonic treks, or hunting expeditions, followed by relaxation at the Dalat Palace Hotel. Combined with sports, such activities constituted Dalat's greatest advantages, boasted about in guidebooks.

Guidebooks dispensed advice on a host of hikes around Dalat: from the simplest— the single file path described by Soullard—to the most challenging. Fernand Millet and Pierre Bouvard's 1920 guide to Dalat explicitly connected accommodations, food, and hikes. According to this source: "Varied walks and hikes that are proportionate to one's strength, these help build a healthy diet, already excited by the cold, and the fine vegetables served at the hotel."[53] After her first long trek in the Dalat area, Beaucarnot scrawled in her diary: "I am tired, but it is a healthy fatigue."[54] She distinguished between exhaustion in Indochina's lowlands and deltas— believed to be caused by anemic torpor induced by the heat—and a genuine fatigue brought on by tonic exercise.

In other words, such walks were anything but trivial. Indeed in 1917, colonial inspector Saurin had used them as an index of Dalat's healthfulness. He barely contained his wonder: "French people from Cochinchina who took an automobile or were carried for even the shortest distance on the way here, are able to hike in Dalat, for the fun of it, between ten and fifteen kilometers a day on the many beautiful paths and forest walks."[55] Saurin echoed sentiments expressed a year earlier by a journalist: "In Dalat one can walk for kilometers, while one struggles to go 200 meters on the rue Catinat [in Saigon.]"[56] Dalat's miraculous tonic was thus believed to make Europeans more autonomous, more energized, and interestingly, less dependent on colonial hierarchies, porters, and technology.

In tandem with the cold and a French diet, these hikes revitalized Europeans who had been reduced to a state of torpor by Indochina's lowlands. The 1926 *Guide Madrolle* to Indochina took this logic one step further: "[Dalat's] pure air excites the appetite. One feels the need for movement, physical exercise, and intellectual work utterly foreign to us in Saigon."[57] Here, crystallized in a single sentence, we find the unifying rationale for Dalat's otherwise disparate functions: military base, educational and later university center, breadbasket of Indochina, sporting hub, and of course sanatorium and resort.

Any modern-day visitor to Dalat is certain to note the prominent place of sport at the resort. Besides hunting, which I will discuss in more detail below, by the 1930s the town boasted tennis courts, riding (on local horses considered too small by some), an eighteen-hole golf course, swimming, diving at the Grenouillère, numerous cycling routes, rowing facilities, as well as a soccer pitch.[58] Madeleine Jacomme recalls of her Dalat childhood in the early 1940s: "The immense lake . . . was our center of activity. [We organized] rowing parties with my sisters, friends, and myself, and on Sunday races between the different schools."[59] In the 1940s, under Vichy rule, a stadium would complete Dalat's sporting ensemble. As in the metropole, sports thus occupied a vital place at Dalat beginning in the 1920s.[60] Because it constituted Indochina's only site where such physical activities were deemed safe for Europeans, Dalat emerged as the colony's main sporting center for the colonizers.

GAMBLING, SOCIALIZING, AND COLLATERAL VICTIMS

As the sun set, sport gave way to socializing at the *cercle,* reminiscent in many ways of the club George Orwell depicts as the center of European society in colonial Burma.[61] Dalat's *cercle* had opened in 1926. It initially occupied part of the Lang-Bian Palace, before the dedicated club structure was completed. Its full title, *cercle des étrangers,* harkened to metropolitan spa towns, where *étrangers* could refer equally to foreigners from other lands, as to visitors from out of town. Dalat's *cercle des étrangers* was highly regulated: "ladies" and "friends of members" were confined to the *salle des fêtes* or banquet hall. Political and religious discussions were banned outright. The club's membership was set at ten piastres per month, and its clientele reserved and controlled. This strict oversight was owed to the *cercle*'s initial function as a gaming establishment. However, within a year of its creation, Governors Varenne and Pasquier closed the Dalat *cercle,* banned gaming, and sent gambling paraphernalia and staff packing. "Under no pretext," Pasquier cabled, "will gaming or *jeux de hasard* be permitted in Indochina."[62] Colonial gambling anxieties, which I will revisit in a subsequent chapter, had stopped the *cercle* in its tracks.

The establishment subsequently reopened, stripped of its most lucrative function. Indeed, it was renamed the *cercle sportif,* or sporting club, its gaming role definitively eclipsed in the new title. By 1937, visiting Europeans could count on a one-time nonmember fee.[63] Sandwiched between the lake and the Dalat Palace Hotel, the *cercle* still represented a privileged site for elite networking.

Other locales also served as both meeting sites and nostalgia flashpoints for Dalat's French visitors and permanent residents. A 1943 guidebook described Dalat's arboretum as "a deliciously cool spot, whose paths, small bridges, and streams make for an ensemble that rivals the loveliest corners of a European health resort."[64] Some preferred the lakeside. Iphigénie-Catherine Shellshear observes that in 1940, "The Grenouillère was a place where young people went to swim and socialize. The bar was well stocked."[65] The name itself carried a profoundly Parisian ring: famous paint-ings by both Claude Monet and Pierre-Auguste Renoir depict a bathing and relax-ation spot of the same name on the banks of the Seine at Croissy, on the outskirts of Paris.

By 1943, Beaucarnot recounts, a former pharmacist in Tonkin had opened a trendy pâtisserie in Dalat—the Pâtisserie dauphinoise, whose name reflected at once Dalat's provincial French ethos, and its alpine aspect.[66] Dominique Mourey specifies that the Pâtisserie dauphinoise was owned and run by a certain Ban Thaï, whose specialty was mille-feuilles—a French layered delicacy. Significantly, this ethnic Viet-namese French pastry expert ceased practicing his craft for good in 1945, a sign that Franco-catering had come to an abrupt end.[67] Indeed, according to one source, all French boulangeries and pâtisseries in Indochina were closed after the Japanese takeover of March 9, 1945.[68] Beaucarnot mentions another favorite Dalat haunt by the lake: the Restaurant la Chaumière, located between the *cercle* and the stadium.[69] By 1949, after the French presence had been restored, Dalat's butcher store was known as "La Lorraine."[70] No nod to Asia here: tastes and references evoked provincial France. As Shellshear recalls, "Dalat was not a particularly tropical, or oriental place."[71]

Dalat's population exploded during holidays, and over the course of the hottest months in Saigon. European visitors thronged to Dalat for Easter.[72] This was a sign of the town's religious significance to be sure, but also of its position as a short es-cape from Indochina's largest city. The 1935 Easter festivities in Dalat are worth re-lating. *La Presse indochinoise* reported in detail the weekend's diving competitions at the Grenouillère, featuring visiting French champions. The article stressed the wonderful weather, the affluence in Dalat's hotels, the fine coiffure of "Saigon beau-ties." The press chronicled the "Venetian celebration," the horserace, tennis tour-nament, golf cup, farm-animal races, and pigeon shooting."

As an afterthought, the newspaper noted that the festivities had been marred by an unfortunate accident: a Vietnamese militiaman had drowned and died during the canoe races on the lake. That the headline should simply read "Easter celebra-tions in Dalat" and not "Tragic accident at Dalat" betrays, no doubt, the marginal-ity of this death to colonial leisure imperatives, and perhaps a colonial perception of Vietnamese foreignness from Dalat.[73]

HUNTING

In his 1920 guide to hunting on the Lang-Bian, Dalat's head forestry official boasted that "the Lang-Bian's hunting grounds can be compared to some of East Africa's in their abundance and diversity of animal species . . . One can be assured of running into some large game." So began a detailed catalogue of gaurs, deer, tigers, panthers, bears, and elephants that sportsmen could transform into trophies within a short distance of the Lang-Bian Palace.[74] Much of this activity took place around Dalat, which, along with the nearby regions of Darlac and Banmethuot, soon earned a reputation as Indochina's finest hunting grounds.[75]

John MacKenzie has suggested that colonial big-game hunting was above all an exercise in power, in value-transmission, masculinity, classification, and elitism. Hunting, he argues, was steeped in heroism, exoticism, and adventure. It brought these frontier values to urban Europe.[76] Certainly, the Dalat case confirms some of these theories. In 1923 journalist and future deputy for the Seine-et-Marne, François de Tessan, scarcely concealed his admiration for Fernand Millet. The hunter, de Tessan boasted, had killed forty elephants, fifty tigers and panthers, one hundred and fifty gaur, and some six hundred deer.[77] As Indochina's "ace hunter," doubling as head forestry guard of the Dalat region, Millet led "eminent sportsmen of all nationalities" on hunting expeditions, outfitting them with materiel and matching them with highland minority guides.[78]

Millet's hunting guide featured a photo of three dead elephants lying at the foot of the Lang-Bian mountain. This may have proven too much of a good thing. Leaving aside the massive toll he single-handedly inflicted on local species like gaurs, elephants, and tigers—the latter two both slow-reproducing—Millet might also have pushed the limits of the unspoken hunting code. MacKenzie notes that by the late nineteenth century, a mid-nineteenth-century vision of hunting as a "hecatomb" had made way to a more moderate ideal. It had become important not to "spoil" natural resources through wholesale slaughter, but rather to share them with others.[79] Conservationism was no doubt a factor; so too was the ideal of moderation.

Even in the mid-nineteenth century, scale of hunting had served as a yardstick of respectability. Thus, on a hunting expedition in precolonial Madagascar in the 1850s, British missionary William Ellis scoffed that the Malagasy royal hunt "surpassed even the murderous battues of the German sportsmen."[80] Hunting conventions, in other words, had long reflected savoir faire and *savoir-vivre* (know-how and lifestyle), and were even marshaled as arguments to support one colonial power against another. Little wonder, then, that even while professing admiration for Millet's hunting prowess, François de Tessan advocated hunting restrictions around Dalat, lest the Lang-Bian's big game go the way of Baria's, Tayninh's, and Bien-Hoa's.[81]

Another factor weighed on moderating Millet and his hunting companions. According to the testimony of an American tourist and occasional big-game hunter at Dalat in 1919, highland minority guides and porters, so critical to the hunt, were steadfastly opposed to the idea of killing more than one tiger per expedition. This, the American voyager, Henry C. Flower Jr., attributed to highland minority religious and cultural beliefs, which he presented as something of a cynical calculation. In his words, "A wholesale slaughter would result in a campaign of vengeance on the part of the surviving members of the tiger's family, and compared with that, what is a buffalo or two, or a child, or a belated hunter, seized at the jungle's edge."

Amid Flower's tales of adventure (he describes tiger hunting, motion sickness induced by elephant rides, and a spectacular train fire, while assuring readers of Dalat's safety), one discerns an interesting minority moderating influence on the colonial hunt.[82]

A SLOW CONSERVATIONIST TURN

This influence notwithstanding, Millet, Bouvard, and the big-game tourists they guided around Dalat were taking a considerable toll on local species. And for all of the purported restraint of the hunt, certain systemic factors encouraged wholesale slaughter. This included the administration's policy of paying—out of Dalat— fifteen piastres per dead tiger and eight piastres per panther pelt brought in by hunters. This policy was still in place in 1917 when the brother of the American governor of the Philippines and avid sportsman, Archibald Harrison, undertook his second hunting trip to Dalat in as many years.[83]

That very year, in the thick of the Great War, Governor General Albert Sarraut broached the topic of overhunting around Dalat with the Ministry of the Colonies. Sarraut explained that the Lang-Bian had once teemed with game, which was being driven away by irresponsible hunters (Sarraut evoked "barbarous and irrational hecatombs"), increased human presence, and the hill station's rapid development.[84] This led Sarraut to pass a decree carving up the Lang-Bian into three hunting areas, including a "reserved zone." There, hunters would need to purchase a special three-month permit for two hundred piastres, and would be limited to shooting only male gaur, male elephants, and male buffaloes. In a second, "protected zone," gaur hunting was prohibited, as was the killing of Eld's deer and female elephants. The new rules allowed a dispensation for "natives hunting with native weapons."[85] Indigenous hunting practices were thereby exempted, as the French colonial administration sought to reconcile, as Caroline Ford has asserted, two imperatives and sensibilities: preservationism and conservationism.[86]

Increasingly, overhunting also ruffled the feathers of metropolitan conservationists, part of an interesting metropole-colony dialogue. In 1927, the National Committee for the Protection of Colonial Fauna (Comité national pour la protection de la faune coloniale) and the prestigious Muséum d'histoire naturelle in Paris joined forces to try to regulate hunting in Indochina. The pressure worked. In January 1928, Cochinchina became the first French colony to enact strict hunting codes.[87]

Within months, the Ministry of the Colonies was studying the possibility of establishing sixteen national parks across Indochina, seventeen if one counts the intriguing idea of turning Poulo Condore—an island penitentiary—into a nature preserve. The National Committee for the Protection of Colonial Fauna's plan called for an outright ban on hunting a number of specific species (elephants, rhinoceroses, gibbons, and a number of bird species, most notably), and for seasonal limits on others. The plan's architects had carefully studied the model of U.S. national parks, including those of Mount Rainier, Sequoia, and General Grant. Their professed desire was to balance the imperatives of "development" on the one hand, and "touristic and esthetic heritage" on the other hand.[88]

Of the sixteen projected Indochinese parks, one was to be located just outside Dalat, and would be devoted to protecting Asian elephants and Eld's deer. The park would be sizeable: at least 500,000 hectares. Yet the Committee understood the importance of hunting to Dalat's economy and reputation. It therefore decided to make the hill station the sole place in Indochina where the impressive gaur could still be hunted.[89]

A decree, signed by Governor Paul Pasquier on December 14, 1931, set aside the entire Lang-Bian plateau, including the city of Dalat, as a *"parc de refuge."*[90] A subsequent decree dated April 18, 1933, would clearly define the limits of the Lang-Bian park. However, the December 1931 decree, along with another one the same month, provided for the protection of fewer species than the committee had recommended, with only female elephants, gibbons, *singes à culotte rouge,* and *capricornes* appearing on Annam's totally protected species list.[91]

A GENDERED PASTIME

Let us return briefly to the golden era of colonial hunting around Dalat. Even more than the *cercle* or the golf course, one would imagine that hunting would have been the preserve, even the bastion, of European males. This cliché rings largely true. However, in some interesting ways, individuals from two other groups—European women and Vietnamese critics—challenged this order of things.

Gabrielle Vassal set out for Dalat in the first years of the twentieth century for the very reason that would soon bring throngs of Europeans to the site: a doctor had prescribed "a change of air [as] necessary for [her] health."[92] In the event, the doctor was none other than her husband, the Pasteur Institute's Joseph Vassal. Gabrielle Vassal's memoirs reveal a keen eye for detail, and a particular concern for the status of women in both Vietnamese and highland minority cultures. She describes with obvious fascination one of the porters who carried her to Dalat: "I had four bearers, but it was only after a minute that I discovered one was a woman. She looked quite as strong and capable of physical exertion as the men; indeed it is the Moï wife who bears the brunt of the day's work while her husband smokes his pipe in peace. Her muscular arms and shoulders and big calves were as fully developed as those of the stronger sex."[93]

No sooner had Gabrielle Vassal arrived in Dalat proper, than Joseph-Jules Canivey (inspector of the Garde indigène at Dalat) and his wife regaled her with a tiger tale over lunch. A tiger had nearly devoured J.-J. Canivey as his wife looked on helplessly;

at the last second a Vietnamese *linh* (militiaman) had saved the day.[94] Gabrielle Vassal took stock of this episode. Days later, when a tiger was spotted near Auguste-Marie d'André's residence in Dankia, she volunteered to give chase. D'André, the lead researcher at the Dankia experimental farm, initially refused on the grounds, in her words, "that it was too dangerous for a woman, that he was responsible for me to my husband, etc."[95] D'André, and a certain Mademoiselle Schein, equally hostile to the idea, eventually relented. On the first attempt to shoot the animal, Gabrielle Vassal was armed with only her Kodak camera. Just attending the hunt had seemed such an uphill battle, she wrote, that she had not insisted on wielding a weapon. The tiger escaped on that occasion, so Vassal tells us, because of the fear it instilled in the highland minority auxiliaries, and because of bad luck. Two marksmen had missed: d'André grazed the animal at short range, while a certain Agostini froze at the crucial moment.[96] After a second botched hunt targeting the same 3.21-meter feline, d'André distributed his entire armory pell-mell—down to his ornamental sabers. Panic had set in after the tiger had been spotted stalking Dankia's dwellings for food. Gabrielle Vassal clutched a Grass military rifle (d'André kept a Winchester for himself) and she eventually killed the great cat—now easily on its fourth life. Her memoirs recount how she and André had fired simultaneously at the tiger, thereby introducing a degree of uncertainty as to who could claim the feat. In any event, Gabrielle Vassal had fought hard to participate in the killing of a beast she deemed "majestic."[97] She ultimately triumphed after several men had attempted to keep her at bay. Are we to conclude that the Englishwoman had been emboldened by the gender roles she witnessed among highland minorities?

In her compelling analysis of gender and marksmanship in colonial India, Mary Procida argues that hunting and shooting were compatible with "an imperial femininity that incorporated traditional masculine attributes without completely eradicating fundamental gender distinction."[98] She challenges another interpretation, according to which most European women remained outsiders to colonial hunting—itself the paragon of colonial masculinity.[99] Instead, Procida views cases of European women hunting and shooting in India as emblematic of "a partnership between men and women as imperialists in the masculine mold."[100]

Turning to our case, Gabrielle Vassal positioned herself adroitly in the unavoidable, crass photograph of the hunter lording over a trophy. That typically masculine visual of "manly victory over . . . native game" adorns only the French version of her work.[101] In a variation on the triumphant pose in which the hunter positions himself atop his victim, Vassal situates herself slightly off-center from the tiger, whereas her male companion (presumably d'André) lifts his boot atop the tiger's bait, in closer proximity to the imposing feline's head. The bearded d'André's body language—smoking, fist planted on his hip, leg raised, conveying a combination of strained relaxation and "mission accomplished"—contrasts starkly with Vassal's more reflexive and guarded pose. Vassal seems to be granting d'André his vic-

FIGURE 8. Hunting
in the Lang-Bian. Post-
card, date unknown,
author's collection.

torious photo opportunity, while simultaneously claiming credit for the decisive
shot. The highland minorities who had time and again helped track the tiger, look
on, relegated to the background, well behind d'André's hunting dog.

There is no doubt that Gabrielle Vassal embraced the frontier mentality of colonial Indochina, and the adventure of the hunt. Yet Indochina was different from
British India in some important ways. For one thing, there is little evidence to suggest that European men in Indochina taught their wives to shoot, as happened in
the Raj. Gabrielle Vassal already knew how to use a weapon before reaching Dalat.
There is even less evidence to conclude that female gun-handling ever became a

FIGURE 9. Gabrielle Vassal (left) in her "hour of triumph." From *Mes trois ans d'Annam* (Paris: Hachette, 1912).

mark of "imperial service" in French colonies, as in the British case.[102] To be sure, some French women in Indochina were involved in hunting. Take the intrepid Berthe Champoudry, one of Paul Champoudry's daughters, who at the age of twenty accompanied her husband Captain Lavit on tiger hunts. Yet the Parisian press, at least, specified that Berthe Champoudry handled some of the tiger tracking; it made no mention of her wielding a gun, and an accompanying drawing depicted her unarmed.[103] Meanwhile, Gabrielle Vassal's account is so compelling precisely because it provides an enterprising Englishwoman's perspective on French colonial Indochina. It is tempting, in other words, to see in Vassal's narrative a rescripting, an alternate ending to Mrs. Canivey's helplessness. By her own account, Gabrielle Vassal slew the beast, upstaged her hosts, and saved the day.

HUNTING AS POLITICAL METAPHOR

According to MacKenzie, "British hunting in India constituted a repeated winning of battles in maintaining a hold upon the sub-continent. As in Africa, sport and war were easily elided."[104] If hunting were a metaphor for colonial domination or a replay of conquest, then it follows that ridiculing or questioning the hunt could equally well undermine said domination.

Such was the gist of Nguyen-Phan-Long's remarkable 1923 opinion piece in his newspaper, *L'Echo annamite*. In a bitingly satirical tone worthy of Voltaire or Swift, the newspaper manager, and cofounder that very year of the moderate Constitu-tionalist Party of Indochina, professed to have been swayed away from his original opposition to the Lang-Bian railway. His supposed change of heart followed the visit of a French deputy, Pierre Valude, to Indochina. Valude was unimpressed by the magnificence of Angkor Wat, and unmoved by much else in the colony, until he went to Dalat and shot two tigers. Likening the elected official to Alphonse Daudet's bombastic and bumbling character Tartarin de Tarascon (who only managed to shoot a weak, aged lion), Nguyen-Phan-Long asked whether the Vietnamese should be humiliated by Valude's priorities. Would the deputy speak only of his trophies when he returned to the chamber of deputies in Paris? After all, Valude's telegram home had been succinct: "Indochina is the most beautiful French colony: I killed two tigers. In friendship, Valude." As a Vietnamese, Nguyen-Phan-Long wrote of feeling like the mother of a woman avidly courted by a young man: the suitor's in-terests lay elsewhere, and the mother was simply a means to an end.[105]

The metaphor was not particularly subtle. The French, be they from France or settled in the colony, cared only for beautiful Dalat, symbol of leisure, relaxation, and sport, at the expense of Indochina's peoples. Tax and monopoly (alcohol, opium) monies—raised at great cost from all Indochinese peoples—were funneled into de-veloping a playground for the colonizers. Meanwhile, a metropolitan representa-tive, traditionally more sensitive to the plight of the colonized than colonial offi-cials on location, displayed in this instance neither concern nor even curiosity for the rest of Indochina. As Joseph Buttinger suggests, a segment of Vietnamese opin-ion was starting to resent the hill station. By the 1940s, Dalat had become a widely shared allegory for waste and Franco-centrism.[106] In anticolonial circles, the resort was fast emerging as a contested symbol of empire itself.

ENNUI

There was no consensus on Dalat even among Europeans in Indochina. For some colonials, Dalat was not just fun and games. Captain Fernand Bernard had con-demned the hill station as ineffective and wasteful. Other objections to Dalat were less lofty. Dalat evidently counted its share of irritants, duly related by visitors and residents alike. One of the very first Frenchmen posted to the Lang-Bian complained of intense boredom. In September 1898, Léon Garnier wrote: "We have been ex-periencing that despair-inducing grey weather of fall days in the parts of France north of the Loire, precisely at the same time as in France. Isolation under such cir-cumstances adds even more to the maddening monotony and boredom of watch-ing fine drizzle twirl and fall to the ground."[107] Dalat's phenomenal expansion in the interwar years seems not to have fundamentally altered this judgment. For all of his generosity towards Dalat, *L'Illustration* contributor François de Tessan ac-knowledged that the resort offered little to do.[108] Ennui did not dissipate. On a February 27, 1932 postcard to a friend, one Dalatois confessed bluntly: "Always the same here: I am very bored. To help pass time on Sundays, I attend mass in the morning and go fishing during the day."[109]

The field of boredom studies is sufficiently developed for a conference to have been devoted to the topic.[110] Suffice it to note here that in their quest to escape the dreaded *cafard*—a chronic melancholy or blues brought on in part by nostalgia for the homeland—Dalat's visitors and residents exposed themselves to other forms of tedium, the very one Nordemann had described as potentially lethal.[111] Garnier bemoaned the lack of distractions and the drizzle. Each exacted a toll on visitors.

DISCOMFORTS

Paradoxically, at a site devoted to health and reinvigoration, some colonials complained of ills, afflictions, and discomforts stemming from the weather. At the very least, the hill station's weather was widely recognized to be overly damp and chilly— especially in certain seasons. One of the first European travelers to the Lang-Bian, the elephant hunter Oddéra, wrote to Hanoi that as he ascended to the plateau he and his escort endured three to four hours of fine, cold drizzle, "that chilled to the bone." Yet Oddéra seems to have taken special European pride in withstanding sensations that "his Vietnamese"—in other words his porters—found "far too cold."[112] In order to make Dalat French, the Vietnamese body had to be construed as not just foreign, but fundamentally ill-adapted to the site.

In his 1904 report on the Lang-Bian, Dr. Grall had expressed concern over Dalat's temperature variations, noting that they could prove especially harmful to those needing to acclimate to Indochina. In this scenario, Dalat could actually prove counterproductive, by forestalling acclimation in Europeans who had recently arrived in the colony.[113] The microclimatic bubble that was Dalat could then only fully function, one assumes, if Europeans could remain in it at all times. Yet it was precisely those who lived there permanently who seem to have complained the loudest.

Unsurprisingly, early settlers dwelled on the prevalence of the cold and rain at Dalat. In 1913, one government official tellingly described the Lang-Bian's climate as "healthy but harsh."[114] Dalat's first mayor, Paul Champoudry, complained bitterly of the weather during the winter months. A doctor who examined Champoudry in December 1901 blamed the mayor's bronchitis on "the abrupt temperature changes and considerable humidity."[115] While his compatriots sweltered in the lowlands, a congested Champoudry shivered in damp Dalat.

Similar complaints surface decades later. In a 1920 review of its trials and tribulations, the company that linked Dalat to the interim rail station by automobile noted that its employees were "in deplorable health" because of the back and forth between warm Krongpha and cool Dalat.[116] Rather than solving a health crisis, altitude created a new set of challenges.

This problem never went away; Dalat's rainy season remains synonymous with mud and mold to this day. At Dalat's zenith in popularity during the colonial era, from 1940 to 1945 when the hill station was bursting at the seams, colonial residents commiserated about the unrelenting wetness. "September 1944" noted a local columnist, "was a record month for rain. Unfortunate summer vacationers found it raining every day. What is more, the temperature has been consistently lower than in 1943, which in turn was colder than the years before." "Is skiing next at Dalat?" asked a local magazine.[117] Yet cold and rain could not deter colonials avid for a taste of the motherland. One source jokingly implied that eager villa buyers followed the trail of handkerchiefs, stalking French residents with chronic colds and other "*Dalatites*" (read Dalat diseases), so as to pounce on their properties the minute they went up for sale.[118] Runny noses, it seems, represented a lesser ill, even an opportunity, for some colonials.

THE RISKS AND PERILS
OF A CONTROLLED ENVIRONMENT

Ultimately, Dalat failed to make the European body safe in Indochina. It was not for lack of trying. Guidebooks prescribed reinvigoration techniques, Europeans internalized codes of healthy behavior, and practiced activities designed to reaffirm their Frenchness. Sport, rest, hunting, socializing, dining, "eating local," and hiking were more than a regimen, they were Dalat's mantra. Yet drizzle, chronic colds, uncooperative tigers, boredom, and other threats eroded European defenses. What is more, by the 1920s, outsiders to Dalat's charms began to clamor for them to be more widely shared. While its setting, its vegetation, its architecture, and even its sounds, smells, comestibles, and temperatures might have seemed French, the clone proved imperfect, often ringing false for colonials. However, the various effects of these Dalat byproducts on Indochinese cultures, either by refraction or appropriation, remain to be seen.

6

Situating the "Montagnards"

There is no shortage of ethnographies of the minority highlanders around Dalat. Gerald Hickey's and Oscar Salemink's archivally based studies also double, respectively, as histories of the minorities of the south-central Vietnamese highlands and of French colonial ethnography. Rather than revisit these fine works, this chapter explores a set of more neglected themes, and specific interactions between colonials and highland minorities in and around Dalat. It ponders Dalat's role as a site of interaction between the colonial state and highland minorities, paying particular attention to power dynamics, spaces, representations, and to a range of practices and administrative realities. Readers seeking a more sustained analysis of the Lang-Bian region's highland minorities themselves, or of the French colonial ethnographers who claimed to know them, can turn to Hickey's and Salemink's books directly. Those interested in the question of highland minority porters and "coolies" should flip back to chapter 4.

Dalat's location was critical to French-minority relations. In the heart of a minority zone, Dalat lay near the crossroads of several different upland groups including the Koho, Sre, Chil, Lat, and Chru. Oscar Salemink has rightly stressed that these categories were and remain fluid.[1] However, to colonial planners, it mattered that Dalat seemed at a strategic point not just in its position vis-à-vis *pays* like Annam, Cochinchina, or Cambodia, but also with respect to different *ethnies* they had classified and categorized.

TRIANGULATIONS OF POWER

From the outset, the Lang-Bian plateau was envisioned as a site of power where the French could pit some of Indochina's ethnic minorities against the Vietnamese. In one variation on this scheme, France would provide the glue with which to forge minority alliances to counterbalance Vietnamese influence. This scheme was certainly not unique to Indochina: the *politique des races* had been widely used in Algeria and Madagascar, for instance. Other colonial powers elaborated similar strategies. Yet the policy is relevant here, as it shaped Dalat's many purposes. In 1903 General Pennequin listed among his rationales for the hill station that "our domination in Southern Indochina will not be complete until we have controlled the highlands . . . where the ethnic Vietnamese have never dared to venture." This notion that the Vietnamese had feared the mountains even in areas under their sovereignty was critical to French colonial strategies.[2] However, Pennequin extended the argument much further:

> Our Indochina is only really comprised of two parts: the Annamese lands and the Cambodian ones. Laos is a reserve for the future, especially if we are strong enough to hold on to the right bank of the Mekong. All of these regions are inhabited by very different races, all of which are easier to assimilate than the Annamese. One day, they will form an important counterweight to Annamese power. But each is remote and divided: the Mekong is not navigable; only a railway will ensure our conquest of these parts. Building a rail link to the Lang-Bian will thus be a first step.[3]

Pennequin envisioned Dalat as the nerve center of a future federation, banding together highland minorities allied against purported ethnic Vietnamese domination. The choice of a site of French colonial health and leisure in the mountainous "Indochinese hinterlands" was thus coded with powerful anti-Vietnamese meanings. Underlying Pennequin's vision was the belief that highland minorities and Cambodians were somehow more apt at assimilation than the Vietnamese, with whom some saw the colonizers locked in a clash of civilizations or even of colonial competition. Indeed, colonial administrators and ethnographers alike ascribed colonial ambitions to the Vietnamese.

In his statements above, Pennequin in many ways reflected established colonial wisdom. He echoed, for instance, Dr. Yersin's earlier idea that the French could profitably serve as the wedge in relations between ethnic Vietnamese and highland minorities. Antoine Outrey, in charge of Upper Donnaï province in 1900 added that "the Moïs fear the Annamites very much, and the Annamites never fail to exploit the terror they inspire in the Moïs."[4] Early administrators to the highlands sensed an opportunity to play the role of arbiters to ancient grievances.

However, more was involved here than the French simply posing as "protectors" of minority groups.[5] The picture was more complex. For all of the emphasis on defending ethnic minorities from the Vietnamese, colonial authorities were also intent on solidly anchoring the Indochinese highlands to their creation, the Indochinese federation, so as fend off competing claims from outside powers. As Frédéric Thomas has suggested, the "Vietnamization" of the south-central highlands, illustrated by the adoption of the pejorative Vietnamese-language term "Moï" (or "savage" in Vietnamese) to denote its inhabitants (in lieu of the Laotian term, "Kha"), as well as the use of Vietnamese auxiliaries to help map and chart the interior, served to distance the highlands from some of their other previous inland partners, notably Siam.[6] Indeed, French colonial officials even followed the entrenched Vietnamese practice of granting Vietnamese mandarin titles to select upland minority elites, thereby once again connecting the highlands to the court in Hué.[7] Thus was invented a "Moï hinterland" to the Annamese lowlands.

FOUNDATIONAL MYTHS

Still, there remained something fundamentally different about the highlands, which allowed colonial officials to view them as a tabula rasa. This colonial impression, and accompanying founding myth were both directly tied to the kind of health anxieties I analyzed in chapters 1 and 3. As Alison Bashford has demonstrated in another context, colonial priorities rested overwhelmingly on whiteness and on colonial place. Making Dalat French meant eliding both the highland minority and the ethnic Vietnamese presence within this space, a colonial place of exception, an oasis in the tropics.[8] Starting with Yersin's diary for 1893, in which he described "a vast, barren, and deserted plateau," colonial narratives insisted that the Lang-Bian was a French creation.[9] As a corollary, they often argued that the vast plateau had never been settled by indigenous populations, even less by Vietnamese. The reason for this supposed state of affairs was that the Lang-Bian, apparently meaning "cursed" or "disinherited" in one minority tongue, was purportedly feared by highland minorities. According to one colonial source, this malediction would prove beneficial for the French, for it spared the trees of the high plateau, whereas those on its slopes had fallen victim to the "vandalism of the Lat."[10] Colonials, conversely, would come to think of themselves as custodians of the Lang-Bian's nature.

Asserting the region's cursedness for minority populations and ethnic Vietnamese alike allowed colonial explorers to lay claim to the area in the name of French reason. Léon Garnier recalled: "When I first got [to the Lang-Bian], Dalat did not exist. Not a soul could be found on the plateau, save for in Dankia." He elaborated: "The Moïs were still unaccustomed to us. A few agreed to work at the nascent Dankia farm, because it lay on their territory; none wanted to come to Dalat."[11] The same theme of isolation recurs in other stories about early Dalat. Mayor Champoudry is described as "alone. . . . No Europeans, no Moïs either; they prudently kept their distance far afield."[12]

Dr. Joseph Vassal saw both advantages and drawbacks in the plateau's underpopulation: on the one hand, he observed, "we need not worry, by settling the Lang-Bian, of having to oust previous inhabitants"; on the other hand, wrote Vassal, one could not count on minority laborers. Despite their "docility," Vassal deemed them insufficient in both numbers and "in intelligence" for the massive construction and transportation projects Dalat required.[13] Dalat-dreamers found themselves in a catch-22, denying the presence or usefulness of minorities, yet desperate for disposable labor.

Close inspection of early reports on the Lang-Bian debunks the myth of a deserted plateau. In 1898, Captain H. Wolf reported, fresh from his mission, that the Lang-Bian plateau counted some 250 highland minority inhabitants, settled for the most part in the villages of Dankia, Bendonn, Prem, and Ankroët, on plateau's western fringe.[14] He sketched Bendonn's dwellings in his report, dwellings dwarfed by the surrounding hills, deliberately represented without their inhabitants, but dwellings nonetheless. How then could colonial reports so consistently evoke a deserted area? To be sure, the plateau's grassy center appears not to have been settled, and no doubt Champoudry and d'André's labor practices drove minority populations away from early Dalat. Yet the idea that the plateau was somehow "deserted" is without basis.

The concept of the Lang-Bian plateau itself as a colonial invention has proven remarkably enduring. In a recent official history of Dalat (1993), the elision of highland minorities is achieved, paradoxically, through the allegory of a young minority woman: "The day when Dr. Yersin set foot on the high plateaus of the Langbian and discovered Dalat, this land was savage like a young montagnarde girl. Only after that moment—like sleeping beauty awoken by the kiss of her charming prince, Dalat awoke from a long sleep to become Indochina's site for fresh, wholesome air."[15]

This quotation from Le Quoc Hung manages at once to exoticize highland minorities and erase their presence at the site, positioning the precolonial era as a long sleep, and the colonial moment as an awakening. This was and remains a recurring allegory. An official English-language volume on Dalat's history, also published for its centenary, chronicled Dalat's transformation: "From a reserved mountainous girl, Dalat changed her appearance to become an attractive and beautiful nurse whose beauty could fascinate Western tourists."[16] As we will see, this gendered mythmaking finds its origins in the many, overlapping, and often conflicting representations of the highland minorities of the south-central Vietnamese highlands in the colonial era.

"A NOBLE RACE"

In the colonial era, minorities of the central highlands fascinated travelers from Europe, local settlers, missionaries, adventurers, and administrators alike. Many of the accounts they left featured what we might label as "positive" stereotypes. These texts insisted for example on highland minority nobility, beauty, purity, and dignity, often contrasting these virtues with supposed ethnic Vietnamese vices. This tendency was certainly neither new nor unique to French colonial Indochina. At British colonial hill stations since the 1830s, colonial travelers considered upland minorities "superior in moral character and social qualities to the people of the plains."[17] The image of minority beauty was also for metropolitan French consumption: an undated French advertisement for "Moï highland tea" featured a highly stylized highlander woman carrying a baby on her back while harvesting tea leaves. To be sure, the image did fit the stereotype of an Indochinese worker laboring diligently. Yet its very representation of "Moï" otherness also marked a break from what Dana Hale has characterized as a monolithic metropolitan French representation of the Indochinese.[18]

Lucien Roussel's 1913 hunting guide to Indochina features implicit hierarchies, in which highland minorities were positioned well above the Vietnamese: "The Moï is more vigorous than the Annamese. He does not have slanted eyes . . . he is a handsome Asian type, sometimes bearing bestial traits like Malaysians sometimes more aristocratic features, like Indians."[19] On his hunting travels through the central highlands before the First World War, the Duke of Monpensier described the highland minorities he met as "intelligent and chivalrous . . . friends," adding that "women Moï are very pure, faithful to their husbands, and comport themselves perfectly." In sum, wrote the duke, in a brew of admiration and condescension, "these are good folks, sympathetic savages." Even their degree of savagery was open to discussion, "the Moïs having become [since the arrival of the French] more adorable, more malleable."[20]

Many colonial voyagers found themselves identifying more readily with highland minorities than with the Vietnamese. Gabrielle Vassal focused on the issue of language, specifically on the nontonal nature of highland minority languages: "The tone of voice, the rolling of the 'r' was so European that it seemed to me that if only I listened attentively enough I should understand what they said. It was the greatest contrast to the monotonous singsong of the Annamese. . . . The language has none of the intonations which make Annamese so difficult."[21] Despite remarking on linguistic commonalities with European tongues, Vassal's text also underscores highland minority alterity: she likens female villagers at Dankia to the witches of *Macbeth*, dwelling on their smoking, and on their long earlobes, distorted by rings.[22]

Generally, Europeans thinking back on their colonial childhoods in Dalat display a similar gaze on minority populations. Reminiscing about her time in Dalat in the 1940s, Iphigénie-Catherine Shellshear recalls that the minority people she crossed "carried themselves with great dignity as they walked in a single file," while Dominique Mourey remembers "the Moïs' enigmatic pride and the sculpturesque beauty of women Moïs."[23]

However, these primitivist, naturalized clichés centering largely on male dignity and female purity and beauty were anything but universal. In 1909, explorer Henri Maitre lambasted those who "depict the Moï [of the south-central highlands] as a

FIGURE 10. Advertisement for Thés des Plateaux Moïs. Date unknown, author's collection.

frank and free soul, endowed with all virtues, knowing neither crime nor lying." On the contrary, asserted Maitre, highland minorities were inveterate liars, as well as being lazy, thieving, vindictive, and "disconcertingly credulous."[24] As Oscar Salemink has argued, Maitre's view of highland minorities was evolutionist, yet, paradoxically, precluded any further evolution on their part.[25] In other words, contrary to Pennequin, Maitre fundamentally denied the possibility of highland minority assimilation under the auspices of France. His vision was no doubt shaped by his particular way of naturalizing minority peoples. In a poetic but ambivalent flourish, Maitre bade adieu to the highlands: "Darlac, perfidious plateau [north of Dalat], I leave your fever miasmas, but I keep in me . . . the unforgettable memory of the bewitching taste of your superb forests, your undulating bush, and your wooly mountains." His words belie a profound ambiguity toward a region whose inhabitants at once fascinated and repelled him, but whose natural beauty he incanted.[26]

This duality was recurring. While conceding the "nobility of their attitude" in 1935, *La Presse indochinoise* accompanied a gratuitous front-page photo of three topless female highland minorities with the following caption: "Without the artifice nor the rescue of makeup, their splendid bodies make for a violent contrast with their often bestial or inexpressive faces."[27] Similarly, the topless highland female minority postcard genre was clearly in demand in Dalat, with soldiers, administrators, sailors, settlers, and tourists writing home on the flip side of the card. Texts varied. Sometimes they commented sarcastically on the beauty of the model, sometimes they flippantly recognized the medium's pornographic dimension, sometimes they failed even to mention the image on the card.

Representations of highland minorities could be powerfully politically charged. In 1941, in keeping with Vichy ideology, Dominique Antomarchi sang the praises of Rhadé society. He especially admired its procreative resourcefulness, describing a scenario in which a sterile wife would provide a young concubine to her husband, so that they might have children.[28]

As late as 1948, at a time when the French administration was carefully trying to earn the favor of minority groups, a major Saigon French-language newspaper ran a column signed by the fictional highland minority character "Kiriho"—a pun meaning "he/she who laughs out loud" in French. Ostensibly lampooning the absurdity of modern Western life, the column entitled "Moï notebook" used the highland minority character as a picaresque, innocent, and naïve onlooker. The genre was nothing new; it modeled itself partly upon early modern travel narratives, including many armchair travel accounts, like Montesquieu's *Persian Letters,* which were likewise aimed more at lampooning French society than the "exotic" cultures they invoked as foils. Thus, during negotiations over the future of Vietnam, the Kiriho column poked fun at the French national assembly's desire for transparency and accountability: "In our tribes, when grave matters are debated, we leave the responsibility for them entirely to our representative, and during the discussions we do not ask them to share their secrets. We trust them, and they pow-wow freely. Only the final result counts."[29]

In other words, common people ought not meddle in state affairs, or in business they knew less well than their leaders. Furthermore, the piece suggested, the ends justified the means. The hierarchical, authoritarian realpolitik message was clear. In another instance, Kiriho commented on the ruinous cost of war for France: "We make war with the means at our disposal, and we fight the neighboring tribe, but for war to begin, it must be for such serious matters, that wars are rare."[30] Here the political gist was quite different: warmongering was cast as Western waste, even insanity. In both cases, however, the conceit remained the same. In these two examples, upland minority common sense was wrapped firstly in the lore of the American far west ("pow-wow" and "tribe" standing in as markers of the U.S. frontier), and secondly in almost primeval simplicity.[31] The highland minority remained at once a nonaligned observer, and a signifier of an undemocratic, unmodern, frank, vigorous, and authentic ideal. This ideal held an enduring appeal to some segments of late colonial society, and was consistently and enduringly contrasted with "dominant" Vietnamese indigenousness, generally presented as perfidious and tyrannical.

DICTIONARIES AND GUIDES

We have seen in previous chapters how colonial Dalat provided "exotic" attractions like big-game hunting—a pastime for which the colonizers relied heavily upon minority scouts and guides. Vocabulary lists, phrasebooks, and dictionaries were used to enable a range of activities for which colonials and minorities entered into contact—hunting especially, though not exclusively. As Bernard Cohn has suggested, lexicons in colonial contexts can be treated as artifacts designed to "mak[e] the unknown and the strange knowable"—while flattening the cultural contexts in which indigenous languages might be understood.[32]

These vestiges of colonial contact reveal some of the shifts and continuities, as well as dominant tropes, of colonial discourses towards minorities of the central highland regions. Most were produced (written or published) in Dalat, capital alternatively of the Lang-Bian, of Upper Donnaï, and for a brief time of Indochina itself, whose administrators were busy managing the businesses of hunting and labor recruitment.

The French-minority phrasebook genre developed over time, informed by previous generations of vocabularies and dictionaries, including the Jesuit phrasebooks from the North American continent and beyond—a genre that was by no means obsolete by the twentieth century. As Johannes Fabian has contended in an African context, these phrasebooks tended to constitute a first wave, the second one being the translation of religious texts. Yet Fabian also notes that the erudition of missionary lexicons (in the case of Katanga, which interests him, these were used to foster a dominant Swahili language) was such that the colonial administration sometimes deemed them impractical.[33] In the case of the Dalat region, although missionaries certainly penned some of these works so as to facilitate conversion, they were not alone on the early phrasebook scene, nor were all of their texts aimed at proselytizing. Indeed, many early lexicons should be read as byproducts of the frenetic quest for labor around the time of the hill station's initial development. As a result, they tended to be less rigorous and exhaustive, and more pragmatic than the exhaustive missionary dictionaries produced on minority languages of northern Indochina, like François-Marie Savina's 500-page *Dictionnaire Tay-Annamite-Français*.[34]

Intended for use across the south-central highlands, administrator Prosper Odend'hal's 59-page 1894 dictionary translated the French word "coolie" into four upland minority languages he listed as: "Tareng, Sué, Ha-Lang, and Churu."[35] The Italian elephant hunter Oddéra's 1899 Cho-Ma-French dictionary, commissioned by the administration with an eye to recruiting workers, featured essential sentences like: "How many coolies can this village provide?" "Make a straight path, not a crooked one," and "Who is the chief of this village? Bring him to me immediately." The text already anticipated some of the specific commands of later phrasebooks. Among the Italian explorer's more practical phrases one finds: "Wash my clothes,"

"Bring me fresh eggs," "How much did this bowl cost you?" and "I want to see the cook."[36]

Although penned by a missionary, Father Cassaigne's 1930 French-Lat-Koho phrasebook posted little religious pretense. It was aimed explicitly at three distinct audiences—tourists, hunters, and planters—an interesting example, then, of missionary-administrative cooperation. Though rudimentary, the phrasebook taught these colonial audiences to issue such orders as "Shut up!" "Hurry up!" "Get out of my way!" "Wake up!" "Leave!" "Be seated!" "Make way!" "Chop down this tree!"; to pass moral judgments including "You are valiant," "You are lazy," and "You are late"; to pose goal-oriented questions like "Where are the elephants?" or "Have you seen the tiger?"; and to convey practical instructions like "Pass the quinine" and "Build an observation tower!"[37] Distilled to the extreme, these concise phrases speak to colonial priorities and practices in the contact zone.

Necessary for the most basic of local interactions, these phrasebooks would endure, even as comprehension of Vietnamese and French increased among minority populations. A 1951 pamphlet entitled *Elements of Franco-Koho Conversation,* while professing a newfound respect for what by then were being described as "montagnard" cultures, still enjoined travelers to ask "you give me two or three porters go next village." The phrase is in a kind of deliberately broken French, patronizingly used in colonial dialogue. In this text, hunting has taken second place to a far more pressing and more recent imperative: veering minorities away from the siren calls of the Viet-Minh. Thus, the reader is taught how to "take advantage of tools that are at our disposal, but which the enemy lacks: money, salt, and gifts." The accompanying caption gives the Koho for "If you tell me lies, I won't give you anything and I will punish you, but if you tell me the truth I will offer you gifts."[38]

Even though they did not impart direct messages intended for minorities in the same way that phrasebooks did, guidebooks allow us to gain insights into the mentality of hunters and tourists towards highland minorities, or at least into the attitudes that experienced colonials expected to instill in them. Roussel's 1913 guide to hunting in Indochina provides a telling metaphor for French ethnic policies in the Lang-Bian. Roussel writes: "In these vast regions we have two precious and remarkable auxiliaries: 1) Autochthonous human savage races, barely known in Europe, and curious to observe, and 2) Indigenous and European dogs, these wonderful servants of man, so prized by hunters."[39] As his narrative progresses, Roussel argues for the creation of a new race—not of humans, but of hunting dogs. He advocates eugenic experiments, wherein the superior intelligence of European dogs could be coupled with the shorter hair and inherited local knowledge of indigenous dogs. In the process, the Dalat area would become the site of "the creation of a new, métis race."[40] Roussel's narrative shifts almost seamlessly from human to dog and back.

The hyper-specialization of hunting roles reflected and even accentuated colonial hierarchies. In his 1948 text on hunting in Darlac, J. C. Demariaux recalls the following advice he received on location: he was to take a European hunting companion, Vietnamese *rabbateurs* (beaters who drove the prey towards the hunter), and Rhadé trackers. "The Moï," explained Demariaux's source, "is admittedly lazy and slow . . . but on the positive side you will be surprised by his memory of place, his extraordinary sense of orientation and the sharpness of his sense of smell."[41] As in Roussel's account, the line between animal and human hunting associates, and their qualities, was blurred.

MINORITY-FRENCH CONTACT

So far, we have considered the place of highland minorities around Dalat in colonial grand strategy, in representations, and in prescriptive literature. Everyday interactions between French and highland minorities are harder, though certainly not impossible, to reconstitute.

Dalat had long featured an "Annamese quarter" present on all maps of the town since O'Neil's plan. Given that this permanent Vietnamese population had arrived along with the wave of French settlement and not before, and given that most accounts agree that Dalat itself was a colonial creation, what, if any, was the place of highland minorities at Dalat proper? In his 1914 report on the hill station, Dr. Joseph Vassal noted that "Moïs only ever pass through Dalat: those who do are either requisitioned, or porters, or prisoners."[42]

In his 1932 urban blueprint for Dalat, architect Louis-Georges Pineau tracked the population of the Dalat metropolitan area according to race. Whereas the number of "Annamese" had jumped from 71 permanent inhabitants and 300 occasional inhabitants in 1922, to 838 permanent inhabitants and 2,662 occasional ones in 1931, the population he listed as "Moï" had remained remarkably stable, going from 116 permanent inhabitants and 150 occasional ones in 1922 to 117 permanent and 220 occasional inhabitants in 1931.[43] To be sure, these numbers accounted only for the closest environs of Dalat. Minority villages further afield were not registered. Still, the numbers suggest that scarcely any minorities lived permanently within Dalat proper.

And yet extensive minority-French relations were being knotted on Dalat's periphery, and sometimes in town. Contact between French and highland minorities usually occurred when upland minority people entered Dalat to shop, trade, or work, or conversely, when colonials ventured into the hinterland to hunt or visit indigenous villages.[44] The contact radius was vast: in 1948, anthropologist Georges Condominas registered the importance of Dalat's market for the Mnong-Gar of Sar Luk, a village some forty kilometers northwest of Dalat.[45] Other kinds of relations were also developed between ethnic minorities and the colonial state: beginning in 1904, the French administration collected a head tax on highland minority people around Dalat.[46] By the interwar years, as Gerald Hickey has shown, colonial authorities were recruiting soldiers among minorities around Dalat. In this sense, Dalat acted as a hub from which colonial influence radiated over the Lang-Bian plateau and beyond. If the Annamese highlands had been "non-state spaces," sites of refuge from colonial control prior to Dalat's creation, Dalat's growing influence in the early twentieth century was fast altering that state of affairs.[47]

It was not so much their own relations with ethnic minorities that most preoccupied colonial authorities, but rather the question of Vietnamese-highland minority contact. Here, another shift is discernable: while in the 1920s colonial officials still considered "preservation" measures aimed at limiting Vietnamese settlement in the highlands, Dalat proper was increasingly exempted from these designs. It seemed that the initial imperative of sheltering highland minorities from Vietnamese control held for the rest of the highlands, but not for Dalat and its surroundings. Dalat, in point of fact, was also being carved out as a nonminority site in the heart of a minority zone.[48]

Nonetheless, colonial authorities ultimately came to rely more and more heavily on highland minorities. One of the main areas of interaction took place in the sphere of labor. Labor shortages had dogged French planners ever since disease had ravaged the ranks of workers during the first wave of construction on the Lang-Bian sanatorium at the turn of the century. A March 1925 report on the realization of the Hébrard plan in Dalat began by bemoaning some of the difficulties the administration faced in bringing Vietnamese laborers to the Lang-Bian. Besides the rapacious practices of intermediaries (coolie providers), the administration quipped that the high cost of living in Dalat was rendering the resort unaffordable to the workers themselves. "Free" Vietnamese workers were hard to come by; in many cases, the administration tried to obtain prisoners to toil on public works projects. This resource too proved limited, as prisoners were in high demand. As a result, highland minorities were used more widely than had initially been planned.[49] By 1925, they too were demanding higher wages. A report notes that "even the Moï's salaries have been raised to 0.50 piastres a day, with that of the Annamese ranging from 0.50 to 0.70 piastres daily."[50] Highland minority labor, though paid in this case, was also widely requisitioned—the two concepts were compatible, for the administration often forced minority people to work, while paying them this lower salary. Indeed, the practice of requisitioning minority laborers by force in and around Dalat only ended in 1952.[51]

As Gerald Hickey has demonstrated, Dalat's educational system was also largely closed to minority populations, or to be more precise, special minority schools were built outside of Dalat.[52] Although a few isolated highland minority people did attend some of Dalat's schools by the 1940s and as we are about to see, French-minority interactions did occur in the realm of tribunals, intercultural contacts were long restricted by the idea of Dalat itself, a city conceived from the start as a European bastion.

FIGURE 11. Colonial-era postcard showing minority people seated by Dalat's artificial lake. Date unknown, author's collection.

The relative visibility or invisibility of minority peoples at Dalat lay of course in the inconsistent eyes of Western onlookers. Frequently, minority groups were relegated to the representational background—as in a 1948 brochure for Dalat's Lycée Yersin, which featured a column of highland peoples on its cover without ever mentioning them in the text—a disjuncture that corresponds to a kind of colonial shorthand: minorities were not to be found at the Lycée Yersin, but they were "around."[53] It seems clear that the rhetoric of highlander absence at Dalat that began in the hill station's earliest days never really subsided. Yet strangely, the initial claims that Dalat was devoid of minority people at its foundation were occasionally turned on their head. Take Claude Perrens's 1943 article that asserted "long ago, the Moïs considered this place [Dalat] theirs; they were part of the scenery; one often crossed them, walking in line, long eared, grave, strange, depending on the season either draped in hand-made capes, or simply nude; they scared us a bit. Nowadays, they reject Dalat: they have given the land up to the whites, who, usually, wear more clothes than they do. Rare are the Moïs who now smoke their pipes near the market. They have become foreign to the décor."[54]

This passage betrays both the denaturalization of highland minorities at Dalat in the local colonial imagination, and no doubt the segregation between highland minorities and French over time. Quotidian interactions, if we are to believe this testimony, were becoming scarcer, or perhaps, simply less noteworthy, now that highland minorities were deemed less frightening. More profoundly, though, the above passage speaks to colonial blind spots, minorities having in fact become to Dalat's white inhabitants "parts of the landscape," contrary to what Perrens asserts.

DISPENSING JUSTICE

A 1900 report on Upper Donnaï province reads: "Exploited until today by Annamese pirates, the [minority] population understood quickly that it could find aid and protection from our administration." The very day that French administrative offices opened in the province, they were apparently flooded with requests from highland minorities trying to settle claims with Vietnamese merchants from Phan Thiet and elsewhere. The report goes on to explain that the highlanders had previously been unable to trust the Vietnamese authorities with their complaints. Now that fair and free justice was being provided by the French, the report concluded, "our administration has been accepted from the north of the province to the south, from Tanh-Linh to beyond the Lang-Bian, from the east to the west, in other words from the foot of the Annamese mountain chain to its Laotian flanks." According to this upbeat official, French justice, more than any other factor, contributed to highland minorities embracing of French rule.[55]

The rosy outlook of these early reports was soon put to lie by acts of rebellion and resistance on the part of some highland minorities. The murders of explorers cum ethnographers Prosper Odend'hal in 1904, and Henri Maitre in 1914, constitute only two spectacular examples of highland minority defiance to colonialism's many intrusions. These intrusions ranged from the massive requisitioning of labor discussed in chapter 4, to in Prosper Odend'hal's case, repeated cultural insensitivity. The defense line taken by Odend'hal's purported Jarai assassins—"Five years [in jail] is a long time; we have some buffaloes in our village if you want to take them instead"—also undermines French claims that their justice system was immediately embraced and understood in the highlands.[56]

In 1913, Governor General Albert Sarraut recognized a decree from the emperor of Annam, organizing justice in the province of Kontum. There would henceforth be three courts, one for cases involving only Vietnamese, a second for cases concerning only highlanders, and a third dedicated to incidents that concerned both highlanders and minorities. In the latter case, the French Résident would have the final word.[57]

In April 1916 the Résident supérieur d'Annam consulted with the governor general in Hanoi about the new province of Lang-Bian's judicial structure. The Résident proposed the freshly established Kontum system as a model. Consequently, around Dalat as in Kontum, highland minorities would essentially dispense their own justice, as would ethnic Vietnamese. However, in cases where a Vietnamese and a highland minority person were pitted against one other, the French Résident would decide and punish, in consultation with members of both ethnicities.[58] French colonial justice had assumed the role of arbiter in a province of French creation, while also limiting direct intervention in the many cases involving a single ethnic group. Here was a combination of direct and indirect rule that sought to render the vastly outnumbered colonial authorities indispensable.

The Lang-Bian was essentially carved out as a province so as to justify the creation and development of Dalat; yet in minority affairs, French colonial planners and jurists were careful to apply to the new province the same rules that governed minorities elsewhere. The choice of Kontum as a blueprint is therefore significant. It associated the Lang-Bian more closely to other highland minority provinces than to zones of direct Vietnamese control. Yet the new local judicial system, because it had been initiated in Hué in 1913, and by its very emphasis on Vietnamese-minority relations, also rooted the Lang-Bian in Annam, and reflected the reality of a growing Vietnamese presence in Dalat. As we will soon see, French colonial rule was enabling another project to thrive: the large-scale Vietnamese colonization of different parts of Indochina, including Laos and the Vietnamese southern highlands.[59] Vietnamese merchants, auxiliaries, and officials were increasingly visiting and settling Dalat. There was a strong paradox here, for in administrative terms, Dalat was fast becoming a capital for highland minority affairs.

DALAT AS CAPITAL OF HIGHLAND AFFAIRS

Though Darlac had been recognized an autonomous province in 1899, and Kontum and Banmethuot could both genuinely claim the title, it was Dalat that gradually emerged as the de facto capital of highland minority affairs.[60]

The process by which linguistically diverse minorities were homogenized into a coherent group by colonial officials has been well documented by Oscar Salemink. In 1909, Henri Maitre had asserted without hesitation that "the Moï nation does not, and has never existed."[61] As Salemink has noted, this first colonial line of thinking held that the inhabitants of the south-central highlands were as torn by linguistic differences as they were by ethnic or "tribal" ones.[62] However, by the 1930s and increasingly in the 1940s the category of "montagnards" ("Moïs" was still retained, but that concept too was being homogenized) was being used to describe minorities of the south-central highlands "as one group, to be opposed to the ethnic Vietnamese."[63] In 1938, the governor general of Indochina, Jules Brévié, writing from Dalat, asserted unambiguously that "despite differences in mores and customs that one can observe among Moï populations, they nevertheless form, from both a geographical and an ethnic standpoint, a homogenous bloc that is clearly separate from the other Indochinese races that have reached a much higher degree of civilization."[64]

This conflation was not simply semantic, ethnographic, or intellectual: it was eventually materialized by French High-Commissioner Thierry d'Argenlieu's creation in 1946 of the Commissariat du Gouvernement fédéral pour les Populations montagnardes du Sud-Indochinois (hereafter PMSI). In some parlance, the region's inhabitants were termed "Pemsians."[65] This semantic shift was partly a way of marking a rupture with the pre-1945 era; thus in 1946, the term "Moï" was finally and formally proscribed in official French correspondence.[66] Still, the new shorthands, like the old, were increasingly lumping together all upland minority peoples.

According to Salemink this reification process was based on a "fictional Montagnard ethnic identity . . . [which] created a 'homeland' for a Montagnard ethnic nation, distinct and detached from a Vietnamese nation-state."[67] I would contend that the actual process of "montagnard" unification began in Dalat in the 1920s. In Dalat's local newspaper, Le Camly, one article down from the results of Dalat's women's tennis cup for 1924, the reader stumbles upon an intriguing column. It attests to the fact that on March 9, 1924, a "Moï loyalty oath" ceremony was held in Dalat. The idea, hatched by then Résident supérieur d'Annam Pierre Pasquier a year earlier, involved convening in Dalat leaders of diverse minority populations from throughout southern Indochina. The ceremony was an elaborate co-opting of elements of highland minority culture; these were then fused into a freshly invented tradition.[68] Delegates swore fidelity to France in front of Résident Cunhac, one of the French founders of the hill station. In his ensuing speech, Cunhac tried to convey what France was, what it should mean to highland minorities, and what it could do for them. The "Marseillaise" then echoed and the tricolor was raised. Le Camly's coverage of the banquet that followed at the Lang-Bian Palace focuses on the party favors and on the attire of the European women in attendance (like Mademoiselle Garnier dressed in Egyptian costume), leaving no sense of whether the minority representatives were even invited to this gala convened in their honor.[69] By 1943, Claude Perrens would try to smooth over such disparities, by claiming a natural alliance between "cocktail drinkers and jar drinkers"—the latter a reference to highland minority culture.[70]

The minority fidelity oaths would be staged in Dalat again, but they would also rotate between other locales in the years to come. Still the idea of Dalat as a site for minority summits endured. In December 1935, the governor of Cochinchina, the Résident of Upper Donnaï and the head of Thudaumot province agreed to meet in Dalat to discuss a variety of highland minority issues. This event, which eventually became annual, marked a continuity with the oath ceremony insofar as it served to further unify highland issues. However, by the same token it also constituted a major break in administrative terms, for it blurred the once sacrosanct divide between a French colony, Cochinchina, and the protectorate of Annam. Even the head of the province of Thudaumot initially seemed squeamish about the boundary-breaking that was taking place, suggesting for example that the matter of a vast hunting reserve at the juncture of Cochinchina, Cambodia, and Annam might be tackled by a special federal committee.[71]

The first meeting, known as the Interprovincial Conference for Moï Regions, took place in Dalat in January 1936, and was organized by Lucien Auger, the Résident supérieur of Upper Donnaï. Unlike the fidelity oath ceremonies, no members of highland minorities were present. On the agenda was the matter of facilitating exchanges between southern inland Annam and Cochinchina. Also a priority was the establishment of reliable tax registries for minority populations, and the harmonization of tax-cards. Interestingly, the question of dictionaries and phrasebooks was raised. Auger announced that Father Cassaigne's French-Koho phrasebook would be reedited, since it fulfilled a vital function. He made a case for transferability, arguing that Koho was comprehended well beyond the Lang-Bian proper, and could be understood by most inhabitants of Upper Donnaï province, including by members of the linguistically further removed Churu (or Chru) people.[72]

At the Interprovincial Conference for Moï regions held at Dalat in 1937, Auger revealed that the empire of Annam had expressed serious reservations over the idea of a supraprotectorate authority that might further erode the emperor's authority. As a result, Auger announced from the outset, borders were not to be moved so much as clarified. Indeed, Auger explained, such a clarification had been rendered pressing because migrant minority people were flouting colonial control by seizing upon territorial ambiguities and ill-defined frontiers, presumably to escape taxes and requisitions. Upland minorities, the Résident remarked, "had taken this joke too far." After some discussion, it became clear that most of these movements took place across the border between Cochinchina and Annam. Consequently, Aurillac, the delegate for Djiring, suggested drawing a "straight line" to mark a cleaner border. The same question was raised with respect to the boundary between the province of Phan Thiet and Upper Donnaï. The delegates concluded this debate by calling for the creation of a geographical service—yet another wish that would materialize in Dalat proper. With amazing nonchalance, and without having consulted the sovereign of Annam, medium-ranking colonial officials had suggested redrawing the maps so as to stem highland minority population movements.[73]

A logical corollary of this new approach to minority questions involved the suggestion from the French Ministry of the Colonies, in 1935, to create a powerful new highland *commissariat,* which would have brought highland minorities in Cambodia, Annam, and Cochinchina under a specific, harmonized new authority, centered in Dalat. In this scheme, the military in highland areas would also form a centralized command. The project was designed in part to quell growing unrest, notably in the border zones with Cambodia and in eastern Cambodia proper. Although at least one administrator admired the almost "Roman" quality of the project—carving out a new country on which to extend a Pax Gallica—all Résidents consulted agreed that the project was highly impractical, and ultimately, undesirable. It was, they contended, bound to undo years of efforts, to gloss over some of the administrative "specialization" and detailed knowledge of local peoples, and to jeopardize existing agreements with the crown of Annam that already permitted direct French control over highland minority issues. In June 1935, Governor General René Robin relayed these grave reservations to Paris, and the project was briefly shelved.[74]

In 1939, the Ministry of the Colonies asked Governor General Catroux to revive the concept in another guise, by creating a "General Inspection of Moï Lands."[75] In addition to harmonizing policies towards upland minorities, the new Inspection was intended to facilitate the raising of minority troops. Finally, in 1946, the project of a supranational highlander bureau was fully realized in the form of the PMSI, which crossed the boundaries of Annam and Cochinchina.

The path towards a unified highland affairs bureau operating out of Dalat was somewhat more sinuous than I have suggested above. In a March 1940 report to Governor General Catroux, Lieutenant Omar Sarraut, placed at the helm of the new General Inspection of Moï Lands, explained that the Résident of Upper Donnaï province could not longer handle the many tasks incumbent on him. Dalat had grown into such a large center that urban planning alone consumed much of his time. As a result, the lieutenant concluded, while Dalat was certainly reaping very positive results for the colony of Indochina, it was paradoxically hampering the governance of minority populations. Sarraut was taking issue in part with the merging of the posts of Résident of Upper Donnaï province and mayor of Dalat. He advocated separating the two, thereby disentangling the governance of the French centre of Dalat from the management of highland minority affairs.[76] For all of the pressure, emanating especially from Paris, to homogenize highlanders typologically and harmonize and centralize highlander affairs bureaucratically, these goals sometimes clashed with Dalat's other raison d'être.

EPILOGUE

In November 1945, a primary school inspector in Banmethuot by the name of Le Gall advised the new French administration to bring an old project to the fore, by creating a single highland minority federation. He wrote that "the idea of a federation of the tribes in the Moï hinterland has recently been put into practice in the educational realm." To Le Gall, the issue was one of cultural survival: "Faced with the Annamese invasion, the native behaves the same everywhere: he cedes his land to the immigrant, who despises him . . . and is left with an infertile laterite soil, dense forests, and swamps infested with malaria. The French Résident, veritable slave-trader, still manages to find him to force him to work on plantations."[77]

The assessment was dire. Yet what caught the eye of the postwar French colonial administration in Saigon was not so much the threat of cultural annihilation, as the possibility of recycling previous plans for such a montagnard federation to new ends: countering this time not so much ethnic Vietnamese influence, as Viet-Minh influence.

Thus, one month before the Dalat conference of April 1946, which will be discussed at length in chapter 13, Minister of the Colonies Marius Moutet mandated the establishment of "an autonomous Moï territory." In a letter to the French high commissioner in Indochina, Thierry d'Argenlieu, Moutet explicitly rooted his decision in Governor Pasquier's earlier rationale of "saving the [montagnard] race and improving the inferior conditions of this population."[78] Dalat would soon become the centerpiece, indeed the official capital, of both a highland autonomous province (PMSI) and, remarkably, of the entire Indochinese federation.

Viet-Minh propaganda immediately seized upon the French resurrection of earlier plans for the south-central highlands. In its April 10, 1946 issue, the newspaper *Cuu Quoc* strongly condemned the French project to form what it called "a separatist movement in the Moï regions of Southern Annam." "Do not fall back into your old mindsets," it urged. By reviving this project, "the French would be breaking their word to mark a rupture with past colonial practices." Lastly, the piece insisted, "The Moï territories . . . are part of Viet-Nam and any attempt to separate them constitutes an attack on the integrity of Viet-Nam."[79]

In fact, this did prove to be at the heart of French strategy until 1949: the two Dalat conferences of 1946 left the city as the capital of a large "autonomous" PMSI region, one that answered directly to the French high commissioner in Saigon. As we shall see, with Bao Dai's return to power in 1949, French colonial planners—together with a relatively new actor on the Indochinese stage, the French foreign ministry—orchestrated an about-face, converting the newly created PMSI into Vietnamese crown lands. In some respects, this meant that French policy had come full circle, with the south-central highlands firmly reconnected to the Vietnamese monarchy. Read another way, however, the southern highlands' separate and unique status was only reinforced by this final colonial twist.

Throughout these many permutations, shifts, and reorderings, Dalat and the freshly invented PMSI emerged as the geographical centerpiece of Indochina's, then Vietnam's, ethnopolitical puzzles. Not only had the colonial state resolutely rooted itself into what one could argue was previously a "non-state space," but also it gradually remade said space into the cornerstone of an admittedly fragile colonial future.

7

A Functional City?

Architecture, Planning, Zoning, and Their Critics

[In Dalat] French determination has created an elegant and harmonious town, developed in such a way that it has become a veritable little paradise, in a setting of flowered gardens and pine trees. . . . In designing the town, we avoided pretentious and unattractive buildings. Everywhere, delectable villas hide behind lovely gardens, gardens full of flowers from Europe. Roads are wide, asphalted, and offer breathing room. On the vast artificial lake's limpid waters, majestic swans swim by. Tennis courts and a perfectly conceived golf course add a sporting note to the resort.
"PHYSIONOMIE DE DALAT EN 1937"

So rhapsodized a French journalist for *L'Asie nouvelle* in 1937. To that commentator at least, Dalat emblematized French rationality, determination, good taste, and quaintness. In other words, Dalat offered much more than just tiger and gaur hunts, the spectacle of highland minority peoples put on display for tourists, a luxury hotel, and a pristine natural setting evoking Europe; it was above all a perfectly designed new resort, where French urban planning made possible a "little paradise," an escape from the tropics. It is noteworthy that the above passage, which dwells so insistently on Dalat's inherent Frenchness—reflected in its vegetation, its aesthetics, and its amenities—fails to make the slightest mention of either local highland minorities or Vietnamese people. This chapter will focus on the themes exposed or suggested in the above quotation: the process of urban planning, the attempt to segregate the Vietnamese at Dalat, as well as questions of style, unity, and modernity.[1]

Much ink has been spilled on colonial planning and architecture since 1965 when Janet Abu Lughod bemoaned that the topic remained utterly uncharted.[2] This chapter will consider the chasm between architectural and spatial discourses on the one hand, and practices on the other. To be sure, there was a guiding principle at Dalat: colonial segregation—but even its implementation gave rise to tensions of all sorts. The most prominent studies on French colonial urbanism to date suggest that the colonies represented "testing grounds" where "master plans" (often unimaginable in the metropole) could be carried out.[3] While Dalat certainly saw its share of master plans in the colonial era—five to be precise—their implementation proved a messy affair. Budget constraints, local pressure groups, and villa owners challenged imposed visions. The Vietnamese bourgeoisie publicly opposed schemes to cordon it off. Freshly created councils endlessly debated questions of style and good taste. There is, in other words, a major paradox between Dalat the quintessentially planned resort—designed from nil—and the chaos or at least dissonances that often seemed to result. In order to investigate this tension, one needs to examine more than the master plans themselves, and delve into municipal council minutes, press reactions, and petitions, reading each against the grain.[4]

URBAN MASTER PLANS

A military report dated December 1900 laid out the original blueprint for Dalat. Early planners conceived of this vast plateau as a tabula rasa, presenting multiple advantages and a few drawbacks. On the one hand, it allowed the colonial administration to establish a European town removed from the traditional seats of Vietnamese power, on the model of the British hill stations in India, which served as summer capitals. On the other hand, everything, literally, needed to be built: transportation routes, infrastructures, buildings, villas, supply networks—all daunting tasks in a remote highland region. Still, the 1900 report envisioned that "with a rail line, comfortable buildings, paved roads, vegetable and fruit gardens, the salubrious Lang-Bian plateau could become a decent little piece of France, and a good colonial sanatorium."[5]

Dalat would experience a prodigious growth spurt between this first vision in 1900 and its colonial zenith circa 1944. In 1913, the hill station consisted of some dozen cottages, one of which doubled as a hotel.[6] By 1944, it counted 750 private villas, numerous government offices, the summer estates of the emperor of Annam, the governor general of Indochina, those of leading authorities from Annam and Cochinchina, and a golf course. The resort town could readily accommodate the 2,537 European visitors who summered there in a single month.[7] Strong central planning lay behind this remarkable expansion. Five major plans stand out: Paul Champoudry's of 1905, Jean O'Neill's 1919 report, Ernest Hébrard's grand model from 1923, Louis-Georges Pineau's from 1932, and Jacques Lagisquet's from 1942.[8]

Paul Champoudry, Dalat's very first mayor, claimed considerable expertise in urban affairs from his experiences in Paris. In his new functions as mayor of the nascent town of Dalat, Champoudry drafted his blueprints in concert with military authorities, who were the first to benefit from the hill station. Accordingly, in his 1905 projection, Champoudry concentrated all public and administrative services in a single quarter, noting that the military authorities had counted on taking up considerable

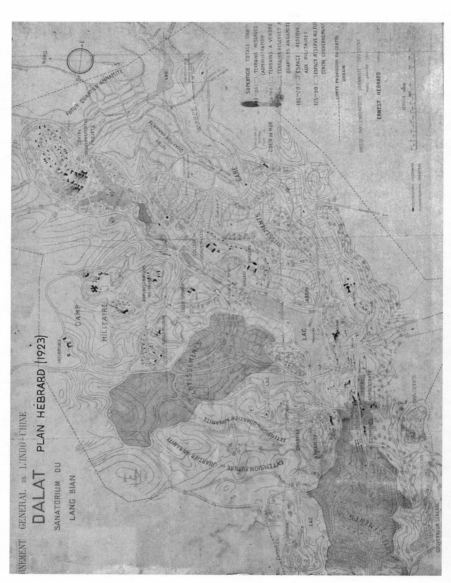

MAP 4. Hébrard Plan for Dalat, 1923. CIAM Archives, Zurich.

space on the vast plateau. Champoudry foresaw a market, situated at the juncture of the town's main arteries, giving onto a public square, itself designed to facilitate traffic. Near the market and in the center of town, he designated spaces for merchant stalls and small businesses. In the heart of the downtown, Champoudry imagined a hotel, featuring a restaurant and a casino. He dedicated a district to the post office and train station, conveniently located across from one another. A school would be placed to the east of the town, on a vast property near the train station. Hygiene was a paramount concern for Dalat's first mayor. The public laundry would be located downstream from the town. Dalat would also be a thoroughly modern center: all buildings and homes would be electrified and would feature indoor plumbing. Reinforced concrete would be the construction material of choice.[9] The main lines of Champoudry's vision would for the most part be carried out by later planners and architects: the separate native village, the site of the future hotel, train station and so on, would all be retained. In 1919, Jean O'Neill, the author of Dalat's next master plan—and of a budget for public works—would build upon Champoudry's initial blueprints. Indeed, it was at the close of the First World War that funds began to flow into Dalat, and that many of Champoudry's visions became realities.

Ernest Hébrard, the advocate of an associationist style of architecture capable of integrating and respecting local forms, was also a strong proponent of zoned planning. The man who had redesigned Thessalonika drafted the following preamble to his 1923 master plan for Dalat: "Instead of leaving the division and concession of lands to fate and the fancy of individuals, [my] plan takes into account the future of this city, which should avoid costly modifications down the road." Zoning lay at the core of Hébrard's vision. He deemed it "intolerable" for a residential quarter to rest near "noisy or uncleanly areas." Hébrard foresaw three towns within one: the administrative quarter, a European residential quarter, and an "Annamite district." Each of these quarters was itself subdivided. Thus the administrative district would encompass a religious center, an educational complex, and a commercial area. Like so many of Dalat's architects and planners, Hébrard drew from a deep well of knowledge on other hill stations around the globe. According to Hébrard, "at Baguio [Philippines], the governmental quarter forms the main axis of the hill station. Given Dalat's configuration, we cannot do the same, but I have situated the administrative quarter, in a place where it will command part of the valley, making for . . . a monumental ensemble, fitting of Indochina's richness and grandeur."[10] Hébrard's 1923 vision proved too grand. As the Depression hit Indochina, his plan was scrapped. As we will see below, financial considerations were not the only factor that ultimately scuttled Hébrard's plan; local actors lent a hand in sinking a project they reviled as inflexible and ill-conceived.

Dalat's meteoric rise occurred over the next two decades. By 1930, a rail line from Saigon reached Dalat's doorstep. As of 1937, one train per day made the Saigon-Dalat trip in each direction.[11] Even Hanoi was within relatively easy reach: when

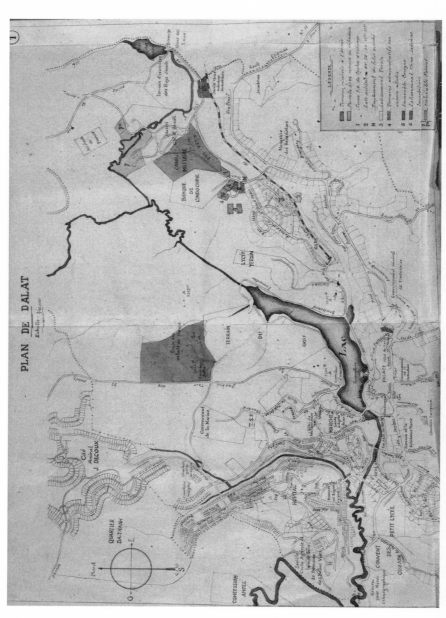

MAP 5. Map of Dalat, 1942. ANOM, ICM 537.

Indochina's archivist-in-chief Paul Boudet undertook the voyage in May 1940, he left Hanoi at 6:30 P.M., and arrived in Dalat the next morning at 7:30 A.M.[12] In 1932, a new road, snaking over the Blao pass, put the hill station just six hours away from Saigon by automobile.[13] The town's population climbed, accordingly, from 1,500 permanent inhabitants in 1923 to some 13,000 in 1940, then 20,000 by 1942. The number of visitors rose accordingly: 8,000 in 1925, 12,000 in 1940, and 20,000 in 1942.[14]

And yet paradoxically, in part because of the Depression, Louis-Georges Pineau's 1932 plan proved far more restrained than his predecessor's.[15] Indeed, while Hébrard had stressed expansion, Pineau emphasized preservation. Pineau, who would leave a stamp on Hanoi, Saigon, and Dalat, was certainly one of the more cosmopolitan French planners in Indochina. He was associated with the pioneering left-leaning CIAM (Congrès internationaux de l'Architecture moderne), and obtained a fellowship to study at Harvard in 1939. Within these circles, he met the likes of Le Corbusier and Walter Gropius. He differed from the former philosophically, noting with amazement in 1930 that Le Corbusier supported the notion that big cities could be highly livable. A careful examination of data, Pineau opined, would show infant mortality rates to be highest in urban settings. "Humankind does not reproduce in cities," he concluded, in a note that foreshadowed the ruralist, preservationist approach he would try to bring to Dalat.[16] Pineau's work in Indochina spans the years 1930 to 1945 (though he would later return in the 1950s to teach at the University of Hanoi).[17] He considered the following guiding principles when drafting his 1932 plan for Dalat: "protecting Dalat's natural beauty, enlarging its artificial lake, developing gardens, establishing zones adapted to the site and the climate . . . open spaces of all sorts, be they parks, hunting reserves, or conservation areas."[18] Pineau clashed with his predecessor in other ways as well: he tended to favor architectural eclecticism and idiosyncratic villas, for instance. Pineau's legacy is thus preservationist in some respects, and pioneering in others, since many of Dalat's villas were built in the era of his plan.

Between 1942 and 1945, Dalat's last colonial grand planner, Lagisquet, would carry out Vichy governor Jean Decoux's ambitious project: transforming the hill station into a de facto summer capital, removed from traditional spheres of Vietnamese, and now Japanese, influence. In one domain, then, all of Dalat's planners found common ground: they all sought to define Dalat as a French city. In so doing, each grappled with the reality that a large Vietnamese community had, like the French, settled in Dalat and its surroundings.

THE PLACE OF THE VIETNAMESE

Champoudry's 1905 plan already broached the thorny question of a native quarter. He explained in a note affixed to his blueprint: "[On the enclosed map,] we have only partially indicated the sites needed for the indigenous population (secretaries, messengers, . . . coolies). We think that these sites will be best assigned as the town grows, by allotting available lands to them."[19] The "indigenous problem"—and there was one from the French *urbaniste* perspective—had been put off to a later date. Who were these "natives"? Champoudry was referring here not to highland minorities, but rather to ethnic Vietnamese auxiliaries. The 1919 O'Neill report recognized the crucial importance of Vietnamese laborers in the bluntest of terms: "a native town is vital to lodge and provide manpower, native employees, and their families."[20]

A European city by design, a *ville d'agrément* or leisure town according to Jean O'Neill, and a *ville hôtel* according to Pineau, Dalat would require indigenous hands to build and run it.[21] According to data provided by Louis-Georges Pineau, it was in 1927 that Dalat's Vietnamese population overtook the European population. By 1932, Pineau estimated Dalat's permanent population at 800 Vietnamese, and 350 Europeans.[22] Taking into account visitors, cottage-owners, and floating population, he advanced the figure of 4,000 Asians for roughly 1,900 Europeans. Thus, although French commentators were undoubtedly correct in considering the ratio of Europeans to Indochinese far more "favorable" in Dalat than anywhere else in Indochina, Dalat was decidedly not, as it was so often described and charted by colonial sources, a strictly "French resort."

Very early on, a Vietnamese quarter emerged near the eastern end of Dalat's planned artificial lake (under construction in 1920), near the market stalls.[23] Again, O'Neill crudely explained that "the native town must be located near the commercial district and downstream from the European town. Its location is therefore predetermined: along the Camly river, just downstream from the lake's dam."[24] This decision would have tragic consequences when flooding caused the artificial lake to overflow in 1932: the seventeen resulting fatalities were all Vietnamese. Colonial sources somehow still pinned the blame on them for "refusing to leave their *paillotes* on time."[25]

Ernest Hébrard's 1923 master plan promised to further demarcate the "Annamese quarter" from the administrative and European residential districts, and even to extend the said "Annamese quarter" to the north. All French parties seem to have concurred on the necessity to identify, then cordon off, a strictly Vietnamese quarter. In a March 1924 missive to the Résident supérieur d'Annam, the commissioner-mayor of Dalat, Léon Garnier, evoked the urgent need to "erect the Dalat market as quickly as possible, as much because it has become a nuisance, as because the neighborhood in which it is located presents the greatest danger to public health, in the absence of any paving." Léon Garnier elaborated that "on your recent visit to Dalat in the company of architect Hébrard, you observed, on location, the need to shoo off indigenous houses, located on the site of the future market . . . "[26] Garnier nevertheless showed some empathy for the Vietnamese who faced expropriation. He requested a relocation indemnity from the Résident supérieur in Hué, and asked

how Vietnamese owners were expected to meet Hébrard's onerous style conditions—
the use of brick in lieu of wood, for instance—if they could not afford it.[27]

Although he decried Hébrard's intransigence, which soon grew to be legendary
in Dalat, Garnier nevertheless shared the belief that Dalat's "little Vietnam" needed
to be both refurbished and sealed off.[28] A year later, in June 1925, the members of
Dalat's Committee of Public Salubrity met to discuss ways of improving health at
Indochina's premier health resort. Dr. Guérin, the director of the prestigious Pasteur Institute, left little doubt as to how to accomplish this goal: "[He] insisted on
the importance of separating as clearly as possible the Annamite village from the
European center. In the event of an epidemic, the Annamite village must be easily
encircled, isolated, controlled, and supervised. From a hygienic point of view, it would
therefore make sense to banish the Annamite village beyond the Huyên Moï, and
to allow only businesses or homes in the style of secretary residences, all hygieni-
cally sound, on the site of the current Annamite quarter."[29]

Not one to bend his plan, Hébrard rejected this idea of confining the Vietnamese
town to the outlying northern suburb only. The "Annamese quarter" around the
market would be rebuilt but maintained, in spite of local calls for its outright removal.[30] At the same time, additional Vietnamese housing would be built further
to the north.

In 1925, Ernest Hébrard supervised the transformation of Dalat's central "Annamese town" around the market. Hébrard considered his new parcel grid, comprised of especially narrow lots, to be "very simple." His margin for negotiation,
however, appears to have been slim. The inter-axes, he noted, could be shifted by a
"few centimeters," but he insisted that the overall divisions be respected.[31] A few
weeks later, Garnier wrote back with a series of pointed questions. The new single-
floor brick structures separated by 2.5 meter paths did not draw Garnier's ire, so
much as the decision to keep "wooden boutiques" adjacent to the market—Dalat's
hygiene committee had ordered these wooden buildings destroyed the year prior.
"Indigenous-styled constructions" Garnier insisted, were proscribed.[32] Once again,
local authorities claimed that idealistic architects operating out of Hanoi had neglected local priorities: in this instance, the leveling of the market area and adjacent
wooden residences. For all of their disagreements, though, the mayor of Dalat and
the master planner shared a common vision of a segregated, modern city.

Nearly the entire discussion over segregation at Dalat was coded in hygienic
terms. In 1925, Commissaire Léon Garnier exposed that it was an "impossibility"
for "Annamites to use garbage bins." In lieu of bins, Garnier ordered the creation
of five concrete garbage platforms in the native quarter, "destined to receive all the
rubbish by a certain time. Garbage will be removed from the platform by ox-dri-
ven carriages." In the European quarter, conversely, "garbage [was] collected by
truck, and individuals thr[ew] their trash directly into the trucks."[33]

If hygiene served as the chief discursive register of segregationist policies, zoning emerged as the main instrument for implementing them. Zoning lay at the heart of Dalat's sometimes contested, often unevenly applied, but strongly held and medically sanctioned segregationist principles. At the June 1925 meeting of the Committee of Public Salubrity, Guérin even advocated the creation of a *cordon sanitaire*: "gardens, public spaces, should be introduced in a neutral zone between the Annamite village and the European center."[34]

In 1926, Dalat formally obtained the status of town *(commune)*. Its freshly minted municipal council included the new mayor, Victor-Edouard-Marie L'Helgoualc'h, two European members, Paul Ancel and Desanti, and two Vietnamese ones, Ho Van Le and Nguyen Ngoc Chuc. The latter two emerged as outspoken critics of the changes to the Vietnamese quarters caused by Hébrard's plan. The disruption had been considerable. Even the dead were relocated, the "indigenous cemetery" moved to the northernmost limit of the new Vietnamese district.[35]

At the November 27, 1926 session of Dalat's municipal council, Ho Van Le demanded some measure of stability. He insisted that the Vietnamese be given a site to settle once and for all, so that they would henceforth be spared "relocations imposed by the execution of urban plans." Unfazed, the mayor and council president retorted: stability Ho Van Le would have. The new Annamese quarter would be strictly defined, encompassing one hundred hectares between the Dankia road and the new indigenous cemetery to the north, the Camly river and new market to the south, the native guard headquarters to the east, and the infirmary and hill to the west. A second native town would be located on the western fringes of town, near the future train station. L'Helgoualc'h did attempt to reassure Vietnamese council members on one matter: relocated Vietnamese people would be granted homes of the same size as the ones they had been forced to leave. Each property corner would henceforth be delimited by a concrete *borne*—thereby presumably offering "natives" a geometric guarantee of sameness.[36]

Nguyen Ngoc Chuc took over where his compatriot had left off, drawing the commission's attention to the narrowness of parcels in the Vietnamese quarter. "If we were to apply the Hébrard plan to the letter," he noted, "homes would end up far too close together. They would take up most of the lot, leaving no room for gardens or sheds. I therefore ask that all lots be 50 x 20 meters; in this way we will attract more villa owners and builders to Dalat."[37] Nguyen Ngoc Chuc had put his finger on yet another vexing feature of Dalat's systemic, deliberate, and indeed minutely planned urban double standard. O'Neill's 1919 plan had indicated that "all houses for Europeans in Dalat must be surrounded by a garden, and enjoy sufficient aeration and views."[38] After all, this was precisely the point of Dalat: the vast plateau allowed for large properties, wide villas, and an escape from the congestion of Hanoi or Saigon. The narrowness of the plots in Hébrard's revamped Vietnamese quarter was therefore no accident, but merely a reaffirmation of O'Neill's principles—betraying the logic that while Europeans would enjoy large plots, Vietnamese dwellings could be reduced to sardine tins.[39] This outcome, of course, was a far cry from Hébrard's purported embrace of associationist principles, as well as his professed desire to understand local architectures and adapt French models to them. In reality, Hébrard's Dalat plan served as the fulcrum of colonial segregationism.

Mayor L'Helgoualc'h could only recognize that Nguyen Ngoc Chuc's complaint was widely shared. Hébrard had hoped, the mayor explained, to dissuade speculation and the further subdivision of lots in the Vietnamese district by making them a single, standard, and modest size to begin with. And it was possible, remarked the mayor, to build a 12 x 12 meter house on such a lot. The mayor even displayed a few examples in a photo album. But he agreed to show flexibility, as he claimed to have done in the case of one Mrs. Hao.[40] Indeed, according to the cadastral map, Mrs. Hao boasted six contiguous lots in the European neighborhood near the train station. In this instance, the two Vietnamese members seized the opportunity afforded by the new municipal council to voice a series of grievances. They expressed the exasperation of a relocated population, and protested the injustice of Vietnamese Dalatois relegated to row homes, a stone's throw away from opulent European villas.

At times, Vietnamese and dissident French interests overlapped, as in the case of the Hébrard plan. Vietnamese and some French locals alike—the mayor notwithstanding—joined in condemning the narrowness of the proposed lots. E. Riberolles' short-lived Dalat newspaper, *Le Camly*, lampooned the Hébrard plan on this very score. In a 1924 "fake news" piece, it reported that Hébrard now called for "10 square meter lots for dwellings, to be built vertically. . . . The hospital will be given 50 square meters, while the slaughterhouse and Masonic temple will each stand on 100,000-meter lots. In the new plan, there will be 83 lakes that drain automatically, and can be transformed instantly either into gardens, or into thick forests, flowery meadows, or swamps to raise mosquitoes that transmit malaria. In this last case, the lakes will be lined with quinine trees and eucalyptus."[41]

The newspaper had previously criticized Hébrard more tactfully, suggesting that on such a vast plateau, one did not have to be stingy with space. In this second attack, the editorial held no punches: Hébrard's unwillingness to consider the views of Dalat's inhabitants, the plan's unrealistic scale, the absurdly grand nature of public buildings next to private lots, Dalat's vulnerability to *Anopheles* mosquitoes, the policy of creating artificial lakes that fostered said mosquitoes, all were connected in this scathing article.

Over the course of the 1930s, many of Dalat's Vietnamese inhabitants remained in real-estate limbo, as it became clear that Hébrard's lavish vision for the city could not be carried out in its totality. Between the Committee of Public Salubrity's August 1923 decision to destroy the previous "Annamese district" and Hébrard's eventual completion of a new one, an urban refugee crisis had unfolded.[42] In 1935, the town's municipal council again took up the question of "displaced Vietnamese

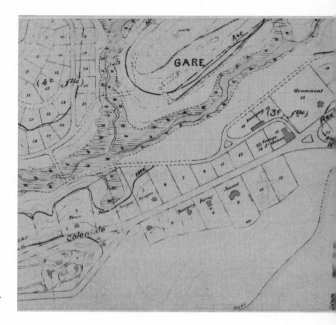

MAP 6. Detail of Dalat's
cadastral plan, circa 1930.
Author's collection.

inhabitants of Dalat." Many had fled the transformation of the market area for the region around the Petit Lycée in the south of the town. Some members of the municipal council sought to regularize their situation, and allow the relocated Vietnamese to buy the lots on which they presently lived. Others, however, expressed concern that by setting a low price for the aforementioned land, the "Annamites might profit from such low prices to undertake speculative profits." When the new mayor, Lucien Auger, reassured councilor Yves Desrioux that this would be impossible, since the Vietnamese could only purchase the lands they presently occupied, councilor Vo Dinh Dung interjected that if this were a policy, it should apply to all, regardless of whether they were Asian or European.[43] Again, Vietnamese councilors directly challenged the iniquity of Dalat's zoning and land allocation. It seemed that even the prospect of creating a small Vietnamese enclave near the Petit Lycée threatened the colonial order.

Dalat's permanent inhabitants only constitute part of the story. Since the hill station attracted an ever more numerous summer clientele, the issue of segregation for visitors seems worth mentioning briefly. Although class seems to have trumped race at the Dalat or Lang-Bian Palace Hotel, where Emperor Bao Dai was certainly welcome, Dalat's hotels nevertheless mirrored the segregated environment of the city itself. A 1930 guidebook listed the hill station's four main hotels: the luxurious Lang-Bian Palace (30 rooms), the nearby Hôtel du Parc (70 rooms), the Hôtel Desanti,

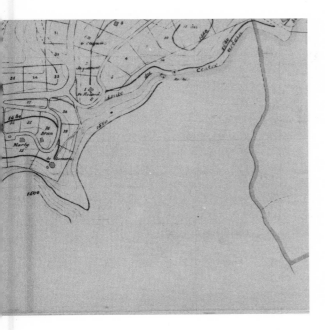

composed of pavilions around the lake, and the Hôtel Annam (25 rooms). It was at this last establishment, the guide noted, that "the native elite congregated."[44] Unsurprisingly, it was located in the Vietnamese quarter, albeit on its southern edge.

Still, it would be much too simple to accept administrative and settler desiderata for total, nearly hermetic segregation, as somehow reflecting reality. By the 1920s, significant exceptions were beginning to emerge. The Vietnamese aristocracy was manifestly exempt from segregationist zoning. Emperor Bao Dai's decision to erect a summer palace in Dalat was in fact well received by French Dalatois, no doubt seeing in the move a token of the resort's desirability. The emperor claimed some of the town's finest real estate, on a hill overlooking the administrative district and the pine forest. Architect Paul Veysseyre began work on Bao Dai's summer "palace" in 1933; when, a few years later, the same architect was commissioned to design the governor general's summer residence, a very similar layout was chosen.[45] At Dalat, power tensions were often expressed through villa emulation or envy.

The emerging Vietnamese bourgeoisie provided an arguably greater challenge to zoning rules.[46] Vo Dinh Dung, just mentioned above, in many ways embodied the rise of Vietnamese interests in colonial Dalat. A member of Dalat's municipal council, which he joined at age thirty in 1932, he also ran a company that oversaw the construction of some of the resort's main public edifices, including the train station, large parts of the lycées, and the hospitals.[47] Ho Van Le, for his part, inhabited a liminal space, his home lying immediately north of the lake, between the golf course and the Vietnamese town. Mrs. Hoa, meanwhile, was neighbor with the likes of the Bruns, the Martys, Jean Funé, and the Bourgerys in the European district to the town's west in the 1930s.[48] Similarly, high-ranking Vietnamese functionaries in the French administration enjoyed exemptions from Dalat's zoning. By 1929, the Vietnamese inspector-in-chief of Dalat's schools was housed in a large house belonging to the government, on the Rue de l'Ecole.[49]

This rise in Vietnamese influence can thus be traced back to the 1920s, when cracks began to appear in the segregationist model. In 1925, Le Phat An requested an exemption from Hébrard's master plan. He proposed the erection of "a handsome building" that would "become part of Dalat's esthetic cadre, since it will be visible from the Dalat Palace Hotel, whence it will resemble a meadow in the pines." Interestingly, Garnier championed the project, explaining to Hébrard that "the precedent of Mr. Le Phat An, who belongs to one of the elite families of Cochinchina and who is French . . . might well lead other Annamites from honorable and rich families to follow his lead. I therefore think this initiative should be encouraged." Le Phat An had asked for a full hectare of land for this property—the type of request that was becoming increasingly difficult to accommodate for anyone as Dalat's popularity rose, and under Hébrard's inflexible, at times hegemonic plan. Garnier continued that "even if we were to assign smaller lots and divide the property I am proposing for Mr. Le Phat An in half, it would be impossible to erect two buildings on it, because of the parcel's layout."[50] In short, Garnier sought to draw the Vietnamese bourgeoisie to Dalat, while Hébrard, who resisted such requests, stuck to the segregationist blueprint.

By the 1930s, bourgeois Vietnamese were increasingly managing to purchase large properties in the "European" districts of Dalat. When in 1934, Le Duong requested a two-hectare lot in suburban Dalat, he was granted it on the same terms that Europeans received. So long as he was able to demonstrate that he had "developed, occupied, and sanitized" the property (which an inspection later confirmed), he was granted the deed.[51]

This is not to suggest, however, that zoning itself was called into question. In fact, with Pineau's plan came a newfound emphasis on *cordons sanitaires* under the guise of open spaces. A 1932 article in the French Saigon press welcomed Louis-Georges Pineau's attempt to safeguard selected green areas. "Aesthetic considerations" had determined that some zones be declared *"non Edificandi."*[52] But in reality, Pineau's vision of a green Dalat was politically charged. In 1932, Dalat's mayor approached the planner, asking him to replace the "wasteland" near the temporary city hall—used heretofore as a nocturnal urinal by administrators—with an elegant square featuring an area "reserved to European children . . . where mothers and nannies could find seating."[53] The urban planner fully comprehended the stakes of his much-vaunted green areas, as evidenced in a letter he drafted to CIAM general secretary Sigfried Giedion in 1932. A mere two years after having set foot in the colony, Pineau wrote to his colleague how local law in Indochina allowed planners to designate "open and free spaces" without so much as paying an indemnity to those expropriated. Although Pineau recognized this new law to be "draconian," he nevertheless welcomed it as a great facilitator of his beautification campaigns.[54]

Under the authoritarian Vichy regime's proconsul in Indochina, Governor General Jean Decoux (in office 1940–45), a new "Annamese village" was created further north of Dalat. This village, known as Da Thanh, attracted two thousand Vietnamese inhabitants within a year of its completion in 1942. Colonial authorities presented Da Tanh as "organized along the rational principles of administration and hygiene." They boasted that "it can be considered a model village."[55] Decoux's administration had revived the segregationist agenda with a vengeance, finally accomplishing the goals local officials never saw fully realized in the 1920s: designating a Vietnamese village well to the north of Dalat proper, so as to avoid further spillovers of the central market area, which was bursting at the seams.

To French planners, the role of the Vietnamese at Dalat had been problematic from the outset. Many of the hill station's original creators had seen its remoteness from centers of Vietnamese influence as its greatest asset. However, already in the first years of the twentieth century it became apparent to most colonial officials that Vietnamese workers and functionaries would be essential to Dalat's development and everyday activities. Confronted with this reality, colonial planners and doctors alike mandated the construction of a "little Vietnam" at Dalat, located downstream from the European district, in an area separated from the administrative and residential quarters by an artificial lake, a dam, and a river. By the 1920s, however, major slippages were occurring—precisely around the time of modest gubernatorial reform in Hanoi (the left-leaning Alexandre Varenne served as governor general of Indochina from 1925 to 1927). This gradual liberalization was accentuated in the 1930s. Interestingly, even some local Dalat authorities, who had long resented the rigidity of plans drawn up by architects *de passage* on whirlwind tours, began contesting the exclusion of elite and middle-class Vietnamese from the good life Dalat embodied: namely its grand villas, its golf course, and its luxury amenities. And of course, Vietnamese councilors seized the limited public space afforded to them to bitterly condemn their ongoing exclusion and constant relocation.

DALAT'S EUROPEAN VILLAS

While the quest to define, seal, and contain Dalat's Vietnamese quarters constituted a nagging challenge for Dalat's colonial officials, most of their energies were directed at the European administrative and residential districts. Since these were

FIGURE 12. A Dalat villa. Photo by author.

literally planned from nil, debates over the function and identity of Dalat were consistently mediated through questions of style, unity, elegance, and modernity. Already in 1905, at a time when Dalat counted a handful of ramshackle cottages, Paul Champoudry raised the matter of architectural diversity versus unity. According to him, "if one wants to build a town with original character, through varied architecture . . . one must commission several different architects. A single architect would inevitably yield a regrettable uniformity of style."[56] The former Parisian municipal councilor had established a principle of architectural eclecticism as the very antithesis of the capital city he left—one that would be strongly but unsuccessfully challenged by the likes of Ernest Hébrard.

At Dalat, Gwendolyn Wright has commented, Ernest Hébrard had sought to "fashion a perfectly harmonized system [through] an architecture supposedly emmbod[ying] scientific reason and cultural tolerance, alluding to a perfect balance between past and future, aesthetics and industry, high art and vernacular."[57] It was this planning, this total control that spelled modernity to Hébrard, regardless of its inherent paradoxes. Absolute harmony would mean controlling not only public buildings, which were certainly within his purview, but villas as well. Here, Hébrard broke with Champoudry's laissez-faire attitude, which had permitted the expression of multiple villa styles. Hébrard's 1923 plan recommended that "in order to avoid ugliness being introduced in Dalat, villas should be based on plans pro-

FIGURE 13. A Dalat villa. Photo by author.

vided by the administration, with guarantees that they be completely followed. Different types could be drawn up quite easily, and entrepreneurs could undertake to construct these standardized villas for a set price. This system has been successful at Welwyn City, near London."[58]

Uniformity was central to Hébrard's vision. Villa owners, he argued, were entitled to expect their future neighbors "to build analogous villas [to their own]."[59] In 1925, Hébrard even submitted a set of blueprints to Dalat's Committee of Public Salubrity. The plans for "houses deemed acceptable on both hygienic and esthetic grounds" were to be distributed to construction and real estate firms.[60]

In spite of the level of detail, the degree of homogenization, and the aspirations of grandeur contained in Hébrard's plan, less of it was carried out than any other of Dalat's five grand designs. The complete serialization of villas would have to wait until the Second World War, which triggered a dramatic rise in Dalat's popularity at a time when trips home to France became impossible. It also marked the advent of a Vichy French administration willing to implement centralized plans where previous regimes had balked.

In the 1930s, as the Hébrard plan was laid to rest, countless regional villas began springing up in Dalat's European residential quarters, to the south and east of the artificial lake. Arnauld le Brusq has noted that Dalat's next *urbaniste,* Louis-Georges Pineau, privileged French regional styles for private villas, while paradoxically favoring modern architecture for public buildings.[61] In 1937, Pineau pondered the questions of French versus Franco-Asian hybrid architecture, syncretism and regionalism. He asked:

> Which architecture should be chosen [for Dalat?] Without a doubt the answer is European and even French, insofar as one can even identify a strictly French architectural school. It is a fact of human geography that when man travels, he takes his form of habitat with him. Tonnelat [in a 1907 article], reports that German settlements in Brazil resemble parts of the Black Forest. At Dalat, one can find many a Basque villa, and alas, some ugly houses reminiscent of the Paris suburbs. . . . Alternatively, French architecture in Indochina could adopt some local influences, as it has so successfully done in Morocco. However, the attempts in Indochina strike me as failures.[62]

Hébrard, an advocate of an associationist Franco-Vietnamese style of architecture emblematized by his museum at the Ecole française d'Extrême-Orient in Hanoi (1926–31), had been roundly condemned by a successor who believed that colonizers were to import their particular national or even regional style. In truth, Hébrard's fusion of Asian and French motifs had been unimaginable in Dalat to begin with, given the town's role as a temperate replica of France in the tropics. Pineau, then, recommended the complete avoidance of Asian architectural influences in Dalat. He endorsed some of the new regionalist villas mushrooming on the plateau in the 1930s: those reminiscent of the Basque country, Brittany, Savoy, and other French provinces seem to have received his blessing, while the suburban *pavillon* style drew his contempt, no doubt on elitist as much as aesthetic grounds.

The highly varied styles of Dalat's villas soon became its cause célèbre, and remain so to this day. The daughter of one of the highest Vietnamese officials in Dalat in the 1930s and 1940s—the school inspector—recalls that functionaries "inhabit[ed] villas of French regional styles." She adds "each one [wa]s different."[63] Clearly, the eclecticism of Dalat's villas constituted one of its trademarks. Some admirers of the hill station seem to have secretly longed for the classicism or stylistic unity of Paris. In 1941, one source remarked that "the freedom [which planners have given to villa styles] has not resulted in too great a catastrophic anarchy: not everything is pretty, to be sure, but originality, coquettishness, and good taste are generally present."[64] Yet rather than rendering Dalat unique, this eclecticism betrayed a vast plagiarism of nineteenth-century British colonial hill stations, whose villas were renowned for their Swiss, Tudor, Gothic, and Scottish styles.[65] This was even reflected in some villa names: alongside villas named Sans soucis, Geranium, or Les

Roses, one finds Mon cottage.[66] Pineau's Dalat of regional villas resonated as much with British colonial Gothic revival as with French *terroirs*.

None of this is to suggest that the villas of the 1930s were somehow "unmodern." As Arnauld Le Brusq has observed, much of Dalat's architecture featured a dialectic between modernism and regionalism.[67] Indeed, the two movements and sensibilities were anything but mutually exclusive. Paul Rabinow has observed that French regionalists deemed their movement to be active, in contrast with the more passive traditionalists. Regionalism, in this sense, involved "systematic but supervised diversity."[68] Shanny Peer, conversely, sees French regionalism emerging as a reaction against "excessive centralization."[69] The degree of stylistic supervision or control at the hill station constituted an ongoing debate among Dalatois keen to give their imaginations free reign over highly personalized villas. It is tempting to see Dalat's regional villas as a direct backlash against the Hébrard plan, and the broader risk of "homogenization [seen] throughout the industrialized world."[70] The modern regionalism of Dalat's villas reflected a coterminous trend in the metropole. There, in 1936, architect René Clozier described regionalism as "nothing but the adaptation of modern architecture to the land where it develops." Similarly, Peer shows, the planners for the 1937 World's Fair in Paris proscribed pastiches or nostalgic reproductions, in favor of these resolutely modern, yet putatively authentic, regionalist forms.[71] Each of these descriptions fits Dalat's villas to the letter. What is so striking at Dalat is that such vernaculars were invariably European—from Picardy, Provence, the Landes—and even as we are about to see, Bavaria. The prevalence of such whimsical regionalist signifiers underscored Dalat's absolute Europeanness.

How precisely were Dalat's idiosyncratic villas conceived? Dalat's architects clearly discussed models with customers. Among the papers of Paul Veysseyre, one of the main architects operating in Dalat in the late 1930s and early 1940s (designer of several religious edifices and fifty-four villas at Dalat alone), were brochures, cuttings, and advertisements from a host of contemporaneous architecture magazines. These were no doubt shown to customers, who could choose from the latest designs, including regional styles, and summer villas of the Côte d'Azur. Interestingly, as with Hébrard, who cited British modular housing projects, Veysseyre appears to have been receptive to other European influences. His collection contained several foreign magazines, including the January 1938 issue of the German publication *Neuzeitliches Bauwessen Heraklith-Rundschau*, from which he had clipped blueprints for mountain chalets or *Berghausen*. This suggests that considerable energy was expended on conceiving current designs, and on drawing from other European schools, rather than merely mimicking French regional elements.[72]

Nordic or Central European forms were by no means restricted to private dwellings. The *Berghaus* style of villas found some resonance in the elegant curved brick shape of the Lycée Yersin and its sleek square tower. In a 1943 article, Claude

Perrens likened the structure to the belfry of Stockholm's city hall.[73] The resemblance is in fact striking. The Scandinavian and Nordic parallel proved a recurring one. Suzanne Coussillan, who stayed at Dalat in 1946, recalls that the place resembled "Switzerland, or even Norway."[74] This result was no accident. Louis-Georges Pineau, for instance, maintained close relations with a network of German, Dutch, and Swiss architects and planners like Cornelius Van Eesteren and Sigfried Giedion. He troubled these counterparts to send their publications to him in Indochina, and regularly sought news in the 1930s from his Dutch colleague Mart Stam, busy designing model worker cities in the Soviet Union.[75] Indeed, it was through Pineau's CIAM contacts that Dalat was showcased as a "functional city" in the "leisure city" category at the fourth CIAM congress, in Athens in 1933. International influences were thus as manifest on Dalat as was the town's increasing international exposure.

To return to villas, not all were privately owned. Various branches of the colonial administration (like the Banque d'Indochine or the Ecole française d'Extrême Orient) purchased and developed summer residences for their employees. So too did private enterprises. In 1934, as the Great Depression sent ripples across Indochina, the Compagnie agricole d'Annam contacted a Saigon lawyer to sell its three Dalat properties. These give a sense of how corporate retreats had hitherto functioned. A large Norman (or Tudor if one prefers) style villa near the Petit Lycée had been reserved for entertaining and housing company cadres. It featured a billiard room. The villa went for sale with all of its contents, including the tiger pelts that adorned the bedroom, twelve bedspreads, and several tea sets. If this first villa was designed for vacations and receptions, the second had been earmarked as a convalescence center for company employees posted at Banmethuot. As with most Dalat villas, the two servant quarters in this second villa were located on the ground floor, near the kitchen and garage. The third and final villa had served as the residence of the company's secretary.[76]

It was under the Vichy regime that Dalat saw a return to Hébrard-style rigid central planning.[77] Circumstances called for it, to be sure, since Dalat experienced an unprecedented vogue at this time. Aesthetics and politics also played a part. An August 1943 article in Vichy's local mouthpiece lamented that Indochina's hill stations "have not yet found their individual personalities." Frequently, the article suggested, a new villa elicited jealousy from its neighbors who then proceeded to "copy it, without fear of plagiarism." This trend supposedly continued until a new style arrived, which in turn was mimicked à outrance, resulting in unattractive architectural strata. Lagisquet's 1942 plan for Dalat, it was hoped, could finally break the cycle of shameless copying and lend Dalat a "harmonious aspect."[78]

At last, in 1942, Hébrard's goal had become a reality. On the northern outskirts of town, Lagisquet oversaw the construction of a wholly planned subdivision soon dubbed the Cité-Jardin Amiral Decoux, in honor of Vichy's Governor General in Indochina. This planned community was to target categories of Europeans who had

FIGURE 14. The Cité-Jardin Decoux under construction, 1942. Archives municipales de Bordeaux, Decoux papers.

previously been excluded from Dalat: those who could afford neither the resort's hotels, nor a villa of their own. A pamphlet on the Cité-Jardin explained: "[Our goal] is to allow women and children, the sick, those who suffer from the rigors of the Indochinese climate, to find reinvigoration, strength, and good health in the picturesque setting of our federation's beautiful hill station."[79]

Different formulas were proposed. Some thirty villas were available for renters already by the end of 1942, to which twenty more rental villas were added the year following. Another fifty villas were put up for sale, again at modest prices, with income maxima placed on potential buyers. The villas bore every resemblance to North American planned communities: renters and buyers could choose from six different models. Each was intended "to evoke Alpine chalets."[80] The homes were considered "simple yet elegant, perfectly planned, and equipped with rustic furniture."[81] Half a world away from metropolitan France, Vichy authorities implemented the kind of new social model that metropolitan authorities could rarely see through to fruition at this time.[82] In Indochina, the result was Dalat's most uniform district, made up of alpine chalets for a French settler community. The Cité-Jardin, and Dalat more generally, could bring redemption to Indochina's *petits blancs*.

Despite the fact that the Vichy years signaled a return to segregationist planning, they paradoxically afforded a greater opportunity than ever to Vietnamese architects. This fell in line with Vichy's policy of admitting more Vietnamese into the public administration. At Dalat, the trend certainly contributed to perpetuating some of the resort's distinctive villa tropes into the postcolonial era. Consider the case of Pham Nguyen Mau. Architectural critics under Vichy credited him with building "solid constructions, with nice finishings, that contrast with some of [Dalat's] shoddy villas cobbled together with insufficient funds, whose owners commission fanciful facades, calling to mind a Nuremberg toy." Pham Nguyen Mau's clean and sharp angles, his use of concrete, drew sufficient praise that Decoux's mouthpiece, the review *Indochine hebdomadaire illustré,* cited only him in the category of villa design.[83]

A FUNCTIONAL CITY?

In 1933, some of the world's boldest architects and planners boarded a cruise in Marseille bound for Athens. These luminaries had assembled for the fourth CIAM congress. Among them was Louis-Georges Pineau, armed with six giant maps. He had long dreamt of presenting at the CIAM, but had been forced to bow out of a previous meeting in Brussels precisely because he had been called away in 1930, as he explained, "to design several cities in . . . Indochina."[84] In 1933 he was finally able to accept the invitation from this prestigious forum. He chose to showcase not his work on Saigon, but rather Dalat. Dalat, then, was exposed at the congress on the same footing as Detroit, Budapest, Paris, and Amsterdam, although in the "rest" or "leisure city" category. Few other colonial cities were entered: Algeria was well represented, and the Dutch submitted plans for Bandung, one of Indonesia's hill stations.

Functionality was the congress' overarching theme. By functionality, the organizers understood liveability, as their manifesto made clear: "the functional city must ensure the proper disposition of the location and size of different quarters: those for work, living, leisure and circulation." Moreover, "urbanism shall fix the relations between the sites of living, work, and leisure in such a way that one's daily activities: domesticity, work, recuperation, can take place with the strictest economy of time." Finally, the city should be considered "in its economic totality, which is to say within its region of influence."[85] Pineau would endeavor to weave each of these threads into his maps. The first showed Hébrard's plan, no doubt by way of backdrop to Pineau's self-consciously more "liveable," "green," and "modern" scheme. Another showed Dalat proper, divided into zones: the market, native housing, European housing, and leisure (the golf course for example). Here, Pineau simply superimposed a layer on the CIAM's quest for compartmentalization: on top of the geographical division of labor and domesticity, Pineau introduced colonial segregation. A third map showcased Dalat's *non-oedificandi* green belts and buffers, of which Pineau was so proud. A fourth presented transportation routes, a fifth displayed construction zones, and a last one Greater Dalat. Photos adorning the fringes of these science-fair like posters displayed variously the native quarter, seminude highland minorities, villa types, ongoing work on the lakes, and the damage done by flooding in 1932.[86] Pineau's presentation of the city underscored its functionality and its degree of planning, to be sure, but also exposed its colonial divisions, its role as a site of leisure, and its pristine nature reflected in its lakes, parks, and indigenous minorities.

THE BLIGHTS OF UGLINESS AND MEDIOCRITY

The allegory of choice among Dalat's planners was that of paradise. No rotten apple, no unsightly blemish, would therefore be permitted to stain the hill station. Here, questions of good taste, of *laissez-faire* versus central planning were formulated around the notion of a pristine European retreat. Maintaining a paradise implied protecting the deer that roamed across the lawn of the Dalat Palace Hotel. It meant preserving vistas of Dalat's unique pine forests, which had reminded the first European visitors of home. And it entailed reinforced segregated zoning, as well as designating *cordons sanitaires* and open spaces, so as to contrast "rational," airy, new, and European Dalat, with the purported chaos of Vietnam's older cities.[87]

Of course, the ugliness so reviled by each of Dalat's planners lay at least partly in the eyes of the beholder. Pineau showed little charity in assessing his predecessor's plan. For all of its grandeur on paper, he wrote, the 1923 Hébrard plan had resulted in a single residential complex. As for that complex, the narrowness of its lots and its poor design yielded an ensemble resembling "a mediocre product of French suburbia."[88] Yet for all of their differences, Pineau, like Hébrard, claimed to "protect Dalat against ugliness." Too often, he wrote in 1937, French colonial towns bear the hallmarks of banality. They are uncomfortable, mediocre, in short, they too often "resemble cheap seaside resorts."[89]

The fiercest critic of Dalat's urban face was without a doubt the anonymous A. D.—likely Auguste Delaval, designer of Saigon's Musée Blanchard-de-La-Brosse, and called upon in 1930 to sketch one of the early blueprints (ultimately rejected) for Dalat's train station.[90] In a 1926 article reprinted in 1930, A. D. lampooned abominable hybrid buildings and homes across Indochina. He ridiculed those featuring, for example: "Norman roofs, Mansard rooftops, medieval corner turrets, Greek porticos, zinc cupolas. . . . What art!"[91] Here was a frontal attack on Hébrard's associationist syncretism.

In 1937, the anonymous critic set his sights on Dalat proper. In an article in *L'Impartial,* he railed against "a criminal attack" on the resort town. After having first allowed developers to erect "some hideous little houses" atop the hill overlooking the Ecole franco-annamite and the cinema, at present private residences were going to rise along the shores of the artificial lake. A. D. continued turgidly: "The lake!

FIGURE 15. Deauville's train station, present day. Photo courtesy of Lawrence Jennings.

To dare the sacrilege of suffocating that emerald jewel, that sapphire or black diamond . . . with a belt of cheap villas." A. D.'s sign-off suggests a fury against Dalat's recent public monuments. He concluded with typical bombast: "After the Lycée and the train station, halt these profanations! Dalat is neither Aubervilliers nor La Courneuve." Like Pineau before him, A. D. conjured up the Paris suburbs to represent the most abhorrent and drab architecture of the 1930s. That Auguste Delaval's own 1930 blueprint for the said train station had been passed up for an alleged monstrosity only added to his rage.[92]

PUBLIC BUILDINGS:
THE CASE OF THE TRAIN STATION

Dalat was and certainly remains famous for its villas. Yet debates over public structures proved equally, if not more acrimonious, from the Dalat Palace Hotel to the long delayed city hall, the lycées, the central market, and the train station. Delaval's outrage over Dalat's railway station needs to be placed in a broader context.

We saw in a previous chapter that trains only began arriving in Dalat proper at the end of 1932.[93] Yet the terminus was not yet in place. The aftershocks of the Great Depression delayed the train station's inauguration. Construction needed to be halted shortly after it had begun in 1935. The station would only be completed in 1938.[94]

FIGURE 16. Dalat's train station, present day. Photo by author.

It had thus been put off, designed, then redesigned—to reflect the times, the atmosphere of the hill station itself, as well as competing interests and aesthetics.

Delaval's original 1930 sketch had called for a country style—interestingly, it would appear that the blueprint, or a close facsimile of it, was adopted for the train station in Pointe-Noire in the Congo. Delval's drawing had evidently been intended to call to mind images of rural France, in everything from its bell-clock to its arcades and windows.[95] As Arnauld Le Brusq has remarked, this regionalist proposal clashed with Dalat's other public buildings, which reflected "international forms."[96] The project was subsequently shelved, and a new design by architect Paul Reveron approved by the municipal council in 1935. The council entrusted Vo Dinh Dang's firm with the actual construction.[97]

Reveron drew inspiration from the Deauville-Trouville station in Normandy, dating from 1863.[98] The choice was no accident. Reveron had borrowed from the golden era of Norman seaside resorts. This seaside style was clearly intended to signal the town's resort-aura to arriving passengers—making the statement that passengers had left the tropics for a microcosm of France.[99]

To some at least, the desired effect was achieved. Iphigénie-Catherine Shelshear, who spent part of her childhood in Dalat, recalls that "the railway station in Dalat was an expression of French architecture at its most creative. Its appearance belied its purpose as a centre of travel, and by stepping on the platform, a sudden change of time, scenery, mood took place. It is as if one passed without warning from one country to another, each having different geography, climate, and customs."[100] Here, Dalat's raison d'être was successfully conveyed through its train station. It served as a gateway to a microclimatic replica of France in Indochina, a site the colonizers claimed as culturally and even naturally French. Although its allusions to Deauville, to the beach, and to the *terroir* cannot be denied, Reveron's railway station was far from strictly nostalgic. Reveron added many variations to his original model. Art deco motifs, splashes of bright color, audacious curves, made this a modern and distinctive structure, visually striking to this day.

CONCLUSION

Looking solely at Hébrard's 1923 plan, one would surely have missed the complexities of, and challenges to segregationist zoning, the dialectic between regionalism and international modernism, the tension between planning and the freedom of ad hoc villa construction, the ebbs and flows of serialized housing, the battles over good taste and the importing of "the worst of the metropole" (the Paris suburbs), not to mention the backlashes against several monumental plans. Indeed, Hébrard's grand vision was barely even implemented before it was scrapped. This point in turn reinforces the importance of urban practices, municipal council debates, the forms and functions of villas, and dissident voices—both Vietnamese and French. Only by setting these practices against the five grand plans for Dalat can some degree of historical relief be achieved. The archives in Ho Chi Minh City, Aix-en-Provence, Paris, and elsewhere yield a complex picture of conflicting interests, between tourists and permanent inhabitants, Vietnamese and French, administrators and settlers, planners *de passage* and vested local interests. Invariably, these tensions were inscribed in the urban face of Dalat: in its train station, which after much wrangling was transformed from a clichéd provincial replica into a modernist jewel; in its residential districts, where a Basque villa sits across from a British cottage, a German *Berghaus* neighbors a neogothic Norman residence, or a Savoyard chalet stares down a functionalist Bauhaus-inspired retreat; in its planned quarters, in its expansion, and most notably, in its zoning strategies. For all of this apparent discord, however, Dalat's French promoters, urban planners, and municipal authorities shared a set of common goals: making of Dalat an oasis of France in highland Vietnam, a sanatorium or rest station for the entire colony, and a summer, if not permanent, capital of Indochina.

In his history of Hanoi, Philippe Papin asks how postcolonial Vietnamese have come to view Hanoi's two hundred colonial-era villas (note the contrast with Dalat's 750 villas by 1944). Although some may dismiss them as "the affected and provincial vestiges of a hated period symbolizing foreign domination and the ostentatious luxury of settlers," he writes, "most seem to greatly admire the villas," to the point that self-consciously neocolonial architecture is experiencing a boom in Vietnam's capital—although as To Anh Dang notes, no law mandates the preservation of colonial-era dwellings.[101] Much the same holds true for Dalat, whose tourist bureau promotes the eclectic, tranquil charm of successive generations of French architecture and planning. Indeed, thanks to Pham Nguyen Mau and a number of young Vietnamese architects plying their trade in the late colonial era, French forms, styles, and plans continued to weigh heavily on post-1954 Dalat. Lagisquet's 1942 blueprint was even dusted off and pressed back into service under President Ngo Dinh Diem.[102]

8

The Dalat Palace Hotel

After disembarking at the graceful art deco train station, a visitor to Dalat in the late 1930s would have passed the Swedish-inspired, brick Lycée Yersin under completion, then skirted the central lake along the Avenue Albert Sarraut. They would have glimpsed the Grenouillère snack and diving stands to their right, and admired the governor general's residence perched atop a pine-covered hill to their left. As it still does today, the smell of evergreens would have wafted in the air, stirring powerful memories for colonials. In the distance, the visitor would have followed rolling hills along the plateau, as far as the eye could see. Some crests were developed, with perched villas or monasteries, others not. Across the lake to their right, the visitor would have made out the emperor of Annam's golf course. Three vistas would then present themselves, offering a stark contrast: straight ahead, the administrative quarter, in which one could discern the gendarmerie, the brick church, pristine white hotels, and tax offices. Further ahead, one of the main European neighborhoods and its whimsical villas, it too set on a slope, along evocatively named streets like the Rue des Roses and Rue des Glaïeuls. The other side of the lake, to the right, offered a less orderly spectacle: the densely built, bustling Vietnamese quarter, site of the central market and the prison. However, what was sure to have captured the eye of a visitor approaching central Dalat from the train station along the Avenue Sarraut was the resort's grandest structure, dwarfing all other buildings: the Lang-Bian Palace Hotel, dominating the administrative district, commanding the lake.

Completed in 1922, this monumental hotel, known at the time as the Lang-Bian Palace Hotel, was designed as a site of colonial leisure and power at the center of Indochina's premier resort. According to geographer Robert Reed, the Palace "function[ed] almost immediately as the nerve center of proper Western colonial society in the highlands."[1] The hotel's monumentalism, modernity, luxury, and location made it a conspicuous symbol of French domination over the Indochinese central highlands. This ostentatious hotel sheds light on a number of interconnected issues, from colonial tourism to urban planning and the quotidian practice of colonialism.[2] The Lang-Bian Palace Hotel constitutes at once a focal point and a fault line for the identity, status, and social relations of French colonizers in Indochina. The Palace Hotel points to other divides between the theory and practice of colonial sites of leisure and power. When one pushes the examination of Dalat beyond initial plans for an oasis of France in the highlands of Indochina, one uncovers more discord and rivalry than unity of goals: the various strata of the French colonial administration could never agree on which should bear the financial burden of keeping the grand hotel afloat. The Lang-Bian Palace Hotel emerged, in other words, as a site where various and often competing colonial ambitions, tensions and visions of Indochina itself were negotiated.

Early French residents in Dalat bemoaned the isolation and drudgery of the place.[3] What were needed were European leisure infrastructures: a grand hotel, a first-class French restaurant, a rowing club, tennis court, stables and riding facilities, etc.—as much as markers of the colonial lifestyle as ways of affirming Frenchness in the "backyard" of the Vietnamese, so to speak. The majestic Lang-Bian Palace Hotel would offer all of these amenities and more.

It is hardly surprising then, that it emerged as the linchpin of post-World War I urban plans for Dalat. The city was literally laid out around its Palace Hotel and its artificial lake. The hotel was positioned at the centre of a European business and administrative quarter, dominated the "native quarters," and served as a buffer between them and the European villas. The Lang-Bian Palace would offer a tranquil base from which to "explore" nearby highland minority villages or set out on big-game expeditions. Most important, as its title of "palace" suggests, this would be a luxurious establishment, competing with the poshest colonial hotels of Southeast Asia, be they the Oriental Hotel in Bangkok or the Raffles Hotel in Singapore.

The Lang-Bian Palace thus mediated between the exotic and the familiar. It provided access to a highland minority setting from a familiar homebase featuring French food and European luxury. Here was a place of multiple escapes: escape back to France (or the best substitute for it), into a "primitive" or trophy-hunting universe, and away from Vietnam and the Vietnamese. Customers were certainly not avoiding other French people, who concentrated their stays at the hotel in peak seasons or holidays. Escape thus had its limits: customers sought *dépaysement* while at the same time pining for reminders of France.[4] They also remained firmly rooted in what was by definition a hierarchical colonial society, one that migrated en masse from Saigon to Dalat during hot spring and summer spells.[5] But the hotel's paradoxes did not end here. The Lang-Bian / Dalat Palace (once known as the Lang-Bian Palace, it became the Dalat Palace after the Second World War, although since the two place names were interchangeable, earlier uses of the latter also exist) also high-lighted a tension between colonial desires for *démesure* and luxury on the one hand, and a more modest reality on the other.

TROUBLED BEGINNINGS

Dalat's grand hotel first appears on paper on Champoudry's 1906 plan for the hill station.[6] The project then disappears from the record until the First World War. In 1917, colonial inspector Phérivong drafted a report calling for Dalat to become not merely Indochina's prime center for rest and reinvigoration, but also a sanatorium for Europeans from all over East and Southeast Asia. A luxury establishment was critical to this vision. In the inspector's words: "Neither in Siam, nor in the Philip-pines is there a hill station like this one; even the British in Hong Kong have ex-pressed interest in it. It is therefore necessary that we immediately create comfort-able establishments that might attract a foreign clientele. Hence, a Palace-Hotel has been planned [for Dalat]."[7] Here, French Indochina's prestige was closely tied to the hill station's jewel in the crown, which was to be a shining example of French grandeur and savoir-faire for all of Asia.

Little wonder then, that the Palace Hotel occupied such a central role and site in Dalat. While British colonial hill stations like Simla or Ootacamund tended to revolve around individual seats of power, such as the viceroy's residence, at Dalat the Lang-Bian Palace was erected fifteen years before the governor general's villa, and dwarfed it in stature. To be sure, this state of affairs also resulted from a gen-eral scaling-back from architect Ernest Hébrard's outlandish 1923 blueprint for Dalat, which featured a projected massive administrative quarter northeast of the main artificial lake. Little of Hébrard's vision was ever realized. The Lang-Bian Palace's incommensurability with the rest of Dalat in 1922 thus stems in part from its construction date: at the height of an economic boom in 1922. When economic circumstances changed later that decade, most plans for government structures in Dalat were scrapped (villa construction, meanwhile, continued unabated), leaving the town with a Palace Hotel as its centrepiece and icon. When the Depression finally receded, only the Palace Hotel was left as a monumental structure. However, such a change of fortunes alone cannot explain why the Palace Hotel would have been built *first:* it is striking that it was erected before a post office, train station, or city hall—even before most of the city's schools. Certainly this sequence must be in-dicative of the French colonial administration's priorities. In 1922, the hotel stood quite literally alone in terms of public edifices.

The Lang-Bian Palace opened in March 1922, after Governor General Long made multiple visits to the resort to accelerate and oversee construction in person.[8] Sev-eral sources suggest that the Lang-Bian Palace experienced a rocky beginning. Be-cause the rail line to Dalat was not yet completed in 1922, construction materials had to be carted for long stretches on foot by "coolies"—at great physical cost. But the colonial administration drew financial, rather than humanitarian lessons from this. In 1923, the governor general of Indochina explained bluntly to the Minister of the Colonies: "The exorbitant prices incurred to build the Lang-Bian Palace . . . led to the adjourning of any further construction [in Dalat] until the completion of the rail line."[9] Delays to the Dalat hotel's opening had become a running joke. In April 1923, one of Dalat's part-time inhabitants, the Saigon press baron Henry de Lachevrotière, opined: "For years the Dalat Palace had been under construction, and there seemed to be no end in sight, since planners demolished one day what they had built the previous day, only to build it again the next. It was the Penelope's web of public works."[10] Worse still, the hotel left in its wake a legacy of near fiscal ruin, so costly had it proven to build a palace in the remote central highlands of Vietnam. In turn, the resulting freeze on construction in Dalat bred discontent— sometimes directed pointedly at the extravagance of the Lang-Bian Palace. A 1923 article in the *Moniteur d'Indochine* complained that the administration had neglected all other hotels in Indochina at the expense of the grandiose Lang-Bian Palace project. This "costly" hotel, whose price tag the author estimated at six million piastres, "had left the administration content, so long as it was inaugurated and kept open some fifteen days or so."[11]

The human cost proved harder to quantify. Colonial-era records may be silent about the sufferings of indigenous laborers who hauled materiel up to the Lang-Bian on their backs. But the local press does relate a tragic accident that underscores the hotel's shaky beginnings. In September 1924 part of the hotel's garage collapsed, killing a chauffeur who was sleeping in his car. The car's owner sued the governor general's office for the cost of his automobile, not for the death of his chauffeur.[12]

The Palace's troubles did not end there. For one thing, clients mourned the loss of the more modest Hôtel Desanti. In 1925, the local press griped that the Lang-Bian Palace had only attracted three or four customers, who "roamed melancholically in its vast halls." In contrast, at the old Desanti establishment, "one had felt at ease," and "mothers could tend to babies without worrying about an overly formal decor." Lastly, the press asked, would the Palace succeed in restoring European children's constitutions, would it feed them hardy fare to boost their red blood cell count? The chic new establishment had put off a large segment of colonial society.[13]

Legal troubles soon added to these woes. Throughout its colonial history, regulations stipulated that the hotel should have either a French maître d'hôtel or a French head cook on hand.[14] In 1920 Mr. Marc Desanti, the very first (and shortlived) manager of the Lang-Bian Palace, recruited a chef from Pau in Southwestern France.[15] Cook Henri Passiot and his wife, who was to serve as *chef de lingerie*, signed a three-year contract which was to begin at the Lang-Bian Palace starting on January 1, 1921. The *cuisinier* cum war veteran and amputee proceeded to sue the Lang-Bian Palace Hotel and Mr. Desanti when the establishment failed to open on schedule in 1921. In October 1921, seeing that the hotel's interior was far from completed, Passiot sued Desanti, who in turn sued the government general of Indochina.[16] Passiot sued for his back-pay, as well as travel expenses to Indochina and back to Pau for himself and his wife.

Infighting and recrimination within the insular French colonial community of Dalat also led to a series of catastrophes shortly after the hotel's opening in 1922. In 1925, escalating tensions, as well as fiscal belt-tightening led to perhaps the greatest calamity of all for a hotel of its standing. A city health inspection revealed that the kitchens and their surroundings suffered from "a condition of considerable filth." A doctor issued precise recommendations to remedy the situation. Yet six months after the initial report, no action had been taken. A second, more sternly worded warning from Garnier lamented the "shameful stain" on the hotel of having flies infest the kitchen. So numerous were the pests that they represented a real nuisance for guests located on the same wing as the kitchen.[17] The hotel's short-lived managers hurried to point fingers at one another over this filth: Mr. Chaillet, newly designated to replace Mr. Morel in 1925, placed the blame squarely on his predecessor, as well as on the hotel's Vietnamese staff.[18] Paradoxically, in spite of these allegations, the hotel would also draw the ire of those who saw in it a metaphor for lavish spending, waste, and luxury.

A SYMBOL OF COLONIAL POWER

Initially featuring thirty-eight luxury rooms, the establishment boasted the most modern amenities of the time, as well as an orchestra, a cinema, tennis courts, private fruit and vegetable gardens, a dancing hall, riding facilities, gymnastic equipment, and a French restaurant.[19] Its managers upheld the establishment's inherent Frenchness. Iphigénie-Catherine Shellshear recalls of the hotel in which she spent part of her childhood in the early 1940s: "It was not by accident that the hotel resembled a French Château! When Monsieur Feraudi [the manager, *sic*] had the hotel built [*sic*] he wished it to be an oasis of French culture for a clientele that lived so far from the mother country. Much more than a hotel, the Lang-Bian Palace was an institution that promoted gracious living."[20]

By 1930, the hotel offered jazz concerts.[21] The original 1922 personnel list called for three European and sixty-one "native workers," including twelve servers for the restaurant, one Chinese cook, one *pâtissier* a hair dresser, three chauffeurs, ten coolies, etc. As for the three Europeans, they would occupy the posts of general manager, maître d'hôtel, and gouvernante. Meals in the restaurant were simple but resolutely French: "*potage, grillades, pain, entremets chauds,*" etc.[22] An emphasis was placed on fresh fruit—and not surprisingly, on French fruits like apples and pears, though litchis and mangoes were also served. As a final mark of French culinary

FIGURE 17. The Lang-Bian Palace Hotel in the 1920s. Reprinted by permission of the Archives Nationales, Centre des Archives d'Outre-mer, GGI 59875.

authenticity, hotel guidelines stipulated that butter, and never grease, would be used for cooking.[23] As for the uniforms of the hotel's personnel, these were described as follows by a 1932 convention: "The attire of domestic personnel must be clean and neat: a white, freshly ironed outfit will be de rigueur for waiters; domestics in contact with visitors must have a complete mastery of their trade, and speak sufficiently fluent French."[24]

Architecturally, the Palace was inspired by metropolitan French resort styles— merging elements of spa towns like Vittel with seaside architectural elements borrowed from the likes of Cabourg or Cannes. In his historical fresco of Indochina during the Second World War, French novelist Morgan Sportès depicts the Lang-Bian Palace as follows: "One could have been on the Riviera, in some elegant seaside resort. This impression was corroborated by the high, white silhouette of the Palace Hotel (a dead ringer for the Negresco Hotel in Nice)."[25] For her part, architectural historian Gwendolyn Wright describes the building's original appearance succinctly: "The Palace Hotel was completed in the rococo style of hotels along the French Riviera."[26]

In 1943, under the Vichy governor general of Indochina, Admiral Decoux, the Lang-Bian Palace's ornate facade was purged, making way for a starker exterior.[27] The new, clean, modernist facade was almost certainly inspired by architect Paul

Vesseyre's two other "Palaces" in town—Bao Dai's and the governor general's, built in 1934 and 1937 respectively, in a style more reminiscent of art deco or even Bauhaus than of the fin-de-siècle spa style.[28] On both aesthetic and political grounds, Governor Decoux abhorred the rococo art that had proliferated across Indochina during the great flourish of construction at the turn of the century. The governor general's secretary noted of Decoux's July 1, 1942 meeting on this topic with Dalat's mayor André Berjoan: "[The hotel's] facades will be rid of those out-dated ornaments."[29] At least one source bemoaned the lost mystique and romanticism of the place, and its replacement by a colder "ski resort" style.[30] The Lang-Bian Palace's modernization in 1943 was in reality part of a much vaster campaign to simplify complex lines, and to excise rococo frivolities. Other examples include the palace of the governor general of Cochinchina in Saigon, whose two caryatids were removed under Decoux, and the famous Saigon theater, whose statues and bas-reliefs were demolished on Decoux's orders.[31] In 1997, renovations undertaken on Saigon's theatre reversed Decoux's modifications, and restored its original details.[32]

ETHNIC MINORITIES ON DISPLAY

Visits to nearby minority villages, attractions which are still offered at the Dalat Palace Hotel today, were a staple of the hotel beginning with its inception. Colonial-era visitors to the hotel felt simultaneously attracted and repelled by the highland minority presence. The attraction resided in romanticized images of hardy highland peoples leading a rustic, ethnologically fascinating existence just beyond the walls of the Palace. The Palace's managers and Indochinese tourism agencies played the card of the "noble Moï" in a magazine ad that ran in 1926 and 1927 in *Extrême-Asie*. The ad juxtaposed a small caption representing the opulent Palace Hotel with a larger image of a muscular highland minority man poised to spear a wild beast. Behind him, a minority woman looks on, half covered by the forest canopy. This advertisement is reminiscent of stereotypical nineteenth-century representations of fierce native Americans, and might just as easily been used to sell a lodge at Yosemite or Banff. A similar motif appears on the colonial-era luggage tag intended for Palace customers. It depicts a highland minority hunting by one of the Dalat region's trademark Camly waterfalls.

Of course, touting highland minorities as fierce warriors or even hunters was a potentially perilous marketing strategy. In his article published in the widely circulated metropolitan French magazine *L'Illustration*, François de Tessan reassured potential visitors to Dalat and its Palace Hotel that the local minorities had been completely "pacified" and that the "age of heroic conquest is over. We have . . . entered into the age of progress."[33] The delicate balancing act used to market Dalat's ethnographic appeal thus consisted of piquing colonial curiosity in "muscled,

FIGURE 18. Lang-Bian Palace Hotel luggage tag by V. Duong. Date unknown, author's collection.

tanned, wild haired, wide eyed [warriors]," while simultaneously reassuring the everyday traveler of their complete harmlessness, stressing that minority "tribes" now constituted attractions, not threats.[34] Making the highland minorities appear either too threatening or too peaceful could ruin the fantasy.

However, the "noble savage" did not always draw travelers. For those preferring a replica of France over a fanciful "far-west" (note that a kitschy far-western theme park can be found at one of Dalat's lakes to this day), the highland minority presence was irritating at best. Witness the following postcard, written to a friend in the Paris suburb of Saint-Cloud by a woman visiting the Lang-Bian Place Hotel on October 4, 1924. The image on the card, entitled "panorama from the Hotel," shows several minority people—scantily clad by European standards—and a minority village in the

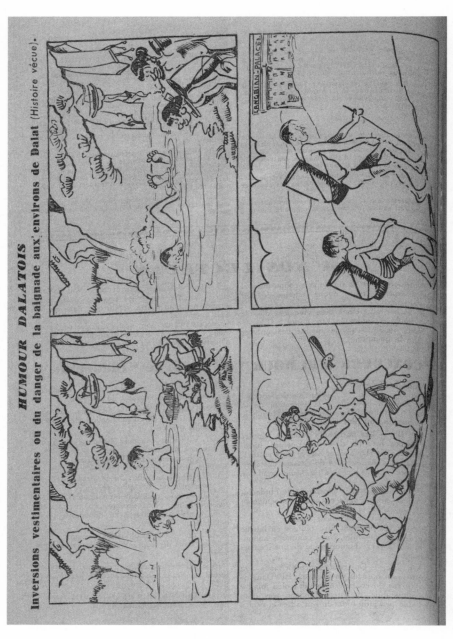

FIGURE 19. "Sartorial inversions or the dangers of bathing around Dalat (a true story)." From *Indochine, hebdomadaire illustré,* July 13, 1944.

background. On the flip side, this female traveler, no doubt a resident of Saigon suffering from the ennui so many French women experienced in Indochina, wrote:

> Dear Nicette, I am sending you a card of Indochina's convalescence site, which is a far cry from Vichy, especially with its inhabitants whose attire leaves a little something to be desired. Nevertheless, there are two handsome hotels, a theatre, cinema, dancing hall, tennis court, and so on. The air is reputedly good here in the mountains of Southern Annam. Let's face it, it doesn't match up to St Cloud, but then again, neither does Saigon. Yours. . . . [35]

This traveler's narrative shifts from a focus on the scant clothing of local minorities, to an unfavorable comparison with Vichy, and later Saint-Cloud (an affluent Paris suburb). Betraying both her Paris-centered worldview and her homesickness, the author explicitly complains that Dalat is not enough of a French clone; in this instance, highland minorities stand in the way of the traveler's fantasy of reintegrating the motherland in the highlands of southern Indochina.

Meanwhile, visitors more curious about local inhabitants could set out on ethnographic visits to minority villages. To these tourists, the opulence of the Lang-Bian Palace was no doubt contrasted with the perceived starkness of minority houses. Certainly, the Palace Hotel served as a poignant reminder of Frenchness—a social landmark that guaranteed that the French would resist any temptation of "going native." This principle was encapsulated in a 1944 cartoon purporting to recount a true story.[36] The captions show two French men letting their guard down as they go for a swim (one manages the feat of smoking while soaking); two members of a local minority proceed to steal their clothes in a classic gag, and an equally classic inversion of European and "primitive" trappings. In the final scene, the two French men are reduced to returning in highland native garb to the Lang-Bian Palace Hotel—elevated here into a monument to whiteness and "civilization." The two unfortunate swimmers look forlorn, bearing the sartorial stigma of nativeness, while the two minority people walk back to their nearby village wearing pith helmets—the markers of colonial status par excellence. Here the Lang-Bian Palace's very presence as a social marker literally shames these two Europeans. And it is precisely because of the Lang-Bian Palace that this anecdote is a nightmare come true for them. It is not the act of losing one's clothes, so much as the return to European high society—embodied by the Palace—that creates this powerful sense of ridicule. The hotel thus provided a relational standard or norm by which to measure one's Frenchness in the highlands.

THE PLACE OF THE VIETNAMESE

The relationship between colonial and Indochinese societies was strained by the place of servants. For the colonizers, having a retinue of indigenous servants was of course a mark of power, and constituted one of the advantages of the colonies. However, the servant—though a necessity and indeed a token of status within the colonial hierarchy—was paradoxically a source of constant anxiety for the colonizers, as a potential enemy within the household. This fear of servants who could communicate "secretly" in their own tongue, who had access to the French private sphere, and could indeed access and shift between both Vietnamese and French registers, sometimes verged on paranoia.[37]

At the Lang-Bian Place Hotel, such fears reached a zenith in the late colonial era. A persistent rumor, described by a recent French guidebook to Vietnam, holds that an underground Communist ring operated out of the Lang-Bian Palace's kitchen in the 1930s.[38] In reality, the incident occurred in 1952, and had little to do with the kitchens. At the height of unrest in Dalat, that year the Sûreté arrested one Tran-Van-Hoang, a secretary at the Palace Hotel. The police quickly linked him to a communist information-gathering cell.[39]

Psychologically, the effect of such an arrest was to reveal the fragility of Dalat's colonial cocoon. The city of rest, lakes, and pines was evidently not immune from "infiltration" by Vietnamese "subversives." Indeed, the personnel ratio must have reinforced such fears: in the colonial era, some sixty Vietnamese worked at the hotel, a figure to be contrasted to the establishment's six European employees, or its thirty-eight rooms for that matter. The cell also reveals an interesting degree of political militancy amongst the personnel of the elite hotel, catering to the colony's wealthiest patrons.

While fears of Vietnamese servants and anticolonial subversion were perennial concerns for French society in Dalat, this is not to suggest that the highland resort remained a playground for the French alone. Vietnamese elites soon found their place side by side with their French counterparts. Like the grand Japanese hotels of the late nineteenth century, the Lang-Bian Palace hotel enabled European and indigenous elites to mingle.[40] Emperor Bao Dai held banquets at the Lang-Bian Palace.[41] As Bruce Lockhart has suggested, Bao Dai's predilection for Dalat in itself reveals more than his legendary passion for hunting and diversions: it implies that the emperor felt estranged from his capital Hué—and even more so from his future capital by default, Saigon.[42] This alienation drew him to a Europeanized highland resort, whose urban layout was arguably more segregated than any other Indochinese city, and where his palace stood atop a hill overlooking the European and administrative quarters.

The Palace Hotel also exposed inequalities. In the establishment's early years, it provided the only purified water in all of Dalat. In 1925, the local Committee of Public Salubrity expressed the hope that the hotel's Lepage machine could be used to purify water for non-French Dalatois, and not simply for hotel guests, as had been the case up to then. Other measures would need to be undertaken, including the condemning of eighteen unhealthy wells. Still, the short-term solution to a public health crisis was to urge Vietnamese Dalatois to come to the hotel for water distribution; the hotel's place as a center of power, modernity, and Frenchness was only strengthened from the resulting queues for clean water.[43]

CLIENTELE

Throughout the hotel's colonial existence, its managers and the Indochinese tourism agency made concerted efforts to woo foreign visitors. An English-language brochure from 1933 advertised: "the Lang-Bian Palace and the Grand Hôtel de Dalat . . . offer every modern comfort, and diversion, including concerts, tennis, golf, walking tours and motor excursions. The sportsman will find plenty of game, large and small, in the nearby hills."[44] Rich adventurers and big game hunters were particularly targeted for attention. Maurice Rondet-Saint, the head of the Ligue maritime coloniale, remarked upon the prominent place of hunting in Indochinese tourism, noting that some fifty million piastres a year were spent by big-game hunters in Indochina. Stressing that Europeans could kill two birds with one stone, Rondet-Saint distilled the Lang-Bian Palace into a balance between the exotic and the familiar: "In the mountains of Annam, at Dalat, there is a sanitarium where Europeans who cannot spend their holidays in Europe come to refresh and reinvigorate themselves in the pure and healthy mountain air. It so happens that Dalat and its Palace are also in the heart of hunting country."[45] This passage underscores the diverse makeup of the Palace's clientele: while some customers were wealthy outsiders visiting Indochina to bring home big-game trophies, others were high-ranking administrators on furlough or long-weekend visits. Unwittingly, Rondet-Saint may also have pinpointed the Palace Hotel's problematic marketing position: as a resort for those who could not afford to return to Europe, colonial Dalat defined itself in part as a "cheap substitute" for France. With wealthy colonials heading back to France at the earliest possible occasion, this left Dalat with middle-ranking administrators, the vast majority of whom could not afford Palace prices. To give a sense of scale, in the early 1930s the Lang-Bian Palace Hotel cost 6 piastres a night, while the town's "lesser hotels" charged a mere 1.20 and 1.75 piastres.[46]

The Lang-Bian Palace was already caught in a price gap, itself the reflection of an expectation gap: the hotel offered a replica of Europe at European prices, when those who could only afford replicas of France could not pay European rates in the first place. To compound the problem, the proliferation of villas in Dalat between 1922 and 1945 meant that the ultra-elite courted by the Lang-Bian Palace already possessed cottages of their own in Dalat. In 1929, the governor general of Indochina summarized the marketing conundrum of the Lang-Bian Palace Hotel. He wrote to his colleague in Cochinchina that the Palace Hotel failed to answer the needs of the "modest clientele of *colons* and functionaries with limited budgets, who are in many ways the most interested in Dalat, for they are the most tired, and hence most in need of reinvigoration."[47] The projected increase in the Lang-Bian Palace's size from thirty-two to one hundred rooms—by adjoining an annex building, later dubbed the Hôtel du Parc—failed to address the problem of middle-class leisure.[48] The Palace, it seemed, reflected more the colonial dream of grandiose standing than the reality of colonial budgets.

CONTESTED LUXURY

In the colonial era, the Lang-Bian Palace Hotel suffered both from poor timing and from its status as a semipublic, then wholly public luxury establishment. Shortly after the Palace's long-delayed opening in 1922, French Indochina was rattled by a series of economic crises, starting in 1928 with a free-fall in the value of rubber, and culminating in an all-out depression by 1934—in line of course with the global Depression.[49] Already in 1927, disputes erupted over public subventions allocated to the Lang-Bian Palace Hotel. Annam covered part of the bill for the Palace, the remainder being paid by the governor general in Hanoi, as well as by a private consortium known as the Société anonyme des Grands Hôtels indochinois that went bankrupt in 1930.[50] The main bone of contention derived from Dalat's geographical situation within the kingdom of Annam. While Annam footed much of the costs of the Palace, it was readily apparent that the luxury establishment catered primarily to the wealthy elites of Saigon and the rest of Cochinchina, which never contributed a cent to its upkeep. Thus, on December 22, 1927, at the first sign of broader financial troubles in Indochina, the Résident supérieur d'Annam announced that he was suspending payment to the Lang-Bian Palace. By May of the following year, the Résident supérieur d'Annam justified his decision to the governor general in Hanoi:

> It is paradoxical to pay a subvention of 24,000.00 piastres to the Lang-Bian Palace, while at the same time paying a subsidy of 6,000.00 piastres to the Desanti Hotel which competes with it. I should add that I have never understood how Annam stood to gain from paying for the Lang-Bian Palace. A stay in Dalat is accessible only to a small privileged elite in Annam, while most of the clientele of these indebted hotels consists of high bureaucrats, *colons,* or industrialists from Cochinchina and Cambodia. I therefore insist respectfully, but firmly, Mr. Governor General, that starting January 1, 1929 the Lang-Bian Palace's subsidy be paid by the Governor General and not Annam.[51]

Clearly articulated here was the idea of geopolitical injustice, the notion that wealthy Saigonese were disproportionately benefiting from Annam's subsidies, and that the government should not keep all of Dalat's hotels afloat in the first place. Competition and capitalism, the mantra of most *colons* in this lucrative colony (lucrative for some), never seemed to take root in the world of Dalat's hotels, situated as they were in an artificial bubble of highland leisure.

By the 1930s the hotel's title of "Palace" cost it dearly in a time of budgetary restraints. Indochina's inspector of finances singled out the Palace as a symbol of waste and excess; the grandeur that had been the establishment's selling point in the 1920s was now held against it. In a December 1931 missive, the inspector of finances argued:

> In countries all around the world, ministers of finance are proclaiming that the state must reduce spending. It is therefore not the time to consider subsidizing a Palace, by definition a sumptuous and frivolous spending par excellence. I am fully aware that this means that the Lang-Bian Palace will have to close. And since the Hôtel du Parc is not open yet, only the Desanti Hotel will be left running. This will no doubt be regrettable, but beggars can't be choosers. The Governor General's office is in no position to pay holidays for Saigonese who themselves are in no position right now to afford a stay in Dalat.[52]

As the Depression hit Indochina, the Lang-Bian Palace Hotel was increasingly castigated as a white elephant by the administration, and its manager portrayed as out of touch with, and insensitive to, the fiscal belt-tightening required around the world at the time.

The hotel's manager in the 1930s, Edouard Feraudy, an Italian with years of experience in the hotel sector in Indochina, appears to have seriously underestimated the administration's desire to close his luxury establishment. At the very time of the inspector's report, Feraudy was clamoring to the administration for new silverware. And when the governor general's office suggested short-term solutions like the elimination of the hotel's orchestra, an indignant Feraudy responded that he had already slashed his own salary by 50 percent and that of his employees by 20 percent. Reducing or eliminating the orchestra, he retorted, was out of the question if he was to maintain the hotel's standing.[53] This document, which made its way to Hanoi, is covered in marginalia, red exclamation marks especially, from administrators clearly dismissive of Feraudy's concerns about his hotel's prestige and standing at the height of the Depression.[54] Feraudy and the administration were evidently speaking different languages: Feraudy's rhetoric revolved around standing, "minimum service" to maintain such a standing, and the government's imperative to defend colonial luxury. Reducing the orchestra, or laying off some of the establishment's sixty-five employees, he wrote, was tantamount to "stripping the hotel's rank." Only Feraudy, it seemed, had remained faithful to the vision of this hotel not as an economically viable resort, but as a marker of status and prestige. The goal of the Lang-Bian Palace, in this view, had more to do with the challenge of building a luxury palace in the "outback," than it did with any capitalist venture. In this sense too, the Palace Hotel encapsulates the delusions of grandeur of French colonial administrators, planners, and architects, for whom aesthetic and power considerations systematically superseded practical ones.

Feraudy would soon lock horns with another level of administration. In September 1931, the mayor of Dalat, facing a financial crunch of his own, complained of paying three hundred to seven hundred piastres per month to light the Lang-Bian Palace at night. The mayor was incensed by Feraudy's constant quip that he need "save the reputation and prestige of the Palace" by illuminating it at night—a burden that was allegedly single-handedly ruining Dalat's municipal budget.[55]

The mayor of Dalat and Feraudy also clashed over the hotel's very function. They were at odds over both the Palace's mission and its market. The level of vitriol reflected in their correspondence suggests that the petty rivalries so common in closed colonial circles were rampant in Dalat. Thus in March 1933, the mayor wrote to the governor general of Indochina:

> Mr. Feraudy's tenure as manager expires on June 30, 1933; the running of the Lang-Bian Palace, as it presently stands, leads to monthly losses usually in excess of 2,000 piastres, and this in spite of a subvention of 1,000 piastres. This situation is not surprising: it is the result of the special rapports between Mr. Feraudy and the clientele he deigns to accept in his Palace. On several occasions, I have received complaints from customers who, after having been the victims of haughtiness, or even insolence on the part of the manager, vowed never to return to the Palace.[56]

The mayor flatly accused Feraudy of driving away customers, attributing this situation to Feraudy's own conception of the hotel as a preserve of the elite. In the fractured and hierarchical colonial system, the Lang-Bian Palace had emerged not as the playground for all Europeans in Indochina, but as the *domaine réservé* of a minute elite, described by one source as Indochina's *"grands pontes"*—or bigwigs.[57] Intimidation, haughtiness, or whatever other character traits the mayor saw in Feraudy, were no doubt radiated by the manager so as to maintain the hotel's standing—a perennial obsession which completely superseded economic viability. No doubt in the world of 1930s French customer relations, Feraudy's distance and "haughtiness" would actually have been perceived as desirable attributes by the crème de la crème of French colonial society. In Indochina, of course, an already hierarchical French social universe was bent and distorted to a paroxysm. Here, after all, the veneer of "equality" in "liberty, equality, and fraternity" was absent, while a correspondingly distorted and inflated sense of self-importance seemed de rigueur, no doubt stoked by coteries of servants, "boys" and *"con-gaïs"* (indigenous lovers).[58]

For all of his purported haughtiness, Feraudy was certainly resourceful and determined to maintain his establishment. As a way of generating funds, he proposed the establishment of a casino, tied to the hotel. This was in reality a reformulation of earlier plans, dating back to the creation of the Lang-Bian Palace, which called for the creation of a casino within easy walking distance of the Palace Hotel.[59] Then, in 1926 the Résident supérieur d'Annam agreed to the construction of a *cercle des étrangers*—a private club where gaming would be permitted, and which would be located steps from the Palace Hotel. During the time that the dedicated club building was being erected, the Résident even granted permission for the gaming operation to operate within the hotel's confines. In an abrupt about-face a year later, during a governor transition, Governor general Alexandre Varenne ordered the new *cercle* to be closed and gambling prohibited throughout the colony.[60] Yet the plan would not die, so tied was it to the idea of Dalat as a world-class resort. In September 1935, a desperate Feraudy again revived the idea of a grand casino, arguing that "having been asked from many quarters to give Dalat (the most beautiful highland resort in East Asia) a Casino that will be required one day or another any way to aid its development, and its appeal on a par with French mountain resorts, [I am studying the possibility of] forming a company to build and run . . . a Dalat Municipal Casino."[61]

Feraudy explicitly compared Dalat to French mountain resorts like Chamonix, noting that only a casino stood between the two. Feraudy also broached the question of who would be allowed to gamble: "we would add Asian gambling in the same conditions as [European gaming]."[62] Here, Feraudy treaded on thin ice. As Erica Peters shows in her analysis of gambling in colonial Indochina, French colonizers portrayed the Vietnamese as innately compulsive gamblers and decried gambling as a local hydra. But, Peters suggests, French positions were in reality more ambivalent, given the place of gambling in French society. What most shocked colonial mores, she argues, was the possibility of Europeans and Vietnamese gambling side by side.[63] And this of course was precisely the Pandora's box that Feraudy had opened. In his highly disapproving letter to the governor general, Dalat's mayor pointed to two reasons to turn down this proposed casino: first it seemed typical of Feraudy's "megalomania," and second, it presented "a moral dimension which you alone can judge." After the governor general's rejection of the casino project on October 11, 1935, Feraudy's options for continuing to run the Lang-Bian Palace were seriously reduced.[64]

The battle to save the hotel had been raging for some time. In 1931, Feraudy was no longer pleading for silverware, new plumbing, or the maintaining of his orchestra as he had in the past, but quite simply for his hotel to remain open. He implored the governor general in Hanoi: "Should you consider the temporary closure of the Lang-Bian Palace, then five European employees (not counting myself) and sixty natives would be left jobless."[65] The following January, the Grands Magasins de Dalat, a luxury boutique rented out by the hotel, and located between the Lang-Bian Palace and the Hôtel du Parc, filed for bankruptcy.[66] Faced with mounting losses, a less frequented hotel, and an irate administration, Feraudy finally agreed in April 1932 that the Lang-Bian Palace would close from 1934 to 1937; the date of 1934 was chosen, for it marked the estimated opening date for the Palace's sister hotel, the Hôtel du Parc.[67] Thus at least one of the two establishments would remain open for vacationers, even in harsh economic times.

Closing one of the two hotels was constantly advanced as a possibility to cut costs.

Seeking to stave off the complete closure of both hotels in the 1930s, and faced with the harsh reality of needing to furnish two hotels with the materiel for only one, Feraudy relented, and accepted the principle that rolling closures could occur in one hotel or the other, depending on demand.[68] Still, Feraudy had to resist several creative attempts by the administration to convert or decommission the Lang-Bian Palace altogether. In 1932, he sent a strongly worded reply to the governor general's office, rejecting a plan to transform the Lang-Bian Palace into a government building. According to this scheme, the Hôtel du Parc would have remained a functioning hotel, while the Palace would have been handed over to the administration. Feraudy replied that "to substitute the Dalat Palace with its annex [the Hôtel du Parc] . . . would be a dreadful mistake. This would leave Dalat with only two hotels—of economy category. And the hotel which represents [Dalat's] main attraction, based on its location, its offerings, its celebrations and social life, in short Dalat's main selling point, would disappear, leaving a vacuum that would hamper the city's development."[69]

Feraudy's response once again underscores the centrality of the Lang-Bian Palace to Dalat's function as a site of French leisure and power. The series of conflicts around the Palace in the 1930s attest to its tenuous position as a symbol of luxury, grandeur, and excess on the one hand, and its status as a publicly run establishment on the other. Moreover, this disjunction between colonial fantasy and economic reality betrays the social ambitions of a colonial society that so valued a Palace in its highland playground, but soon realized that this "Indochinese dream" was unattainable for all save the colony's plutocracy.

THINGS FALL APART

On March 6, 1943, the grand covered staircase entry to the Palace Hotel abruptly collapsed, killing three Vietnamese workers—two male masons and a woman "coolie" by the name of Ngo. Paul Veysseyre, the architect called upon by Dalat's judge to lead a technical inquiry, held no punches in his report. The tragic collapse— at least the second in the hotel's short existence—was a direct result of shoddy workmanship during the rush to renovate the hotel, he argued. One can deduce that the rush involved renovating the establishment in accordance with the aesthetic revolution promoted by Admiral Decoux, by introducing more right angles and straight lines, and eliminating baroque frivolities. The new, massive, no-nonsense entrance had just been erected in January of that year, with finishing touches made some two weeks before the accident. Veysseyre deduced that the accident resulted from three main causes: calculation errors on the actual weight of the huge concrete slab covering the entrance; the insufficient time given to the concrete to set; and the "irrational" use of materials like brick to support heavier concrete. The consequence, he wrote to the judge, was the collapse of eighty tons of concrete on the Vietnamese workers who had been laboring on this embellishment project. Although Veysseyre noted that it was not his place to judge the aesthetic of the projected grand entrance, his tone suggests reproval of this as well. The collapse of 1943 in many ways restaged previous conflicts and recriminations over the hotel, but rather than resulting in plumbing failure, clashes with the mayor, or hotel closures, it ended in tragic loss of life, and doubtless in serious bitterness on the part of the families of the deceased.[70] In fact, some of the workers had previously refused to continue the renovation because they had warned that the slab in question had already begun to slump some time before the accident. Negligence at the center-point of French colonial Dalat was a serious allegation indeed. The literal collapse of the hotel prefigured the momentary collapse of French colonialism in Dalat two years later, as we will see in following chapters.

RENOVATION AND INDOCHIC

In the early 1990s, American tycoon Larry Hillblom became fascinated, if not obsessed, with the Dalat Palace Hotel. In 1993 he embarked upon a lavish restoration project.[71] Robert Templer's trenchant analysis of Hillblom's motivations and achievements is worth quoting: "[In the early 1990s, the Dalat Palace Hotel] was remade to evoke a time of brilliantined hair, Vuitton trunks and tennis whites all set in the luminous and mythical landscape of 'Indochine,' a place as distant from the realities of French colonialism as it was from contemporary Vietnam. The original hotel had never taken off, indeed the grand building overlooking the town's lake was a mirror of the economic dreams and failures of French colonialism in Indochina."[72]

Certainly the original hotel had reflected at once colonial dreams of grandeur, the contradictory objectives of its various promoters, and the fractures of a French colonial society torn between adulating and loathing the hotel. Barbara Crossette has noted that "the hotel's history . . . ha[d] not been a particularly happy one."[73] But as Templer suggests, Hillblom had little interest in the historical reality of a hotel that had struggled to attract clients. In the early 1990s, the American billionaire (the "H" of the DHL courier empire) invested some forty million dollars into reopening the Dalat Palace Hotel, which had languished since the end of the Vietnam War in 1975. Hillblom's disappearance after his plane vanished in the Pacific in 1995 adds a twist worthy of a detective novel to the story. Hillblom barely had a chance to see his cherished hotel renovated before his death. His disappearance brought still more mystery, with its ensuing paternity suits, assorted court cases, alleged foul play, and DNA tests involving some of his presumed offspring, not to mention the University of California's stake in the inheritance.[74]

As for the results of Hillblom's restoration, they are at once fanciful and historically consistent: consistent because the Palace's more reasonably priced twin, the Hôtel du Parc (today the Novotel Dalat) continues to attract a more diverse

FIGURE 20. The Dalat Palace Hotel, 2001. Photo by author.

and larger clientele than its flagship partner. Consistent also because of the Palace's Westernness—down to the wood-burning fireplaces, whose necessity at Dalat never ceased to draw wonder and nostalgia from homesick *colons*. The more fanciful side has to do with the nature of renovations itself, which transformed a rather plain dining room seen in old photos of the hotel, into a *grand restaurant,* which it had never been before.

In many respects then, the latest incarnation of the hotel actually far outshines the original in its luxury. This new luxury is rooted in a wistful vision of Indochine—a vision that conjures up the filmic myth embodied by Catherine Deneuve rather than the starker legend encapsulated by Marguerite Duras; to some extent, they represent the flip sides of an "Indochic" phenomenon which is beginning to draw French tourists to Vietnam in droves, through tours organized by the Maison de l'Indochine in Paris.[75] Indochic has even spread beyond the French-speaking world. Take for instance this glowing review of the Dalat Palace Hotel in an American guide-book: "[The Dalat Palace Hotel is] a truly divine establishment with spacious, elegantly furnished rooms to kill for. If you stay in only one grand hotel, it should be this one. The empty corridors seem to echo with ghosts from the days when dressing for dinner was de rigueur and ballrooms came alive every Saturday with full orchestra."[76] The hitch, of course, is that many of the Western tourists visiting Vietnam in the past decade have done so on early Durasian rather than Deneuvian budgets. Budget guides for backpackers suggest visiting the hotel, rather than actually staying in it.

Despite the illusion of remaining static, the Dalat Palace's trappings and meanings have shifted over time: at its opening in 1922 it stood as a monument to French colonial power, and a keystone for French plans in the Indochinese interior. Over the course of its colonial existence, it was decried by some in the administration as a colonial white elephant (delayed in its inauguration, prone to leaks, budget deficits, kitchen fiascos, and collapses), and defended by its backers as the ultimate marker of Frenchness and prestige in Indochina. By the 1990s the Dalat Palace Hotel had become a nostalgic monument to French comfort and an ambitious gamble at drawing high-end tourism, a category of travelers who had previously vacationed in Indonesia or Thailand rather than highland Vietnam.

9

Vietnamese Dalat

A central irony to a resort initially conceived as inherently French is that the project itself required considerable Vietnamese support and legwork. Looking back on the golden years of the resort, Dalat's last French mayor, Jean Rouget, observed that "he who calls [Dalat] a French town should also speak of an Annamese one. The European drags behind him an entire population of auxiliaries, domestics, clerks of all ranks, masons, building specialists—all of those beautiful villas have to be built by someone! The rice cultivator of the plains followed this migration wave, turning into a fruit and vegetable farmer so comfortable with his crops that one would think he was born among cabbage and carrots."[1]

Dalat did indeed see its ethnic Vietnamese population rapidly expand between 1900 and 1945. In some ways, the phenomenon is reminiscent of the hill stations of the British Raj. As Dane Kennedy has commented, "One of the paradoxes of the hill stations is that their success as places where the British imagined it possible to get away from Indians depended on the contributions of Indians."[2] The question of labor, which was considered in chapter 4, was central to such an irony in Dalat as well. However, the archives also reveal the extraordinarily wide spectrum of colonial-era Vietnamese people with stakes in Dalat, many of whom are not reflected in Rouget's remarks. From some of these social strata, and the traces they left, one can glean shifts in sensibilities and comportments that served to fuel Dalat's popularity in a range of Vietnamese circles, especially in the period between 1920 and 1945. After considering the variety of Vietnamese professional occupations in and around Dalat, and tracing growing political mobilization at Dalat, this chapter will evoke elite Vietnamese uses of Dalat, before assessing the impact of colonial leisure and tourist practices on a new Vietnamese generation.

VIETNAMESE ALTOPHOBIA?

The cliché that ethnic Vietnamese people feared the highlands was solidly embedded in French colonial thought. An 1892 report from Prosper Odend'hal outlined this belief: "The Annamese prefer to take their roots along the coastline. There they have settled around . . . Nha-Trang, where cultivation and fishing allow them to eek out a living, rather than brave the tigers and the woodland fevers [of the highlands]."[3] Geographer Paul Vidal de la Blache did not hesitate to generalize that "the Chinese and the Annamese, nations of the plains, detest trips to the mountains, where the Lolos, the Moïs, and other tribes have been able to adapt."[4] In 1934, Dr. Serge Abbatucci affirmed that Indochina was divided into two parts, the highlands and the lowlands, the latter being "the traditional lands of the Annamese, where they have for millennia cultivated their daily rice."[5] As late as 1972, geographer Pierre Gourou maintained that in East Asia, "cultural and climatic zones coincide almost exactly," adding, "the [Vietnamese] peasant of the deltas experienced a legitimate repugnance to settle in mountainous areas."[6] The trope would eventually shape French policy during the Indochina War. Colonel Roger Trinquier, charged with forming minority guerilla groups against the Viet-Minh, recounted mater-of-factly in 1976 that "the [North Vietnamese] army was comprised mostly of Annamese from the Delta, whose adaptation to life in the highland areas was long and hard. They were able to occupy the upper regions only because they had found them empty."[7]

These virtually immutable assertions came with several corollaries. For one thing, they posited the homogeneity of the category "Annamese," a fallacy Wynn Wilcox debunks by pointing to the cosmopolitanism of Emperor Gia Long's court.[8] For another, they presupposed a Vietnamese incapacity to migrate or to acclimatize, a supposition studied by Andrew Hardy. Finally, the schema rested on topography, the Indochinese highlands being seen as a kind of natural barrier, hindering ethnic Vietnamese expansion, and by the same token protecting a wide range of ethnic minorities.[9] This web of clichés had obvious implications for colonial strategies: presenting the highlands as a terra incognita to "the Vietnamese" was tantamount to considering the mountainous interior as a land of colonial opportunity and adventure.

The degree to which these clichés held any validity can be endlessly debated. To be sure, highland areas near the border with China had for centuries been considered by Vietnamese emperors as a kind of buffer zone, over which they ruled only very indirectly.[10] However, reductionist claims of Vietnamese aversion to the mountains have no doubt been overstated: after all, contacts between highland minorities and ethnic Vietnamese had been established for centuries. Mostly, these claims need to be situated within the chronology of ethnic Vietnamese expansion: ethnic Vietnamese contact with highland minorities in the North was historically deeper rooted and longer-established than in the South.

On balance, ethnic Vietnamese movements into highland areas did of course occur, as for example when Ton That Thuyet and Emperor Ham Nghi took to the hills in 1885 to fight off the French in what some historians have described as "a tradition in Vietnamese history."[11] Evidence also suggests that the mountains north of the Red River had been used as health retreats for many centuries, as sites to escape cholera and malaria in particular. Mountains carried deep and long-established religious meanings as well. In 1298 Emperor Tran Nhan Tong had climbed Yen Tu Mountain near Hanoi where he founded the Truc Lam Buddhist sect, site of an important monastery.[12]

Admittedly, Steve Déry is correct in pointing out that pre–twentieth-century ethnic Vietnamese penetration of the regions that concern us here, the south-central highlands, was less pervasive and occurred far later than in mountainous areas north of Hanoi. This said, even Déry recognizes that Vietnamese settlements at An Khe and Kontum (both north of Dalat), go back to the eighteenth and nineteenth century respectively, and that the "opening" of the south-central highlands to Vietnamese interests had therefore "timidly begun" well before the arrival of the French.[13] And paradoxically, under colonial rule, in spite of an averred policy of "protecting" highland minorities, ethnic Vietnamese migration to the highlands was explicitly encouraged, even organized, by the colonial authorities.[14] The degree of Vietnamese influence over (or aversion to) the highlands before French rule lies beyond the scope of this book. What should be underscored here are both the colonial consensus on the highlands as a terra incognita to ethnic Vietnamese, and the chronologically, geographically, and contextually sensitive nature, not to mention the uses, of this claim.

A GROWING VIETNAMESE COMMUNITY

Stereotypes of Vietnamese aversion to the highlands notwithstanding, colonial sources were correct in arguing that the Dalat hill station was a colonial project, and that the Vietnamese who came to inhabit Dalat did so in the wake of this colonial scheme to establish a European health settlement. In 1907, Dr. Joseph Vassal estimated the ethnic Vietnamese population of Dalat at between sixty and eighty individuals, "almost all of them itinerant salespeople."[15] Vassal's subsequent 1914 report on Dalat broke down the town's ethnic Vietnamese population as follows: eight to ten indigenous guards, some interpreters, and "a whole village" of merchants.[16] Vassal also sketched a grim portrait of Vietnamese existence on a plateau so isolated that Europeans commandeered columns of porters to supply them in foodstuffs, rendering such goods both scarce and expensive. The scientist observed: "the Annamese don't have too much difficulty finding rice here. All other foods cost too much for them. They live a miserable existence and consume opium to great excess as soon as they earn some money. They have made no effort to adapt to the climate here. . . . Therefore pulmonary diseases are common among them. Malaria, reawoken by the cold, claims many victims."[17]

I have already examined at length Vassal's unwillingness to recognize that malaria was actually being contracted on location on the Lang-Bian. Here, the scientist fed off of ambient clichés—like Vietnamese maladaptation to the highlands—to paint a portrait of a Vietnamese underclass withering in an inclement, "unnatural" setting.

And yet, Dalat must also have presented opportunities. How else could one account for the rapid rise in the number of Vietnamese merchants, catering to both French and highland minority populations? Andrew Hardy suggests that economic push-factors to highland zones, while significant, need be considered in unison with factors like "social frustration" and the "spirit of adventure."[18] Whatever the reasons for their migration to the Lang-Bian, it is certain that ethnic Vietnamese were heading there in ever-larger numbers. And colonial authorities seem to have encouraged this. Despite his pessimistic outlook on Vietnamese living conditions in Dalat, even Vassal deemed Vietnamese migration to the Lang-Bian plateau highly desirable, in large part because he mistrusted highland minorities as laborers.[19] This bias was widely shared. And so, as Dalat grew, so did its Vietnamese population. Over the course of 1920s, it rose rapidly, increasing from 71 permanent inhabitants and 300 migrant ones in 1922 to 838 permanent inhabitants and 2,662 "itinerant" ones in 1931 (though one source evokes 4,000 Vietnamese in Dalat in 1925).[20] By comparison, Dalat counted a mere 300 permanent European inhabitants, and 1,599 seasonal ones in 1931.[21]

This said, the Depression did drive some Vietnamese away from Dalat. A 1932 gendarmerie report attested to the departure of large numbers of Vietnamese workers from the resort, following a marked decline in construction.[22] With the departure of a significant part of the laborer population, other sections of Vietnamese society began to emerge in Dalat: 9 percent of the resort's Vietnamese population in 1931 was made up of "functionaries," 7.6 percent of merchants, and 6.4 percent of agriculturalists, specializing in fruits and vegetables.[23]

As early as 1923, Vietnamese entrepreneurs had launched several transport companies at Dalat. They purchased fleets of trucks that carried both passengers and supplies to Dalat. A 1925 article in *L'Echo annamite* attributed a drop in marketplace prices to this new, thriving sector.[24]

Vietnamese retailers and merchants also maintained a strong presence in Dalat. A 1934 article in *Công Luân Báo (The Journal of Public Opinion)* chronicled the troubles this group faced during the Depression. In the process, the piece provides a glimpse into some of the community's members: Nguyen Huu Vinh, owner of Dalat's "Grand Bazaar," was considered a "well-known business man." Mrs. Nguyen Thi Thuong and Mr. Nguyen Dinh Khiêm also owned stores in Dalat. The article reveals that their customer base was composed largely of Vietnamese workers, whose salaries were being slashed to 0.40 or even 0.30 piastres a day. In these circumstances, Dalat retailers complained, their profits were falling drastically.[25] Still, the shop sector remained largely in Vietnamese hands. Indochina phone books published between 1945 and 1949 list Vo Cong Khoa on Rue Maréchal Foch as one of the few grocery stores in town, along with Vinh Hoa, which doubled as a bakery.[26]

After being initially the preserve of the Dankia experimental farm, the bustling fruit and vegetable sector began shifting to Vietnamese hands in the 1930s. In 1938 seven families comprising some forty Vietnamese people came from Tonkin to the village of Hà Đông, just outside Dalat, to start a gardening company with the help of a loan from a mutual aid committee.[27] The village's name was significant: Mr. Võ-Hiến Hoàng Trọng Phu, concerned about overcrowding in Tonkin, recruited its inhabitants from Hà Đông province, just outside of Hanoi. The hamlet, in turn, was developed with the support of the Central Committee of Mutual Aid and Social Assistance of Tonkin. Farmers were trained in cultivating "European" fruits, vegetables, and flowers. They overcame several hurdles, including a vaccination requirement, as Dalat's colonial administration wished to keep disease out of the European health station. By the early 1940s, migrants from other parts of Tonkin were arriving in Hà Đông, which kept its Northern Vietnamese character well into the 1950s.[28] All signs suggest that this community was busy organizing. By the 1950s, the powerful Lang-Bian fruit and vegetable cooperative collected a 5 percent tax on all fruits and vegetables dispatched from Dalat to the rest of Vietnam.[29]

Other social categories and professions were represented at Dalat.[30] As in British colonial India, many servants accompanied Europeans to Dalat—indeed Dalat's villa blueprints frequently show multiple servant quarters.[31] However, unlike porters, rail workers, plantation workers, or even tourists, Vietnamese servants only rarely surface in official records. As for the press, it only noticed them when sensation erupted, as in a high-profile theft case, when a servant was considered the usual suspect in the burglary of a Dalat nun in 1925.[32]

PLANTATION WORKERS

It is impossible to disconnect Dalat from its hinterland. Over the course of the 1920s and 1930s, plantations made their appearance in and around the Lang-Bian.[33] Since 1932, the rail line had lent Dalat critical commercial and agricultural importance. Soon the area's fruits, teas, and vegetables all transited out of Dalat. So too did seasonal and permanent workers, and of course plantation owners and managers. By 1957, the Upper Donnaï counted 199 plantations, compared to 43 for Darlac and 5 for the Pleiku/Kontum region. Unlike other areas dominated by rubber production, the Dalat region specialized in fruit, tea, and coffee cultivation. By 1957, 3,150 hectares of Upper Donnaï province were planted with tea.[34]

Until the 1950s, virtually all of the Lang-Bian's plantations relied primarily on "imported" Vietnamese labor. A rich source has survived which illuminates aspects of plantation life around Dalat in the late 1930s and early 1940s: the impeccably maintained business archives of Indochina's head librarian and archivist, Paul Boudet. In 1932, Boudet had purchased the Darnom coffee plantation near Dalat.

In April 1940, the association of coffee growers from the Dalat region, to which Boudet belonged, wrote the Résidents in Dalat and in Hué. The group warned that while the Dalat region possessed immense agricultural potential, and its number of coffee plantations was steadily growing, this potential was being undercut by serious labor shortages. The document presented two solutions: bringing more ethnic Vietnamese laborers from Tonkin, or relying more on highland minority labor. The letter spelled out many of the costs associated with the former scheme: paying recruiters, covering health care costs, lodging, and salaries. The calculations reveal that some ninety-three "coolies" were required on a 10-hectare plantation, workers who were paid on average 0.40 piastres a day to work on average twenty-three days a month. And yet it was proving extremely challenging to recruit even a hundred "coolies," given that the new plantations alone required in total roughly five thousand new workers. Military and worker recruitment for the metropolitan war effort had conspired to drain local labor pools. The coffee plantation owners suggested using highland minority labor instead, on the condition that the forced labor system be streamlined and strengthened. In passing, the group mentioned that minority workers could be paid less than their Vietnamese counterparts.[35]

Little seems to have come of this plan, and in the early 1940s, Boudet's plantation employees were still all ethnic Vietnamese. Analysis of his records reveals the precarious situation of Vietnamese plantation laborers in the Dalat area. In 1940, Boudet's nine ethnic Vietnamese plantation employees earned between 0.40 and 0.60 piastres a day. The senior employee, Nguyen Van Dinh, who served as group leader, was at age forty-six a veteran of both the police and the army. The most junior, a baby-faced boy listed as being seventeen years old, was none other than the group leader's son. Another employee was listed as Nguyen Van Dinh's cousin, another as his brother, and yet another as his other son.[36] Boudet had, in essence, hired a Tonkin family to come to Darnom. This occurred on a massive scale in the rubber sector, but has been less chronicled in the coffee and tea industries.[37]

Yet Nguyen Van Dinh, for all of his seniority, was evidently low on the plantation hierarchy, as would soon be revealed when tensions flared. In October 1941, Forli, Darnom's French manager, and the everyday master of the estate, unceremoniously fired three of the plantation's employees, including two of Nguyen Van Dinh's sons. They immediately sent an appeal to Boudet. After observing that Forli did not have the authority to dismiss them, they outlined some of the miseries they had faced on the job: they often fell sick, they wrote, "because of unhealthy water," and were not paid for sick days. Moreover, the cost of living in the highlands was prohibitively expensive. When Forli was displeased with their performance he withheld pay, leading them to go hungry. Still, the three implored Boudet to take them back.

A July 1940 letter in Boudet's records, presumably an intercepted missive from one of his plantation workers, complained that nearly all of the laborers suffered from fevers. The letter's author had already paid 0.80 piastres for traditional remedies and more still for automobile rides to the city for treatment. Foodstuffs, wrote the worker, cost three times more than in the lowlands. He concluded that he had been wrong to migrate to the mountains for the lure of an initial payment. Boudet had indeed hired his workers in Tonkin and given them advances, which he expected to see paid off. He even appears to have charged workers for the costs he incurred in obtaining their paperwork. Complaints soon streamed into Boudet's archive office, and not simply from within Darnom. For instance, the Tonkin families of some of the plantation workers wrote Boudet to complain that they were receiving no support from them, and to express grave worries about their relatives' health.[38] Under these circumstances, it is scarcely surprising that plantation workers were beginning to organize in the 1930s and 1940s.

STRIKES AND POLITICAL OPPOSITION

In a 1922 political report on Annam, a local French administrator displayed a degree of cockiness. "Never, in the course of its history," he wrote, "has Annam better deserved its title of Pacified South."[39] This wink at the *longue durée* of Vietnamese history glossed over the many conflicts that had already hit the region up to then— like the 1908 tax revolt in Annam—and certainly failed to anticipate the kind of widespread revolt that would rock both Tonkin and Annam in 1930: the Yen Bay rebellion in Tonkin, and the Nghe-An and Ha Tinh rural soviets in Northern Annam, not to mention a series of strikes and peasant revolts across Indochina.

The cockiness of the 1922 report derived perhaps in part from the degree of detailed local policing and espionage conducted by the Sûreté and gendarmerie alike. The Dalat police (Sûreté) and gendarmerie, like their counterparts in the rest of Indochina, were supersensitive to the slightest sign of dissent. An August 1928 gendarmerie report, for instance, singled out a tailor, Lê Thanh Dón, as "very politically suspicious." The report claimed that he was tied to "the Annamese extremist party" and that he tried to proselytize amongst "coolies, hairdressers, and tailors." However, as in many of these cases, evidence was slim: the report cites Lê Thanh Dón's native province Quang Ngai as a hotbed of unrest, and adds that the tailor was "too adroit" to be caught in the act of fomenting revolt. Still, the gendarmerie recommended close surveillance of the suspect, and his expulsion from Dalat at the first opportunity.[40] This was no isolated case; the local gendarmerie was manifestly ultrasensitive to any signs of sedition. Later in 1928, it reported that shortwave Soviet radio from Siberia might be audible from Dalat.[41]

As a result of this tight, even paranoid, policing—but mostly because of the resort's tranquil reputation and its sizable French presence—one might expect the bucolic hill station Dalat to have been relatively sheltered from turmoil in the 1920s and 1930s. And yet, as school protests, hunger strikes, and armed revolts mounted across Indochina over the course of those two decades, Dalat would not be left behind. Though certainly not the epicenter of unrest, Dalat too experienced a series of shockwaves in the 1930s. Already in 1930, crudely produced Communist leaflets had been distributed in Dalat on the occasion of May Day, and to mark the anniversary of the Russian Revolution. Within a year, the French Sûreté cracked down on a Communist school and cell that had formed in the region.[42] That troubles were surfacing even around this colonial enclave speaks to the social ebullition of the period in Indochina.

In February 1937, the thousand (mostly ethnic Vietnamese) workers at the Entrerays tea plantation outside of Dalat walked off the job, demanding a raise. That same summer, as Saigon's youngsters were about to leave in droves for the hill station, Vietnamese rail workers went on strike at Entrerays and at Dalat proper. They severed telephone lines. The Sûreté suspected one Tran Van Ut, soon to be laid off as station manager at Arbre Broyé, of being behind the movement. By July 11, the colonial administration began breaking the strike by running several trains a day, each train "escorted by Moïs bearing spears." Soon, the handful of workers still on the job complained of reprisals. One reported that a striker's wife had lacerated his clothes. With food prices rising, some also began to vent their exasperation against the strikers. Police forces were sent to dislodge the strikers on July 18, and the next day, eleven alleged leaders were arrested.[43]

On September 9, 1938, workers on Dalat's many construction sites followed suit. The administration initially attributed this new strike to guild interests—pointing to a September 6, 1938, article in *Tin Tuc,* calling for Dalat's carpenters to unite so as to "defend their common interests" and "eliminate competition."[44] The following year, the Sûreté reported that the carpenter's guild was in reality a front for an organization named "Tiên-Bô" (progressive or progress group), which the administration suspected of being "revolutionary."[45] A Vietnamese-language history of the region's worker movements depicts this "Progress Group" as follows: "a semipublic association with separate regulations and rules—its public goal was to offer help among its members, and to form a group for studying and reading newspapers." The association, then, seems to have featured a strong corporative, *mutualiste,* or associative spirit.[46]

Strikes recurred at Dalat in 1939, though again in a different sector. This time, according to colonial records, female market stall vendors went on strike on June 7, 1939 to protest the temporary closure of the market, which was due for a thorough cleaning. When the local administration mobilized militiamen to escort butchers into the market, tensions flared. A Vietnamese tinsmith was badly beaten in the en-

FIGURE 21. Dalat's market, built in 1937. Postcard showing vendors, 1939. Author's collection.

suing scuffle. The situation apparently de-escalated after Dalat's mayor made it clear that the market—a brand new concrete structure later replaced in 1959—would only be closed very briefly.[47]

What are we to make of these four strikes, involving plantation, rail, and construction workers, as well as market vendors? To be sure, they were limited compared to others in the colony. What is perhaps most revealing is how the French administration understood them. Writing about the wave of strikes in 1937, the Sûreté d'Annam noted that "the demands of the strikers, when they were even formulated, since at Dalat-Entrerays workers simply walked off the job, these demands were only moderately professional or corporative. . . . I agree with the Résident of Phanrang that these strikes are 75 percent protest-oriented and Communist and 25 percent professional."[48]

Based on the reports in the files, this seems a very curious reading of what appear to be quite targeted strikes. The police reports made no mention at this point (1937–39) of Communist texts, tracts, influence, or even formulations. Indeed, the 1938 Dalat carpenter strike and the 1939 Dalat market vendor strike appear to be eminently "professional" and "corporative." To the 1939 strike, one could add the adjective "spontaneous."[49]

And yet, as in a self-fulfilling prophecy, increasingly Communist elements were spreading into Dalat. An official history of the region describes the birth of a new three-member Indochinese Communist Party cell in Dalat itself in December 1938. Nguyễn Văn Chi served as secretary of this short-lived group, which was broken up and disbanded by the police less than a year later.[50]

With the Communist Party briefly snuffed out in Dalat, outside elements were sent in to rekindle it. In August 1940 Hoàng Kim Ảnh came to Dalat from Hội An, and Hồ Đắc Bật from Saigon with a mission to organize.[51] Others soon followed suit. The Sûreté reported in February 1941: "We proceeded on February 10, to arrest Lê-Tu-Cuôc, an important Communist agitator. You will recall that this Communist militant was a leading member of the city committee of Hué in 1940, and escaped last August's crackdown."

During "interrogations," Lê-Tu-Cuôc apparently declared that he had been hiding for months in several plantations in the Dalat region, as well as with friends in Dalat proper. This information led to three more arrests, as well as the seizure of "abundant communist documentation."[52] That the dissident had been able to find shelter for a year in the tranquil European rest station seems to have especially rattled the Sûreté. By 1942, agitators crucial in the Nghệ Tỉnh and Thanh Hóa revolts would make their way to Dalat, where they would liaise with remaining revolutionaries.[53] We will see in a coming chapter how a few years later, civil war and guerrilla warfare finally reached Dalat.

ELITE DALAT

This is not to suggest that Dalat was the site of major, sustained unrest prior to 1945, nor that the city itself presented vast numbers of disgruntled workers, peasants, or revolutionaries. Indeed, Dalat was still reputed from the 1920s to the 1940s to be a tranquil elite resort, whose comforts and amenities some Vietnamese could enjoy.

In her memoirs, Xuan Phuong remembers that during the time she grew up at Dalat (1929–1942), "life was much jollier than elsewhere." To be sure, Xuan Phuong belonged to the elite: her father was a mandarin, and served as educational inspector at Dalat. She recalls Sunday picnics in the woods, her father going on tiger hunts, and Saturday balls at her parents' house which drew her father's hunting and tennis partners, many of them French. European music, including tangos, rumbas, and the songs of Tino Rossi and Josephine Baker, echoed in the halls. The family's "impeccably shined black Citroën" was "a sensation in town." A retinue of twelve servants set tables, ironed clothes, cooked, and gardened. Each child had a nanny. Xuan Phuong's mother considered herself modern; she held a diploma, and could drive an automobile and ride a horse, though she made a point of not dressing in Western clothes.

The young Xuan Phuong was soon made keenly aware that this privileged, dare one say colonial lifestyle, was not to everyone's tastes. Her paternal grandfather professed to "detest Dalat. For him it was the city of the hooked nosed, and blue eyed." For her uncle, Dalat epitomized colonial rule and cultural alienation. However, for Xuan Phuong, who would go on to join the Viet-Minh as an explosives-maker, then subsequently become a war correspondent and filmmaker, the colonial hill station was not without its charms.[54]

While Dalat made some Vietnamese uneasy, it purportedly provided a convenient cover for others. In any event, it rarely left people indifferent. In his *Journal of a VietCong*, Truong Nhu Tang explains that as a young man, so as to "further the image I was seeking to project . . . I began to mold my private life on the pattern of Saigon's fun-loving and frivolous upper classes. . . . Weekends I would spend . . . in the mountain resort of Dalat, socializing, playing tennis and swimming."[55] Was Truong Nhu Tang merely playing along, or did he actually relish this official bourgeois cover for his clandestine double? Here Dalat seems bound in a mix of nostalgia and guilt. The hill station, it seems, could facilitate "passing."

ROYAL DALAT

Emperor Bao Dai certainly used movement to and from the hill station to signify his willingness to reform the empire of Annam. The young monarch made no secret of his love for Dalat, matched only by his passion for hunting. In 1936, an article described the vacationing habits of this "westernized" emperor of Annam. It explained that every summer "the young sovereigns head to Dalat, under the cool shade of the Lang-Bian, to escape the hot winds . . . which make Hué unbearable. One by one, every week, one of the ministers of the court in Hué joins the hill station. Received in the villa belonging to the Empress, he brings files that are submitted to the Emperor."[56]

Bao Dai's Catholic wife Nam Phuong shared her husband's predilection for the hill station. Indeed, it was at Dalat that she and the emperor first met in 1933.[57] Their marriage, which took place after lengthy negotiations on March 20, 1934, further consecrated Dalat's status as an elite Vietnamese destination.[58]

What exactly did Bao Dai and Nam Phuong see in Dalat? Did they explicitly view it as a way of escaping the court in Hué?[59] Bao Dai's memoirs are silent on the issue. What seems certain is that both members of the royal couple had spent many years of their childhood in France, and saw in this French resort a marker of their own modernity. The colonial press for its part reveled in the trope of a modern westernized couple basking in the beauty of French Dalat. *La Dépêche coloniale* noted that after their heavily ceremonial marriage (read antiquated, byzantine, and Vietnamese, in the eyes of the French press), the couple honeymooned in simple, uncomplicated Dalat.[60] Nor was their penchant for the hill station the only symbol of their modernity.[61] The French press likewise suggested that the emperor had fallen in love with Nam Phuong after she addressed him with a straightforward greeting in French. Thereafter, marveled *Paris-Soir,* he married her for nondynastic, non-pragmatic purposes and broke with traditional polygamy.[62]

By 1933, the couple stayed at Dalat's shining new imperial villa, featuring a large balcony on which the emperor is said to have read poetry. Other connections heightened Dalat's magnetic pull over the imperial couple. While Bao Dai was fond of hunting around Dalat, Nam Phuong paid several visits to the local branch of the Couvent des Oiseaux boarding school. At the age of thirteen, she had attended the prestigious main branch of this institution in Paris, and her ties to the institution remained strong. She would in fact send her daughters to the Dalat chapter of the Couvent des Oiseaux. Three of the couple's children were born at Dalat: Phuong Mai (1937), Phuong Lien (1938), and Bao Thang (1943), current pretender to the throne. Here, Dalat's role as an elite nursery was not only embraced, but actually furthered, by the imperial couple.[63]

It seems safe to deduce that the imperial couple's infatuation with Dalat served to enhance the resort's reputation, much as Napoleon III's taste for Vichy or Arcachon contributed to their prosperity in the nineteenth century. The link between Bao Dai and Dalat would only tighten after 1945. In 1949, for his return to power, Bao Dai made a point of landing neither in Saigon, nor Hué, nor Hanoi, but rather in Dalat. As we will see in a following chapter, the Dalat region and the broader PMSI would at this point become crown lands, a kind of imperial redoubt in Vietnam's south-central highlands.

THE LURE OF THE MOUNTAINS

Up to now, discussion has focused on Dalat's permanent Vietnamese population. But Dalat was known especially as a tourist site. One might be tempted to equate tourism with white colonials, given the supremely uneven playing field of French colonial Indochina. Yet ethnic Vietnamese tourism too was undeniably on the rise in the 1920s and 1930s, and Dalat was at its heart. Vietnamese society underwent profound and numerous transformations during this period. Among them, historians have studied many interconnected trends, from the explosion in *quoc ngu* publications, to shifts in education, garb, gender roles, literary, sporting, and artistic tastes.[64] Peter Zinoman has written of the "progressive language and modernizing ethos that dominated public discourse" in the late 1930s, specifically under the Popular Front (1936–38).[65] He notes how contemporaries palpably experienced these changes, and recorded the impact on their everyday lives.[66] However, the rise of Vietnamese tourism, and in particular the popularity of mountain resorts among Vietnamese during this period, has gone largely unnoticed.

A 1923 French-language article in *La Tribune indigène,* already exhorted the Vietnamese to emulate European tourist practices. Focusing on seaside and highland resorts, the article began by claiming that the Vietnamese, like the French, were

bound to benefit from escaping the heat of the deltas. The article distinguished between Vietnamese bureaucrats on the one hand, and private travelers on the other
hand. For the former, the article complained that while the lowest ranking French
official earned 250 piastres per month, the highest ranking Vietnamese one brought
in no more than 200 piastres a month. The imbalance, argued the article, seriously
impeded the ability of Vietnamese officials to vacation. Still, the piece suggested,
new moderately priced hotels aimed at Vietnamese customers were beginning to
make these trips to the mountains and the beaches possible.[67] Dalat's accessibility
to Vietnamese government officials was no small matter. With Vietnamese functionaries barred from the regular triennial trips to France enjoyed by their French
colleagues (a discrimination based once again on climatic determinism), Dalat, the
France substitute, seemed within easier reach.[68]

The year following, a French Indochinese economic journal again invited Vietnamese tourists to vacation at Dalat. Seeking to explain their limited numbers at
the hill station to date, L'Eveil économique de l'Indochine suggested that cost might
not be the only obstacle: a Vietnamese clientele, the journal opined, might prefer a
simple dormitory, a private, homey area *(cai-nhà)*. Luxury and European hotels,
the argument went, were not for all.[69]

The question of cost was taken up again in a 1925 article in L'Echo annamite
focusing specifically on Dalat. With the disappearance of the lower-priced Hôtel
Desanti, lamented V. M., the anonymous journalist, Dalat was within reach of only
the wealthiest Vietnamese. Still, the article conceded, "for two years now, Dalat has
become better known by the Annamese. To flee the oppressive heat, rich Cochinchinese families make short or long stays in this Indochinese Eden." The Eden drew
repeat customers, if we are to believe the article: "All those who have stayed here
keep a fond memories of the hill station, and vow to return as soon as possible."[70]

By 1929, the Vietnamese publication Vê Sinh Báo (Journal of Hygiene Popularization) explicitly incited the Vietnamese to emulate Parisians. Parisians, the article declared, deserted their city in the summer. Even lower-income city dwellers
got away. "People in our country should follow the custom of taking vacations," the
piece contended. Children especially could profit from the change of air and from
relaxation. The article concluded by recommending the establishment of summer
camps on Indochina's highlands and beaches, camps which would present the added
benefit of spreading and lowering costs.[71] Here was an intriguing broth comprised
of Saint-Simonian philosophy, hygienic popularization, hints of colonial reformism,
and a discourse of social amelioration.

Such articles promoting the emulation of European modern leisure practices
were not the only sources driving Vietnamese tourism. As Christopher Goscha has
suggested, a wide range of travel accounts also served to incite Vietnamese people
to discover Indochina in large numbers in the 1930s.[72] Although written in French,

Nguyen Tien Lang's *Indochine la douce* was aimed at least in part at a Vietnamese audience. Following the traces of Indochinese travel memoirs such as that of Roland Dorgelès, the author depicted Dalat as entirely worthy of its reputation. He remarked that "Dalat, so highly praised in tourist propaganda, Indochinese paradise that has become the dream of so many honest families, Dalat does not disappoint. It is a restful resort, an Indochinese Simla. Beautiful and luxurious, with around its Palace some hundred and forty villas. . . . "[73] Especially striking in this passage is the idea of Dalat as an increasingly affordable dream for "honest families," presumably Vietnamese and not just French.

Nor were guidebooks any longer the preserve of the colonizers. A 1930 Vietnamese-language guidebook for travelers in Annam sang the praises of Dalat, as "a good place to enjoy mountain breezes. There are many beautiful places . . . Cam Ly waterfall, Ankroet waterfall, Lam Vien [Lang-Bian] summit, trails to watch *ca-tong* [Eld's deer]." The guide stressed Dalat's natural, romantic allure, an emphasis that anticipated the region's present-day aesthetic appeal as a site of natural, Alpine beauty.[74]

Colonial statistics confirm this rise of Indochinese tourism amongst Indochinese people themselves. Across Annam in the 1930s, this rise is particularly striking, especially in light of the economic crisis that affected the colony for much of the decade. A 1938 report shows the number of Indochinese tourists in Annam growing from some 475 in 1933–34 to over 3,000 in 1937–38.

This surge in tourism followed a previous wave of increased automobile ownership. As with tourism, automobile ownership was admittedly still limited to Vietnamese elites, but was definitely growing in the 1920s. François de Tessan remarked in 1923: "There are two to three thousand cars in circulation in [Saigon]. A mere 68 were registered in 1914 . . . Europeans are not alone in having acquired a taste for automobiles. Out of a thousand cars imported into Indochina over an eighteen-month period, 500 were acquired by whites, 262 by Annamese, 149 by Chinese and 14 by Hindus, Cambodians or Laotians."[75]

De Tessan believed that these figures demonstrated how "fortune has smiled on everyone in this privileged land"—a statement so removed from fact that it casts doubt on its author's judgment. Still, the point remains that Vietnamese elites were beginning to drive in ever-larger, albeit still modest, numbers. And many, like Xuan Phuong (see above), or Truong Ngoc Hâu, who proudly posed next to his car in Dalat in 1938, considered driving to and around Dalat an important symbol.[76] As Marguerite Duras's novels make clear, automobiles were rapidly emerging as markers of wealth and influence in colonial Indochina.[77]

Many of the articles cited to date make a point of referring to metropolitan French tourist practices as models. What was the precise relationship between French and emerging Vietnamese tourist practices? To what degree were the

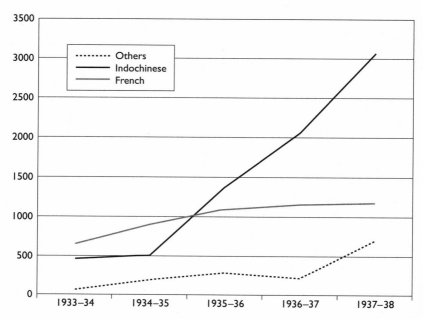

FIGURE 22. Tourism statistics, June 1, 1933, to May 31, 1938. Source: Protectorat de l'Annam, *Rapport d'ensemble sur la situation du Protectorat* (Hué: Imprimerie Phuc-Long, 1938).

claims of wanting to emulate French leisure practices coerced, or at least the product of a system that forced Vietnamese elites to profess admiration for the colonial power?[78] There can be no doubt that the colonial administration used French tourist practices as yardsticks by which to measure merit—or in this case assimilation— among Vietnamese subjects. Hue-Tam Ho Tai and Emmanuelle Saada have both uncovered and analyzed lists of questions that assessors were to ask Vietnamese candidates for French citizenship, the former dating from 1915, the latter for the 1930s. While the 1915 questionnaire featured such lines of inquiry as: "Do your wife and children speak French?" "Do they wear Western dress?" "Does your house have beds, cupboards, mattresses?" the 1930s version had added such queries as: "Which sports do you practice?" and tellingly: "Do you make trips to the sea or to the mountain?"[79] To be sure, the 1930s questionnaire still delved into issues of dress, distinction, and refinement; but critically for our purposes, trips to the mountain had now become an essential component of cultural modernity. By 1937, even the legal decree on the naturalization of Vietnamese included the clause that candidates "should have embraced French civilization through their lifestyle and social habits."[80]

Though precise modes and degrees of colonial cultural influence or appropriation are hard to establish, it seems evident that French norms were increasingly utilized to measure modernity and vice versa. A 1934 *quoc ngu* scientific vulgarization journal explicitly exhorted Vietnamese people to "live in a more scientific manner" by embracing the practice of mountain and seaside vacations.[81] There can be little doubt that modernity and European tourist practices were powerfully twinned.

The colonial medical rationales that had buttressed Dalat's creation, and that proved so enduring, were also embraced by Vietnamese publications promoting a new era of Vietnamese tourism. The 1934 article in *Khoa Hoc Tap Chí* (Scientific Journal) first asserted the cleansing effects of fresh mountain air. Mountain cures were recommended for victims of tuberculosis, of course, but also for anemics. As a general rule, the article insisted, a stay above 1,000 meters in altitude could guarantee an increase in red blood cells, and hence in vitality.[82] Here the European notion of mountain cures as reinvigorating, and as stimulating red blood cell counts, was wholeheartedly embraced. Although France was manifestly not the only model of modernity (Japan too, exerted a powerful influence, especially after 1905), and although many of the medical beliefs just described are actually strikingly unmodern, a strong colonial mimetic influence in the realm of leisure and health tourism seems undeniable.

These shifts occurred fairly swiftly, in a matter of a decade or two. As a result, they caught the attention of contemporaries. Consider for example, a June 9, 1933 cartoon in *Phong Hoa Tap Chi*. Entitled "Two ways of taking summer vacations or the clash between East and West" it featured two juxtaposed scenes. On the left, fast cars zoom to the hill stations of Tam Dao and Sapa, as well as to the beach at Do Son (the piece appeared in a Hanoi paper, hence the reference to local, Northern resorts). The caption reads: "Westerners experience the cool weather in these locations." On the right, "traditional" Vietnamese activities, including a theater performance and prayers, draw the caption: "But in what strange ways we pray for the cool!" At a time when colonial hill stations were becoming far more accessible, and when an emerging Vietnamese bourgeoisie, too, was beginning to drive its Citroëns to Indochina's resorts, the piece's opposition between colonial leisure and Vietnamese culture came precisely as the lines between the two were increasingly blurred. The moral valence of the drawing remains open to interpretation, but it does seem to posit the strangeness of older Vietnamese ways, in contraposition to rational, modern, and elite Western tourism. Then too, the piece can be read as a commentary on the ways in which "traditional" Vietnamese medicine's emphasis on hot and cold either intersects or clashes with modern tourism's quest for cool microclimates and sea breezes.

The impact of these cumulative societal and cultural shifts on Dalat was profound. Though the resort may not have been strictly speaking "democratized," it did attract growing numbers of Vietnamese tourists. Taking their lead from colonial corporations and branches of the colonial administration, which arranged for

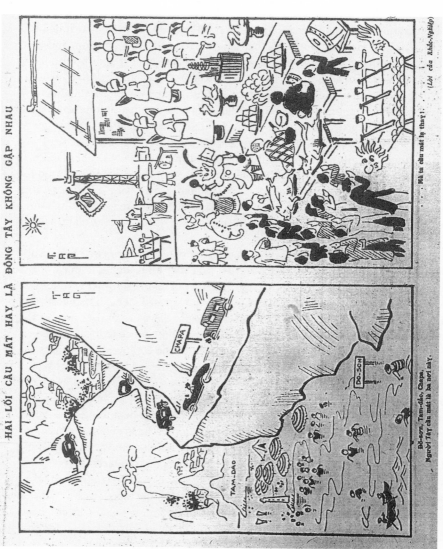

FIGURE 23. "Two ways of taking summer vacations or the clash between East and West." From *Phong Hoa Tạp Chi*, June 9, 1933. Courtesy of Christopher Goscha

employees to share time at the hill station, Vietnamese mutual aid societies were formed to share the cost of accommodations at Dalat. A 1936 article in *Tân Tiên Bao* set the ground rules of one of these time-shares *avant la lettre*. The society, based in the sweltering delta town of Sadec, set very precise membership contributions and categories. Full membership guaranteed access to the Sadec Mutual Assistance vacation house in Dalat. Nonmembers could also apply, but would be considered on a first-come-first-served basis. The article doubled as an advertisement, vaunting the "opportunity to enjoy the beautiful scenery and wonderful weather in Dalat."[83] Such private initiatives emulated public ones. Since 1936, Vietnamese functionaries from Cochinchina were able to reserve places at a "rest home" reserved for them on the outskirts of Dalat.[84]

An interesting 1938 series penned by Nguyen Trung Thu in *Tân Tiên Bao* traced the author's visit to Dalat for a tennis tournament. Tennis appeared to be something of a pretext. The real prize here was Dalat itself, described from the first installment as "the Queen of all resorts," a title it borrowed from the spa-town of Vichy. Rich in details—including descriptions of the cramped train car from Saigon to the hill station—the article reads like a slightly hyperbolic version of a modern-day travel column.[85] Nguyen Trung Thu waxed that "words are not enough to describe the beauty of the Lang-Bian region," and again, "swans swim peacefully and small boats glide along the lake." The author was particularly smitten with such natural sites as Cam-Ly waterfall and the "love forest," although architecture and urbanism also caught his attention. Thus the regional styles of Dalat's villas, and their glorious gardens both earned mentions. The athlete found little to improve at Dalat, save for the following suggestion: "I wish there were an ancient pagoda under the pine forest and close to the lake. This would create a picturesque mountain-water-pine-temple scenery."[86]

This request would in fact soon be realized; within months of his column appearing, Linh Son pagoda would be opened just outside of Dalat. Many other Vietnamese religious and commemorative structures would follow. In 1941, an imposing mausoleum on a hill outside of Dalat was dedicated to Pierre Nguyên-Huu-Hao, the father of Empress Nam-Phuong, herself a Catholic. The French press described the structure as "the first great monument bearing a truly Annamese character in Dalat." A stele included a verse about the deceased "maintaining a reputation as durable as the waters and the mountains of this land"—an interesting passage reflecting the linkage of Dalat's mountain landscape with Vietnameseness.[87] Over the coming decades, Dalat would witness the proliferation of explicitly Vietnamese monuments and temples: Thien Vuong Co Sat pagoda was inaugurated in 1958, and in 1994 a large Truc Lam Buddhist temple was completed near Dalat.

Nguyen Trung Thu's 1938 narrative includes detailed descriptions of his extracurricular activities. These included hikes in the forest, horseback riding, and bathing under waterfalls. Dalat excited each of his senses in turn. He evoked the powerful scent of pine, the cool evenings, the mist, the fresh milk and butter. Finally he pondered the reasons for the resort's success: "tourists come to Dalat purely because of sightseeing" he marveled. This tourism he portrayed as highly individualized: sport enthusiasts could ride bikes or horses, hunt, or even sail; romantics could stroll through the forests; those interested in development could admire the region's farms; the "cultural curious" could "see the living style of the savage tribes" around Dalat.[88] In short, the resort offered something for everybody, lovers included.

A ROMANTIC DESTINATION

As this testimony suggests, Dalat was being increasingly reinscribed as a romantic site. To be sure, Dalat had long been known for its charming setting and quaint architecture. However, its explicitly romantic ambiance appears to have struck contemporaries with ever-greater frequency in the 1930s, which coincided with an era of exuberance in Vietnamese literature and poetry. Vietnamese romantic poet Han Mac Tu (1912–1940) penned the following verses about Dalat:

> To hear water sizzling on the bottom of the lake
> To hear the willows trembling in wind
> And to see the sky explaining love
> The row of pine stands in silence
> With their branches and leaves unmoved.[89]

Another bard, Quach Tan, also immortalized the Dalat he knew in the 1930s:

> With moon's shadow shining on silent lake's surface,
> Time races to sink under.
> Leaning on mountains, stars and a jade stream,
> Drunken soul drifts into soft dream.[90]

Dalat's artificial lake, mountains, and its trees all occupy a central place in these renditions. The hill station's natural charms and its bucolic atmosphere seem to have served as especially powerful agents in attracting Vietnamese tourists.

CONCLUSION

Though hardly "accessible," this "Indochinese Eden" was etched in many Vietnamese imaginations by the 1930s, as much, if not more than in the colonial consciousness. This said, behind the façade of a romantic destination lay some other realities. Vietnamese Dalat was in this respect even more fractured than French Dalat: plantation workers within a short range of Dalat toiled under terrible conditions, and for miserable pay. Rail workers and construction workers mobilized and organized. And of course, Vietnamese elites, and increasingly, members of the middle class, vacationed at Dalat, leaving their imprint on the site, even formulating desiderata for improving the hill station. In the thirty years that separated Dr. Vassal's hardly neutral observations on the wretchedness of Vietnamese traders in Dalat and Nguyen Trung Thu's tennis diary, the site's functions had fundamentally shifted and multiplied, revealing and reflecting some profound changes in Vietnamese society.

Some Colonial Categories

Children, European Women, and Métis

A 1930 guide to Dalat described the resort as "a paradise for children."[1] The context makes clear that the remark meant by that, French children. Within colonial logic, Dalat's powerfully transformative setting made it a natural site for educating a new generation of colonizers, for fostering European domesticity, and also for Frenchifying métis youngsters. Indochina's premier hill station was thus conceived as a potent and controlled environment, in which the colony could be remade in the image of an idealized motherland.

SCHOOLING THE COLONIZERS

We have seen that Dalat's different functions evolved over time. European children—and certainly Vietnamese, Laotian, Cambodian, and métis children—did not figure in the first colonial visions of the hill station. Initially conceived as a sanatorium and rest station, Dalat's imagined clientele was initially adult, white, and military. While doctors and other specialists saw in Dalat a major asset for empire, their degree of optimism fluctuated: early on, it was believed that Dalat would allow Europeans to extend their stay in Indochina by perhaps a matter of years. Gradually, a majority of colonial doctors (under the influence of hill station promoters) became convinced that Dalat could help perpetuate the French presence in Southeast Asia, and was therefore destined to become a "colonial nursery," much like the hill stations of India.[2]

Thus, in Dalat's earliest planning stage, while the blueprints for the hill station featured a military base, a hospital, and so on, they lacked a single school. This reflects in part a demographic reality: few colonial families braved Indochina's reputation until the early years of the twentieth century. As a result, Indochina's pre-1900 colonizers were predominantly single males, much to the regret of colonial moralists. The Doumerian plan for a more active and denser administration on the ground, not to mention the real improvement in survival rates among settlers, changed this state of affairs. With the arrival of French women and children, Dalat would emerge, thanks also to its role as a health station and temperate oasis, as one of the colony's main sites for European domesticity.

This shift took place progressively. In 1901, none other than Paul Doumer expanded Dalat's role when he asserted that "in addition to the garrison and the permanent administrative services that will be permanently established on the Lang-Bian, settlers and administrators will easily be able to seek rest there, and to bring their families, and send their children to school."[3] A 1906 article in the *Annales d'hygiène publique et de médecine légale* printed the advice of Dr. Grall "on the usefulness of organizing Indochinese hill stations . . . and of ensuring that they receive women and children, for whom the stay in the colonies is so harsh."[4] Thus was established Dalat's reputation for protecting supposedly the most fragile colonizers, those embodying the long-range colonial future of Indochina, women and children. That same year, while competing interests still wrestled for a piece of Dalat, a summit brought together the colony's leaders. For Governor General Paul Beau: "It would be desirable for the school planned for Dalat to open as quickly as possible, even before the rail link is finalized. There is a real need for young people to be able to pursue their studies in a serious manner in the colony, which can only take place, in healthful conditions, in Dalat's temperate climate. It would be impossible in Saigon or Hanoi."[5] In this way, Dalat's weather and its atmosphere, its Frenchness and its salubrity all destined it to become a school site. Its charms, be it the hill station's remarkable calm, its lakes, its reputation as a "Switzerland in Indochina" are all conflated in this logic with its climate, and its putative non-Vietnameseness.[6]

Though the change was gradual, it proved definitive. By the 1920s, Dalat had been transformed from a military rest station and convalescence center, to the colony's premier educational hub. In 1929, Governor General Pierre Pasquier went so far as to rebuke the military for coveting Dalat when "the presence of an important European garrison would generate such problems in a rest station reserved first and foremost for women and children."[7] Educational imperatives had triumphed over the original vision of a reinvigoration center for spent troops. A 1926 planning document for the hill station's future lycée (which at this early stage was being named Lycée Alexandre Varenne) explained: "Dalat, destined to become a European city and a health station thanks to its climate that is so close to the metropole's, is a natural site for a large French teaching establishment." Because the establishment would serve almost exclusively white children from other parts of Indochina, it was conceived from the start as a boarding school.[8]

THE SCHOOLS

Between the two world wars, schools of all types rose on the shores of Dalat's lake and on the crests of its gentle hills.[9] A French primary school was promised in 1923; teachers started arriving in 1926; the prestigious Lycée de Dalat was established in 1927 and renamed Lycée Yersin in 1935.[10] In 1927, a second lycée was opened, named more plainly the Petit Lycée de Dalat.[11] While the Lycée Yersin served as a secondary school or lycée in the proper sense of the word, the Petit Lycée served rather as a primary and secondary school. Dalat also boasted several private religious schools, among them the famous Couvent des Oiseaux, an outlet of the Congrégation Notre-Dame's prestigious Parisian institution, reserved for girls. In 1936, the administration claimed that 450 European children were schooled at Dalat, between the lycées, the Couvent des Oiseaux, and other religious schools.[12] The following year, the representative of the Popular Front Government, Justin Godard, noted in his report on Indochina that Dalat's schools were overflowing, and regularly had to turn back applicants.[13]

In the past decade, a host of pre-1945 Dalat childhood memories have been put to paper. Madeleine Jacomme, born in 1930; Xuan Phuong, born in 1929; Iphigénie-Catherine Shellshear, born in 1934; and Dominique Mourey, born in 1926, have all described their Dalat student experiences in some detail. Each of these testimonies is, as could be expected, steeped in nostalgia, be it the memoirs of the future Viet-Minh, Xuan Phuong, or those of the Australian of Franco-Greek origin, Iphigénie-Catherine Shellshear.[14] Each provides insights into a cloistered universe, at the very time that it was beginning to open.

PRIVILEGE AND EXCLUSION

From the outset, the Petit Lycée, directed between 1928 and 1934 by Bernard-Martial Lagonelle, was defined as a space for white offspring. Segregated schools were not unique to Dalat, of course: as Gail Paradise Kelly and Hue-Tam Ho Tai have shown, since the First World War, some settlers had pressed for the total exclusion of Vietnamese children from French schools in Indochina, wanting to relegate them to so-called "Franco-Annamese" establishments. Such schools were for the most part paltry second-tier institutions; the degrees they dispensed tended to close, rather than open doors.[15] At Dalat, climatic determinism was employed to justify this state of affairs. A 1930 booklet devoted to the Petit Lycée explained that "[the school] answers the natural preoccupations of our administration which is anxious to allow young Europeans, placed in a position of weakness in the lowlands, to follow a full secondary curriculum in conditions, in comfort levels, and in a climate favorable to their physical and intellectual development."[16]

In this way, the school could compensate for the bio-climatic handicap Europeans supposedly faced in the rest of Indochina. Consequently, according to the booklet, "the Petit Lycée admits only European students." It added, by way of explanation: "Natives, who can undertake their secondary studies in French in their own climes, whether at the Lycée Chasseloup Laubat in Saigon or at the Lycée Albert Sarraut in Hanoi, and who also have at their disposal two large franco-native lycées in these towns, these natives have no special reason to come to Dalat. In fact, statistics drawn up by Dalat's city hall show that [Dalat's] climate and altitude are actually detrimental to them."[17]

The very spot that served as a climatic remedy for the colonizers was thus perceived as nothing less than toxic for the Vietnamese. This amounted to excluding non-Europeans (in the above logic, even Vietnamese holding French citizenship were excluded) from one of the three establishments in all of Indochina that offered the prestigious *baccalauréat* exam.[18] At the same time, we can discern in this text a clear effort to avoid a Vietnamese backlash. Consider the following passage: "this then is the school that the Administration . . . created for the education, instruction, and health of young Europeans, for whom there was previously no dedicated establishment, the colonial efforts having naturally focused first on the creation and the development of native schools."[19] No mention, of course, of the fact that Vietnamese schooling rates lagged far behind those of Indochina's neighbors.[20]

The same pamphlet also insists on the absolute Frenchness of the school's curriculum, its lunch menu, etc. The school's program of study was that of "lycées in France."[21] As Dominique Mourey recalls, "the [Lycée Yersin's] program and activities were those of any local French school. We learned Ronsard and translated Seneca with the same conviction as we would have in a French provincial school."[22]

The setting was considered equally French: Dalat's school environment, pine trees, and scenery were all likened to the metropole. They enabled both physical and moral health in the eyes of the authorities: "to see the children under the clear shade of the pines, on the soccer pitch, one would imagine oneself back home at a convalescence center, more than in the kind of barrack-school that Governor General Pasquier warned us against in his visit to Dalat in 1929."[23] As a result of these optimal conditions "children can . . . work just as in France; schedules and study programs are the same; the level of study is therefore normal. Actually, we observed that students coming directly from metropolitan schools did not outshine the students who have been in our establishment throughout."[24] In sum, Dalat offered a putatively metropolitan environment. Thanks to these boarding schools, settler potential would no longer be eroded by the climate and the colony.

On this last point, school officials seemed aware that a colonial mentality—a sense of entitlement stoked by the colonial context and its retinues of servants—had managed to contaminate Dalat's young boarders. So as to justify his emphasis on "the establishment of sound moral habits," the principal of the Petit Lycée depicted average boarders as "sickly children, who only parted from their parents as a result of an ultimatum from a doctor: 'France or Dalat.' These children were too often spoiled precisely because of their precarious health, and generally obeyed blindly by domestics, and sometimes even their parents themselves."[25] Sapped by the climate, spoiled on all sides, afflicted by the spirit of the colony, these young Frenchmen required an especially potent tonic.

As present-day headlines regarding healthy versus unhealthy cafeteria food remind us, the conflation of moral and hygienic discipline is especially pronounced in debates around school diet.[26] Milk, rightly identified by Erica Peters as an agent of Frenchness later recommodified for Vietnamese consumption, turns out to have been central in the elaboration and gradual disintegration of an explicitly European school milieu at Dalat.[27] In an article published in *L'Impartial* in 1935, an anonymous author lambasted the administration's decision to cut costs by depriving Dalat schoolchildren of their fresh milk ration. This milk, produced at the Dankia farm, had heretofore constituted a staple of Dalat's French schools, while Vietnamese students were not entitled to fresh milk in schools reserved to them. The author lamented that under the pretexts of saving monies and, notably, "of abolishing inequalities in the diet of Indochina's lycées," young French children would be reduced to "a diet of condensed milk, when just a few kilometers from their cafeteria some of the most beautiful cows in all of Indochina . . . are reduced to giving their milk to their calves."[28] The tone may have been tongue-in-cheek, but the subject was serious. As Luc Boltanski has shown, the precise nature and quality of cow's milk destined for French youngsters remained, well into the 1960s, an issue that concerned all social classes.[29] In the case before us, the cost-cutting measure of replacing real cow's milk with condensed milk seems to have marked a turning point, the beginning of the end of the cafeteria's absolute Frenchness, itself auguring the end of strict segregation in Dalat's schools.

CLASS AND RACE

Despite the much-heralded educational reform projects of the 1920s, the face of Dalat's student body only began to change noticeably in the 1930s.[30] In 1934, a "group of Annamese parents" demanded in the *Presse indochinoise* that Vietnamese students be eligible for entry to the Grand Lycée de Dalat. The complaint should be situated within the broader pattern of grievances on the part of teachers, parents, students, and the educated Vietnamese public; many such grievances focused on the lack of job opportunities for non-European degree-holders.[31] This particular group of parents displayed considerable determination. The current situation was stacked against them, argued the parents, "for this lycée only has a section A . . . and the program in section A includes Latin." And, "since students are only admitted to this lycée through exam competitions . . . involving Latin, [Vietnamese] students will never be able to write the exam, and hence won't be admitted."[32] Here was a direct challenge on the part of Vietnamese elites, seeking to school their children in what was then considered the educational jewel of colonial Indochina. The petitioners were foiled insofar as no sizeable influx of Vietnamese students was permitted; however, the administration appears to have bent slightly, making a number of exceptions beginning in 1934.

Certainly Latin continued to serve as a selection tool, but it was increasingly deployed within an inner circle that included a small number of elite Vietnamese, Laotians, and Cambodians. It did remain, however, a perceived bulwark with which to kept out the vast number of other indigenous applicants. Why then were exceptions even considered? Perhaps colonial educators were responding to a new colonial imperative of "inventing a cultural tradition for . . . Vietnamese pupils" in the 1930s, as Herman Lebovics has contended.[33] For colonized elites, however, any degallicization of the curriculum proved double-edged. In 1936, at least, previous rules remained in place: all students registered at the Lycée Yersin were required to take Latin, unless they obtained a special dispensation from the colony's director of education.[34]

Shifts in racial thinking in the 1930s can be registered both in Dalat's educational trends and in colonial discourse and policy around schooling. Whereas in 1930 colonial authorities had argued that Dalat posed a menace to the health of Vietnamese children, by December 1936 Dalat's municipal council had changed positions radically, asserting that "the climate of Dalat is quite favorable to young Annamese children, who are just as healthy here as French children."[35] A combination of factors can no doubt help explain this about-face: the reformist spirit of the second half of the 1930s, reflected in the hope elicited by the arrival of the Popular Front government in 1936; as well as the fact that scientific racial determinism came increasingly under attack in the 1930s, as suggested by some of the Guernut commission's findings.[36]

This same 1936 municipal council report even registers a smattering of diversity, limited though it might have been: "Dalat, educational center, has begun to attract children from nearby countries: there are young Siamese children among the students at the Lycée Yersin."[37] Non-European elites were thus managing to penetrate the previously closed and segregated milieu of these schools. Dominique Mourey remarked on the growing number of "native" elites at the Lycée Yersin in the 1930s. By 1942, Mourey noted, the sons of the Cambodian minister of finance were enrolled at the school.[38] In fact, Mourey suggests, Vietnamese and Cambodian youngsters often ended up at the top of the class.[39] Madeleine Jacomme, meanwhile, recalls that in the early 1940s, Emperor Bao Dai's daughters were schooled at the Couvent des Oiseaux, to which they were driven in a Rolls Royce. The school's identity rested on class, she suggests, far more than race. She explains that "many of us at the Oiseaux came from well-to-do families: we were the daughters of doctors, notaries, lawyers, high-ranking officers, bankers, engineers."[40] Colonial education, it seemed, was allowing for a set of exceptions, which is to say a varied indigenous elite educated at Dalat's premier institutions.[41]

FIGURE 24. The former Couvent des Oiseaux, 2001. Photo by author.

During his well-publicized visit to Indochina in 1937, the representative of the left-wing Popular Front government, Justin Godard, underscored the social stratification of Dalat's schools. Although describing the resort's religious schools as "private and very luxurious establishments," and "aristocratic," Godard nevertheless stuck to the standard line about their vocation as bastions of Frenchness. He remained persuaded that "thanks to its geographical situation, Dalat constitutes a favorable milieu for Europeans, especially for European children."[42]

Xuan Phuong provides a unique testimony. Daughter of a Vietnamese mandarin who served as head school inspector in Dalat between 1930 and 1942, she recalls that her father enforced colonial censorship. She also remembers his insistence that she attend the Couvent des Oiseaux, where her father doubled as a Vietnamese-language teacher.[43] She further notes that during the first years of the Vichy regime, "there must have only been a dozen Vietnamese girls [at the Couvent des Oiseaux]: mostly the daughters of landowners in the South, and the three princesses [daughters of Bao Dai]."[44] Instruction was virtually entirely conducted in French, and represented a challenge at first. In fact, the school left some bitter memories: the taunts of French girls are etched in the author's mind. So too is the fact of being renamed "Helen" by one of the nuns, "to make things easier."

Be this as it may, the numbers of nonwhite students trained at Dalat's schools was on the rise in the late 1930s and 1940s. Whereas in its opening year at Dalat in 1936–

37 the Couvent des Oiseaux only counted five Asian boarded pupils, in contrast, between 1938 and 1945, 127 Asian girls would board at the prestigious establishment. The vast majority of these were ethnic Vietnamese, although two "Siamese," two Cambodian, and five ethnic Chinese pupils were enrolled as well.[45]

By the late 1940s, then, Vietnamese youngsters were graduating in large numbers from Dalat's elite schools. Of the forty-two students from all Dalat secondary schools to pass the then-prestigious *baccalauréat* in Dalat in 1949, fifteen had recognizably Vietnamese names, and another two bore names that evoke a possible métis background (Pham Victor and Jean-Daniel Quang).[46] The year following, twenty-six of the fifty-four baccalaureate winners bore discernibly Vietnamese names, another five likely métis names, and one possible Cambodian name.[47] Dominique Mourey notes that in 1948, five graduates of Dalat's lycée entered the prestigious Parisian engineering school, the Ecole Polytechnique. They included three Frenchmen (including Jacques Salles, son of the Lycée Yersin's principal) and two "Indochinese": Hoang Chan from Saigon, and the Cambodian Thioum-Moum.[48]

Although one can certainly not speak of mass democratization of Dalat's colonial-era schools (the French represented a tiny percentage of Indochina's population, yet more French than Vietnamese passed the *baccalauréat* at Dalat even in 1950), one must recognize significant turning points in the city's educational vocation. Initially intended for adult French convalescents, Dalat soon became a nursery for the colonizers at large, a place for European domesticity, even the site of the colony's finest schools. Beginning in the 1930s, and then increasingly in the 1940s, Indochinese elites began to penetrate this once-closed European milieu, a milieu still presented, as late as 1930, as being as hostile to the Vietnamese body as it was revivifying to the European's.

A WHITE FEMALE ENCLAVE

As we have seen, the capacity for both European children and European women to thrive in the colonies had been challenged prior to 1900. The arrival of white women in Indochina in large numbers followed the establishment of a hill station on the Lang-Bian in 1897. There had been no consensus in France on the wisdom of this emigration wave. Supporters, among them Joseph Chailley-Bert, the indefatigable colonial lobbyist, saw the step as critical to maintaining the empire for which France had toiled. He explained in 1897 that "thanks to [colonial women], households and families can be founded without the idea of returning. A new race of settlers born on location will henceforth rise and propagate."[49] Detractors, on the other hand, perceived this expatriation as profoundly harmful. According to the right-wing nationalist newspaper *La libre parole* in 1898: "There might be something better for these young ladies, armed with degrees, to do than to expatriate themselves, like vulgar criminals, to the colonies."[50] The disagreement stemmed in part from opposing appreciations of the role of women at the turn of the twentieth century. This debate pitted social conservatives against feminists, to be sure, but it in turn should be situated within internal French battles over colonial expansion, in which heady progressives or self-proclaimed radicals intent on colonial expansion often found themselves at odds with fiscal conservatives or Europe-oriented nationalists, each espousing quite different gender perceptions. Thus these cleavages also resulted from different readings of the colonies themselves. Lands of opportunity for some, to others the colonies remained deeply associated with the *bagne* (the colonial penitentiary), disease, and death. For single women to emigrate to the colonies could spell only *déclassement,* decadence, degeneration, and demise.

European women did in fact arrive in numbers, though perhaps not the sorts of numbers that migration advocates and colonial leagues had hoped. In Tonkin, Gilles de Gantès has established that the proportion of European women to men rose from 1:7 in 1907 to 1:4 in 1907, and 1:3 in 1922.[51] As Marie-Paule Ha has noted, the social composition of this migration wave was itself the subject of much interest at the time. Promotional literature promised rapid social ascension and paid jobs for *émigrantes,* effecting a transformation so spectacular, that Ha describes it as "Cinderella-like."[52] Once in the colony, French women regardless of their social rank, were expected to assume the trappings of the bourgeoisie: overseeing servants, tending to the home, maintaining social niceties.[53] While historians still debate whether European women were empowered by the colonial context, it seems clear that the pressure for maintaining traditional gender roles was often more intense in the colonies than in the metropole, in part because of the perceived need to uphold French female codes of honor and respectability.

Indeed, one has only to glance at some of the guides aimed at women leaving for the colonies, to detect strong normalizing pressure to tend to the domestic hearth. Clothilde Chivas-Baron's 1929 manual stressed marrying and setting down roots: "presently the French couple can, if it wishes, build something [permanent] in the colonies, and no longer just set up tents."[54] Further, this author counseled, a voyage to the colonies could and should cement the bonds of a European couple, there being "no female rivalry to consider"—native women posing no viable threat to this author—"only a mutual culture and tastes to share and foster."[55]

How was such advice received? In her 1934 review of one such advice manual for *La Presse indochinoise,* a certain S. Guay chides the author for thinking of the French couple as mere procreators. However, what begins as an emancipatory feminist critique soon veers in an altogether different direction. Guay proceeds to depict the colonies as a bastion. Whereas in Europe, women are increasingly expected to work both as mothers and in the factory, in Indochina, she asserts, "there is a chance to save the family." She explains that "this colonial home must feature the absolute equality of rights." But, she adds, "I would like the Frenchwoman, cornerstone of the home, to cease being her husband's competitor in the office and the factory, and stay at home to tend to the children that she could then, finally, raise in peace." Thus, Guay hoped, in remote Indochina, European women could buck the trend of what she ironically dubbed "progress," and safeguard the sacrosanct familial hearth.[56]

Dalat, more than any other space, became synonymous with this bastion mentality. As we have seen, the resort was considered not just safe for women, but actually conducive to European health and family life. It naturally drew European families on both short and longer stays. Yet as colonialism entered a crisis-point in the Second World War, Dalat became for all intents and purposes a white female space, with empowering possibilities of its own.

Madeleine Jacomme remembers her childhood in 1940s Dalat partly as a liberation from her "father's intransigence."[57] Indeed, Jacomme's father, like that of her best friend Claire, carried on with his business in other points of Southeast Asia, leaving his family in the climatic and geopolitical safety of the Lang-Bian resort. In the event, Jacomme's father worked in Phnom-Penh, while Claire's was posted in Singapore. These were anything but isolated examples. Dominique Mourey's just-widowed mother found a post as a boarding school overseer at Dalat in 1937, and brought her two children to the bucolic resort for a long-term stay that lasted the duration of the war.[58] These mothers, tenderly and touchingly remembered in otherwise quite different narratives, came to play roles that would have been inconceivable in a dual-parent context in Hanoi or Saigon. These strong and independent women worked, ran the home, and made life-and-death decisions as the Japanese occupation loomed. They did so not as part of the partnership imagined by Chivas-Baron, but entirely on their own.

A EURASIAN SITE

Some of the earliest social engineering schemes for Dalat involved the settlement of métis children in this site resembling France. Owen White and Emmanuelle Saada have shown how métis children were alternatively perceived as a source of anguish, as threats to the colonial order, as auxiliaries of empire, or as a category in need of *reclassement*—full immersion in a French cultural milieu in order to sprout roots and avert degeneration.[59]

Both the French colonial administration and the clergy had long bemoaned the conduct of French men in Indochina, seen as fathering then abandoning scores of métis offspring. These young Eurasians were often raised by organizations like the Fondation Jules Brévié, which later became the Fondation de l'enfance française d'Indochine (FOEFI).[60] In a case of state-church convergence, the administration and religious orders in Indochina often cooperated on Eurasian matters (even within the ranks of the Brévié Foundation / FOEFI), and more fundamentally, shared a common vision of Eurasians as the fruit of colonial sin.[61] "*Les péchés de ces messieurs"* — "the sins of [colonial] gentlemen" — whispered a nun as she showed visiting parliamentarians the ward for abandoned Eurasian babies.[62]

DALAT'S TRANFORMATIVE POWERS AT WORK

It is in this light that one should consider a certain Brother Louis's offer to the French secular authorities in February 1900. Louis petitioned the Résident of Upper Donnaï to enable the creation of a farm on the Lang-Bian, to be staffed by métis children from Cochinchina.[63] This was seen as a way of putting métis youngsters to work, of grounding them, and of giving them moral purpose. The unstated goal was surely redemptive. Though nothing came of the initiative, it shows that the Lang-Bian was believed to exert a powerful neo-Lamarckian influence on Eurasians, not to mention a hygienic one.[64] These influences were deemed capable of making Eurasians morally, culturally, and civically French, while at the same time serving a French colonial cause. Brother Louis's project would prove to be merely one of many attempts to reroot Eurasians by assigning them to farming and agricultural tasks.

Milieu, Saada argues, was deemed critical in the acculturation of Eurasians. Dalat, as a France replica, came to be seen in the colonial era as an ideal site for their upbringing.[65] Indeed, David Pomfret has shown that Dalat soon emerged as *the* alternative to sending métis children to metropolitan France.[66] Organizations based in the cities of the deltas sought to send their charges to the fresh air of the mountains, whenever possible. When conditions allowed, the Fondation Brévié dispatched Eurasian children to summer camp in Indochina's hill stations. Hill stations being in such high demand, organizers sometimes had to settle for seaside resorts instead.[67]

The Fondation Brévié/FOEFI also directed some Eurasian youngsters to reside permanently in Dalat; others came to Dalat independently from the foundation, no doubt encouraged to do so by their families. Public institutions not necessarily aimed at métis children thus drew Eurasians: a 1938 report indicates that Lycée Yersin schooled "numerous" métis children.[68] By the 1940s, several orphanages aimed explicitly at Eurasians had also been established in Dalat.[69] In addition, the FOEFI often farmed out Eurasian schooling to Dalat's religious orders. In 1948, the Sisters of Saint Vincent de Paul housed 139 Eurasian boys and 50 Eurasian girls, while the Sisters of Saint Paul de Chartres in Dalat were home to eight Eurasian boys and five girls.[70] Each of these orders received funding from the FOEFI, based on the number of Eurasian children cared for per institution.[71] That same year, nearly all children in the Société d'assistance aux enfants Eurasiens d'Annam were brought to Dalat.[72] The year following, the FOEFI even discussed the possibility of moving to Dalat another school for Eurasians, this one located outside of Saigon (the Collège Eurasien de Cholon).[73] The hill station was deemed the perfect spot for Eurasian upbringing, an ideal proxy for "home."

In her memoir, Kim Lefèvre recalls what it was like to grow up in Indochina as a girl of Franco-Vietnamese descent. She remembers feeling rejected by Vietnamese and colonial society alike. A turning point in her own upbringing came when a benefactress offered to pay for her schooling at the prestigious Couvent des Oiseaux, just prior to the Franco-Vietnamese Geneva Accords of 1954. Long after the events, the hill station's smells and sites remain engraved in Lefèvre's memory. Of her arrival at Dalat, she remembers the pines, evoking Christmas trees she had never before seen with her own eyes, as well as "the temperate climate, the carrots, the potatoes that were grown there—all these things brought something like a scent of France." There she tasted *café au lait* for the first time, but found it inferior to noodle soup. There she was also torn between her Vietnamese friends, and French or assimilated children who played French music and consumed all things metropolitan. Lefèvre evidently considered her Dalat experience a major turning point. In her words, "two months lived in this protected site, in a kind of cultural haze where we studied the language of Racine but spoke in Vietnamese amongst ourselves, had erased my familiar images [of Vietnam]. I was starting, progressively, to lose my roots." If this testimony is any indication, Dalat's Frenchifying magnetism was powerful enough to be consciously noticed by those subjected to it, although whether it fostered the sprouting of roots or, conversely, instilled a sense of alienation, was of course profoundly subjective.[74] The French upbringing of Eurasian children like Kim Lefèvre was no trivial matter. Indeed, as in British India, offspring of mixed ancestry, and especially girls, were considered crucial, in part because of their purportedly greater emancipation vis-à-vis their indigenous counterparts, and in part because of their future maternal role, itself highly charged with anxieties tied to identity and domesticity.[75]

Eurasian boys, too, were of perennial concern to the colonial administration in Indochina. They constituted potential go-betweens who could serve the colonial administration, and increasingly as the twentieth century progressed, the military. Thus, when General Alphonse Juin plotted the reconquest of Indochina in December 1945, after months of Japanese occupation and the birth of a new Vietnamese state, he gave the issue center stage. Carving out a French zone in the highlands around Dalat, Juin's advisors noted, would create "a durable basis for our influence in Indochina, and would resolve in some ways the problem of métis *reclassement*, a problem that is bound to return with greater urgency after the arrival of the French expeditionary force."[76]

THE ECOLE DES ENFANTS DE TROUPE
EURASIENS AND ITS AVATARS

It was in 1939 that an institution was created in Dalat specifically for Eurasians. The Ecole des enfants de troupe Eurasiens de Dalat served as a boarding school and military academy for boys between twelve and twenty years old (in 1951, it began taking boys as young as eight).[77] Its averred goal was to prepare a pool of intermediaries for the army, who could serve Frence while drawing from local knowledge, cultures, and languages.

The school admitted both Eurasian children recognized by their parents, and those abandoned, presumed to have had a French parent (a French father, in the vast majority of cases). In academic terms—far less slippery than these ethnic ones—admission to the school was based on a simple set of entrance exams that involved demonstrating some basic proficiency in French and in algebra.[78] For the sake of convenience, the exams were held in different parts of Indochina.[79] The school's success hinged on the triple action of Dalat's milieu, a strict military discipline, and a French curriculum (though Indochinese languages were also taught), a brew believed to exert a powerful moral force on youngsters deemed to be sitting on an identity fence. Come graduation, students were expected to enroll in the French army.[80] In essence, Eurasian boys were subjected to the most potent Frenchifying and homogenizing influences the French Third Republic had mustered: school, army, and place.

Yet the army, at least, still considered graduates of this program as potentially valuable go-betweens capable of aiding French forces in Indochina, thanks to their presumed knowledge of Indochina's cultures and languages. The school's mission statement included the phrase "The Ecole des Enfants de Troupe de Dalat's goal is to favor the recruitment, for the French army, of French elites hailing from this country, knowing its languages and local customs, and adapted to life in Indochina's particular climate."[81] For all of the rhetoric of Frenchyfing métis children through the influence of Dalat's climate, the idea of Eurasian otherness remained potent for colonial, and especially military, authorities.

Though material conditions were difficult at first, the school expanded quickly. It opened in 1939 with some fifty students, drawn mainly from the Fondation Brévié, as well as from a number of Ecoles de Troupes Annamites—similar military academies for young Vietnamese—that Eurasians had hitherto attended by default. By 1942, Dalat's Ecole des Enfants de Troupe Eurasiens counted 150 students. The head of the institution, Colonel (then Lieutenant) Savani, recalls that in its early years the academy impressed all residents of Dalat with its "folkloric parades," its navy blue uniform, and the "magnificent physical and moral health" of its cadets.[82] The Ecole des Enfants de Troupe Eurasiens closed briefly near the end of the Second World War, and was subsequently moved to Saigon in 1946, before finally being transferred back to Dalat in 1947.[83]

Emmanuelle Saada has analyzed some of the confusion caused by the Ecole des Enfants de Troupe's original mandate. A variety of candidates and administrators wrote to ask whether the sons of Vietnamese elites (French citizens in some cases) could be considered; the answer was negative. In response to a question about

FIGURE 25. Students at the Ecole des enfants de troupe de Dalat, 1950s. Photo by Jean Petit. ECPAD/France/Petit, Jean, ANN 53 51/20.

whether a French child whose parent hailed from Pondicherry could be considered, the administration responded that race, not citizenship constituted the chief criterion for admission.[84]

At the end of the Second World War this question was posed anew. The legal category of Eurasians hinged on a racial identification. Though this might not have been problematic in the 1920s and 1930s, it became so after 1945.[85] In a note to the Commissaire Général de la France en Indochine, the colony's judicial services warned that the term "Eurasian" itself had proven confusing, because "French law grants French citizenship to the offspring of Europeans and Asians . . . and any discrimination beyond that is therefore superfluous." In the case of the "Ecole des enfants de troupe eurasiens," the legal department asked, why not drop the mention of Eurasians altogether, since all other Ecoles d'enfants de troupe would specify "Vietnamese, Cambodian, or Laotian."[86] Three months later, the judicial department counseled the general in charge of French troops in Indochina to "[come] up with a term that would not be seen to visibly discriminate racially, but that nonetheless allows us to define accurately on ethnic and social lines. . . . Thus the 'Ecole des Enfants de Troupe Eurasiens' could simply be named 'Ecole Française des Enfants de Troupe.'" In the intervening three months, the word "French" had been added for good measure. The judicial branch recommended that in the future the army, and the administration in general, cease to use the terms "Eurasian" and "métis" altogether, and replace them instead with "*Français d'Asie*."[87]

Based on a 1928 decree, some Eurasians could already apply to become French in Indochina.[88] However, here the transformation took place wholesale. Regulations issued in 1952 for the Ecole des Enfants de troupe stressed that the school authorities should ensure that children become French citizens before they turn 18, if they were not already at the time they entered the school. Their subsequent recruitment into the French army depended on it.[89]

Nor was the shift limited to the realms of law and citizenship. In 1949, an inspection of the school drew attention to the poor diet dispensed in its refectory. General Blaizot unleashed a wave of correspondence, seeking to secure essential foodstuffs for the Ecole des Enfants de troupe. Each of these, in its own way, confirmed the Frenchness of these young pupils: butter, milk, cheese, and chocolate. That a general in a war environment—1949 Indochina—would persevere to secure these nutrients for a Eurasian educational facility speaks to this venture's importance.[90] Eating French, with copious rations of butter, chocolate, and cheese, was central to the Ecole Française des Enfants de Troupe's new identity.

A new set of rules governing the school beginning in 1952 shed light on its everyday operation shortly before its move to France in 1956.[91] Eurasian students applying for admission were to submit both a birth certificate and an official administrative report about their family situation, or in the case where students were the ward of a humanitarian organization, whatever known information there might be about the biological father.[92] The school itself featured a general curriculum (language, math, etc.) supplemented by physical education and moral training, deemed especially important given that many of the pensioners were essentially fatherless.[93]

By the 1950s, the Indochina war led to a heightened sense of urgency at the Ecole des Enfants de Troupe. French military leadership in Saigon urged the FOEFI to select and direct the finest eight-year-old physical specimens to apply. The averred goal was to "prepare good noncommissioned officers, and eventually officers" at the school. In a bid to boost the size of the student body, and to adapt to the circumstances, the French military considered allowing "Afro-Asians" to be admitted after 1951, even though, in many such cases, neither the pupil's mother nor father was a French citizen.[94]

The war had thrust Dalat's Ecole des Enfants de Troupe to the center of a maelstrom; to the French administration, only the Ecole seemed likely to train "reliable" insiders, aware of Indochina and loyal to a geopolitical entity under fire: *L'Indochine française*. Here Dalat's Frenchifying powers were harnessed in a last bid to save *Indochine*.

DALAT'S LAMARCKIAN LIMITS

At Dalat, colonial control proved elusive, colonial blueprints fallible. However frequently the metropole was invoked, be it to set educational standards or gender norms, or to exercise French magnetism over métis youngsters, Dalat deviated from such norms in subtle but revealing ways. Dalat's functions evolved over time. Its schools certainly embodied colonial privilege, but they gradually came to represent other values as well. Its much-vaunted family-friendly atmosphere likewise reflected something the metropole supposedly no longer could offer. Its main center for young Eurasians deployed strong assimilationist practices, while at the same time training Eurasians to serve as cultural intermediaries in the French army. Dalat, the France replica, reveals both the unity of empire and metropole and, ultimately, the surprising elasticity of colonial structures, categories, and master plans.

Divine Dalat

Saigon, not Dalat, bore the title of "the Paris of Indochina." In his description of Saigon in the 1880s, the colonial official Albert d'Anthouard de Wasservas already wove moral condemnations into his sketch of Indochina's, and now Vietnam's, largest city. He claimed that behind the facades of the rococo and neoclassical monuments, the theaters and cafés festered moral decay and debauchery. Administrators with a record of probity in France became compulsive gamblers and embezzlers of public monies in Saigon.

To make matters worse, European women were extremely scarce in the city: one for every ten men, according to the baron. The reason for this state of affairs was simple: the climate was considered incompatible with their temperament and fragile health. This gender imbalance came with terrible consequences: *laisser-aller,* moral turpitude in the form of relationships with local *con-gaïs* or Vietnamese lovers—relationships which left in their wake "alluvial flows of métis children." Bereft of a white female presence, the city was rife with rudeness, "nomadism," homesickness, and harsh mores.[1] Anxious to escape with his soul unscathed, Baron d'Anthouard dreamed of exploring the hinterland and mountains of northern Cochinchina and Annam—a dream that materialized in 1882.[2] Saigon, he feared, eighty years before the city's reinvention into a site of G.I. entertainment, might corrupt his soul.

How had leaders of the navy and the civil administration, whom d'Anthouard recognized as previously upstanding Frenchmen, failed in their bid to recreate a moral replica of France in Saigon? Three answers can be gleaned from the baron's memoirs. According to him, Indochina was to blame; its nefarious influence was powerfully transformative. An equally important factor had to do with the essentially masculine nature of early colonization. Last but not least, the secular, Third-Republican administration drew the baron's ire. He was persuaded that "sectarian freemasons" were responsible for an all-out war over the place of Catholicism in the colony—and indeed freemasons and missionaries *were* locked in an intractable conflict that culminated in the 1890s.[3] According to the baron, this war had resulted in education being transferred from the hands of benevolent fathers into those of petty criminals sent to teach the colonized. This change had been mandated by a new secular regime in Paris, in the name of "democracy," and in keeping with the values of the French Revolution.[4]

To d'Anthouard, Saigon bore the same stigma as the Paris to which it was often compared—a capital the baron associated primarily with the Commune of 1871.[5] D'Anthouard was ten years old when he followed in terror the events of the Paris Commune from his native Versailles.[6] To like-minded colonial administrators, the colonial solution to Saigon's ills would eventually lie, as the baron suspected, in the highlands northeast of Saigon. There, a space could be carved out that could accommodate the growing number of European women in the colony, and thereby make possible the domesticity d'Anthouard so craved. There, religious missions could escape the wretched moral and thermometric climate of Saigon. There, monasteries could be erected far from the colony's Sodom and Gomorrah. There, minority peoples, heretofore supposedly beyond the reach of any organized religion, awaited conversion. There, in short, an alternative, moral, and Catholic France could be fashioned in the pure air of the highlands, breaking from both Saigon and the metropole, each of which had strayed from the flock. Converting highland minorities and ethnic Vietnamese around Dalat could vicariously compensate for the sins of French Indochina.[7]

Escaping to the Vietnamese highlands to ensure physical and moral safety proved an enduring concept, and not merely for the devout. In her scathing 1935 critique of abuses in French colonial Indochina, left-wing journalist Andrée Viollis presented Dalat as follows: "Its atmosphere is certainly purer, in every sense of the phrase, than is Saigon's."[8] Similarly, in his award-winning 1993 historical novel *Annam,* Christophe Bataille tells the story of eighteenth-century French missionaries forced to seek salvation and shelter from persecution at "Gai Lai Kon Tum, or the great plateau." Kontum, located in the same south-central mountain chains as Dalat, provides a setting in which Bataille's protagonists could live "a pure life in the high mountains of Annam."[9] The idea of seeking safe haven, solitude, perfection, or the divine atop remote mountains has deep historical roots in a variety of cultures and faiths. Here we find a very specific and recurring linking of purity of air and purity of soul atop Vietnam's mountains, and among its highland minority peoples.

SACRED HILLS

In the span of some forty years, between 1914 and 1954, Dalat emerged as one of Indochina's dominant Catholic sites, probably the dominant one per capita: in 1935, the Congrégation Notre-Dame arrived in Dalat, and a year later, its monastery and the Couvent des Oiseaux school were erected among the pines; in 1936, Benedictine monks established a monastery at Dalat; that same year, the Filles de la Charité Saint-Vincent de Paul expanded what had been a rest center for the sisters into a convent known as the Domaine de Marie.[10] Father Céleste Nicolas, for his part, soon welcomed clergymen from the entire colony; his Dalat residence became known as "Saint Nicolas cottage."[11] This was only the tip of a surprisingly large iceberg. In addition to unofficial rest stations like Nicolas's home, by 1958, Dalat counted twenty-nine chapels and churches, fifteen different Catholic orders, and nineteen separate religious schools.[12] Many of these orders occupied individual hills within Dalat, commanding breathtaking views over the hill station and surrounding mountains. Dalat had developed a Catholic, and especially a missionary, vocation. And since the Church moved relatively early, as Charles Keith has shown, to a policy of Vietnamization, Dalat's Catholic faithful, be they priests or parishioners, were increasingly ethnic Vietnamese.[13]

DALAT'S MAGNETISM AND DRAWBACKS

What initially brought missionaries to Dalat, besides its vaunted innocence? The resort's reputation for luxury and relaxation seems at first blush to run contrary to the missionary ethos of suffering and abnegation. Part of the answer to this apparent paradox is that to missionaries, Dalat did present its share of hardships, despite its relative comfort. Certainly, missionary literature emphasized the challenges of setting up sites of worship and conversion "in the bush, among the high grasses, where Moï paths zigzag, but little else is to be found."[14] The barrenness of the Lang-Bian plateau constituted a recurring missionary theme. "In the immense brush, all is arid; the Holy Presence breathes life into everything; In the immense brush, what isolation! But here come from France the Virgin and the Child."[15] So ran a hymn composed by the Congrégation Notre-Dame in 1935. It evokes not only the almost monastic isolation of the plateau—itself a potential hindrance for missionary conversion work—but also the intertwining of French patriotism and missionary zeal.

Hardships came in all forms. When the sisters of the Congrégation Notre-Dame first voyaged to Dalat in 1935, they complained of the poor conditions on board the train, noting that they were "shaken like salads" by the time they arrived.[16] Another text reveals the sisters' surprise at tasting Vietnamese food—although they certainly used far greater tact and charity, describing the dishes as "surprising" and "ineffable," than most freshly arrived colonists.[17] Language posed a daunting challenge as well. The sisters noted that learning Vietnamese required a "good ear, memory, and perseverance."[18] In one of its regular circulars to other "nests" or branches around the world, the sisters of the Congégation Notre-Dame in Dalat regaled their readers with tales of wild beasts, including an enormous snake that had recently bitten one of the establishment's servants.[19] Some years later, in 1945, a Couvent des Oiseaux student would actually die from a snake bite at Dalat.

Hardship was certainly not the only "incentive" bringing clergymen to Dalat. As J. P. Daughton has argued, early–twentieth-century French missionaries were also in tune with the zeitgeist: they used modern fundraising techniques and the latest tools to proselytize.[20] It follows, therefore, that they embraced and sometimes appropriated the scientific language of acclimatization and climatic exceptionalism that surrounded Dalat. Thus, for Christmas 1935, the sisters of the Congrégation Notre-Dame wrote of the sacrifice of "expatriating their bodies, [and] acclimatizing their souls."[21] If these were the challenges of missionary expatriation, then surely a cultural and climatic recompression chamber like Dalat could facilitate adaptation.

The Québecois chapter of the Redemptorist order has retained among its archives extensive discussions of Dalat's perceived merits and drawbacks. The Canadian Redemptorists, whose *maison mère* was located in Sainte-Anne de Beaupré, east of Québec City, first arrived in Indochina in the 1920s, whereupon they rapidly learned Vietnamese. The French colonial administration deemed them to be "accomplishing an eminently French task," even commenting on their "pure French" and on the fact that the Vietnamese easily confused them with French missionaries.[22]

Shortly after their arrival in Indochina, the Redemptorists considered moving to Dalat. In a 1927 letter, one Redemptorist lobbied for a Catholic Study center in Dalat, on the grounds that "in Dalat one can study as seriously as in Canada."[23] Later that same year, the same missionary, Constantin Aiutti, wrote home to Father J. Pintal in Sainte-Anne de Beaupré: "I knew that in Saigon there would be opposition to us going to Dalat, especially from those who have never visited. . . . [Arguments against it included:] a difficult climate for the Annamese, and a high cost of living." Having gone to see for himself, Aiutti pronounced these drawbacks to be, respectively, inaccurate and overblown. If the climate was too cool for the Vietnamese, he asked, then why did two thousand ethnic Vietnamese inhabit the hill station? Furthermore, Aiutti pointed out, "thousands" of Vietnamese lived and studied in Paris, where the climate was "much cooler than in Dalat." As for the cost of living, it might be higher for some goods, Aiutti recognized, but it was certainly lower for others: milk, vegetables, and chickens.[24]

Each of these perceived drawbacks is interesting in its own right, Aiutti's needing to respond to them equally significant. The concern that Dalat was foreign to, or even physically hostile to the Vietnamese was certainly a critical point, if the objective of moving to Dalat was to evangelize ethnic Vietnamese. As for Dalat's expensiveness, it no doubt encouraged the perception of the hill station as an elite destination, hardly the sort of place that rhymes with missionaries. Aiutti countered each of these points with climatic and geomedical rebuttals—Dalat's Canadianness, its healthfulness and serenity all made it an ideal training site for Christians.

None of Aiutti's rather abstract climatic rebuttals were trivial; rather, they reflected ongoing and much more pragmatic concerns over acclimation. A quick perusal of the tome dedicated to Redemptorists who served in Indochina reminds us that disease and death still lurked at every turn: Father Georges Bélanger's hepatic ills led him to be repatriated in 1932, Father Marcel Bélanger's fainting spells prompted repatriation in 1946, Father Edouard Blais suffered from malaria, tapeworm, and typhoid fever, before a doctor prescribed a cure at Dalat, and finally a trip home in 1952—and that only accounts for some names starting with the letter B.[25] The Redemptorists were, in part, following in the footsteps of the Filles de la Charité Saint-Vincent de Paul, who had first established a rest center in Dalat before founding a place of worship there. In this sense, many missionaries, like colonists, and especially colonial soldiers and bureaucrats, came to Dalat first for health cures, before coming to fancy the place on other grounds.

The Redemptorist fathers' debate over settling at Dalat continued, even after the order finally purchased a plot in Dalat in 1942. The question of a study center was still unresolved. In 1946 correspondence, Father Georges Galipeau wrote that "Dalat is ideal for intellectual work. Situated at 5,600 feet, Dalat is both in terms of climate and vegetation, like a little piece of Canada dropped in the heart of Vietnam."[26] The Redemporists' massive Noviciat and Studentat buildings were finally inaugurated in Dalat in 1952, after the order withdrew from Hanoi in 1950. This ongoing missionary debate over Dalat reveals that the hill station resonated much the same way to missionaries as it did to the civil administration: it provided a powerful reminder of home—in this case Canada. And, not incidentally, it was believed to foster the appropriate conditions for study and serenity. Be this as it may, how did missionaries square these lofty, almost monastic, ideals with their main mission: evangelization?

SAVING HIGHLAND MINORITY SOULS

Conversion was by definition the prime objective of missionaries. But which souls should be targeted around multiethnic Dalat? Surprisingly, and in contrast to the situation in other regions of Indochina occupied by minority populations, missionaries turned relatively late to the highland minorities on and around the Lang-Bian plateau. Indeed, this chronology is all the more intriguing when one considers that the first conversion attempts on the highland minorities of interior Annam date back to the 1760s.[27] This said, Jean Michaud rightly underscores that this initial wave of enthusiasm was followed by a period of relative indifference towards highland minorities—lasting roughly until the 1870s.[28] By that decade, the Missions étrangères were quite active in the Kontum area further north in Annam, yet nonexistent in the Lang-Bian region.[29]

According to missionary history, it was Father Jean Cassaigne who first received the official order from Monseigneur Isidore Marie Joseph Dumortier, in 1927, to head to the Djiring and Lang-Bian regions to convert highland minorities. Cassaigne, described in a bishop's report as "full of virtue, capable of leading a mission," reportedly learned his minority language skills from a thirteen-year-old boy, who doubled as his servant.[30] He gradually earned the trust of local Koho-speaking people, offering tobacco and medication to further his cause. He oversaw his first minority baptism in 1929, and claimed his first conversion in 1930.[31]

In December 1935, Cassaigne was elated to see a highland minority chief and his wife near the altar at Christmas mass. The chief invited Cassaigne to attend a sacrifice—and apparently held out the hope of a large-scale conversion. In such situations, missionary ethnographic fieldwork—"incidental" and untrained though it might have been—could reap concrete rewards.[32] In point of fact, Cassaigne attended the sacrifice, and happily reported that he could count on at least forty conversions in the near future, as a direct result of this turn of events.[33]

Cassaigne was one of the few missionaries in the 1920s and 1930s to have mastered some of the minority languages of the Dalat region well enough to proseltyze. In her 1936 circular, Mother Marie-Antoinette of the Congrégation Notre-Dame in Dalat called not speaking "Moï" one of her greatest regrets. She added, however, that Vietnamese alone was already proving a monumental challenge, noting that she and her companions "were working assiduously" to master the language, even if it meant "forcing our mouths to make contortions."[34] Still, language barriers alone did not prevent women of the cloth from meeting and reaching out to highland minorities.

In reality, then, Cassaigne was far from alone on the scene. In 1920, Father Céleste Nicolas, Dalat's parish priest, opened a school aimed at minority children. However, Nicolas was a busy man, as Dalat's European and Vietnamese congregation took up a considerable amount of his time.[35] When in 1927 his superiors asked him to leave Dalat, ostensibly for a promotion, so as to represent Cochinchina and Cambodia at the central council of the Missions étrangères in Paris, he objected strongly that he and Cassaigne had only recently founded the "Mission sauvage du Lang-Bian." This project, still in its earliest days, required his language skills. He explained: "I am the only missionary . . . who knows what to do there, knows several hundred words of the Moï language, and is known by the region's savages, who come almost every day to request something or other from me."[36] Nicolas, in other words, was indispensable. A decade later, he again complained of not being able to focus sufficiently on highland minorities. This time, it was Dalat's Saint Nicolas Church that consumed his time. Finishing the centrally located church, a vital necessity for Dalat's growing French and Vietnamese congregation, ought to be the bishop's task, he insisted.[37] Dalat's competing roles as a French center of health and power clashed, in the religious sphere as in the civilian one, with its function as a contact point with highland minorities.

Another conversion attempt on highland minorities near the Lang-Bian took place as early as 1922 at Lien-Son, on the road to Dalat. The Missions étrangères in Paris attributed this admittedly isolated success to the fact that Lien-Son lay at the intersection of Vietnamese and minority zones of influence, two kilometers from the largely Catholic Vietnamese village of Rung-Lai. According to this account, the "deeply Christian life" of the local Vietnamese had rubbed off on local minorities, thereby "sheltering them from the dangers of superstitious rites, so popular among purely savage villages." The fact that this area was "mixed" also meant that conversion could be undertaken in the Vietnamese tongue.[38]

Yet Church histories recognize that the conversion efforts undertaken by Nicolas and Cassaigne on the Lang-Bian and by others at Lien-Son, were not only exceptional, they also proved somewhat futile. One missionary text bemoaned that the bulk of Father Nicolas's time was consumed by "non-Montagnard" issues, a reference no doubt to the ongoing saga of Dalat's parish church, which was taking longer to complete than religious authorities had imagined. The piece added: "We had to wait until 1948 to see any real missionary work undertaken towards the natives [highland minorities]."[39] Another article stated bluntly that Nicolas and Cassaigne's efforts failed when converted minority children vanished into the forests, never to reappear again. "Things remained that way until 1948, when a conversion wave began at once, without my being able to specify exactly why, at least not in human terms."[40] The increasing competition of Protestant missionaries in the area likely had as much to do with this new wave of conversions as did divine intervention.

Whatever the precise cause, Catholic missionaries began intensely concentrating on minority populations around Dalat in the 1950s. In 1953, missionaries Octave Lefèvre and Boutary had registered some 1,447 catechisms among some sixteen villages within a twenty-kilometer radius immediately north of Dalat. The missionary publication *Les Lettres communes* enthusiastically relayed the following story: during a buffalo sacrifice, a young woman, having only recently received her catechism, intervened to free the beast, before intoning a prayer to the "real God."[41] By 1957, the Camly "Montagnard Center" led by Fathers Desplanque, Boutary, and Kermarrec numbered some twenty villages totaling some two to three thousand people, of which 650 had been baptized.[42] Still the process proved arduous. One missionary recounted that "missionaries on the high plateaux must constantly stimulate those already converted, for they do not yet have Christian atavism and seem to follow custom more easily than the teachings of missionaries."[43]

The Redemptorists too, joined the 1950s frenzy to convert Dalat-area "montag-

FIGURE 26. Sister from the Congrégation Notre-Dame with highland minority people, 1950. Courtesy of Congrégation Notre-Dame.

nards." Father Sylvère Drouin's first contact with Dalat came while on vacation. Thereafter, he returned to the area, authored a Koho-French dictionary, and undertook converting no fewer than forty-five villages, operating out of Fyan, near Dalat.[44] His visits to these hamlets were often as medical as they were spiritual, and missionary history recounts that he became known as the "finest sorcerer among the Montagnards." In 1955, Drouin helped establish a Montagnard Center in Fyan, comprising a monastery, a dispensary, and a school.[45]

CONVERTING ETHNIC VIETNAMESE

In a 1949 article, Fernand Parrel tried to dissipate a myth. Admittedly, Dalat was "covered with European villas" and had been selected for a possible administrative capital of all of Indochina. Yet, the missionary added: "One would be wrong to think that Europeans comprise the majority of the missionary's flock [in Dalat]. The Vietnamese element is in fact far more numerous. Then there are the montagnard or 'Moï' masses, who live in surrounding villages, and whom one could not legitimately overlook."[46] Parrel's ordering is revealing: Dalat, he insisted, was no missionary sinecure. The hill station's many ethnic Vietnamese merchants, workers, farmers, bureaucrats, and the ethnic Vietnamese plantation laborers in surrounding regions all required spiritual attention.

After 1945, missionaries petitioned the local administration to create a "new Catholic Vietnamese village" outside of Dalat, known as the Village Saint-Jean. By 1949, the village was taking shape. Fathers Parrel, Octave Lefevre, and a Vietnamese vicar, Father Bo, blessed the grounds, and articulated their designs for the village. It was to "live according to the formula of the early church, forming a veritable community whose members would be united by the spirit of Christ, in an atmosphere of true fraternity, based on the primacy of sharing communal goods."[47]

DALAT IN MISSIONARY LORE

As J. P. Daughton remarks, the output of missionary literature relating to the French colonial empire far surpassed anything produced by geographic societies or other traditional mouthpieces of imperial expansion.[48] And unlike geography reviews or popular travel literature, missionary texts made for active reading. Indeed, the many orders present in Dalat communicated regularly with their home organizations, thereby creating a dialogue between metropolitan faithful and the colonial periphery. Thus a girl from Verneuil, one of the Congrégation Notre-Dame's metropolitan girl schools, wrote to the attention of the Congrégation Notre-Dame in Dalat in 1935: "Dalat contains all that is dearest to us: our Mothers and our Moïs. But one must be very brave to go to Annam. One could be eaten by ferocious beasts!"[49] Two years later, a grade six student wrote to Dalat: "We read together the review on Dalat and wanted to sponsor a conversion. So we broke into teams and each team has a box where we collect our savings for the cause."[50]

The dialogue worked both ways. While girls at religious schools in France and beyond wrote on a regular basis to the sisters in Dalat, the order in Dalat also asked members of the congregation back home to canvass for musical instruments, religious postcards, and recorded religious music, all useful instruments and technologies of conversion on the ground on the Lang-Bian plateau.[51] Besides this, each Congrégation Notre-Dame outpost around the world drafted regular *circulaires*, which were as their name suggests circulated to sister establishments. Dalat's chapter proved especially prolific. These circulars, containing tales of everyday trials and tribulations, were read carefully by superiors, then excerpted in missionary reviews, some of which, again, were intended for a younger public. Thus a self-referencing, dialogical circuit fueled missionary pedagogical literature.[52]

MISSIONARY-CIVILIAN RELATIONS

J. P. Daughton has shown how missionary claims to primacy in Indochina—where they had been saving souls long before any secular Republican administrator set foot in the region—and a wide range of tensions with the *république laïque*, came to a head in a headline-grabbing incident in the 1880s. During this affair, some missionaries came to support Charles-David Mayréna's quixotic and usurpatory claim to a highland minority "kingdom."[53] This famous scandal, which occurred in the Kontum region north of Dalat, had lingering consequences on relations between missionaries and civil authorities.[54] Still, as Daughton argues, by the twentieth-century missionaries increasingly saw themselves as the allies of colonial authorities, and although on occasion they did not refrain from criticizing secular republican officials, they nonetheless felt bound to them in a common "civilizing" and patriotic cause.[55] To be sure, some simmering tensions persisted well into the 1920s and 1930s over the place of private Catholic education, over the broader issue of state-church relations, and more specifically over administrative support for some missionary activities.[56]

Certainly, the archives contain numerous examples of lingering difficulties between missionaries and civil authorities at Dalat. For instance, the Congrégation Notre-Dame encountered a string of problems with Dalat's mayor. In 1935 the mayor insisted, for example, that the sisters improve the beauty of their projected buildings before a construction permit could be granted.[57] Annoyances persisted even after the permit was obtained. In early 1936, Dalat's Committee of Public Salubrity inspected the Congrégation Notre-Dame's temporary quarters. A doctor, a veterinarian, an engineer, and an architect all descended on the place of worship, ostensibly searching for mosquitoes.[58]

The sisters elaborated a variety of schemes for coping with bureaucratic obstruction. The simplest, and probably the most effective, involved climbing to the top of the civilian chain of command. In one circular, the sisters wrote of lobbying both the Résident supérieur and the governor general in person simply to garner "support in our small difficulties."[59] Their task was facilitated by the fact that the governor general's daughter attended the order's famed Dalat school, the Couvent des Oiseaux. Yet overall, these were minor conflicts, proving that the days of major rows in Indochina between secular republican administrators—often freemasons—on the one hand, and religious orders on the other hand, were consigned to the past.

Boundaries nevertheless remained in flux, positioning towards indigenous peoples contentious. Missionaries sometimes found themselves in awkward positions vis à vis the colonial bureaucracy. Thus in 1952, Father Fernand Parrel wrote of his first encounters with minority people around Dalat, some four years earlier: "It would be wrong to say that I received a warm welcome during my first visits [to minority villages]! I was reproached with being a poor agent of the administration." Parrel elaborated: "It was imperative that I clear up this misunderstanding—All the more, since the montagnards still thought, in their primitive brains, that I could help them in their quarrels with the administration. And God knows these quarrels were numerous: the question of corvées, that of mandatory schooling, the future dam, military recruitment, and others still. . . . These poor people thought that thanks to my intervention, all of these obstacles would be lifted at once."[60]

Parrel could not perform miracles with the colonial administration. And he found himself in a conundrum: he certainly wished to distance himself from a colonial civil administration that was proving a source of unrelenting anguish for villagers. This distance he sought not merely for strategic reasons, or for ideological ones—Parrel did seem genuinely concerned about the colonial state's growing intrusion in minority villages—but also to uphold missionary independence and legitimacy. Yet it was no doubt tempting for Parrel to utilize his understanding of the French administration, if only his language skills, to assist villagers in some way. Such an act could only enhance his own credibility and standing, hence his likelihood of achieving conversions.

COMPETING FAITHS

For all of their reservations about Catholic missionary activities, twentieth-century colonial authorities certainly did not police Catholic missionaries—even foreign ones—as they tracked faiths they considered more menacing: Protestantism and Cao Daïsm.[61] For Dalat had emerged as a multifarious religious center. Although available sources do not permit a detailed analysis of the important Buddhist pagodas that were established in Dalat starting in 1938, we saw in chapter 9 that these came to play an important role for ethnic Vietnamese people all over Vietnam.

In a 1926 colonial police report on the arrival of the Canadian Redemptorists in Annam, the colonial Sûreté hypothesized that their sudden appearance in Indochina was the result of a clear though secretive Church grand strategy. It involved "reinforcing French missionaries whose numbers are insufficient, [thereby] counterbalancing in Indochina the influence of evangelical American missionaries."[62] Concern over Protestant American missionaries would mount from that time forward. Sûreté agents were sent to attend a Protestant missionary synod held in Dalat on May 11, 1936, though they found scant subversion to report.[63] A year later, the colonial police revealed that the Christian and Missionary Alliance, led by Reverend Herbert Jackson, was planning on opening an oratory at Entrerays, near Dalat.[64]

By 1949, French officials observed with some alarm the spread of the American Protestant Church in the Dalat area. In Dalat proper, the Christian and Missionary Alliance now owned the "Alliance villa." It offered classes and was, according to a colonial report, brimming with initiatives, with new missionaries from America, and with new equipment.[65] During a synod held in Dalat in June of that same year, Pastor Alfred C. Snead felt the need to reassure French officials, "remarking on the fine influence of France in the Far-East." This positive impression he promised to share widely after he returned to the United States.[66] In this game of cat and mouse, American missionaries gladly paid lip service to France so as to placate the Sûreté. The colonial police, however, was not reassured.

Protestant missionaries were indeed making major inroads. While in 1942, the

American Protestant missionary presence in Indochina was limited to thirty-one pastors, a decade later, it had risen to ninety-six. By 1950, some three hundred highland minority people of the Dalat region had converted to Protestantism. The Alliance villa seemed to be outperforming its Catholic rivals. The Alliance's Dalat press published thousands of copies of brochures, pamphlets, and magazines. The French administration, at least, was persuaded that this religious penetration augured a political one. The missionaries were squarely accused of "making people believe that the Americans will bring happiness to the Indochinese population, be it by modernizing cities, increasing productivity, or industrializing." One U.S. missionary in particular was said to have called France a "secondary power."[67]

If Protestant evangelizers were perceived as dangerous threats from without, colonial authorities were persuaded that "sects" like Cao Daïsm presented a menace from within. The syncretic religion, founded in 1926 at Tay-Ninh, was rapidly gaining converts in parts of Cochinchina and Annam in the 1930s. By 1939, Truong Van Ngo requested permission to preach Cao Daïsm in Upper Donnaï province. His request was flatly turned down. When that year Truong Van Ngo entered the Dalat region in spite of this interdiction, the colonial police escorted him out of the province, only to have him return, and be kicked out once again. Colonial police bulletins kept track of rumors that were purportedly enhancing the religion's popularity in the Dalat region. In particular, they registered a rumor according to which followers of the Cao Dai religion would be exempt from military service, an important consideration in late 1939.[68] Cao Daï, whose hierarchy would forge an alliance with the Japanese occupiers during the Second World War, had already at this stage been singled out as a political menace in religious clothing.

CONCLUSION

Strolling down Dalat's Avenue du Docteur Yersin or the aptly named Rue des Missions, in the 1930s, 1940s, or 1950s, one was just as likely to come across a man or woman of the cloth as to rub shoulders with a uniformed civil servant, soldier, or sailor. Dalat may have initially been a creation of the French colonial administration, bent on perpetuating colonial rule in Indochina. Yet it was soon appropriated for other ends by other actors, among them religious orders that came to see the hill station as the consummate site for serenity, contemplation, and conversion. Mostly, they saw in Dalat a fresh start in Indochina, one morally and physically removed from Hanoi and Saigon. To be sure, they struggled with the hill station's reputation for luxury, its remoteness, and even with the question of whom precisely to convert, and in what order. But Dalat still emerged in the span of thirty years as a major site of worship, even pilgrimage—perhaps Indochina's largest Catholic center, if only in the number of orders present.

This is not to suggest that Dalat's religious functions necessarily clashed with its colonial one, but rather that the meticulously planned resort was taking on new guises, and in the process, new significance. By the 1940s, Dalat was as much a religious center and an educational hub, as it was a rest station or a resort. And, notably, the religious orders in Dalat would survive the maelstrom of the Second World War relatively unscathed, largely sheltered from the worst of the turmoil that shook Indochina over the course of 1945 especially. If one is to believe a 1945 colonial report, the main damage incurred by the Indochinese church during the Second World War was moral in nature: the Vietnamese clergy in particular, had found itself torn between its quest for national independence and a reputation as a "foreign" religion, enduringly bound to colonialism.[69]

The Maelstrom, 1940–1945

The Second World War marked a peculiar, paradoxical time for Dalat. On the one hand, the hill station reached its zenith of the colonial era, attracting thousands of French civilians who were unable to return to a besieged metropole, as well as growing numbers of Vietnamese. On the other hand, it ushered in a period of uncertainty, with Vichy French, Japanese, and Viet-Minh interests all vying for control of a hill station that had become Indochina's nerve center.

DALAT'S COLONIAL GOLDEN AGE

Dalat's population rose spectacularly during the war, jumping from thirteen thousand inhabitants in 1940 to twenty thousand in 1942. By 1942, the town boasted 730 villas, a far cry from the handful of cottages it counted at the beginning of the century.[1] Even the luxurious and pricey Dalat Palace Hotel was now bursting at the seams—a sign that short-term visits were also on the rise.[2] Dalat's growth spurt in 1940 was certainly not spontaneous; rather it was the result of rapid political and social change.

Governor General Jean Decoux, who emerged over the course of 1940 as loyal to Marshal Pétain's emerging Vichy regime, came to reside in Dalat with greater and greater frequency between 1940 and 1945. He knew the merits of the hill station: already in the 1920s, he had lobbied for the rapid construction of naval barracks and officer villas in Dalat.[3] Now at the helm of the colony, he ordered the improvement of communication links to Hanoi and Saigon, so as to render Dalat an effective point of governance.

His choice of residences was therefore no coincidence. No doubt it also served to extract him somewhat from the Japanese microscope.[4] Japanese forces had been present in northern Indochina since September 1940—after French authorities arrived at an agreement with Japan under the barrel of a Japanese gun.[5] On July 21, 1941, the two parties formally ratified another deal that came to be known as the Darlan-Kato pact. This was followed by a detailed military accord between France and Japan ratified after Pearl Harbor, again under intense Japanese pressure. The deals came about partly because of aggressive Japanese tactics and the asymmetry of military might, but also by virtue of Vichy's subservience to Nazi Germany, and Japan's 1940 treaty with fascist Italy and Nazi Germany. In practice, Japanese forces had entered Southern Indochina in July 1941, and were henceforth posted in the entire colony. Indeed the December 1941 deal would confirm that the "defense" of Southern Indochina was in Japanese hands, while Northern Indochina was to remain the responsibility of French troops.[6] Japanese forces would soon use southern and central Indochina as a launching pad for further conquest in Southeast Asia.

Decoux's increasing presence at Dalat also fell in line with the values of the regime he served: historians have chronicled the Vichy love affair with mountains, nature, fresh air, and all things earthy. Meanwhile, one of Decoux's right-hand men, charged with relations with the outside world, speculated that Decoux's passion for Dalat stemmed simply from his own need to seek refuge from Indochina's terrible heat, and to mend his health.[7] Anti-Decoux resistor René Poujade saw several factors at work, hypothesizing that Decoux both relished Dalat's clement weather and preferred its "atmosphere" to Hanoi and Saigon's.[8] Whatever the root cause, Decoux made Dalat into more than his place of predilection. We will see in the following chapter that he contributed to making it the de facto capital of Indochina.

As early as July 1940, the governor general's office ordered Dalat's naval villas to be handled and allocated directly by the director of health services. This extraordinary measure was justified by the fact that "European personnel [was] stranded in the colony."[9] With Indochina once again cut off from the motherland by global war, Governor General Jean Decoux issued new decrees increasing the duration and frequency of leaves in Indochina's hill stations.[10] The decree of August 6, 1940 (inspired by another from the First World War) extended the twenty-one-day medical leave for functionaries to three months per year at a hill station. As before, bureaucrats on rest leave at Dalat continued to receive their full pay. This was considered a medical leave of absence, distinct from and combinable with the annual *permission*.[11]

Flooded with requests for such medical leaves of absence, in 1941 Decoux ordered the creation of a special form, to be signed by a doctor before setting off to the hill station, then by another doctor every fifteen days at the hill station itself.[12] As for the now-standard annual leaves to hill stations, Decoux thought it wise to specify that they should only be granted to the extent that they would not completely deplete an administrative unit, to the point of shutting it down. Barring this, Decoux added, such leaves should be granted as often as possible.[13]

FIGURE 27. The children of the Cité-Jardin Jean Decoux, July 1943. Note the smaller flag of the Kingdom of Annam floating besides the French tricolor. Archives Municipales de Bordeaux, fonds Decoux.

The cessation of trips home clearly weighed on the governor's mind. Dalat was beginning to suffer from overcrowding. Officially endorsed hill stations now numbered ten: Chapa (or Sapa), Tam Dao, and Bavi in Tonkin; Bana, Bach-Ma, and Dalat in Annam; Bockor in Cambodia; and the Bolovens Plateau, Phou-Khoun, and Xien-Khouang in Laos.[14] The problem of furloughs was so acute, these hill stations in such demand, that Decoux set his sights elsewhere. With Indochina now in imperial Japan's orbit, in May 1941 Decoux reopened the nineteenth-century option of sending colonial officials in Indochina on furloughs to Japan. This measure, contemplated by Decoux in 1941, would have been available to any official who had spent three years in Indochina.[15] With Dalat experiencing record popularity to the point of having to turn back administrators, and Decoux engaged in a version of collaboration with imperial Japan, it seemed time consider new—or rather old—outlets like Japanese sanatoria, hill stations, and spas.

Decoux endeavored as early as 1940 to render Dalat more affordable and accessible to all French inhabitants in Indochina. This he accomplished by creating low-cost housing in a suburban *cité-jardin* named after himself. He also encouraged French youth from across the colony to congregate in Dalat. By 1943, the Cité-Jardin Decoux counted 130 children—the result of Decoux's policy of favoring applications from large families.[16] Summer camps flourished on the Lang-Bian, with priority given to "children whose length of stay in the colony or whose health justifies an altitude cure."[17] A number of new institutions aimed at youth, like a female physical education training center (L'Ecole supérieure des Monitrices d'Indochine, founded in 1942), a female "household science" school (L'Ecole supérieure ménagère, founded in 1944), and the Ecole des Enfants de Troupe (founded in 1939), and the arrival of a host of scout groups (Decoux even planned a youth camp for children of the merchant marine!), soon gave Dalat the reputation as a "city of youth."[18] In other words, Dalat's growth seems to have occurred across the board, attracting both young and old, rich and less well off, even colonizers and colonized.

Indeed, under Decoux, an interesting semantic shift took place. Leaves at Dalat were no longer framed as the exclusive precinct of the colonizers. In a 1942 article, Decoux professed to make Dalat "the great resort of Indochina, where all French and Annamese will come to draw new strength in the Lang-Bian's revivifying climate."[19] In reality, the new Da Thanh Vietnamese quarter hatched by Decoux's administration in 1942 served mostly in the governor's eyes to "decongest" Dalat's downtown. Within a year of its creation, the new Vietnamese suburb counted two thousand inhabitants.[20]

LÀ-HAUT SUR LA MONTAGNE

In 1943, Dalat's mayor, André Berjoan, described Dalat as a site where one could feel "the spirit of the National Revolution," the Vichy regime's state ideology. Better still, he wrote, Dalat's recent facelift reflected the genius of "renovated France."[21] Among her memories of Dalat in December 1940, Iphigénie-Catherine Shellshear rekindles verses from the song "Là-haut sur la montagne" ("Up There on the Mountain")—lyrics in line with Vichy's alpine ethos.[22] Although composed by a Swiss clergyman in 1929, after 1940 the song became closely associated with Vichy's campfire values.

Vichy's xenophobic, reductionist, nostalgic ideology had reached the highlands of Indochina. In the metropole, the National Revolution ushered in a purge of the French republic and its values, a professed desire to return to the soil and to the countryside, the restoration of "French values," and the relentless pursuit of scapegoats blamed for France's 1940 defeat. On a much smaller scale, most colonials in this isolated hill station would enthusiastically embrace these tenets.

As if scrolling down an ideological checklist, Decoux's administration enacted each National Revolutionary ideal. On the critical issue of French fertility (Marshal Pétain blamed the defeat on France's low birthrate), Decoux applauded a "magnificent" couple from Tonkin, who brought their twelve children on holidays to Dalat's cité-jardin.[23] Institutionally, Dalat received the visit of the Vichy regime's vanguard, the Légion française des combattants et volontaires de la Révolution nationale. One Légion-endorsed speech at the Hôtel du Parc in May 1944 dealt with Pétain's labor charter, which introduced a measure of Mussolini-style corporatism into the French economy.[24] Another took on the "historical foundations of French civilization and the message of our ancestors," a clear nod to Vichy's obsession with the distant, preindustrial past.[25]

It was in the mobilization, regimentation, and indoctrination of youth that Dalat most closely followed the lead of Vichy France. Scores of uniformed youngsters hiked the Lang-Bian's pathways. Jean Rouget, at the time associate mayor of Dalat in charge of the "youth-sport" portfolio, recalls how he was responsible for organizing swimming, rugby, and athletics. He claims that he was able to delegate processions, rallies, and other more ideological events to a specialized agent who then liaised with the resort's many religious orders to mount elaborate mise-en-scènes.[26] Adventure, suffering, and effort were some of the leading values of the day. Dominique Mourey remembers Captain Jean Le Pichon berating Dalat's youngsters for being soft colonials, in need of ideals, effort, and suffering.[27] Scouts wrote wistfully about "reaching the orchid mountain, the summit of the forest of leeches, after getting lost in the mysterious valley."[28] In addition to the scouts, a number of youth camps sprouted at Dalat: some organized by the caisse des écoles de Saigon, others by Notre Dame du Lang-Bian.[29]

Fantasies of ancient France were played out in the shadow the Lang-Bian. Youngsters in the garden of the Dalat Palace Hotel reenacted Joan of Arc's siege of Orléans; to ensure historical accuracy, the children dressed as Englishmen were asked to die easily.[30] In 1944, Dalat's homage to Joan of Arc was combined with that of the Trung sisters, who circa 39 A.D. briefly but successfully ousted the Chinese from Nam Viet. This ominous portent somehow escaped Vichy youth officials, who followed to the letter Vichy directives asking officials to promote local pasts and stoke local folklore throughout France and its empire.[31] Similarly, female scouts were divided into revealing groups: Trung-Trac and Trung-Nhi (the same Trung sisters), the "Legion of the Little Flowers of Annam," and the " Little Homemakers."[32] Female physical education was encouraged, although Decoux's officials simultaneously posed revealing limits on it, as evidenced by this description from the Ecole supérieure des Monitrices d'Indochine: "Careful! Force is good, but so too are grace and gestural beauty, elegance in one's attitudes."[33] Embodying elegance included stretching out one's right arm in unison, part of the proliferation of the Olympic salute in Indochina under Vichy.[34]

A local magazine chronicled the sea change that had taken place, both in Dalat and in France: "Before, we [young people] dreamt of the easy life, of cowardice and selfishness before effort. Did these soft, muscle-deficient . . . adolescents, really embody French youth?"[35] The head of sport in Dalat, Captain Jean Le Pichon, took pride in the city's impressive new sporting complex, built on the model of the Colombes Olympic stadium outside Paris.[36]

Lest the political purpose of such inaugurations go unnoticed, Decoux's press services waxed eloquent, as during the graduation of the first cohort of *monitrices* from Dalat's school: "The Madame Jean Decoux promotion [Ecole des monitrices] is now graduating from the quaint school perched atop one of Dalat's hills, and . . . will go on to teach the principles of physical and moral education which the Marshal, head of the French state, asks youth of the empire to follow in order for imperial France to be stronger and more beautiful."[37] Were it not for the reference to "empire," this scene could easily have been set in a metropolitan youth camp under Vichy. The twinning of moral and physical health, the alpine ideal, the cult of the Marshal, and the need to obey, all fall in line with the precepts of Pétain's National Revolution. During these war years, Dalat and Vichy France were one, a mirror-effect that no doubt reinforced Dalat's role of "little France."

Was this all for show? In the administrative realm, in December 1942 when the local gendarmerie conducted its usual background check on Dalat inhabitants who wished to marry French military personnel, it now included the clause: "Miss X, of French nationality, does not belong to the Jewish race."[38] At least one witness from the era remembers Vichy's ideology carrying considerable sway in Dalat between 1940 and 1945. Dominique Mourey recalls one of his teachers, Jean-Marie Abadie, "denouncing Anglo-Saxon Jewery." Mourey also describes seeing a heavy-handed propaganda film relating how the English "pig," Lord Kitchener, had defeated Marchand at Fashoda in the Sudan. And he evokes an English teacher at the Lycée Yersin composing an ode to Marshal Pétain, as late as the summer of 1944.[39]

Indeed, in this mountain time warp, Pétain's regime remained in power, and popular, well after the liberation of Paris and the forced exile of Marshal Pétain to Germany. This said, any overt sympathy for General de Gaulle (there was some, though covert for the most part) might have drawn the ire of Japanese forces, which were stationed all over Indochina, including at Dalat.

COHABITATION WITH IMPERIAL JAPAN

We saw above that Vichy France entered into a series of agreements with imperial Japan between 1940 and 1941. With Japan's lightening advance across Southeast Asia, these accords soon left the French as the sole colonial power operating within the expanding Japanese orbit. Because of Vichy's loyalty to an ally of Japan, but also because Japan stood to gain by letting the French administer Indochina themselves, until 1945 the French experienced a very different fate from European colonizers in Singapore, Malaysia, Indonesia, and Hong Kong. Still, the occupation was in many ways ambiguous, the tension palpable, long before Japan's sudden attack on Indochina's French forces in March 1945. Dalat, the privileged European enclave, reveals some of the implications of the Japanese presence, on both colonial rule and on Vietnam itself.

Most European testimonies recall that the Japanese presence at Dalat between 1941 and March 1945 had been discreet. In the words of Iphigénie-Catherine Shellshear, a child at the time, " their arrival was most unceremonial . . . in my recollections they did not interfere with our daily routine at all."[40] Be this as it may, the imperial Japanese army had expressed interest in Dalat early on. A document reveals that among the many construction projects undertaken in the colony in 1942 was a Japanese military hospital in the suburbs of Dalat, built under French auspices.[41]

This last point elicits two observations. The first is that the Japanese army clearly shared French climatic visions of Dalat as an ideal rest and recovery center for fatigued and diseased troops. A second observation has to do with the nature of the Vichy-Japanese relationship. While some historians still refuse to define Japan's presence in Indochina as an "occupation" and many others consider Decoux's relations with Japan something short of outright "collaboration," there was certainly a high degree of complicity here.[42] This was especially true in certain spheres like trade, until March 9, 1945.[43] Indeed, Indochina's currency was soon aligned with the yen, one of many signs that the colony was increasingly integrated into Tokyo's self-proclaimed coprosperity sphere.[44] In a recent book, former Indochina resistor René Poujade has enumerated some of Vichy's acts of "collaboration" with Japan in wartime Indochina, including extensive commerce, the handing over of ships, the granting of technical advisors in the petrol sector, and the attempt to recapture New Caledonia from Free France.[45] Yet even Poujade concedes that Nazis and Japanese occupied differently, and that notwithstanding strong "parallelism," French experiences differed as well.[46] We will see that collaboration and resistance in Indochina, and at Dalat in particular, were and remain loaded terms, consistently filtered through the lens of this fresh, albeit geographically distant, reference: Nazi occupied France.

A seemingly innocent incident, recorded in the French colonial archives, speaks to some of the stakes of the delicate cohabitation between Japanese and French at Dalat. We have seen that after 1940, Dalat was in high demand among French administrators and military personnel stranded in the colony. As a result, in 1942 General Eugène Mordant, at the helm of French ground troops in the colony, ordered the expansion of the Camp Saint-Benoît, on the outskirts of town. Unfortunately for Mordant, such an extension meant that the camp would now border the new Japanese military hospital. He therefore ordered the construction of a 1.8-meter wall, so as to "avoid contact between French and Japanese forces." Governor Decoux was incensed by this decision taken by a general with whom he frequently crossed swords. The governor general insisted that the wall be lower, on aesthetic grounds. If privacy were a concern, why not grow rose or blackberry bushes along the property line, he asked. In reality, between June 16 and June 24, 1942 Decoux had gone from advocating barbed wire to vegetation atop this lowered wall; one can deduce that political sensitivities crossed his mind in the interim.[47]

This conflict is certainly symptomatic of a larger trend. Under the guise of enforcing civic beauty and suburban hedge codes, Decoux no doubt sought to avoid provoking the Japanese. Mordant, who would later be contacted by a Gaullist agent, wished for his part to minimize Japanese espionage and maintain some autonomy.[48] In his memoirs, Mordant relates that he had ordered as early as 1941 that French bases should reinforce their perimeters, that "no entry" signs in Japanese should be placed around them, and that Japanese troops should be prohibited from so much as visiting French infantry installations. Decoux allegedly refused to do the same for the units under his control: the navy and the air force. Mordant hints repeatedly that he waged a constant struggle—presumably against Decoux as much as the Japanese—to interdict fraternization between French and Japanese forces. The tensions between the men culminated in June 1944, when Mordant offered his resignation to Governor Decoux at Dalat.[49]

It was in everyday affairs that Franco-Japanese coexistence seemed most strained. Thus in June 1942, a French soldier named Hinderschid scuffled with several Japanese soldiers near Dalat's Chic Shanghai Hotel. The drunken French serviceman had turned on his rickshaw driver, who apparently had failed to deliver him to his desired destination, one of the resort's several brothels. As Hinderschid publicly berated the rickshaw driver, several Vietnamese onlookers took the latter's side. The soldier tried to shoo them away. At this point, Japanese troops intervened to protect the Vietnamese bystanders, and forced the drunken French soldier to retreat into the hotel. Though no blows were exchanged, even the French gendarmerie seemed to acknowledge that that the Japanese had scored a public-relations coup, while the French experienced a public humiliation.[50]

Even when the tables were turned a few months later (December 1942), and a Japanese soldier caused a drunken scene, the fallout was arguably even less favorable for the French. In front of other patrons at Dalat's Truong-Xuân restaurant, the Japanese soldier had produced an "obscene mime while pronouncing the word 'French.'" The gendarmerie report could only applaud French soldiers for having kept their sangfroid.[51]

Another Dalat-related incident sheds light on the nature of the Franco-Japanese relationship. In September 1942, Decoux had been proud to report that all foreigners in Indochina were at once free and under his protection. He was, in other words, abiding by Vichy's putative neutrality.[52] The following month, Vichy even considered a British request to evacuate British captives in Thailand (where Japanese troops were present as of December 1941) to the relative safety of the "Indochinese highlands."[53] Nothing came of this. In fact, in November 1942, the Japanese asked that all "enemy foreigners"—mainly British citizens, and American and Canadian missionaries—present in Indochina be jailed in Jarai, a known malarial zone. The issue was a thorny one: these were purported enemies of Japan, not of Vichy France. Had Decoux given in on this matter, he would have relinquished a measure of French sovereignty, not to mention violated official neutrality. The Decoux administration negotiated, proposing instead that "enemy foreigners" be placed in secure, supervised areas at Dalat. Thereupon the Japanese counterproposed that the "enemy foreigners" be placed under direct Japanese guard in Phnom Penh. After considerable discussion, a compromise was reached, and some so-called enemy foreigners were placed under French supervision in Mytho, in the Mekong Delta. The case shows both how Dalat continued to be seen as a safe white preserve, and how French and Japanese negotiated in a truly delicate situation—with a major power imbalance and a de facto military occupation.[54]

Given the presence of Japanese troops in Indochina between 1941 and 1945, and the Decoux administration's economic accords with imperial Japan, it is hardly surprising that the French public equated the Decoux administration with Pétain's, and more important, Nazi Germany's occupation with Japan's. When examined carefully this second parallel proves messy. For one thing, Decoux's administration maintained considerable autonomy until March 1945, even while Japanese troops were present in all of Indochina. This situation was quite different from metropolitan France, which had been carved up in two zones, one Vichy-controlled, the other occupied outright, between 1940 and late 1942 (between 1942 and 1944, the Nazis were present in both zones). Chronologies, contexts, and degrees of agency all differed in subtle but important ways.

Immediately after the war, the binaries of collaboration versus resistance were similarly projected onto the Indochinese context. Again, the exercise proved imperfect. Decoux's administration had for all intents and purposes collaborated until March 9, 1945, when, attacked by Japan, it put up a brave though short fight. These skirmishes earned the accolades of some longtime Free French fighters, who were willing, for the time being, to turn a blind eye and glorify as "resistors" some of Indochina's diehard Pétainists who earned their resistance medals at the eleventh hour, with only months left in the war.[55] Only the French Resistance newspaper *Franc-Tireur* dared point out that Decoux and his consorts "who had [previously] handed Indochina over to Japan, now reinvented themselves as anti-Japanese, and no doubt, as 'Gaullist.' "[56]

Then again, the recent historiographical emphasis on "grey areas" in Vichy France might invite new, nuanced parallels. In dismissing the concept of collaboration between France and Japan in wartime Indochina, Philippe Franchini points to Decoux's efforts to counter Japanese propaganda and to fight Japanese spies. Yet we now know, thanks to the recent work of Simon Kitson, that Vichy likewise waged covert battles against Nazi spies in metropolitan France.[57] The present case, too, suggests that collaboration and suspicion could coexist, in a Southeast Asian context.

CONFLICT AND ACCOMMODATION WITH JAPAN

None of this is meant to detract from the gravity of the Japanese surprise attack of March 9, 1945 against all French forces in Indochina.[58] In the ensuing days and months, scores of French and Vietnamese soldiers, civilians, and administrators were killed, many tortured, many summarily executed after surrendering, and others still left to die in appalling conditions.[59] Historians have yet to agree on what precisely triggered the Japanese attack on French forces with whom they had previously cooperated, or why it occurred precisely when it did—though Ralph Smith has noted that the main Japanese hesitation over the bold move involved a possible adverse Soviet reaction.[60] There is a consensus, however, that the attack was well planned, and ruthlessly carried out. The purge left nearly no French people in administrative positions; French colonialism had been stopped in its tracks.[61]

Compared to their comrades in other parts of Indochina, French civilians in Dalat proved fortunate, for the most part. Three French eyewitness testimonies are particularly useful in reconstituting the chaotic state of affairs at Dalat between March and December 1945: those of Dominique Mourey (a student at the Lycée Yersin), Louis Salles (the principal of the same school), and an anonymous French woman, whose detailed diary is reproduced by Marius Borel. All three evoke the panic that spread over Dalat after the rapid Japanese takeover of March 9, 1945.

Several European witnesses share a revealing observation: shortly after the Japanese coup, their Vietnamese servants, including Vietnamese Catholics, left without notice, joining the anticolonial resistance.[62] At the same time, Vietnamese nurses at Dalat's hospital walked out and joined the swelling ranks of the insurgency.[63] According to David Marr, in the days after the Japanese coup, one hundred members of Decoux's youth leagues fused with thirty-two scouts and Viet-Minh party members at Dalat. Joining forces, they enrolled a thousand more members into the resistance in a matter of days.[64]

Decoux's legacy, that of youth leagues and of the cult of the Trung sisters, remained palpable between March and August 1945: stoking Vietnamese patriotism under Japanese auspices, the new authorities, like the old, promoted a host of politicized youth activities under the guise of camping, scoutlike movements, and musical and theatrical performances. Highlights included a lecture on the Trung sisters, and a play about the thirteenth-century Diên Hồng conference that had assembled Vietnamese sages in a bid to counter foreign domination.[65]

March 1945, perhaps even more than August of that year, proved the decisive turning point in Dalat. The situation was as explosive as it was complex: from March to August 1945, a new nationalist Vietnamese government collaborated with imperial Japan, the Viet-Minh sought to fight both the new government and the Japanese alike, and sparse French elements tried to regroup and survive the Japanese occupation.

Within days of the Japanese *coup de force,* the roughly five thousand French people remaining in Dalat were represented by a liaison office (the BFL or Bureau français de liaison), comprised of Lycée Yersin principal Louis Salles; architect Paul Veysseyre; the director of the Pasteur Institute, Dr. Henry Morin; and C. Brun-Buisson, head of the Cité Decoux.[66] The group communicated as best they could, mostly in English, with the Japanese. Very quickly, the screws were tightened on the French and foreign community. After initially considering Dalat one of the spots where French civilians could be grouped, the Japanese army reversed course, and ordered the departure of most French civilians to Saigon. Exceptions were made for religious orders, for essential services, and for some fifty foreigners, including the young Iphigénie-Catherine Shellshear. Shellshear was fortunate that the Japanese confused her Hellenic citizenship with the neutral "Helvète," (meaning Swiss) which allowed her and her family to be considered nonenemy Europeans. Only six hundred Europeans (six hundred "souls" Salles writes revealingly) remained in Dalat, half of them children.[67] On April 6, the Japanese authorities concentrated the remaining Europeans into two sites: with the exception of religious orders that were allowed to stay put (including the Couvent des Oiseaux boarding school), all French citizens were crammed into the Cité Decoux, all European foreigners from nations not at war with Japan into the Cité Bellevue.[68]

The Couvent des Oiseaux provides an interesting example of successful negotiation with the new occupiers, overcoming an uneven power relationship. On March 29, 1945, Father Céleste Nicolas wrote to the head of the Couvent des Oiseaux, warning her of an imminent Japanese demand that a list be drawn of the establishment's possessions and inhabitants. Nicolas, however, advocated rebuffing this request, by invoking the institution's ties to the Vatican. The strategy worked: on April 1, 1945, signs went up outside the Couvent des Oiseaux, pronouncing the site to be property of the Vatican, answering directly to Pius XII. Soon thereafter, the Japanese authorities affixed another placard, in Japanese, warning soldiers not to enter.[69]

Overall, then, Dalat's remaining French population endured a "softer" treatment than that of its compatriots elsewhere in the colony. A postwar inquiry, aimed at granting French inhabitants of Indochina the titles of "Resistor" and "Prisoner of War," calculated that across the colony 1,500 French civilians were interned in Japanese cells and another 2,500 in camps, while some 5,000 French military personnel were interned in cells or punitive camps. Treatment for these 9,000 was harsh indeed. Meanwhile another 19,000 French civilians and 7,000 military personnel were placed in assigned residences, barracks, or under house arrest.[70] Dalat's remaining French population fit into this latter category. Still, with Nazi genocide singed on Europe's collective consciousness, even the more lenient practice of perimeters and assigned residences was hastily lumped in with the creation of "ghettos." Amongst other ominous symbols, metropolitan French sources commented on the marking of European dwellings with special symbols.[71] The Nazi and Japanese occupations were conflated once more.

Several signs suggest that the new rulers of Indochina intended to appropriate for themselves some of Dalat's previous vocations, including its leisure and educational functions. In June 1945, they established a Japanese language school at the hill station, which trained some two hundred Vietnamese students.[72] All the while, they recruited widely for workers and auxiliaries.[73]

Certainly, Dalat's villas were rapidly seized. One testimony relates that in very short order the occupiers covered French villa name plaques with rising sun symbols.[74] At Dalat, the policy of assigned residences had left the posh French residential quarters vacant. The Japanese occupiers claimed the choicest villas for themselves, and Japanese officers commandeered the grand Palace Hotel for their headquarters.[75] Marius Borel, a self-described "old colonialist," recalls being placed in a delicate position as he crossed a Japanese officer in the halls of the Lang-Bian Palace Hotel:

> I found myself in the great hall of the Lang-Bian Palace Hotel, where I saw the Japanese officer who had [previously] come to requisition our cars at Dankia. He was leaving an office that gave onto the hall. He recognized me, and came to me with his hand outstretched. I could only return the gesture. This did not prevent a French observer from saying: "I would rather have spat in my hand than given it to him." That's easy to say when one has nothing to fear, but when one has a family and personal stakes, it is preferable in my opinion, to be polite.[76]

The power inversion was as palpable as it was complete.[77] In the span of a month, the hotel had been transformed from the preserve of French colonial high society into a site where the French were not merely on edge, but actually outsiders. The above passage also suggests that already in the thick of events, divisive issues of collaboration and resistance were raised in the small remaining French community.

The Japanese were also locked in a struggle with a rapidly emboldened Viet-Minh movement. In Dalat, a four-member Viet-Minh front committee was formed in May 1945. Within a month, however, its leaders, Nguyễn Huy Diễn and Nguyễn Thế Tính, had both been arrested by the Japanese, apparently following a denunciation.[78]

In the coming months, as Japan's defeat drew near, rumors and chaos spread: French settlers fretted that the Viet-Minh had poisoned French water supplies. Europeans were reduced to a handful of holdouts in Dalat; even there, they feared for their lives. Dominique Mourey, a young man at the time, recalled that "we had fallen from our status of white lords to a herd that got parked here and there in Dalat."[79] Or, as Bernard Fall put it succinctly, "The spell of French overlordship in Indochina was broken forever."[80]

THE AUGUST REVOLUTION

In early August 1945, yet another regime change seemed in the cards. A French source vividly, if floridly, described the last hours of the short-lived Viet Nam De Quoc government, born out of the March 1945 Japanese coup: "Faced with a decomposing state, lost before public opinion, [imperial delegate] Phan Ke Toai and his accomplices awaited only the opportune time to flee in a whirlwind of tablets and silk robes. In eight days, the government, the mandarins, the bourgeoisie, the nationalist parties, the pro-Japanese elites would vanish, snatched off the scene as if they had fallen through a trap door on a theater stage."[81]

Emperor Hirohito's announcement of Japan's surrender on August 15, 1945 would indeed trigger a remarkable chain of events in former French colonial Indochina. The vacuum left by the Japanese defeat and the collapse of Tran Trong Kim's pro-Japanese Vietnamese government paved the way for the Viet-Minh to seize power on August 19, to form a government on August 29, and for Ho Chi Minh to declare the Democratic Republic of Vietnam's (DRV) independence on September 2.

Local revolutionaries in the Dalat region wasted no time in acting. On August 23, 1945, youth movements took the lead of a revolt comprised of some ten thousand people, chanting "Down with imperialism"—an interesting equation of the Tran Trong Kim government with colonialism—and "Long live the Viet-Minh front!"[82] Some in the crowd were armed with weapons seized from the Japanese guard post at Liên Khang the previous day.[83] The group accepted the resignation of the short-lived governor Ung An, opened the prison gates, and raised the red flag with its single yellow star over the hill station.[84] Three days later, the old administration, born of the March 9, 1945 *coup de force,* was officially "leveled by the Viet-Minh." "Ardent posters" vaunting the Viet-Minh were affixed to Dalat's public buildings.[85]

In many parts of Vietnam, Ho Chi Minh's government swiftly replaced municipal authorities with its own. In some cases, breakaway elements of the Japanese army joined or cooperated with Viet-Minh forces.[86] In Hanoi, a French doctor described the situation as "total anarchy."[87] However, at Dalat, the Viet-Minh and the Japanese would continuously jockey for power. The remaining French in Dalat would be one of the objects of contention.

On August 18, according to one account, the BFL "begged" the defeated but still armed Japanese not to leave, and urged them to continue guarding them against emboldened Viet-Minh elements.[88] On August 28, 1945, the leader of Japanese forces in the hill station, Colonel Hatifuji, organized three-party talks. Around the table were ten Japanese officers, the four BFL members, and five representatives of Ho Chi Minh's new Vietnamese government.[89] The parties agreed on little, except for the need for direct French–Viet-Minh talks on September 1. There, the local representatives of the Vietnamese government informed the BFL of their need to install a DRV youth camp at the Cité Decoux; they then attempted to imprison the members of the French delegation in Dalat's naval barracks. By the next day, however, the Japanese had liberated the French.[90] And as an official history of the region recognizes, the Japanese, not the Viet-Minh, controlled the Pasteur Institute, the banks, the treasury, and the post office.[91] In Dalat, at least, the August Revolution was finding it difficult to take root, even after having successfully toppled the Tran Trong Kim regime.

Why was this? The outcome has to do in part with the localized nature of post-surrender Japanese responses; whereas elsewhere in Indochina Japanese forces lacked the authority or desire to take a stand—and in some cases Japanese "desert-ers" joined the Viet-Minh—in Dalat, conversely, the bulk of Hatifuji's forces took their August 1945 surrender convention to mean that they should actively support French interests.[92] The outcome also stems from Dalat's position in the highlands. As David Marr has shown, the August Revolution reached the central highlands somewhat tentatively. Marr implies that Viet-Minh officials proceeded cautiously in regions where ethnic Vietnamese were in the minority. Whereas administrations were often purged in other parts of Vietnam, in the highlands it seems some offi-cials from the short-lived pro-Japanese regime remained in place.[93] A French re-port noted that by October 1, 1945, most provinces, municipalities, and villages in Northern and Central Vietnam were effectively managed by "people's committees"; the one exception lay in the highlands, where such committees sometimes existed, but rarely wielded effective power.[94]

This is not to suggest that the Viet-Minh sat by idly in Dalat. On August 28, 1945, Hồ Nhã Tránh led a show of force to the city's Decoux-era stadium. He delivered a speech in which he declared the region officially won over to the August Revolu-tion. In the wake of this assembly, Hồ Nhã Tránh emerged as leader of the regional Viet-Minh committee.[95] Still, most of the town's institutions remained in Japanese hands. And the tide was about to turn further in favor of the Japanese.

On October 3, 1945, Japanese and Viet-Minh forces clashed violently in and around Dalat: flash points included the Institut Pasteur, the Banque d'Indochine, and the electrical plant.[96] The Viet-Minh later claimed to have killed some twenty-five Japanese soldiers in what was coming to resemble an all-out insurrection.[97] Do-minique Mourey, stepson of one of the BFL members, Dr. Morin, recalls that Japa-nese forces rescued French civilians on several occasions.[98] Even though they never controlled the besieged Palace Hotel or the Institut Pasteur, the Viet-Minh were managing to seize valuable infrastructures, setting up checkpoints on the railroad to Dalat, and cutting off electricity to Dalat's villas.[99]

After the series of firefights at the Pasteur Institute and the bank, Hatifuji assigned most remaining French people—with the exception of religious orders, whose safety the Viet-Minh guaranteed—to the Lang-Bian Palace on October 8, 1945.[100] The BFL would later claim that this decision was a French one, taken in the face of the alter-native: wearing armbands assigned to them by the Viet-Minh. Since agreeing to the armband scheme would imply recognizing Ho Chi Minh's government, the French allegedly refused them, which in turn led to the French being holed up at the Palace Hotel.[101] Regardless of the precise manner in which the French found themselves there, in the final months of 1945, the hotel was transformed into a "bunker" in which Japanese forces sheltered the former colonizers. Mourey remembers being handed an 1886 Lebel rifle to defend the hotel's main stairwell should the Viet-Minh strike.[102] Viet-Minh and Japanese elements continued to vie for control of the city until November 1945, when Japanese forces finally took the upper hand.[103]

Around November 10, 1945, Japanese units from Saigon (Saigon had been in Anglo-Indian hands since September) set out to reinforce their compatriots in Dalat. On their way to the hill station, they were ambushed by the Viet-Minh.[104] However, by November 15, the now-strengthened Japanese elements had managed to disband the Viet-Minh's Dalat police force, and to arrest a number of DRV officials. They also freed eighty-two "pro-French" Vietnamese imprisoned in Dalat's jail. The red flag, which had been raised in town every morning at 7:30, floated no longer.[105] Ho Chi Minh's government, never in complete control of Dalat to begin with, had been uprooted in a matter of days. The Japanese even oversaw the reelectrification of Dalat's European villas. An article in the *Journal de Saigon* noted with satisfaction that the French in Dalat had returned to their homes, and recovered their personal articles, which had been carefully stored by the Japanese. Notwithstanding a brief aside on the ransacking of villas by the Viet-Minh, the article seemed to applaud a return to the status quo ante.[106]

By December 1945, the new government in France observed that the former Japanese enemy "was ensuring and maintaining order in Dalat."[107] That same month, advance Allied elements reached the Dalat region, followed by General Leclerc himself in late January 1946. Sporadic combat between the mechanized French expeditionary force and remaining Viet-Minh fighters was reported between January 28 and 29, 1946.[108] Iphigénie-Catherine Shellshear remembers the "liberation" of the hill station as singularly anticlimactic, a far cry from the liberation of Paris she seemed to want reenacted in highland Indochina.[109] For her part, a sister at the Couvent des Oiseaux attributed quotation marks and no capital to Dalat's "liberation," marking a clear distancing from events in the metropole, or perhaps from divine liberation.[110] Indeed, one could genuinely ask from whom Dalat was being liberated, since the Japanese essentially handed over the keys to the city. Besides, to many Vietnamese, Leclerc's forces arrived as reconquerors intent on reimposing colonialism. As it happens, Dalat would experience nine more years of more or less direct colonial rule, until the events of 1954.

The fact that Dalat was taken by French forces is nonetheless significant. South of the sixteenth parallel, most cities saw the Japanese hand over their arms to the British, while north of the parallel, it was to the Chinese. Although a handful of Allied elements did reach Dalat prior to Leclerc, and the Japanese certainly toppled the local Viet-Minh on November 15-16, it was Leclerc who oversaw the formal transfer of power.

Dalat had been insulated from both the worst of the combat that raged across Indochina in 1945, and from the terrible famine that ravaged Northern Vietnam between February and May 1945.[111] Prior to March 9, 1945, the only major conventional clash reported around Dalat involved an Allied strafing of the locomotive that served the Lang-Bian.[112] A missionary referred to the resort as "an isle of peace, of serenity, even of joy" between 1940 and March 1945.[113] Yet the city's insulation soon revealed its limits. After the August Revolution, the DRV diverted Dalat's rice stocks, presumably north to Tonkin; food prices skyrocketed as a result.[114] Medical sources evoke outbreaks of bubonic plague and typhus in and around Dalat respectively. In 1946, the Viet-Minh in the areas surrounding Dalat would actually lose fighters to plague.[115] Malaria was on the rise in Dalat and elsewhere: the need for antimalarials in the colony was so acute that a Free French report from 1944 assigned top priority to secretly parachuting quinine to French in the colony.[116] By 1947, when French medical authorities again began registering disease rates, they treated 597 cases of malaria at Dalat (for a variety of reasons, not all patients infected with malaria would have sought treatment). The disease was disproportionately affecting Vietnamese and highland minority populations.[117] In 1948, plague claimed two lives within Dalat proper.[118] Despite the *Journal de Saigon*'s desire to turn the clock back to before the war, the situation in Dalat had fundamentally changed, be it in the realms of public health, institutions, or governance.

THE BFL'S CONTESTED LEGACY

In the political arena, the dizzying series of regime changes in 1945 had come full circle. As the French regained control, once again, metropolitan reference points of collaboration, resistance, and revenge were mapped onto Indochina. As early as November 1945, newspapers in Saigon proclaimed the upcoming purge of Pétainists from the French administration. Even more pressing in 1945 was the question of "collaboration" with the Japanese. Dalat's BFL therefore came under intense scrutiny. Had the BFL volunteered to negotiate with the Japanese? Had they assisted the enemy? Had French honor been compromised?

Between June and August 1946, former BFL members lobbied High Commissioner Georges Thierry d'Argenlieu to clear their names publicly.[119] This was part of an avalanche of requests received by the new French administration, ranging from postwar "maneuvers" to denunciations and settling of scores.[120] In this particular instance, the admiral relented, and on September 25, 1946 the *Journal de Saigon* duly reprinted a note from the high commissioner, expressing his "satisfaction" with former BFL members.[121]

The need for this statement is telling in itself. In a letter to the high commissioner dated June 1946, the former BFL members had outlined the many ways in which they had "saved, often in spite of themselves, the honor of our compatriots." Their correspondence betrays the fact that many Dalatois did not share this judgment. The June letter reveals the deep hostility of many Europeans at Dalat towards the BFL, which they plainly accused of collaboration with the enemy. Especially vexing to former BFL members was the fact that the new mayor of Dalat, Auger, had demanded the BFL's immediate resignation when he came to take office in December 1945. This summary dismissal only reinforced the perception that the BFL was being punished for "collaboration"—which it no doubt was. The BFL, in turn, accused its critics (denouncing them by name) of "venomous" and "backhanded" attacks, motivated by a host of factors ranging from jealousy to personal animosity. They mounted a strenuous defense, pointing out, correctly, that Europeans in Dalat had received far better treatment from the Japanese than their compatriots elsewhere in Indochina.[122] To the Free French Admiral Georges Thierry d'Argenlieu, cool to say the least towards an organization seeking to rehabilitate Decoux in Indochina, this must have seemed eerily reminiscent of Pétain and Laval's justification for collaborating with Germany.[123] Ultimately, beyond the grey zones between accommodation and collaboration, this episode reveals mostly the deep fissures left by the war in Dalat.

EPILOGUE

In June 1946, those French civilians, officials, military personnel, and their families who had spent at least six years in Indochina prepared to return home. In light of their hardships under the Japanese occupation, the Red Cross thought it wise to take them to rest centers in Dalat, Nha-Trang and Cap Saint-Jacques before their repatriation to France.[124] In some ways, this was business as usual. Dalat had served as a French safe space even at the height of the Japanese occupation, and it now resumed its role as a convalescence center. However, in many other respects the war had fundamentally altered colonial equations. The Japanese presence, the pro-Japanese national government, and the Democratic Republic of Vietnam had profoundly shifted the power dynamics in all of Indochina. Already compromised, the French community was now deeply split by divisive issues of collaboration and resistance, nowhere more evident than in the judgment of the Bureau français de liaison de Dalat. As colonialism in Indochina reached a crisis point, Dalat's position had become strategically more critical than ever. Weakened on all sides, colonial officials plotted to make tranquil, bucolic Dalat into Indochina's capital.

Autonomous Province or Federal Capital?

Historians have largely ignored the process by which Indochina's capital city was chosen.[1] No doubt the question has escaped attention because it has always seemed self-evident: Hanoi went from serving as Indochina's capital prior to 1945, to serving as the Democratic Republic of Vietnam's capital thereafter. To be sure, it is common knowledge that the relationship between two of the region's dominant cities, Saigon and Hanoi, had been strained by rivalry long before Vietnam's partition in 1954. In 1907, the colonial press likened French colonials in Saigon to the inconsolable Calypso after Ulysses' departure: Saigon's French population could not accept the transfer of government to Hanoi some years earlier. There was even mention then of shifting the capital to a more neutral, geographically central location, like Hué, the former seat of imperial Vietnamese power.[2] Nothing came of this, no doubt because such a move could have stoked anticolonial royalist sentiment. To most observers, then, Hanoi remained the only viable option for a capital city until Vietnam's partition in 1954.

However sound this received wisdom might be with respect to the three constituent parts of Vietnam (Tonkin, Annam, Cochinchina), it neglects that Indochina was a federation encompassing not only the three entities that comprised Vietnam, but also Laos and Cambodia. When one considers the impact of powerful and plural colonial-era federalist currents so sharply identified by Christopher Goscha, the question of capitals takes on new meaning. After 1931, Goscha argues, a host of groups, including a variety of nationalists, Communists, and French colonial officials, embraced a federalist vision of Indochina, which served in some cases as a counterweight, and in other instances as a buttress, to national solutions.[3]

Federalism usually implies a new, neutral, seat of government. For a decade between 1937 and 1947, Dalat emerged as the leading candidate for Indochina's. This protean plan, embraced by certain colonial sectors as of 1937, and then briefly pressed into service in the aftermath of the August 1945 Revolution, called for Dalat to serve as federal capital for all of Indochina, relegating Hanoi to the role of Tonkin's administrative center.

The plan to make remote Dalat a capital sheds light on a concrete federalist alternative, on colonial adaptation strategies, and on questions of pluralism, identities, boundaries, space, and territoriality as they sprang out of the cracks and fissures of the 1930s and 1940s. Analyzing the scheme also allows us to reestablish the profound interconnection of three thematic strands that historians have tended to considerer in isolation: federalism, triangular Vietnamese-minority-French relations, and the decolonization process.

TERRITORIAL AMBIGUITIES

Though the hill station of Dalat may have been a French creation, it nevertheless lay clearly within the borders of Annam—"clearly" at least on maps drawn up by the time of the First World War. Although fully recognizing, and often instrumentalizing the ethnic, religious, and cultural distinctiveness of the highlands, French officials paradoxically justified their own claims over the region by pointing to ancient tributary ties between highland minorities of the south-central highlands and the court in Hué.[4] By tying the highlands to Annam, colonial officials appropriated existing tributary relationships, thereby successfully factoring themselves into a regional equation.[5]

In spite of these seemingly coherent colonial aims, the actual process by which the south-central highlands became tied to Annam had been particularly messy, even haphazard. Darlac, Pleiku, and Kontum provinces had initially been linked to Laos in 1895, only to be shifted to Annam's control thereafter. Darlac was tied to Annam by decree in 1904, Pleiku in 1905, and Kontum in 1913. Oscar Salemink suggests that these many realignments stemmed from military imperatives: connecting these highland areas to Annam guaranteed faster French military intervention in the event of unrest.[6] But even these measures remained ambiguous. As late as 1920, the Résident supérieur d'Annam asserted that Darlac province around Dalat was still "politically" tied to Laos, despite the 1904 decree.[7]

This hedging of colonial bets is better understood if one considers that situating the highlands under Annam's jurisdiction presented potential pitfalls of its own for colonial rule. On paper, at least, by virtue of the treaties of 1874 and 1884, the empire of Annam maintained some measure of autonomy from France in matters of governance and sovereignty.[8] Where did this leave the south-central highlands? At times, the strategy of tying the southern highlands to Hué so as to cement French control over them seemed to backfire. In 1942, Tran Chanh Thanh used unrelenting logic to turn the French position on its head.[9] If the south-central highlands were under Annam's sovereignty rather than that of Laos, it followed that indigenous highlanders were *protégés français* and in fact nationals of Annam. Tracing Hué's historical influence over the highlands back to the seventeenth century, Tran Chanh Thanh asserted Annam's historical claim over the area, all the while referencing French legal and historical sources to make his case.[10]

The contested and at times hazy status of the south-central highlands was also reflected in cultural terms. Goscha cites the Vietnamese novelist Nguyen Tien Lang writing of the area in 1935: "It's Annam, but it's not Annam. I don't know quite how to explain it. One doesn't quite feel Annamese in the Highlands."[11] The south-central highlands, it seemed, exercised a powerful capacity for identity-blurring: French and Vietnamese alike felt at once at home and alien in these mountain ranges.

LANG-BIAN PROVINCE

In 1899, Dalat had been incorporated into the Upper Donnaï province along with several other towns, but that administrative unit dissolved only a few years later. Subsequently, Djiring was temporarily connected to Phan-Thiet and Dalat to Phan-Rang. Here was a clear effort to link the coasts with the minority hinterlands.[12] However, in 1915, as Dalat's development surged, colonial authorities abruptly changed strategies, and rushed to create a new inland province for Dalat, now dubbed Indochina's future sanatorium or health center. The need for this change was threefold, explained the French Résident supérieur in Hué to the members of the protectorate of Annam's council, assembled in November 1915. Expediency demanded that different provinces on the road to Dalat be merged, lest local interests stall the resort's development. Thrift mandated that monies be concentrated in a single budget, in this new "autonomous" province. And most important, in the words of the French Résident, the new province promised to bring together for the first time "all Moïs under a single authority, thereby facilitating the penetration of our influence over them."[13]

The reform was ultimately approved and signed by Governor Ernest Roume in January 1916. The province, with Dalat as its capital, absorbed both the existing Djiring district, as well as the "Moï populated" areas previously belonging to the province of Phanrang. Beyond its obvious implications for Dalat, the reform profoundly shifted relations between French, Vietnamese, and highland minorities of the south-central highlands. The Lang-Bian was henceforth an "autonomous province" within the empire of Annam. By undoing their previous reforms and dividing the previous Phanrang district into two parts, one populated predominantly by highland minorities, the other by Vietnamese, colonial authorities had sought to achieve several goals: diminish perceived Vietnamese domination over highland minorities, position themselves as arbiters in conflicts between the two groups, and distance the new province entirely from ethnic Vietnamese political control.

The Lang-Bian's 1915 boundaries proved short-lived. By 1920, Annam had re-

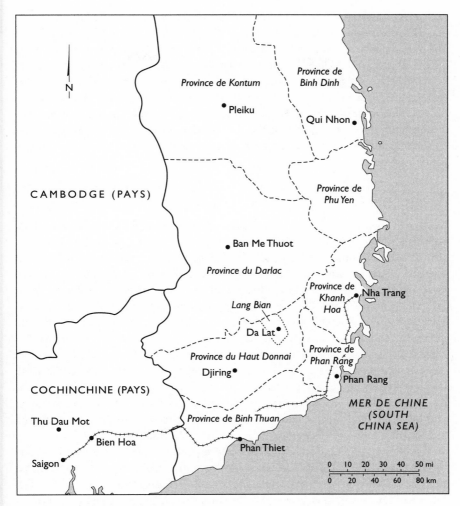

N

Province de Kontum

Province de
Binh Dinh

• Pleiku

Qui Nhon •

CAMBODGE (PAYS)

Province de
Phu Yen

• Ban Me Thuot

Province du Darlac

Province de
Khanh
Hoa

• Nha Trang

Lang Bian

Da Lat •

Province du Haut Donnai

Province de
Phan Rang

Djiring •

• Phan Rang

COCHINCHINE (PAYS)

MER DE CHINE
(SOUTH
CHINA SEA)

Thu Dau Mot
•

Province de Binh Thuan

Bien Hoa

Phan Thiet

Saigon •

0	10	20	30	40	50 mi
0	20		40	60	80 km

MAP 7. Dalat and the Lang-Bian autonomous district within Upper Donnaï province, 1928. Map by William Nelson, based on a map from *L'Atlas de l'Indochine,* Hanoi: Imprimerie d'Extrême Orient, 1928.

claimed control over parts of the area. Indeed, by royal ordinance of October 11, 1920, the Lang-Bian was redefined as an "autonomous circumscription," rather than a full-fledged province. In this new schema, Dalat was reconceived as the capital of a resolutely French Lang-Bian enclave (roughly 10 km in diameter around Dalat) within a broader Haut-Donnaï province.[14] French control may have been exerted over a smaller zone, but this zone was more than ever excised from Annam.[15]

Thus, whatever victory the crown in Hué might have scored over outlying areas, it certainly lost the crucial battle over the hill station itself. A 1923 law placed both the municipality of Dalat and the broader autonomous circumscription under the direct control of the Direction des services de la station d'altitude de Dalat et du tourisme dans la région du Lang-Bian, which was to receive its orders from the governor general. As a net result of these reforms, Dalat lay more clearly than ever outside of the empire of Annam's scope.[16] These many shifts speak not merely to a lack of constancy in colonial planning; they point also to the ongoing recasting of issues of sovereignty and control within a complex framework of protectorates, colonies, and kingdoms.

A FEDERAL CAPITAL

We saw in chapter 4 that even in its earliest days Dalat featured a Cambodian-style *sala*. Cochinchina, another of Indochina's constituent parts, was also leaving its imprint on the hill station. One of Dalat's early villas belonged to the city of Saigon. It even bore an ostentatious red "S" on its roof tiles to remove any doubt as to its ownership.[17] Soon, a Dalat street bore the title Rue des Saigonnais. Furthermore, Cambodian, Tonkinois, and Laotian elites and administrators, not to mention Vietnamese emperor Bao Dai, and increasingly in the late 1930s and 1940s the French governor generals, likewise made Dalat their home away from home. Dalat, in other words, was gradually emerging as a pan-Indochinese space.

None of this was lost on those who argued for Dalat to serve as federal capital: they pointed to Emperor Bao Dai's penchant for the site, its long-standing role as de facto summer capital for governors, its modern access routes overland to Saigon and by rail to Hanoi and Saigon, the hill station's thriving administrative district and existing centers of power, to name only a few factors.[18]

It is difficult to pinpoint the project's precise genesis. Certainly, as Caroline Herbelin has noted, the idea of creating an administrative capital at Dalat can be traced to some of the earliest writings on the hill station, including those of Governor Paul Doumer.[19] However, in large part because of delays in Dalat's rail link, the project remained dormant until the 1920s. It resurfaced in 1923 in the pages of *L'Eveil économique de l'Indochine*. "Settled in Dalat" the journal observed, "The Government General would be less prone to excessive centralization."[20] Emulation of the British model played an important role in shaping Dalat's capital vocation. A 1925 French-language article from Dalat basked in Governor Alexandre Varenne's recent visit, noting that "[The Governor General] observed that Dalat would become the summer capital of Indochina in the same way as Simla in India serves as summer capital for the British."[21] In September 1928, Governor René Robin called for Dalat to become "not merely Indochina's sanatorium, but also Indochina's administrative capital."[22] At this pre-1937 juncture, however, discussions focused on "summer" or "administrative" centers, rather than upon Dalat as a "federal" capital.

One article suggests that the idea of making Dalat "the capital of the Indochinese Federation" was born with the arrival of Governor Jules Brévié in 1937.[23] Brévié, named by the left-wing metropolitan Popular Front government in 1936, did have a mandate for reform, although outside of some prominent prisoner releases and the relaxing of press censorship, he failed to deliver on the hopes pinned on the Popular Front in Indochina.[24] Still, the notion of making Dalat a federal capital seems in keeping with a certain reformist spirit, and certainly would have broken with the rigid policies of harder-line governors.

As they had when they first selected Dalat as a hill station, French technocrats carefully considered the experiences of other empires and countries with respect to federal capitals. Most studies on the matter refer to the examples of Canberra, Washington, New Delhi, and Ottawa. Pineau, for instance, writes: "We have seen . . . in the cases of Washington and Canberra that federal states require—in fact more than other states—a centrally positioned capital city."[25]

Like these other federal cities at their birth, Dalat offered a fresh start. Unlike existing centers of indigenous power, be they Saigon, Hanoi, or Phnom Penh, Dalat could claim a measure of strategic and geographical neutrality. Dalat's leading planner, the influential architect Louis Georges Pineau, made this clear in his important 1937 article promoting Dalat as "capital of the Indochinese Union," an article which launched the debate in earnest.[26] The architect, who had tellingly first trained at the Ecole libre des sciences politiques (as Sciences Po was then known), ran through a long list of practical factors: the speed of modern communications made the selection of Dalat possible, while the hill station's "central location" made it the "necessary" choice. Here, Pineau invoked the examples of Canberra and Washington, to show how functioning federal capitals necessarily occupied negotiated spaces.[27]

Pineau then touched upon a point crucial to colonial federalist thinking. Citing Governor General Varenne's September 1926 speech, he insisted that Vietnamese lands "are not all of Indochina" and that "next to the Annamites, there are other races and other peoples on this vast region, peoples to whom we have promised protection." Dalat, he reasoned, would bring the colonial administration closer to "three of them."[28] Which three? Laotians and Cambodians accounted for two, as established constituent ethnicities of Indochina. The third, significantly, were the local highland minorities, whom colonial authorities increasingly viewed as a single entity or "race." This was a recent typology, the "ethnicization" and homogenization of the montagnards into one of Indochina's constituent "races" having begun only in the 1930s, according to Salemink.[29]

What kind of federalism was this? Federalism tends to convey heady idealism, pluralism, and equality. As Goscha has shown, Indochina from 1930 to 1954 witnessed competing federal projects, some of which were quite remote from these values. Dalat, it seems, was at the heart of a French colonial federalist vision, while it enjoyed less popularity, understandably, in Vietnamese circles, especially revolutionary ones. The attempt to craft Dalat into a capital needs to be understood in these terms. As Goscha notes, Indochinese federalism still had something "artificial" about it.[30]

The discussion over moving the capital to Dalat was anything but abstract. Highly technical aspects of relocation were discussed at length. Thus in May 1937, *L'Avenir du Tonkin* pondered whether it would be best to create a single, massive government building in Dalat, so as to facilitate communications and contacts between different layers of the federal administration in its new mountain setting. The Hanoi newspaper gave the example of Algiers, where such a single-edifice model had been adopted.[31] Federalists were thinking in both practical and grand terms.

It was, in fact, under Decoux that the Dalat capital project received the governor general's blessing. Decoux's memoirs—silent on some issues, like his anti-Gaullist, antimasonic, and antisemitic measures, or his violent quelling of uprisings—accord significant attention to his vision for Dalat. They explain that "the new urban plan for Dalat called for the government general to move there. With this goal in mind, I ordered the construction of villas for leading officials, and the construction of a building for Indochina's geographical services." Decoux also identified Dalat's main asset: the town was a "strictly French creation."[32] In 1939, Georges Pineau had raised another motive, which Decoux might not have dared mention: Dalat would make a "more central and safer capital" than Hanoi.[33]

POSTWAR PLANS

After August 1945, both the Viet-Minh and General de Gaulle's expeditionary force sent to reconquer Indochina set their sights on Dalat. As they did so, each side pondered and primed both their federalist and their minority policies. In April 1946, the Viet-Minh organized an important congress of southern minority groups in Pleiku. The Viet-Minh was orienting itself as a multiethnic organization, although as Goscha has shown, Ho Chi Minh's party was tapping into both nationalist and federalist registers, envisioning a multistate federation of its own.[34]

Meanwhile, in 1944, at a time when the Free French exerted no control over the region, de Gaulle's Fighting French considered these same issues. De Gaulle's Indochina hand, Léon Pignon, promoted a pan-Indochinese federalist ideal featuring greater autonomy for Indochina's various parts.[35] Even as General Leclerc's reconquest mission was taking shape, Gaullist officials spilled a surprising amount of ink on montagnard issues. A dossier in the French foreign ministry files sheds new light on aggressive French contingency plans for the south-central highlands in 1945–46. In a December 1945 brief to the newly named Commissaire général to Indochina,

Admiral Georges Thierry d'Argenlieu, General Alphonse Juin wrote: "In law, and in fact, nothing prevents France from asserting its full sovereignty over the Moï lands." Juin, fresh off his Second World War victories in North Africa, at Monte Casino, and in Provence, offered a wide-ranging justification. He first invoked history: the Vietnamese had little knowledge of the highlands prior to the French conquest. Next, he turned to geography, pronouncing the decision to link the highlands to Annam rather than Laos or Cambodia to have been "arbitrary." He next turned to racial theory: "The Moïs are still at a very backwards stage of civilization." He played on antagonisms, and even alleged "cultural genocide" *avant la lettre,* contending that "the Moï race exists, distinct from those that neighbor it and plot its extermination." Juin's conclusion was unambiguous: "If large autonomy must be granted to the different lands that currently constitute the Indochinese Union, it would be unwise to place the Moï races or the Tonkinois highlanders under their authority."[36] The south-central highlands, in other words, ought to be considered a separate *pays,* under direct French "protection." This idea had already been floated in 1939 under Governor Catroux, but had been scuttled because of opposition from the Résidence supérieur d'Annam.[37] This time, as part of a grand reform imagined after the war, the plan was carried out. In March 1946, as negotiations were taking place with the Viet-Minh and Chinese occupying forces in the North, Paris cabled d'Argenlieu asking that he consider "the creation of an autonomous Moï territory, before the establishment of the final statutes defining the Indochinese federation."[38]

Dalat, as aspiring federal capital and existing regional capital, had been thrust into the limelight. Leclerc's armored forces had just taken it in January 1946. Fierce fighting continued in the highlands well after the March 1946 agreement between France and Vietnam. Pleiku was leveled in July 1946. The fighting, in turn, provided the justification for d'Argenlieu to establish "a Federal Commissariat for Southern Montagnard populations."[39] French authorities were following through on the idea of making the inhabitants of the southern highlands a party on equal footing with Laos, Cochinchina, Cambodia, and Vietnam, at any future talks. Historians have duly noted how d'Argenlieu promoted the concept of Vietnam as a "free state" within an Indochinese federation, itself part of a *union française;* conversely, the plan to create a countervailing montagnard state at this same time seems to have gone largely unnoticed.[40]

French officials set about recasting Indochina into a federal mold in 1945 and then more concretely in early 1946. Stein Tønnesson has shown how Charles de Gaulle's March 24, 1945 declaration on the future of Indochina set a federalist tone. By the following year, de Gaulle's nominee for high commissionner, Georges Thierry d'Argenlieu, would prove deeply attached to this concept of a "pentagonal federation."[41] In many ways, Daniel Hémery has argued, this postwar federalism rekindled the spirit of colonial reform from the 1930s.[42]

Figuring prominently among the elements retained from the 1930s was the idea of Dalat as federal capital. Starting in February 1946, several French legal experts and colonial specialists feverishly worked out constitutional texts for the new federation.[43] They drew inspiration from other federal models, including the United States.[44] Roger Pinto's relatively "liberal" constitutional project extended full French civic and individual rights to all of Indochina, and advocated a dual-chamber system of representation. In turn, René Morizon's constitutional blueprint called for Dalat to play the role of federal capital, and for French to serve as the federation's official language. That neither evoked a future montagnard zone (Morizon's scheme did involve ethnic minority delegates) suggests that this was Admiral d'Argenlieu's agenda, no doubt inspired in part by Juin's report.[45]

THE DALAT CONFERENCE 1: APRIL 1946

Specialists on international relations, Vietnam, and decolonization alike have examined in some detail the two Dalat preparatory conferences of April and August 1946. As they have noted, Ho Chi Minh was highly skeptical of the two conferences d'Argenlieu planned at Dalat, first between France and Vietnam in April, then between France and different parties of a putative Indochinese federation in August. The Vietnamese Communist Party considered both meetings to be diversions plotted by d'Argenlieu, ways of reneging on a March 6, 1946 commitment to hold future talks in either Hanoi, Saigon, or Paris.[46] Given the intractable expectations of both sides, Stein Tønnesson has deemed the conference "doomed almost from the outset."[47] What concerns us here, however, are the places of federalism and of Dalat itself at these summits. Rather than constituting a subplot, I see the conference's venue and the issue of federalism as the main interconnected dramas unfolding in these negotiations.

In March 1946, with Northern Indochina still occupied by Chinese forces, as Leclerc prepared to enter Hanoi (he did so on March 18), French authorities strategized about where precisely to hold direct talks with Ho Chi Minh on the future of Vietnam. On March 8, only two days after hammering out a tentative deal, which had listed Paris, Saigon, and Hanoi as the sites of future negotiations, d'Argenlieu cabled Paris: "I deem . . . Dalat to be the most favorable location for a conference . . . Dalat is neither in Cochinchina (which is the target of a referendum) nor in Tonkin proper. The conference will consequently be able to take place in a calm and serene atmosphere."[48] As Philippe Devillers has suggested, d'Argenlieu had thereby, for all intents and purposes, asked Paris to order him to hold the conference in Dalat.[49] On March 29, Georges Bidault cooperated, seeing only two possible alternatives: delaying the conference until Chinese troops had finally left Indochinese soil or "locating the talks in Dalat, far from the current unrest."[50] On March 12, d'Argenlieu offered the frankest reason of all for choosing Dalat: the city was destined to become Indochina's federal capital.[51] He apparently did not hide this motive from his interlocutors in Hanoi. General Vo Nguyen Giap recalls that on March 24, aboard a French war vessel in Ha-Long Bay, d'Argenlieu had explained to Ho Chi Minh that Dalat would make a fine site for a conference since it was destined to serve as Indochina's federal capital.[52] Ho Chi Minh resisted.[53] With none of these arguments working, d'Argenlieu finally played on personal relations to persuade a skeptical Ho Chi Minh: in a letter, he explained that he had been ordered to take a cure at Dalat on doctor's orders (pretexts can also double as truths; d'Argenlieu's doctor story is likely, given how many officials were sent to Dalat with medical referrals).[54] In the spirit of friendship, and for the sake of his own health, d'Argenlieu bade the Vietnamese head of to state join him at the health resort. Clearly, the French high commissioner had invested considerable energy and diplomacy into making Dalat the venue for the summit.

Place mattered. Here Dalat's functions as a health center meshed with its role as a colonial bastion and a federalist symbol. To summarize the various arguments marshaled in favor of Dalat: it was deemed to offer France its best chance because of its projected role as federal capital, because it was considered far removed from current turmoil, and because it occupied a key location outside of contested Cochinchina (yet it was close enough to Cochinchina, historically and geographically, to please the French), while sitting at the federation's crossroads. No doubt French officials were also leaning on fifty years of history, and on Dalat's reputation as a miniature France in highland Indochina, a closed, private colonial retreat, a place that would favor them in direct negotiations. Indeed General Raoul Salan, a French military delegate at the Dalat conference recalls a Dutch Indonesian official nodding his approval at the site of the conference. "Dalat, far from the sound of combat and of human excitement, is located in a charming site, it is a beautiful French accomplishment," reportedly stated this Dutch official, whose own empire was in its death throes.[55]

In reality, conditions were far from propitious for negotiating. A Viet-Minh document reveals the party's main motivation for participating in the talks as follows: "(1) Maintain our strength intact, while outfoxing the ruses of the white Chinese, the French fascists, and the traitors; (2) Allow us to gain time to rest and prepare for the next struggle for total independence, in which all the population will participate."[56] Vexing protocol issues ultimately kept Ho Chi Minh away from the conference. He had asked to stay at Emperor Bao Dai's villa, interestingly assuming the mantle of imperial Nguyen continuity in the process; when d'Argenlieu responded that he would instead be the admiral's guest at the newly renamed "federal Palace," Ho Chi Minh declined.[57] French trust was just as low, if not lower still. In a memorandum leading up to the conference, d'Argenlieu likened the Vietnamese delegation's arguments about the linguistic unity of Vietnam to Hitler's justification for Grossdeutschland, one of many allusions to Nazism that lace the record on both sides, and remind us of the ubiquity of the Second World War as a referent in the

Indochinese conflict.[58] As for the detailed biographies prepared by French services on the different members of the Vietnamese delegation, these reveal complete consternation. How, they ask time and again, had affluent, elite, francophilic, French-married, French-educated men (Trinh Van Binh, for instance, was a graduate of the École des hautes études commerciales), in some cases French military veterans, turned anti-French?[59] Of the conference delegates, only Giap seems to have been credited with lofty ideals; most of his peers were branded opportunists. Fingered for particular attention was Dr. Pham Ngoc Thach, for his role as founder of the avant-garde youth movements in March 1945.

On the question of minority groups, the French delegation put forward General Juin's earlier scheme to divide montagnards into three main categories. For the inhabitants of the south-central highlands, the plan called for "the creation of an autonomous territory, tied to the Indochinese federation directly." Since the French high commissioner was to serve as the federation's president (as was in fact decided at Dalat 2), this was tantamount to placing the "autonomous" central highlands under direct French authority.[60] The Vietnamese delegation rejected these measures out of hand, arguing that the question of minorities was not even on the table. Even if it were, Giap contended, the Viet-Minh had "been the first to stand as defenders of ethnic minorities," and this long before Vietnam's declaration of independence in 1945. Minority rights, Giap continued, were a concern of his government; only they were a matter of state sovereignty, not a federal issue.[61]

Irreconcilable differences of opinion also arose on the broader conception of federalism. A Vietnamese counterproposal dated May 10 suggested that the new federal council's purview be limited to currency levels and customs policy. Georges Gayet, a member of the French negotiating team, scribbled perplexedly in the margins that federal laws, finances, budgets, and communications had all fallen off the table.[62] The French delegation went to great length to persuade Hanoi that its federal model was benign, and that the French Union's relations with the various parts of Indochina would be harmonious. Pierre Messmer even suggested that the French Union could be compared to the Soviet Union's brand of federalism, no doubt seeking to score points with the Viet-Minh.[63] The Vietnamese representatives remained unconvinced.

However, the Vietnamese delegation seems not to have directly challenged the French project of making Dalat a federal capital, though the importance, nature, and mandate of the federal government itself remained hotly contested. The following clause slipped in by the French delegation appears not to have met special opposition: "through its geographical situation, Dalat seems particularly well placed to become a capital. In order to ensure connections with the outside . . . the federal territory will span the Lang-Bian Plateau, and include an access to the sea between Phanrang and Nhatrang."[64] Here the buffer zone around Dalat, inherited from earlier colonial schemes, actually extended as far as the ocean.

Overall, the April 1946 Dalat conference proved a failure by any standards.[65] Dr. Thach was arrested and jailed for the duration of the talks. On the main issues before the delegates, the verdict was equally grim. The major stumbling block had involved federalism and of course the status of Nam-Bo, which the French still called Cochinchina. From the French standpoint, "the conception of Viet-Nam at the conference differed from France's insofar as [Viet-Nam] sought to neutralize, if not outright eliminate, all federal authority." Internal fractures also came to light. Within the French ranks, rifts had formed between metropolitan delegates on the one hand, and d'Argenlieu on the other. The former favored a "flexible federalism based on economics and finances, likelier to be palatable to the other party" and the latter a much harder line, reminiscent, by the Quai d'Orsay's own reckoning, of the colonial-era government general.[66] Here, two very different conceptions of federalism clashed. These tensions set the stage for a second Dalat conference focusing entirely on the issue of federalism.

If the two delegations saw any silver lining to the April 1946 talks, it involved the setting. The delegates were lodged at the Dalat Palace Hotel, their associates at the Hôtel du Parc. French and Vietnamese flags floated above the two buildings. Sessions took place at the Lycée Yersin and the Hôtel du Parc.[67] A French conference summary lauded the "cordial atmosphere," which it attributed to the delegates sharing the same hotel and dining around the same tables. Among leading delegates, the less formal revolutionary "*tu*" supplanted the more formal "*vous*."[68] D'Argenlieu even invited Giap to hike with him on a break from the conference.[69] Interestingly, Giap reached a similar conclusion as the French report—at least with respect to the conference's setting. With hindsight, the general wrote wistfully about the Lake of Sighs, the accommodations at the Dalat Palace Hotel, and the Lycée Yersin conference site. For all of his contempt for the French delegation, and despite his realization that Dalat was a colonial creation and instrument of power ("Dalat was a health resort, a tourist city reserved for the French and the Vietnamese belonging to the so-called 'upper classes'") he could not help but profess his love for the bourgeois leisure site.[70] He heaped praise on its every turn, pine tree, villa, river, and boulevard. "Magnificent" and "beautiful" Dalat beguiled the revolutionary.[71] Yet the unstated French aim of leveraging this setting into favorable results had failed dismally.

THE DALAT CONFERENCE 2: AUGUST 1946

Dalat's discrete charms would be enrolled once again at the August conference, where a federalist system would be elaborated, complete with a federal capital.[72] Historians have tended to view the pan-Indochinese second Dalat conference of August as a diversion orchestrated by d'Argenlieu, aimed at sinking the direct Democratic Republic of Vietnam (DRV)-French negotiations that had been taking place at Fontainebleau since July 6. In this reading, the admiral's salvo was aimed as much at Paris as at Hanoi. Such was their surprise, in fact, that Parisian government officials found out about the plans for this second Dalat conference from Ho Chi Minh, rather than from their high commissioner in Saigon.[73] The strategy certainly worked; it prompted the Vietnamese delegation at Fontainebleau to suspend the talks in protest. However, viewing Dalat 2 as a mere stratagem misses an important point. Here was a final attempt at forging an Indochinese federation—albeit an explicitly anti-DRV one—comprised of different ethnicities and states, a bona fide alternative to the nationalist framework.

D'Argenlieu carefully prepared the ground for Dalat 2. Days before the conference was convened on August 1, 1946, French delegates met behind closed doors to reach a common position on the question of federalism. This proved challenging. One member underscored the DRV's hostility to the Indochinese federation. He explained: "The Government of Vietnam fears, and I understand this fear to some extent, that the Indochinese federation is in reality little more than the reincarnation of the colonial Gouvernement Général de l'Indochine."[74] As discussion turned to an autonomous Cochinchina and an autonomous highland zone, tensions flared, with some condemning the admiral for "duplicity" and "hypocrisy," sensing that d'Argenlieu had used federalism as a ploy to scuttle any chance of negotiations with Hanoi.[75]

Once it opened, the conference had a very different flavor without the DRV present. For example, Cochinchinese delegate Colonel Nguyen Van Xuan exhorted the federation to adopt a business model.[76] Yet Hanoi was still on everyone's minds. So important was it to distinguish the constituent states of the Dalat 2 federation from the Democratic Republic of Vietnam, that one Cochinchina representative, Nguyen Thanh Giung, stated that "at the second tier of teaching . . . the French language will be replaced by the Cochinchinese language," in effect classifying Southern Vietnamese as a separate tongue.[77]

The delegations themselves shared very little in common with those of Dalat 1: even the French team had been completely disbanded, and was made up this time primarily of local administrators. The list and composition of the other delegations shed light on the balance of power imagined by d'Argenlieu: Cambodia, Cochinchina, and Laos were all present as *pays*. So too were the "Montagnard peoples of South-Annam" represented by Ma Krong and Djac Ayun (a medical assistant), and the Chams, represented by the mandarin Luu Ai.[78]

On August 4, the minority delegates expressed the following wish: "Our main goal is to unite in a single unit all of the people who wear loincloths: the Rhadés, the Bahnards, the Sedang, the Jarai, the Khô, the Kau, and so on. In other words, the provinces of Darlac, Pleiku, Kontum, Lang-Bian, and Upper-Donnaï must be protected directly by France."[79] Two days later, a follow-up motion elaborated: "our goal is national unity under the direction of France," adding that three thousand montagnards now served in French armies."[80] The message was unambiguous: an autonomous highlander country and force were poised to counter DRV influence, and play a key role in a non-Communist federation of Indochinese peoples.[81]

After eight days of discussions, the delegations announced their top three resolutions: "(1) The capital of the Indochinese federation will be Dalat; (2) The city of Dalat will be surrounded by a federal territory, (3) French will serve as the official language of the Indochinese federation."[82] With the DRV out of the picture, Dalat had been chosen by consensus. Its proximity to all the zones and peoples defined at Dalat 2 made it a unanimous choice. The concept of a federal territory around the capital borrowed from outside examples (Washington's District of Columbia comes to mind), but also from the legacy of Lang-Bian autonomous district. At Dalat, a federal assembly would bring together parliamentarians from each state. Provisions even allowed for "states not represented at the conference" to become involved thereafter, although each state, including France, would be limited to ten delegates, thereby placing North Vietnam on the same footing as sparsely populated Laos.[83] On the suggestion of Nguyen Van Xuan, a military school was planned on Dalat's "federal territory," which would train the armies of the federation's different states—this in spite of Laotian Prince Boun Oum's insistence that Laos could not afford, and did not need, an army.[84]

Dalat had emerged as a federal capital on paper. The military school, at least, did materialize in 1950. However, the highland resort also proved to be a pyrrhic and ill-fated capital; events, including turmoil in Laos and Cambodia, not to mention war in all of Vietnam, soon doomed the pan-Indochinese federal model. Within two years of the Dalat conferences, the French themselves had abandoned federalism in favor of an "associated states" model. Yet in the end the idea of Dalat as federal capital was more than a fleeting colonial calculation. It was also the ephemeral realization of a much earlier goal, shared initially by different elements within Indochina, of creating a viable federal framework and space.

CONCLUSION

Those familiar with Dalat in 1937 would have recognized the amount of work still required to make the town a viable federal capital. We have seen how Hébrard's grand plans for a future administrative quarter never really got off the ground. In this sense, transforming an Alpine village replica into a federal capital required either utopian vision or a measure of blind faith. Yet what can this Simla-, New Delhi-, and Canberra-inspired plan tell us about colonial strategies and their shifts in the final decades of empire?

A modern, planned highland capital within a Canberra-like federal capital territory, such was the final incarnation of a multivalent plan to crown the French resort, and lend it federalist meaning. This meaning, in turn, rested on the history of Dalat's early status as an autonomous province, but also on attitudes towards montagnard populations, coded as counterweights to Vietnamese or Communist power. In this sense, Dalat mediated and channeled a range of projects, from colonial reformism to pluri-national imaginings. While Salemink sees the 1946 federalist scheme of Dalat 2 as hardening minority identities, I would suggest that in some interesting ways, it also conjured up a fanciful vision of overlapping and multiloyal precolonial space.[85] Here we have an inversion of Thongchai Winichakul's model, in which "modern geography displaced . . . the indigenous knowledge of political space."[86] Within the Dalat federal scheme, one detects multiple sovereignties, territorial overlaps and ambiguities, and a recentering of previously marginalized spaces, as part of a colonial scheme avowedly aiming to counter a dual Communist and nationalist threat.[87]

Dalat, for its part, served as a logical focal point for this French colonial reordering. A potent symbol of colonial power, cast as an autonomous province within Annam, engineered as a zone beyond Vietnamese control, Dalat was at once closely associated with French prestige, and sufficiently removed from the DRV that it could harbor capital pretensions. As such, the Dalat scheme mirrors similar French plans to make the spa-town of Antsirabe the colonial capital of Madagascar.[88] One could also liken the Dalat-capital project to late colonial Dutch uses of federalism "to outflank the infant Indonesian republic."[89] Yet as tempting as it is to view it as a last spasm of empire, the plan also sheds light on an alternative conception of Indochinese space.

14

Dalat at War and Peace, 1946–1975

In 1949, with the first Indochina war raging, with French and American interests over the region clashing, a journalist recounts that all of Saigon seemed consumed with a strange collective bet. Would the French persuade the former emperor, Bao Dai, to forsake the casinos of the French Riviera and return to power? If so, under what conditions, and within what framework—bilateral relations, full independence, or as part of the French Union? Even more to the point, bets were taken on where and when Bao Dai would return to his native land. The journalist, Lucien Bodard, remarked that if anyone had placed money on Bao Dai making Dalat his point of return to Vietnam on April 27, 1949, they would have made a fortune.[1] As we will see, Dalat continued, perhaps against the odds, to serve as a powerful symbol, as a strategic point, and a prominent prize in the war years between 1945 and 1975.

Current restrictions on archival sources make it impossible to contemplate the years between 1946 and 1975 at Dalat—even less the period between 1975 and the present day—in the same way, or in the same detail, as the colonial era. They do, permit, however, a series of microhistories of military clashes and war crimes at and around Dalat. They also allow some reconstitution of Dalat's ongoing role as a center of leisure and power. The Viet-Minh's determination as early as 1948 to shatter Dalat's reputation as a bucolic, safe retreat demonstrates that the two thematic threads are more closely connected than they might at first appear.

Using materials that are accessible, this chapter also focuses on ruptures and continuities between the colonial and postcolonial eras, intertwining these with dramatic flashpoints when Dalat came to the forefront of the two Indochina wars. It considers in turn the resort's reputation as a bastion of royal power, and as a safe harbor in a region at war. It explores in detail a 1951 massacre that shone international attention on Dalat. Such traumas, for all of their significance, should not detract from Dalat's continuing role as Indochina's prime resort. Despite a series of regime changes over the course of these decades—the most dramatic occurring in 1954 and 1975—despite the era's carnage, Dalat continued to exert a powerful attraction over tourists, pilgrims, and political actors alike. Although it lost some of its centrality beginning in the 1960s, the hill station still held considerable appeal and significance for multiple constituencies during the Indochina wars. Most notably, the resort alternately struggled with, and thrived off of, the contested heritage of the late colonial era, when the city had become the keystone to federal, national, and minority "solutions" in Indochina.

BAO DAI'S KINGDOM WITHIN A STATE

The 1946 Dalat conference between France and the DRV, and the Fontainebleau sequel, both ended in deadlock. In November, French and DRV forces clashed violently in Northern Vietnam, with heavy loss of civilian life in Haiphong, a tragedy that engulfed Vietnam definitively into war. From the outset, the DRV controlled vast zones of Indochina. French forces, waging what amounted to a war of reconquest, faced challenges on multiple fronts. The political situation evolved rapidly, and the French response along with it: after initially promoting Indochinese federalism in the wake of the 1946 conferences, then a version of Cochinchinese secessionism, then an equally ill-fated quadripartite scheme, French authorities turned to a possible Bao Dai solution—betting on bringing back the emperor, who had abdicated in August 1945.

Once again, Dalat lay at the very heart of this plan. When Bao Dai finally returned to power under French auspices in 1949, he made Dalat his unofficial capital. The former ruler returned to Vietnam on April 28, 1949, landing in Dalat amid relatively little fanfare. Lucien Bodard, who was no supporter of the monarch, noted that Bao Dai left the Dakota aircraft "with the pace of an automaton. . . . Within minutes . . . his majesty entered an enormous limousine that took him to his villa in the woods. It is as if he had returned so as to vanish."[2] For its part, Agence France Presse reported laconically that the former emperor's pilot waved an imperial standard out of the aircraft's window as it taxied down the runway.[3] In his memoirs, Bao Dai claims to have landed in Dalat rather than Saigon "out of courtesy," no doubt wanting to steer clear from the imbroglio of Southern separatism.[4] But Bao Dai was also keenly aware that he had negotiated with France for Dalat and the south-central highlands to become an effective kingdom inside a state. That Dalat was chosen for his point of return to Vietnam was therefore anything but coincidental or strictly diplomatic.

Dalat was no consolation prize; it reflected a particular conception of power.

Within days, comfortably seated in the imperial villa, Bao Dai began to form a government that would operate out of the hill station, and rule over two constituencies in two distinct ways: nominally over all of Vietnam, and effectively over the south-central highlands. After arduous negotiations with France over issues of sovereignty and national unity, the new state, with Bao Dai at its head, became known as the Etat du Vietnam or the Vietnamese State. The French strategy of creating a Bao Dai state, of carving off minority zones from the rest of Vietnam, and of isolating the DRV, in many ways prefigured another elaborate partitioning, attempted by the French side during negotiations with the FLN (the Algerian Front de liberation national) in the late 1950s and early 1960s.[5]

We have seen how the idea of a formally recognized Indochinese highland minority zone straddling different *pays* had been floated in French colonial circles with ever-greater frequency in the 1930s, before finally materializing with Marius Moutet and Georges Thierry d'Argenlieu's creation in 1946 of the Commissariat du Gouvernement fédéral pour les Populations montagnardes du Sud-Indochinois (PMSI). The announcement that the PMSI were being placed under Bao Dai's authority came on March 9, 1949.[6] A subsequent imperial order and decree of April 15, 1950 confirmed the transfer of sovereignty of "non-Vietnamese populations traditionally under the Crown of Annam" to Bao Dai's control.[7] By May 21, 1951, the "Montagnard Regions of the South" were given their new status. The goal of these many texts was purportedly to "guarantee at the same time the eminent rights of Vietnam and the free evolution of [minority] populations in the respect of their traditions and of their customs." Again, Bao Dai's May 21, 1951 order insisted on ancestral connections between minority people and ethnic Vietnamese: "The territories of the PMSI, which have always been dependent traditionally on the Crown of Annam, are and will remain attached directly to our person."[8]

This language was on some level stunning, for countless colonial era schemes to create an autonomous highland minority zone had insisted precisely on distancing the region's minority inhabitants from the crown of Annam. Yet now, as Indochina was plunged into war, as the need to drive a wedge between ethnic Vietnamese and highland minorities had given way to a new imperative of distancing minorities from the lure of Communism, a major break was achieved with the past. Read another way, however, Bao Dai's PMSI can also be seen as the culmination of colonial panmontagnard thinking, as the realization of General Pennequin's counterweight strategy under a new guise, or as the final emanation of increasingly homogenizing colonial and ethnographic discourses towards the south-central highlands' minorities.

In his memoirs, Bao Dai makes clear that his rule over highland minorities was designed in part to achieve a piecemeal consolidation of power, by pulling what he seems to have considered to be favorably predisposed groups, first minorities, then Catholics, away from the siren calls of the Viet-Minh.[9] Whatever his motivations, Bao Dai's government did deliver some major reforms in the realm of minority policies. That these reforms were largely aimed at winning hearts and minds can leave little doubt. That they were undertaken with some French input seems equally certain. On November 1, 1951, for instance, the French foreign ministry queried the French high commissioner in Saigon about "how montagnard labor is employed in the French plantations on the plateaus."[10]

On December 31, 1952, Bao Dai abruptly abolished forced labor in all its forms in the PMSI. Colonial rule in the area had largely run on *prestations,* corvées, and other unremunerated labor practices. Contrary to authorities in Paris who sensed the public relations benefits of such a measure, the French high commissioner's office in Saigon deemed the abolition too radical and hasty, foreseeing the collapse of the highlands' economy.[11] Over a hundred years after the abolition of slavery in overseas French colonies (in 1848), echoes of antiabolitionist scaremongering endured. So too did the details of the dire warnings. A 1953 French report on the problem of montagnard labor spelled out that although highland minorities were generally "sympathetic" they remained "dirty," "disorderly," and above all "lazy."[12] Still, even French officials in Saigon acknowledged that *prestations* had become terribly unpopular, especially after they were ramped up in the wake of the Second World War. According to one report, French planters came to think of the *prestations* as a right, even begrudging the administration for diverting forced laborers away from their private plantations so as to repair the damage caused by typhoon Vae in 1952. In 1953, then, unremunerated labor practices made way to "team contracts." These group contracts bound workers to an estate or plantation; in some ways they call to mind the "contract laborers" that both the French and British introduced in the nineteenth century, after the abolition of slavery, in a bid to maintain production levels. Bao Dai's government even sent labor inspectors to verify that the reform was implemented. Warnings, then fines were issued. Yet neither the French nor the Bao Dai government seemed to have pinned much hope on the team contracts; they agreed instead that only an influx of ethnic Vietnamese could "resolve" the "labor problem" of the PMSI. Bao Dai's ministers advocated introducing some 1,500 to 2,000 ethnic Vietnamese per year to the central highlands; in 1952, only 227 arrived.[13] As Oscar Salemink has noted, these still ineffective strategies anticipated some of the massive internal migrations subsequently implemented under the Diêm government.[14]

That Bao Dai's regime should even have labor inspectors suggests that the new government, consistently decried as a puppet by the DRV, was at least trying to undertake reforms and to enforce them in the highlands. Bao Dai delegated minority governance issues to some of his most trusted advisors, Nguyên-Dê for highland affairs, and Colonel Didelot, whose family was bound with Bao Dai's, for the southern zone.[15]

Other fundamental changes can be discerned. A degree of Vietnamization was certainly occurring at Dalat. Thus in November 1950, the keys of city hall were handed from Jean Rouget to Dr. Tran Dinh Que.[16] In September 1952, the Bao Dai regime opened a new Vietnamese high school in Dalat, that would vie with the Lycée Yersin.[17] The quest for independence took on other forms as well. Bao Dai's ministers seemed prepared to play the U.S. card in Dalat. As part of his highland affairs portfolio, Nguyên-Dê invited the U.S. embassy to establish a rest center of its own in Dalat. Baronness Didelot's cottage was quickly selected and rented out to the Americans for this purpose.[18] Bao Dai had managed to gain an American ear near his palace.

At the time, Dalat was discernibly gaining in importance, making major strides to challenge Saigon and Hanoi as a center of power. In 1950, Bao Dai oversaw the opening of an officer's training school in Dalat, a Vietnamese equivalent of Saint-Cyr. The school was established at Camp Saint-Benoît, and although funded by the French, its creator, André Gribius, made a point of flying primarily the flag of the Vietnamese State—a yellow standard cut by red lines.[19] Two years later, Dalat witnessed the inauguration of a national administration school.[20] When added to growth at the resort's preexisting schools, like the Lycée Yersin, this made Dalat at the time the fastest-growing training center anywhere in non-Communist Vietnam.

However it also seems apparent that such reforms alone could not win Bao Dai the propaganda victories he needed in his battle with Ho Chi Minh for national legitimacy. In most other respects, Bao Dai did little to shake his reputation as a creature of luxury, a nightclub king, as the foreign press reprovingly dubbed him. Dalat itself only made matters worse. Lucien Bodard took Bao Dai's choice of capital to signal: "I wash my hands of what is going on." The journalist interpreted the move, in short, as a "self-quarantine," a quarantine from his own people, but also from French attempts to control his government.[21]

Though Bao Dai may have sought isolation, autonomy, and safety at Dalat, his choice of a de facto capital ultimately compounded some of his image problems. Bao Dai's estate at Dalat featured a large private menagerie, boasting some of the emperor's favorite trophies in living flesh: elephants and tigers.[22] In 1950, Bao Dai berated the French gendarmerie for failing to enforce hunting restrictions based on 1930s-era laws, so passionate was he to maintain game reserves.[23] Such a measure, which in time of peace might have been received as sage conservationism, might well have smacked of unacceptable entitlement in time of war. He was also fond of showing visitors to Dalat's imperial villa the gun he had been offered by Francisco Franco.[24] Here was another dubious portend for a self-styled reformer and modern ruler. Even his regime's holidays seemed somehow futile. They included April 28, to commemorate Bao Dai's return to Vietnam at Dalat—a fairly hollow moment, as we have seen—and May 24-25 to celebrate Vietnamese unity, when such a goal at the time was at best hopelessly optimistic.[25] In short, Bao Dai's Dalat suffered an almost Roman reputation for decadence, a reputation that the Viet-Minh relentlessly exploited. For all intents and purposes, Dalat had turned into the new "imperial city," intrinsically linked to the emperor's person.[26] Whatever tarnished Bao Dai stuck to Dalat, and vice versa.

THE 1948 AMBUSH

By 1948, the French expeditionary corps in Indochina was trying to secure a variety of zones across the country. The force would grow steadily, from 67,106 men in 1946 to 183,945 in 1954.[27] In 1948, the Viet-Minh had not yet been emboldened by the victory of the Communists in neighboring China, which would occur a year later, or by the recognition of the DRV by both China and the Soviet Union, which would take place in 1950.[28] And yet, already in 1948, the Viet-Minh was taking the initiative, doing so increasingly in the southern half of Vietnam.[29] Some of its attacks that year were marked by a dual sense of potential ubiquity and brazenness. The Dalat ambush of 1948 constituted a turning point in this war within a war: the struggle for initiative.

The 1948 ambush was certainly not without precedent. In fact, a year prior, the Viet-Minh had attempted to attack an earlier convoy to the hill station, only to see their plans thwarted by French forces, which stumbled upon the plot on September 23, 1947.[30] Nor should one receive the impression that Dalat was somehow at the epicenter of combat during either the first or the second Indochina war. In fact, many sources claimed that Dalat stood as "an oasis of peace in a world out of control," to cite a missionary testimony from December 1949.[31] A 1953 French report still affirmed that the city "lives in absolute peace."[32]

This said, close inspection does suggest that the Viet-Minh was aware of Dalat's symbolic value as a purported sea of tranquility, as the seat of Bao Dai's regime, and increasingly, as an important military base. Indeed, in 1947, the French army opened a commando training school in Dalat. The city counted among the five "principal military bases" in all of Indochina listed in an August 1947 French military report.[33]

Indeed, Dalat served as far more than an oasis: it also constituted the main hub of the SDECE, the French secret service's counterespionage wing, in Indochina. Here again was a parallel with the hill station of Simla, which as early as 1905 had become a major headquarter for British intelligence services.[34] At Dalat, after 1947 dozens of agents under Colonel Maurice Bellaux worked in total isolation, "like monks," at cracking Viet-Minh radio messages in Dalat.[35] The city, in other words, now served increasingly important military functions.

Whether or not the Viet-Minh was aware of this last secret activity at Dalat, it clearly set its sights on Dalat. The Viet-Minh would twice catch colonial defenses around Dalat off guard, first during a large-scale ambush on a convoy to Dalat in 1948, then in a set of attacks in Dalat proper in 1951. On March 1, 1948, after it passed the Lagna bridge in a densely forested area, a long French convoy headed for Dalat, composed of both civilian and military vehicles, came under heavy attack.[36] The

FIGURE 28. The aftermath of the Dalat convoy attack. ECPAD/France/InconnuCOC 50–18/R06.

convoy had already traveled 115 kilometers from Saigon at the time of the ambush. According to military historian Philippe Gras, the attack's significance lay in the fact that it was the first major convoy ambush of the Indochina war.[37] General Raoul Salan, for his part, described it as the perfect ambush. He noted at the time its "minute preparation, as different groups of rebels were in radio contact, obeying a single order."[38] He remarked on the convoy's vulnerable length, adding that it was composed of "numerous civilian vehicles, merchants, and people going to rest at Dalat. At the head of it were the officer jeeps, followed by female personnel." All told, the multikilometer convoy was composed of some two hundred vehicles. The well-camouflaged Viet-Minh destroyed some fifty-nine of them, and according to Gras, claimed 82 fatalities, 11 of them military. Salan, however, provides the quite different figure of 49 dead, 28 of them military.[39] By all accounts, the Viet-Minh also walked away with scores of prisoners. A French survivor who managed to crawl to safety recounted seeing "thousands" of Viet-Minh assaulting the convoy, yelling in Vietnamese, but also in Japanese and in German. This further spurred rumors about the role of both German legionnaire deserters, and refractory Japanese fighters, in Viet-Minh ranks.[40]

The ambush proved psychologically potent. The French gendarmerie reported that the attack had succeeded in striking terror in the heart of Dalat's residents, and in disrupting the local economy. Within days, gas and certain foodstuffs were lacking in Dalat. News of the ambush traveled quickly. Civilians began avoiding the road, taking aircraft instead between Saigon, the hill station, and back.[41] This option's safety would soon be called into question: on July 7, an Air France jet flying between Saigon and Dalat crashed, killing all 21 on board. Already before, Saigonese hoping to sojourn at Dalat had had to take part in inconvenient, cumbersome convoys. Now that a well-defended convoy had come under sustained attack, and that air travel proved similarly hazardous, Dalat's sense of invulnerability was fast evaporating.

THE 1951 MASSACRE

Despite official French and Vietnamese State pronouncements to the contrary, Viet-Minh activity continued unabated in and around Dalat in 1949 and 1950. In September 1950, a Vietnamese-language poem signed by "Lang-Bian's Viet-Minh Information Committee" was sent to several branches of Dalat's administration, urging Vietnamese employees to join the ranks of the resistance.[42] On December 14, 1950, three members of the French High Commissioner's security unit were killed in Dalat near the Redemptorist building.[43] On January 10, 1951, Viet-Minh agents shot to death a minority guard outside of Dalat's electrical plant.[44] Another two Vietnamese officers serving in the French security forces were lured to Dalat's Trai-Ham villa and killed on February 8, 1951.[45] Two days later, fire consumed Dalat's "information hall"; the gendarmerie concluded that Viet-Minh arson was responsible for the blaze. Two more Vietnamese officials were murdered in Dalat on March 21, 1951: one a member of Bao Dai's imperial delegation, the other a member of the city's security forces. One of the two victims, Bui Thach Ngu, was found floating on Dalat's Lake of Sighs, bearing dozens of stab wounds to his neck. The gendarmerie suspected a seventeen-year-old student at the Lycée Yersin of being responsible for the last of these attacks, after blood stains were found on his personal effects.[46] There was, in other words, a sense of foreboding at Dalat in 1951. The war, which was at once a civil conflict and a guerilla campaign, had undeniably reached the resort.

The latest victim in this string of Viet-Minh attacks was the Eurasian Sous-Brigadier Victor Haasz of the French security forces. Haasz was killed on May 11, 1951, at his home on 17 Rue des Roses, Dalat. His attackers had tied up the domestics, and lain in wait in the garden. The assassination complete, they left with Haasz's car, handgun, and other personal effects. During their getaway, they stumbled upon a truck full of French soldiers, and showed their nervousness or perhaps their brazenness by opening fire on the far more numerous soldiers. Still, they managed to escape.[47]

Why had Haasz been targeted in the first place? According to a Viet-Minh pamphlet found in Dalat on June 1, 1951, Haasz had a reputation for employing particularly brutal torture techniques during investigations.[48] Yet Haasz was also, as we have just seen, one of many executed by the Viet-Minh that year in Dalat. His murder, in addition to constituting a clear statement against the use of torture, was no doubt also part of a deliberate Viet-Minh escalation at Dalat.

On the evening of May 11, 1951, three hours after Haasz's death, and in direct reprisal for it, twenty Vietnamese hostages—in effect twenty unfortunate people who happened to find themselves in Dalat's jail, most of them for minor crimes—were dragged to the Camly airfield and summarily shot. Fourteen of the victims were men and six were women. A woman by the name of Nguyen Thi Lang miraculously survived, riddled with eight bullets. She would testify at the perpetrators' trial.[49]

As details emerged, the events seemed to fit the pattern of vengeful rage. Court records would show that only seven of the executed prisoners were even considered dangerous, thereby reinforcing the randomness and senselessness of the act, and lending credence to the idea that common prisoners were being treated as hostages. Soon, some twenty-three suspects were arrested in connection with the massacre, although only the chief of Dalat's police forces, Henri Jumeau, and Dalat's mayor, Dr. Tran Dinh Que, were retained for long.

The press, both in France and in Indochina, seized upon the tragedy. Part of the Saigon French press presented it as a case of an officer cracking after seeing so many of his colleagues fall at the hands of the Viet-Minh. L'Union française of May 22, 1951 read: "the unforgivable execution on the night of May 11 finds its origins in previous multiple bereavements: a cold, implacable, and blind rage crystallized by Haasz' murder." The piece added that the Viet-Minh too routinely practiced summary executions.[50] Such attempts to relativize the massacre drew criticism from other quarters. La Liberté heaped scorn on the journalist Marinetti for suggesting that only someone immersed in Vietnam's climate of terror could understand the massacre.[51]

The tragedy also led to considerable finger-pointing and recriminations between the French Haut-Commissariat on the one hand and Bao-Dai's government on the other, as well as within French ranks. An intercepted letter from a teacher, R. Fauchois, at the Lycée Yersin to a relative in Cherbourg, reads: "The execution order was given by the Vietnamese Government and officer Jumeau had been given a blank check by Bao Dai to undertake severe reprisals in the cases of assassinations. But the order was verbal and not written, and that day Bao Dai was the first to cry out his indignation. Jumeau will be the one to pay."[52] This rendition also appears, interestingly, in Viet-Minh statements. In June 1951, Viet Minh radio reported: "This execution was carried out by the French officer Jumeau who was given the order to accomplish the deed and who now will pay the price himself. Alas, the poor Jumeau has inadvertently sown insecurity on the beautiful and peaceful Lang-Bian plateau, where French colonialists and their puppet scion once quietly fattened themselves up."[53] The equation of Dalat with a French colonial bastion, a symbol of bourgeois and aristocratic gluttony, could not have been any clearer. So too was the message that the time for Dalat's "gluttonous colonials" and their purported allies was up.

Bao Dai's entourage soon lashed back at the accusation that it had masterminded the massacre, countering that Jumeau was solely responsible for it. In this version of events, Dr. Tran Dinh Que had tried to calm an overexcited Jumeau, who announced "things cannot go on this way," then "threatened to kill everyone," before impulsively carrying out the threat.[54] In an interesting turn of events, Le Xuan, Ngo Dinh Diem's future sister-in-law (popularly known as Madame Nhu), also lived on the Rue des Roses at the time, and heard Haasz being shot. She commented on the dreadful coincidence that the Bao Dai cabinet was meeting at the very time of the ensuing massacre. This increased suspicion that the government had ordered the killing. At the very least, the timing of cocktails clinking as families screamed their grief made the Bao Dai government seem callous. Le Xuan added that the entire affair gave the impression that one Eurasian life was worth twenty Vietnamese ones. She concluded cuttingly that if Haasz had been "entirely French," rather than métis, forty Vietnamese would have been shot instead of twenty.[55]

Le Xuan was certainly not the only one to feel outrage. Within weeks, thousands of broadsheets and bright red graffiti adorned walls and electrical posts across Dalat. The principal of the Lycée Yersin noted inscriptions on the Cercle Sportif, the lycées, and the Institut Pasteur. At his own school, graffiti strongly condemned the "military-colonial clique" and the "Bao Dai puppet regime." Lycée Yersin teacher Fauchois related the text of one flyer, left all over town: "It is an abominable criminal act, worthy of the butchers of Buchenwald and Dachau. Dalat compatriots! The debonair mask of French colonialism in Dalat is broken. The hideous face of true colonialism has finally shown itself."[56] A keen educator, Fauchois could not help but notice that some of the inscriptions found at the Lycée Yersin, condemning the massacre and calling for a celebration of Ho Chi Minh's birthday on May 19, were drafted in excellent French.[57]

The Viet-Minh made maximum reference to the tragedy in its propaganda across all of Vietnam. The death toll was sometimes exaggerated, as in a radio broadcast from "The Voice of Nam-Bo" from Sept 20, 1951, which cited the figure of 108 Vietnamese hostages shot, including "some close relatives of [Bao Dai's] puppet regime."[58] The Viet-Minh also took care to justify the initial killing of Haasz as follows: "traitors are always punished, even in Dalat where they feel safe."[59] Here again was the recurring and blunt point that Dalat was no longer a safe haven.

As the previous mention of Buchenwald and Dachau makes plain, Second World War referents proved ubiquitous on the Viet-Minh side. "All social classes liken this odious act to the summary and savage executions used by the Japanese fascists at the time of the occupation," hammered Viet-Minh radio on May 19, 1951.[60] And again four days later: "When the Nazis occupied France, they used the same tactics towards French patriots."[61] Finally Viet-Minh radio asserted on May 18, 1951: "twenty Vietnamese executed at once. This has reminded the French . . . of the Nazi occupation and the executions of the now immortal Jacques Ducourt, Gabriel Péri, Pierre Senart. In Vietnam, French colonialists are playing the role of Nazis, whose methods they have learned."[62] In this savvy juxtaposition, French Communist resistors in the metropole were likened to the twenty Vietnamese victims at Dalat, while the French administration in Indochina was ascribed the role of Klaus Barbie and his consorts.

In metropolitan France too the summary executions at Dalat were widely condemned. Once again the Nazi occupation cast a shadow over much of this reaction. The article on the Dalat massacre in the Communist newspaper *L'Humanité* bore the unequivocal title "Nazis!"[63] At the National Assembly, a deputy from the Vaucluse, René Arthaud, took the stage on behalf of the Communist group. He hit hard: "recycling Hitlerian methods, the government has just proceeded to execute twenty Vietnamese hostages at Dalat." Arthaud then turned his focus to the initial murder of Haasz by "Vietnamese patriots," comparing Haasz's killing to "French patriots executing Gestapo agents during the occupation."[64] On a more measured tone, yet still implicitly referencing the world war, on May 18, 1951 *France Soir* maintained: "Our country, that keeps the painful memory of so many innocent victims, cannot tolerate that crimes of this nature be committed under our flag."[65]

On location in Dalat, tensions flared. On the French side, Jumeau was not alone in displaying a vigilante spirit. An anonymous French letter soon reached police. It threatened revenge for Haasz's death. Its author bemoaned that Indochina had become "an unfortunate land full of asses *(de cons)*, where there is no justice." Soon police were able to crack the mystery of the note's anonymity, ascribing it to a certain Jean Dacruz, an employee at a nearby plantation. They dismissed it as harmless and him as a "simpleton."

On the other side, a number of anonymous threatening letters signed by the Viet-Minh were received in Dalat. Some included business cards for casket sellers, as well as the motto: "The Viet-Minh settles scores quickly, settles them well."[66] Assassinations continued: notables of the Vietnamese State were murdered on May 17 near Dalat. On May 25, a Vietnamese interpreter was killed as he left the Lang-Bian cinema. On June 14, a firefight erupted in Dalat's hospital, killing one Viet-Minh and one policeman.[67] On July 25, 1951, the Viet-Minh abducted a highland minority man in Fyan.[68]

Rumors began spreading in the French community that the Viet-Minh would seek "an eye for an eye" by killing six European women and fourteen members of the French security forces—the precise gender balance of the Vietnamese victims. A June 1951 police investigation revealed this rumor to be baseless, and attributed it to ambient tensions and "psychosis."[69] An intercepted French letter evoked putative threats to French children, adding that as a precaution religious orders were keeping French children indoors. Vietnamese elites too, were afraid. Le Xuan wrote on May 15, 1951 that "Dalat's atmosphere has changed. One no longer feels the calm that one did before. For a month now, one doesn't dare venture into the Camly forests, and in town one feels an atmosphere of suspicion and worry." Dalat, once an "oasis of peace" she wrote, "will become a terrorized and unbreathable city like the other cities."[70] In these conditions, guards lost their cool: in October 1952, a drunk French foreign legionnaire was accidentally shot and killed by a guard at Dalat after the former entered the villa of a member of Bao Dai's cabinet.[71]

Jumeau did eventually stand trial for the massacre, though the trial proved a sham. Of the twenty-two witnesses at Jumeau's trial, seventeen were his own accomplices and colleagues, most of them his subordinates. The light sentences that ensued led one Vietnamese inhabitant of Dalat to conclude that his compatriots' lives were worth "less than lentils."[72]

Ultimately, the massacre further polarized opinion. Colonials in Dalat seem to have been largely sympathetic to Jumeau. Take this intercepted letter from one Monsieur Adam in Dalat to a correspondent in Southwestern France: "The Dalat Affair is being settled, and of the twenty-two arrested, only two are still in jail, the mayor and the head of police. De Lattre finds this situation ridiculous, for we are the ones being shot at in the back, but in France they see everything upside down. Once the Russian juggernaut invades France and deportations begin, many of these hotheads will change their minds."[73]

Another inhabitant of Dalat, a certain Legras, wrote that the outcome of the Dalat affair confirmed that "everything done in France since Pétain is enough to make one disgusted for being French."[74] Taken together, these testimonies suggest a conflation of leftism with anticolonialism, a nostalgia for Vichy, a repudiation of a motherland perceived as soft and corrupt, and a solid commitment to waging a rearguard battle to reestablish the status quo ante in Indochina. There were dissonant French voices, to be sure. One intercepted letter from a Monsieur Levy in Dalat acknowledged that the Vietnamese victims were altogether innocent, many of them apolitical. Levy deemed the execution of the twenty Vietnamese hostages "sickening." Even the French gendarmerie acknowledged that the massacre had undone overnight "several years" of police and propaganda work.[75]

The Dalat massacre would have other long-term consequences. For one thing, it seems to have made both sides reconsider their strategies. While applauding the death of Haasz and other "harmful insects," a May 20, 1951 DRV document recommended that patriots exercise greater secrecy and guard their optimism.[76] Indeed, the military tide in Dalat was, for the time being, turning back against the Viet-Minh.

Several documents vindicate the theory that Dalat had been deliberately targeted to demonstrate that there was no safe haven left for colonials and for Bao Dai's regime. These include a Viet-Minh pamphlet found in October 1951. It reads: "The murder of Haasz, Sûreté Inspector in Dalat, which shook the world, has proven that Dalat is not a site of perfect security for the French enemy."[77] Another Viet-Minh pamphlet, found in Dalat on June 1, 1951, claimed that the string of Viet-Minh attacks in the city "had for the first time shattered the secure zone that the enemy has boasted about for many years."[78] Taken figuratively, Dalat's reputation as a safe harbor harkened back to 1897. Here was final proof, the Viet-Minh boasted, that Dalat was tranquil and bucolic no longer.

The destabilization strategy seems to have worked, if briefly. Bao Dai's advisors deemed the situation to be sufficiently dangerous for him to leave Dalat. On June 24, 1951, Agence France Presse reported that a conference was taking place in Dalat to determine the cause of the town's "growing lack of security" and to find ways to stem the problem. The meeting brought together Nguyen Van Tam, minister of public security, General Cogny, the French high commissioner's cabinet director, and Perrier, head of the French security services. The report added that Emperor Bao Dai had left his Dalat residence for Nha-Trang because of the violence in Dalat.[79]

Yet by the time the emperor left the resort the momentum had already swung back against the Viet-Minh. On June 24, 1951, Bao Dai's national security forces set up shop in Dalat. Nguyen-Van-Tâm, minister of security, made the resort's pacification his top priority.[80] He liaised closely with French forces in the highlands. Four days later, the security forces claimed to have found the Viet-Minh cell's headquarters, at the residence of a nurse, Trân-Nhu-Mai. Two Viet-Minh members and one French security officer were killed in a bid to storm her residence. Another security official was gravely injured.[81] On July 1, 1951, a member of a Viet-Minh cell allegedly turned himself in, and pointed authorities to two camps outside of Dalat, both of which were quickly raided. In February 1952, another former "death volunteer" *(Cam tu Quân)* squad member defected. As proof of his identity, he offered up Haasz's handgun.[82] This turn of events allowed the French to infiltrate the local Viet-Minh movement further, and to make several arrests, including that of Tran-Van-Hoang, a secretary at the Lang-Bian Palace Hotel.[83]

The urban counterinsurgency succeeded for the short term. Reports evoke relative calm in Dalat in 1952 and 1953. In the greater Dalat region in 1953, mobile cinema units scoured the countryside, projecting anti-Viet-Minh propaganda films.[84]

The Viet-Minh too was waging a series of battles for public opinion. This war within the war was fought increasingly in the south-central highlands, which the DRV had established as a priority zone as early as November 1953.[85] We have seen how in Dalat proper the Viet-Minh utilized graffiti, pamphlets, letter-poems, and the like; this should not make us lose sight of the fact that propaganda campaigns were being staged in Dalat's hinterland as well. One Viet-Minh poster distributed in the highlands depicted a straight line of Viet-Minh flags running across Vietnam's interior highlands, including Dalat. In the foreground, a stylized highland minority man and woman raise their fists in the Communist salute.

FIGURE 29. Viet-Minh propaganda poster intended for circulation in the highlands. One interpretation of the text is that it constitutes a phonetic and simplified adaptation of *quoc ngu* Vietnamese, aimed at a highland minority audience. The original Vietnamese would have read *Mỗi tổ tạo nên: Việt Nam,* meaning that each component (Hanoi, Kontum, Dalat, Saigon, etc.) comprised Vietnam. Service historique de la Défense, France, 10H 2369. Photo courtesy of David Marr. Interpretation courtesy of Thuy Linh Nguyen.

The ebbs and flows of war did not completely consume Dalat or its economy. In some spheres the city continued to operate under relatively normal conditions. For instance, the resort cemented its colonial-era function as Vietnam's prime vegetable-producing zone, that is, for reputedly "French" fruits and vegetables like carrots, strawberries, or artichokes, by now fully integrated into Vietnamese cuisine. In the month of November 1951 alone, Dalat shipped some 356.5 tons of "fresh French vegetables" to Saigon.[86] That decade, the Lang-Bian region exported in total some six thousand tons of fruits and vegetables per annum, as well as another six thousand tons of pinewood. The latter was essential for the pulp and paper industry, and relatively scarce in the rest of Vietnam.[87]

THE DIEM YEARS

In the wider Indochina war, French forces and resources were being stretched thin. In 1950 the first major French defeat occurred at Cao Bang. By March 1954, French forces were being surrounded at Dien Bien Phu. Viet-Minh zones of control now sprawled over ever-vaster parts of Northern, Central, and Southern Vietnam. In early April 1954, the Viet-Minh again made major inroads in the south-central highlands, seizing two outposts near Blao and Djiring, on roads to Dalat.[88] By July, two months after the resounding French defeat at Dien Bien Phu, An-Khe, some 200 kilometers north of Dalat, was under assault. On August 1, 1954 a cease-fire went into effect, in keeping with the accords signed in Geneva on June 20. Vietnam was divided along the seventeenth parallel. The French colonial era was reaching a definitive end.

Dalat lay well south of the divide, and now took on a staging role. Released French and Vietnamese prisoners congregated at Dalat, where they were cared for at the Lycée Yersin and other venues.[89] Dalat's role as a safe harbor endured, although this also augured the beginning of a new function: Dalat as a destination for refugees from other parts of Vietnam. The Geneva accords stipulated that refugees would have three hundred days to pick their side of the seventeeth parallel. Nearly a million Vietnamese left the North for the South during this time, two-thirds of them Catholics.[90] Dalat's population ballooned briefly to sixty thousand inhabitants.

In July 1954, Ngo Dinh Diem returned from exile in the United States to become premier of the Vietnamese State—a regime that Willaim Turley describes at this juncture as a "sinking ship."[91] In a little over a year, Diem squeezed out his rivals in government and emerged victorious on the streets as well, thanks to the backing of two influential sects in the South, the Hoa Hao and Cao Dai. In October 1955, he orchestrated a referendum on whether South Vietnam should remain a constitutional monarchy, or become a republic under his rule. Bao Dai was swept from power.

What did this mean for Dalat? Unlike his predecessor, Diem ruled from Saigon.

No sooner had he come to power, than Diem moved the National Administration school from Dalat to Saigon. Also in 1955, the central highlands were absorbed into the Republic of Vietnam, marking the end of Bao Dai's fiefdom within a state. Admittedly in 1955 a new Directorate of Economy for the Highlands of Central Vietnam was created at Dalat and in 1957 a new Highlands Bureau replaced Bao Dai's old Ministry of Highland Affairs at Dalat. But the net effect of these many reforms was to reduce Dalat's stature within South Vietnam.[92]

Much has been made of Diem's Catholicism, and it is certain that the religion thrived in Dalat under Diem, between 1955 and 1963. A Redemptorist document, dated February 1958, evoked a major religious revival. That year, Dalat became an episcopal see. Of its 51,380 inhabitants in 1958, 14,174 were Catholic. This works out to 27.6 percent of the population, when the overall proportion of Catholics for South Vietnam at large was closer to 10 percent. The Dalat figures represent a massive increase, if one considers that the town counted 6,141 Catholics in 1952. In other words, the center's Catholic population had more than doubled with the arrival of Northern refugees in 1954. There was in any event no shortage of places to worship: Dalat now registered no fewer than twenty-nine Catholic establishments, fifteen Catholic orders, and nineteen Catholic schools.[93] The latter, Father Parrel remarked in 1959, proved popular among many non-Catholics as well, with 80 percent of their students non-Catholic upon entry.[94]

However, this religious wave was only part of the story. Dalat also experienced a nationalist revival in this era. The new nationalism was diffused not only in public schools, but also in Catholic ones. Witness some of the teaching resources utilized by the Redemptorists at Dalat in 1959. Among them one finds poems by Pham Dinh Chuong, glorifying god, but also the motherland. Three of these verses read: "Remembering those days when we departed / to offer one's body to defend our fields / to offer one's blood to color the Red River." These recent traumas were sometimes juxtaposed with ancient triumphs, as in the "Song of the Bach Dang River," which students were expected to memorize. It chronicled and twinned two Vietnamese victories over the Chinese in 93 and 1288 A.D. Together, they were depicted as having "opened Vietnam to the era of independence and prosperity."[95]

So too did the Diem years mark a turning point in minority policies. Unlike Bao Dai, who had cultivated a sense of montagnard difference, Diem's government favored the assimilation of highland minorities. Coupled with the wave of ethnic Vietnamese migrants arriving in ever greater numbers in 1955, this assimilation attempt fuelled considerable opposition and outright resistance among minority groups.[96]

Despite these developments and shifts, and despite the escalation of war, all signs point to the fact that Dalat remained en vogue among elite circles and beyond. Indeed, the Diem regime also made conscious efforts to sell Dalat as a tourist destination. A set of posters dating from the Diem years reveal some of the ways in which Dalat was being increasingly naturalized and romanticized. Produced by the national tourism department of Vietnam, the series graced public buildings and new-stands in Saigon and beyond, enjoining Vietnamese people to vacation at Dalat. One poster in particular elides both the colonial legacy and the ethnic Vietnamese presence at Dalat altogether. Instead the visual depicts a highland minority man taking aim at a deer with his crossbow. Nature dominates. The scene is set against the backdrop of Dalat's signature pine trees, rolling hills, and waterfalls. What had been coded during the colonial era as a site for invigorating strolls, a place to recre-ate the Alps in Indochina, or a destination for pseudoethnographic romps, was now repackaged in romantic terms. No doubt harkening back to Vietnamese poetry on Dalat from the 1930s, this advertizing campaign also served to contrast relatively tranquil Dalat to both hyperurban Saigon and to the parts of the South under con-stant military threat.

Dalat remained rife with contradictions. At precisely the time when tourists were being encouraged to climb to the resort, refugees too were thronging to the hill sta-tion. By 1956, South Vietnamese authorities calculated that some 13,368 refugees had settled in the Dalat region. By 1968, the total would reach 16,000. Many were assigned to agricultural tasks: some 500 new hectares near Dalat were cultivated by these new arrivals between 1954 and 1956. Newcomers were estimated to have pro-duced 200 tons of cereals, fruits, and vegetables in the year after their arrival. Among the refugees were some four thousand highland minority people from Northern Vietnam. The Diem government even organized integration ceremonies to mark local solidarity with the refugees.[97]

By the final years of Diem's reign, as the second Indochina war escalated, Dalat became an important piece of the Kennedy administration's "strategic hamlet pol-icy." This massive and sometimes forced internal migration was designed in theory to remove villagers from Viet-Cong influence, and to protect vulnerable popula-tions. Thousands of such hamlets were set up throughout South Vietnam. Because in the Lang-Bian region highland minority people made up the majority of the ru-ral population, they bore the brunt of relocation. In the spring and summer of 1962, thousands of minority people congregated on Dalat. In April 1962, the U.S. Com-mittee on Province Rehabilitation in Vietnam reported: "[we have learned] of the movement of a large number of montagnards to an area close to Dalat. According to the report, the Montagnards left their villages and moved to Dalat to escape the Viet-Cong and to take advantage of the additional security provided near Dalat."[98] By July, the Dalat area had been singled out as a site bursting with internal refugees. A CIA memorandum noted: "With the exception of Tuyen Duc Province (Dalat), where there are 10,000 refugees, many of whom seem in need of immediate provi-sions, foods, and other essentials, most provinces visited to date are not considered to have emergency situations in terms of Montagnard needs."[99]

The strategic hamlet program, as applied around Dalat, involved more than merely protecting minority groups from the Viet-Cong. In an August 1962 telegram

FIGURE 30. Diem-era tourist poster for Dalat. Author's collection.

to the State Department, the U.S. ambassador to South Vietnam outlined "the definitive decision taken to encourage by all means possible the exodus of Montagnard populations from areas controlled by the Viet-Cong to areas controlled by the Government of Vietnam." Ambassador Frederick Noltin then revealed that South Vietnamese officials had expressed concerns that the highland evacuations "had . . . left many growing crops available for Viet-Cong harvesting and use, and the current plan to encourage movement would augment this." The ambassador's South Vietnamese interlocutor directly called for abandoned cultivation areas to be sprayed with defoliating chemicals.[100] Thus, around Dalat, as in other parts of South Vietnam, the strategic hamlets went hand in hand with a scorched earth policy.

American officials soon debated the wisdom of broadcasting news of montagnard relocation worldwide. Their concerns had not so much to do with the unrelenting napalming of evacuated highland areas, but rather with the fate of the refugees themselves. The American committee in charge of the hamlet program ultimately decided in September 1962 that broadcasting would be a poor idea, given that the United States had no guarantee that the Vietnamese government "would carry out its announced decision to support and care for the refugees."[101] The risk was clear: unwittingly generating international outrage at seeing highland minority people uprooted from their villages, only to find their new accommodations wanting, and their lives upended.

In contrast, South Vietnamese authorities showed little such compunction in their public relations. In August, 1962, General Truong Vinh Le asserted at the close of a meeting at the Saigon Municipal Hall: "The fact that montagnards have abandoned their homes is a historic event telling everyone Communism is a mortal danger. . . . This is a great victory for a just cause."[102] Truong Vinh Le's had managed to reinvent flight into victory. He accomplished this feat by leaning on popular representations of montagnard immutability and sedentarism. If the montagnards had been willing to move, the logic went, the threat they were escaping must have been terrible indeed.

By the time Diem was assassinated in 1963, Dalat had undergone some drastic transformations. Its population had exploded following two distinct refugee flows: the first from Northern Vietnam in 1954; the second, a massive internal migration of highland minorities towards Dalat as part of the strategic hamlet policy starting in 1962.

DALAT, 1963–1975

Ngo Dinh Diem and John F. Kennedy's assassinations in November 1963 would have two long-term consequences in Southeast Asia at large: an increased U.S. involvement in the war, and decreased stability in South Vietnam. An aide of Lyndon B. Johnson famously pronounced that the post-Diem South Vietnamese government should make a turnstile its emblem.[103] Another major escalation in the war arrived in 1965, with the onset of the U.S. Operation Rolling Thunder, the systematic bombing of the DRV, as well as stepped-up American involvement in the South. In the Dalat region, that year marked the arrival of American combat troops, who would soon use the city as a base and, unsurprisingly, as a site for rest and relaxation.[104]

At Dalat the years 1963 to 1975 featured both continuities and ruptures. Among the former, the tourism sector once again stands out. Despite Dalat's transformation into a refugee center, it continued to attract tourists from across Southern Vietnam and beyond. In December 1971, 41,794 visitors made their way to the hill station. In March 1972, Dalat broke a record: 45,733 tourists braved the war to visit the resort that month alone.[105]

South Vietnam tourism officials were not content with targeting Vietnamese tourists. A glossy English-language pamphlet, featuring on its cover a highland minority woman, an *ao-dai* clad ethnic Vietnamese woman, a deer, colonial architectural elements, and the Lang-Bian summit, served to vaunt Dalat's romance to a potential Anglophone market: "Lying out against a backdrop of undulating hills and mountains, [Dalat's Xuan Huong Lake] makes a scenery for which superlatives are wholly inadequate." The Lake of Sighs received similar praise: "beautiful and romantic lake reflecting in its water the graceful pine-trees and the renchanging [*sic*] outline of massive hills. It is . . . peaceful and enjoyable." Less romantically, the pamphlet enjoined travelers to take in the brand new U.S.-built Atomic Center (opened in 1962), as well as the South's military academy. Souvenir suggestions included "animals stuffed by taxidermists."[106] Here was a sign that colonial-era hunting remained de rigueur, or perhaps that its fruits could now be consumed as souvenirs without having to expend the time, energy, and money required to actually hunt in person.

However, Dalat's relative tranquility would be abruptly shattered once more, this time by the 1968 Tet Offensive. Historians and contemporaries alike have debated the degree to which the Tet Offensive caught American and South Vietnamese forces by surprise. What seems pertinent here is the postattack excuse invoked for not anticipating that Dalat in particular would have been targeted in the first place. According to one U.S. report: "It must be noted that during the twenty-two years of war in Vietnam, Dalat had never been under any kind of attack."[107] This, of course, completely elided the events of 1951, seemingly unknown to the U.S. army. Once again, Dalat's defenders had been caught flat-footed, persuaded of the resort's safety—or perhaps, this time around, of its diminished strategic and symbolic importance.

Although the Viet-Cong controlled central Dalat only from February 1 to February 6, 1968, the fact that the resort fell briefly during the Tet Offensive undoubtedly contributed to the sentiment that the Viet-Minh could strike at will. Dalat's cadets at its vaunted military academy struggled to retake the city's central market from the guerillas. The attack and counterattacks left considerable wreckage in their wake. The city had been badly damaged, reduced to "a smoking ruin" according to Gerald Hickey.[108] Some twenty thousand people were left homeless, roughly one thousand homes were destroyed and a further two thousand damaged in the fighting.[109]

One more aspect of Dalat during these years seems worth noting. The resort saw a return to some of the contestation it had experienced in the 1930s and 1940s. In November and December 1964, residents of Dalat demonstrated in the streets to demand the removal of Tran Van Huong's government.[110] Later, Dalat seems to have served to stage internal opposition to Nguyen Van Thieu's increasingly authoritarian regime. William Turley points to the importance of Redemptorist Catholic opposition to Thieu; Dalat's studentat and noviciat training centers remained the chief Redemptorist training centers in all of Vietnam.[111]

In 1975, the year South Vietnam collapsed, Dalat counted 105,072 inhabitants.[112] The South's fate was decided partly in the central highlands. Ban Me Thuot fell surprisingly rapidly in March 1975. Coupled with Communist victories in Phuoc Long in January, and on the coast at Da-Nang in March, these sealed the South's defeat. In a mere two weeks, the South lost 40 percent of its weapons and some twelve provinces counting roughly eight million people.[113] Viet-Minh staff members complained of not being able to draw maps quickly enough to keep up with advancing troops.[114]

Xuan Phuong, who had grown up Dalat in colonial times, now returned in the tracks of the triumphant Northern army. As Dalat fell on April 4, 1975 she observed with regret some of the acts of retribution that almost invariably accompany the end of a civil war. For one thing, local Viet-Cong forces imprisoned her, convinced that her companion had worked for the South. Xuan Phuong also relates in detail how the city was ransacked. Many of Dalat's foreign language books were amassed into pyres and burned.[115] It seems the troops had not heeded their officers' purported warnings about leaving the city's cultural and intellectual resources intact.[116] Xuan Phuong also points out that she initially found it hard to find her bearings in the city, so different was it from her childhood days. Thirty-five years of rapid growth, and the damage incurred during the Tet Offensive, had made the French colonial hill station in some ways unrecognizable.

Proof soon came that the South would be treated as a vanquished land in need of punishment for having collaborated with two enemies. This was made plain at the 1975 twenty-fourth plenum of the Vietnamese Communist party's central committee. The plenum, the first for reunited Vietnam, was held at Dalat in the summer of 1975. Though it was called in principle to exchange Northern and Southern perspectives on reunification, the South was represented by none other than Pham Hung, the North's deputy Prime Minister. The net result, as Truong Nhu Tang has implied, was a dialogue amongst Northerners about the South's fate. With little suspense, the meeting consecrated and cemented national unification.[117]

Current research conditions, not to mention the scope of this study, make important aspects of Dalat between 1975 and the present day impossible to track here. They include the experiences of highland minority people in and around Dalat, the question of how Dalat's many learning academies fared after 1975, and the local economy's struggles during the era of restrictions that lasted until the advent of Doi Moi in 1986.

However, a rapid shift to present-day Dalat can yield some rewards. Recent attempts to both commemorate and reinvent the colonial era reveal a number of grey zones, amnesias, reformulations, appropriations, and to borrow Ann Stoler's concept, aphasias, concerning the recent and the deeper past. Dalat's colonial legacies have been sometimes retooled, sometimes erected into totems, and sometimes targeted or erased.[118]

Epilogue

In recent years, elements of Dalat's colonial past have been harnessed to repackage the city as a nostalgic, idyllic destination, reminiscent of the Vietnamese Switzerland Alexandre Yersin had invented a century earlier. This is Dalat at its most performative, and at its most wistful.

Barbara Crossette sees Dalat as the "only major hill station in Asia remaking itself . . . faithfully and deliberately in its historical, colonial image."[1] I am inclined to disagree with the second part of her statement; contemporary Dalat does not strike me as a restoration project, so much as a fascinating cauldron of memorial shifts. While Dalat is certainly being remade, the impetus for the transformation seems largely commercial and nostalgic, rather than "deliberately historical." As Graham Huggan remarks, it is colonial nostalgia's "very falseness" that guarantees its appeal.[2] At Dalat, the horseback rides offered in the Valley of Love alongside fanciful cowboys and Indians, the group weddings and the queues at the region's waterfalls, the highly structured visits of local minority villages, the guided tour of Bao Dai's palace, all contribute to the sense that the former colonial hill station has become a formulaic site of romantic tourism. No doubt its reputation for exclusiveness, for refinement, its rarified air, have paradoxically contributed to fuelling this mass appeal.

Many a Western tourist has remarked on twenty-first century Dalat's purportedly kitsch quality. Some have reveled in it. James Sullivan has described the resort's most idiosyncratic hotel—the Hang Nga Guesthouse, also known as "Crazy House," as "brilliantly kitsch," lending Dalat itself the title of "Capital of Kitsch."[3] Others have tried to see past it. Bradley Winterton, a journalist for the *Taipei Times*, wrote in 2008: "And then there's the Valley of Love. Initially it looks like an amusement park, with Peter Pan statues and pixies on toadstools. The celebrated Dalat cowboys hang out here, likely lads sitting astride tightly reined-in ponies hoping to take you for a ride. But soon you discover the hidden lake surrounded by forested hills. The awnings of the swan-necked pedalos flap lazily in the light breeze . . . "[4]

Another reporter, Pip Morgan, writing for *Time Asia* chose to look the other way. After visiting the resort, he observed in 2003: "In downtown Dalat, love is almost always in the air. Dalat has evolved into Vietnam's honeymoon capital. At hot spots like the scenic Vally of Love park and crescent-shaped Xuan Huong Lake, you'll find a lot of Disneyesque diversion, such as swan-shaped paddleboats. They may not be to everyone's taste, but there's no denying the romantic appeal of the town's evergreen forests, waterfalls, and lakes."[5] To this reporter at least, Dalat's lure lay in its nature, as it had to countless chroniclers in the colonial era. In the twenty-first century, however, Dalat's evergreens might not evoke quite the same wonder as they did for homesick French colonials in the 1920s.

In each of these testimonies, Dalat's paddleboats, its Valley of Love, its costumed cowboys and Indians seem almost too much to bear. This has led some to comment on Dalat's Las Vegas or Niagara Falls-like quality—a "strangely fun," kitschy escape, commodified for romance.[6]

To be sure, some tourists also ascend to Dalat in an unadulterated quest for authenticity or to turn back the clock. They tend to be Westerners, and to stay at either the high-end Sofitel Dalat Palace Hotel or at the Novotel Hôtel du Parc. Here one uncovers a pining for colonial-era Dalat, for a time when the resort was still allegedly pristine and orderly. Both the hill station's many internal tensions and its segregation are elided in such visions. Upon returning to the hill station, Françoise Huguier, who spent part of her childhood in Dalat, lamented that the city's urbanism was beginning to resemble that of Ho Chi Minh City. Her hotel room, she bemoaned, gave onto "a magma of buildings, erected at random."[7]

Saigontourist Travel Service has organized alumni group visits to Dalat's famed Lycée Yersin, now a teacher's training school. The company promises not only tours of the region, but more importantly: "the highlight of the tour for many of the former students . . . [is] the gala dinner at the Hotel Sofitel Dalat and all the food, dancing, and nostalgic chit-chat."[8] Even those not making the journey to Dalat can embark in virtual reunions online, thanks to a proliferation of websites bringing together alumni from the Oiseaux or the Lycée Yersin.

A new, younger generation of Westerners is also drawn to Dalat, ensnared in the glamour of what Panivong Norindr has dubbed "Indochic." This generation's impression of Indochina has been largely shaped by Régis Wargnier's film *Indochine* and by Jean-Jacques Annaud's adaptation of *The Lover,* both released in 1992. Indeed, Samantha Coomber, writing for Air Canada's *En-Route* magazine, explicitly made this link as she took her seat in the Dalat Palace Hotel's vintage Citroën: "I feel like I've been transported (in the height of luxury) back to the first half of the twentieth century, like Catherine Deneuve on the set of *Indochine.*"[9]

Writing in 1993, the year after *Indochine* and *The Lover* were released, French traveler Jean-Luc Coatelem fantasized as follows about residing in Dalat: "Ah, to live here. . . . To play golf in the morning, drive a Peugeot 203 at slow pace, to row a flat-bedded boat on the lake, to hunt tigers in the mountains, and to sip strawberry liqueur. . . . And then, in the evening, to write nostalgic, syrupy and kitschy novels on these terraces, flanked by pine forests . . . [near] the roaring waterfalls."[10] These stock themes evoke a specific colonial dolce vita, to be sure, but they also flatten and conflate its purported charms. The nods to golfing, tigers, waterfalls, and Peugeots, not to mention to strawberry schnapps, read as so many markers of *Indochic*. The result is a cocktail whose kitschy decorations fail to mask a pronounced taste of nostalgia. Indeed, the very invocation of kitsch seems here to provide a license for neocolonial fantasy.

For its part, a glossy French travel magazine that dedicated eight pages to Dalat in 2008 began by conjuring up "a voyage in the memory of these colonial years perfumed by France, a voyage into nostalgia." The article then proceeded to enumerate residual French influences in Dalat: the cultivation of artichokes, the streets still bearing the names of Pasteur, Curie, and Calmette. Conveniently forgotten was the vast renaming undertaken in 1954, when Maréchal Foch Street became Duy Tan Steet, the Lac de la Cité Decoux became Van Kiep Lake, or the second name-purge conducted in 1975, for that matter. Meanwhile, the article systematically denigrated Vietnamese influences: Trai Mat pagoda was deemed "Vietnam's kitschest pagoda . . . a monument to bad decorative taste." The "communist bulldozer" was squarely blamed for Dalat's downturn after 1975.[11]

However, it would be wrong to think of *Dalatstalgie* as generated exclusively from without. Vietnamese authorities have carefully crafted the resort's image. Infrastructures have also been expanded. In 2002, Vietnam spent some 15.8 million U.S. dollars to improve Dalat's airport and allow it to receive international flights, making it the country's fourth international airport after Hanoi, Ho Chi Minh City, and Da-Nang.[12]

Vietnamese tourist publications on Dalat systematically vaunt its poetry and romance. According to an article in the glossy English-language *Vietnam Review*: "Each phrase on Da Lat, in Vietnamese or in a foreign language, the metaphor or comparison always sounds like a couple of verses extracted from some lyric poem [sic]. For instance, Da Lat: A city of singing pines, A city of misty dew, A city with ninety-nine beauties, and A city of Love."[13]

To some Vietnamese tourists, it would seem, Dalat's French and minority pasts both exert powerful, exoticized forces of their own. A study of the resort in the year 2000 noted that Xuan Huong Lake "displays a Western gracefulness: the blue water reflects the pink cherry flowers when spring comes. . . . It is hard to believe that 107 years ago the lakebed used to be the villages of the Langbian native people."[14] Here the language of colonial progress is unequivocally embraced.

Results have more than met expectations. In 2005, Vietnamese officials hoped that Dalat would receive a staggering 1.2 million tourists, of whom a full million were to be Vietnamese.[15] In addition to Dalat's vaunted romance, climate, flowers, handicrafts, and waterfalls, the lure of indigenous people also figures prominently in current advertizing for the resort. In April 2003, three hundred performers from twenty different ethnic groups converged on Dalat for an "ethnic festival."[16] In December 2007, as part of Dalat's flower festival, authorities organized a "Miss Ethnic Vietnam Beauty Contest." In addition to singing, contestants donned traditional costumes, then bikinis, before engaging in riding, hiking, cooking, and floral composition.[17]

How do Dalat's inhabitants confront the colonial past? To be sure, the airfield massacre and the quotidian vexations of empire still matter deeply to several generations. However there also seems to be a desire to turn the page while simultaneously conjuring up Dalat's unique colonial spirit. Here colonialism is whitewashed by the descendents of the colonized. A book published by Dalat's tourist office to mark the hundredth anniversary of Yersin discovering the site in 1893, clearly portrayed early French colonials as the place's inventors, or at the very least as its midwives, in flowery rhetoric that might well have made even Yersin, Doumer, Sarraut, and their consorts blush: "After nearly a hundred years being in the pregnant stage, Dalat was delivered with the assistance of foreign doctors and the Indochinese Governor General."[18] The volume goes on to eulogize Alexandre Yersin, "the man who has discovered the Lang Bian plateau, given birth to Dalat, defeated the plague."[19]

From its inception, Dalat was riddled with ironies and paradoxes: as a planned resort, its implementation was messy at best; as a health center it proved vulnerable to the very diseases it was supposed to alleviate; as a white city, it came to serve as a point of triangular contact between Europeans, ethnic minorities, and Vietnamese; as a resort, it rested upon the labor of local people who literally carried leisure-seekers up the mountain; once a colonial bastion, it was ultimately appropriated for other ends by Vietnamese tourists and anticolonial resistors alike.

At Dalat today, the colonial past is at once ubiquitous, profitable, and hazy: the city's identity is clearly bound up in colonial vestiges and landmarks: its hotels, villas, lakes, golf course, public buildings, even its flowers and artichokes. And yet many of its historical features—its role as a colonial nursery, as a métis site, as a furlough destination, or as a religious center, to name only a few—seem largely erased. In their stead, colonialism is channeled via images of Alexandre Yersin, distilled in Dalat's flower beds, and reflected in its Lake of Sighs.

On my first visit to Dalat around the turn of this century, I was kept up all night by festive song and celebration. Having no doubt succumbed to my subject, I had booked a room at the former colonial governor general's residence, now a hotel. There, Dalat's honeymooners made merry among desiccated colonial hunting trophies (the sun bear had definitely seen better days), fleur de lys detailing, grand staircases, and high ceilings. Did any of the revelers know or care that Governors Brévié and Decoux, and Admiral d'Argenlieu had once made this their residence, within easy reach of Bao Dai's palace? Marketing colonial symbols of power as postcolonial sites of romance is certainly not unique to Vietnam: the phenomenon is widespread in India, for instance.[20] However, in Communist Vietnam, in the wake of Dalat's seizure/liberation by the Viet-Minh in 1975, and given the latter's vision of Dalat as a decadent site for fattened bourgeois, the city's nostalgic colonial aura, indeed its intense popularity, seem especially jarring. Were the revelers at my hotel dancing on the ruins of empire? Or were these young people, far removed from both Indochina wars, now toasting a melancholy, campy, and romantic spirit, born of the resort's position in Vietnam's mountainous interior, in the heart of a highland minority zone, and from its lingering yet vague reputation as a colonial haven? I would hazard to guess some version of the latter. In the process, the former Chamonix, Simla, Petropolis, or Bandung of Indochina has been recast into a city of misty dew, and a city of love.

NOTES

ABBREVIATIONS AND TERMS

Abbreviations

ACND	Archives de la Congrégation Notre-Dame, Fontenay-sous-Bois, France
AFFPOL	Fonds ministériels, Affaires politiques
AGEFOM	Agence de la France d'outre-mer
AIP	Archives de l'Institut Pasteur, Paris
AMB	Archives municipales de Bordeaux
ANF	Archives nationales de France, Paris
ANOM	Archives nationales d'outre-mer, Aix-en-Provence
ARSAB	Archives des Rédemptoristes, Ste Anne de Beaupré, Québec, Canada
BFL	Bureau français de liaison
BNF	Bibliothèque nationale, Paris
CIAM	Congrès international d'architecture moderne, GTA-Archiv, Zürich
CUKL	Cornell University Kroch Library, Manuscripts, Cochinchina records
CONSPOL	Fonds du Conseiller politique du Haut-Commissariat en Indochine
DDF	Documents diplomatiques français
DRV	Democratic Republic of Vietnam
GGI	Gouvernement général de l'Indochine
HCI	Haut-Commissariat en Indochine (série continue)
IAF	Indochine Ancien Fonds
ICM	Indochine, Cabinet militaire
IFA	Archives de l'Institut français d'Architecture, Paris
INF	Fonds ministériels, Indochine Nouveau Fonds
JOIF	Journal officiel de l'Indochine française
LDPL	Lam Dong Provincial Library, Vietnam

MAE	Archives du ministère des archives étrangères, Paris
NLV	National Library of Vietnam, Hanoi
PHARO	Institut de Médecine Tropicale, Le Pharo, Marseille
RSA	Résidence supérieure d'Annam
RST	Résidence supérieure du Tonkin
RSTNF	Résidence supérieure du Tonkin, Nouveau Fonds
SHAT	Service historique de l'armée de Terre, Vincennes, France
SHG	Service historique de la Gendarmerie, Vincennes, France
SHM	Service historique de la Marine, Vincennes, France
SPCE	Service de Protection du Corps Expéditionnaire
USNA	U.S. National Archives, College Park, Maryland
VNA1	Vietnamese National Archives. Center 1, Hanoi (Trung Tâm Tài Liêu Luu Tru 1)
VNA2	Vietnamese National Archives. Center 2, Ho Chi Minh City (Trung Tâm Tài Liêu Luu Tru 2). *Note on RSA sources at the Vietnamese National Archives:* The RSA collection I consulted at VNA2 in Ho Chi Minh City in 2004 has since moved to the National Archives #4 in Dalat. Unfortunately, the call numbers of the files I consulted in 2004 have now changed. When Hazel Hahn generously looked up some RSA documents for me in the Archives #4 in 2008, she gave some of the new call numbers. Subsequently, another colleague provided additional information on the new RSA classification. For many calls numbers in the 4000 range, the offset between the old and new designation is +22 (for example: RSA 4087 from 2004 has become RSA 4109 in VNA4 in 2008). However, there are variations even in the 4000 range. For example: RSA 4069 has now become RSA 4090. Beyond the 4000 range, the offset varies considerably. For instance, RSA 3700 from 2004 has become RSA 3721 in 2009. And RSA 2751 has now become RSA 2762. The footnotes therefore systematically list both the call number as I found it in 2004, and the new call number as it can be found today in the RSA *fonds* of the Vietnamese National Archives #4 in Dalat.

Notes on Terminology

There were numerous colonial-era variations for the spelling of the Lang-Bian (Langbian, Lang Bian), the plateau region in which Dalat is located. For the sake of consistency, I will use the hyphenated version. Conversely, since "Dalat" and "Dankia" were seldom spelled with a hyphen, I have used the nonhyphenated spelling of those two terms throughout.

Until 1946, French colonial sources unfailingly referred to minorities of the south-central highlands as "Moïs," meaning "savage" in Vietnamese. I will use the umbrella term "highland minority" and only retain "Moï" when it is used in a quotation.

To avoid confusion, the colonial-era terms "Annamite" and "Annamese" will appear only in quoted passages. Instead I will use the term "Vietnamese" in spite of the problems this poses: "Annam/ite" and "Annamese" refer at once to a *Ky*, a kingdom, and an ethnicity, while

Vietnam/ese does not convey the same meanings. Moreover, "Vietnam" was not used in official colonial correspondence until 1942, nor even in mainstream Vietnamese parlance prior to 1945, and hence carries with it the risk of anachronism. (Goscha notes that between 1930 and 1945 "the word Viet-Nam remained largely unknown to the common folk." Christopher Goscha, *Vietnam or Indochina: Contesting Concepts of Space in Vietnamese Nationalism, 1887–1954* [Copenhagen: NIAS, 1995], 67.)

INTRODUCTION

1. In 2005, Dalat vied for several world records with giant wedding cakes, dove releases, and mass weddings. See "Dalat Love Festival to Mark Several Vietnam Records," *Vietnam News Brief Service,* October 14, 2005.

2. Norman Lewis, *A Dragon Apparent: Travels in Cambodia, Laos and Vietnam* (London: Jonathan Cape, 1951), p. 58.

3. *Le Guide du Routard Vietnam,* (Paris: Hachette, 1999), p. 301, and (Paris: Hachette, 2006), p. 284. Interestingly, the conic hat, rice bowl references, and stereotypes survived in the latest edition.

4. Déodat du Puy-Montbrun, *L'Honneur de la guerre* (Paris: Albin Michel, 2002), p. 127.

5. See Clifford Geertz, "Thick Description: Toward an Interpretive Theory of Culture." In *The Interpretation of Cultures: Selected Essays,* ed. Clifford Geertz (New York: Basic Books, 1973), pp. 3–30.

6. On this topic, see the excellent book by Romain Bertrand, *Mémoires d'empire: La controverse autour du 'fait colonial'* (Paris: Editions du Croquant, 2006).

7. Antoine Audouard, "L'Indochine, ni gloire, ni honte," *Le Monde,* November 28, 2006, p. 23.

8. If anything, the polarization of the memory of the Indochina war, in particular, seems ever growing. See Kathryn Edwards, "Le Mal Jaune: The Memory of the Indochina War in France, 1954–2006," PhD Thesis, University of Toronto, 2010. For an unabashed rehabilitation attempt of the colonial era, see Paul Rignac, *Indochine, les mensonges de l'anticolonialisme* (Paris: Indo Editions, 2007). For an example of equating genocide and colonialism, see Olivier Le Cour Grandmaison, *Coloniser, Exterminer: Sur la guerre et l'Etat colonial* (Paris: Fayard, 2005).

CHAPTER 1

1. Le soldat Silbermann, *Cinq ans à la Légion étrangère, Dix ans dans l'infanterie de marine, Souvenirs de campagne* (Paris: Plon, 1910), p. 302.

2. Dr. Auguste-Pascal-Marie Danguy des Déserts, "Considérations sur l'hygiène de l'Européen en Cochinchine," Medical thesis, University of Paris, 1876.

3. Dr. A. Léon, *Souvenirs d'un médecin de la marine 1853–1867,* deuxième partie, première période 1858–59 (Paris: L. Bataille and co., 1896), pp. 175, 187.

4. Dr. François-Eugène Bernard, "De l'influence du climat de la Cochinchine sur les maladies des Européens," PhD thesis in medicine, University of Montpellier, 1867, pp. 15, 16, 31.

5. Ibid., pp. 17, 30, 55.

6. Ibid., p. 56.

7. See Charles Fourniau, *Vietnam: Domination coloniale et résistance nationale, 1858–1914* (Paris: Les Indes savantes, 2002), pp. 62–63, 74.

8. Charles Meyer reaches the figure of a 9.9 percent fatality rate in 1861 but is perhaps referring to the population in general. Meyer, *Les Français en Indochine, 1860–1910* (Paris: Hachette, 1995), p. 99. The figure I give here is drawn from Dr. Bonnafy, "Statistique médicale de la Cochinchine, 1861–1888," *Archives de médecine navale 67* (mars 1897): p. 168, and appears in Philip Curtin, *Death by Migration: Europe's Encounters with the Tropical World in the Nineteenth Century* (Cambridge: Cambridge University Press, 1989), p. 188.

9. Dr. Fontaine, "Notes sur la mortalité des troupes d'infanterie et d'artillerie de marine casernées en Cochinchine (1890 à 1896)," *Annales d'hygiène et de médecine coloniales* (Janvier-Mars 1898), p. 115.

10. ANOM, GGI 11458, Médecin-en-chef, Saigon, July 14, 1882.

11. Dysentery and malaria accounted for more than half of all deaths from disease in Cochinchina between 1863 and 1888. Dr. Bonnafy, p. 189 and table in article (non-paginated).

12. Dr. Fontaine, "Notes sur la mortalité," p. 114.

13. Ibid., pp. 114–16.

14. ANOM, GGI 22212, "Mission Odend'hal dans le Sud de l'Annam," p. 22.

15. Paul Gaffarel, *Les colonies françaises* (Paris: Félix Alcan, 1888), p. 350.

16. Dr. Fontaine, "Notes sur la mortalité des troupes," p. 117.

17. Adolphe Armand, *Médecine et hygiène des pays chauds* (Paris: Challamel aîné, 1853), pp. 295–300.

18. Baron Albert d'Anthouard, *Mes souvenirs: Cochinchine, 1881–1885* (Brioude: Watel, 1927), pp. 65–67, quotation from p. 67.

19. Danguy des Déserts, p. 7.

20. Gilles de Gantès, "Coloniaux, Gouverneurs et Ministres: l'Influence des Français du Vietnam sur l'Evolution du pays à l'époque coloniale, 1902–1914," PhD thesis, University of Paris VII, 1994, p. 24.

21. Drs. Kermorgant and Reynaud, "Précautions à prendre pour les expéditions et les explorations aux pays chauds," *Annales d'hygiène et de médecine coloniales* 3 (July-September 1900): p. 408.

22. Lazare-Gabriel-Marie Palud, "Un Transport-hôpital au point de vue hygiénique et thérapeutique." Thèse pour le doctorat en médecine (Bordeaux, 1886), p. 20.

23. Ibid., p. 52.

24. Ibid., p. 53.

25. Dr. Fontaine, "Notes sur la mortalité des troupes," pp. 125–27.

26. ANOM, INF 984.

27. This is corroborated by other evidence. Historian Charles Meyer notes that Cochinchinese hospitals were very concerned about "registering as few deaths as possible" in the 1860s and 1870s. And when an epidemic struck in 1877, the main newspaper *Le Courrier de Saigon* stopped printing obituaries with an eye to maintaining morale. Meyer, p. 103.

28. Palud, p. 54.

29. Georges Treille, *Hygiène coloniale* (Paris: Masson et Cie., 1899), p. 253.

30. Palud, pp. 56, 58.

31. Robert Aiken, *Imperial Belvederes: The Hill Stations of Malaya* (Kuala Lumpur: Oxford University Press, 1994), p. 2.

32. Danguy des Déserts, p. 50.

33. Ibid.

34. Dr. Alexandre Kermorgant, "Sanatoria et camps de dissémination de nos colonies," *Annales d'hygiène et de médecine coloniales* 1899 (July-September), p. 359.

35. Many of Courbet's men had contracted cholera while fighting Chinese forces in modern-day Taiwan. See Fourniau, p. 339.

36. ANOM, IAF 325, Minister of the Colonies to Président du Conseil, Paris, September 24, 1886.

37. Laurence Monnais-Rousselot, *Médecine et colonisation: L'aventure indochinoise, 1860–1939* (Paris: CNRS Editions, 1999), p. 22; and Anonymous, *Hommes et destins* (Paris: Académie des sciences d'outre-mer, 1988), vol. 8, p. 237.

38. ANOM, INF 289, Mècre to Decrais, Minister of the Colonies, June 6, 1899, and the April 1893 contract, signed Mècre and Lanessan.

39. French doctors were not the only ones to view Japan as a possible site for a sanatorium, a safe-zone and medical base for European troops and officials posted on the Asian mainland. In 1863, the British army doctor and deputy inspector-general of hospitals Charles Alexander Gordon posited that Nagasaki would make an admirable sanatorium. He cited the region's climate, which he claimed was cooled by a marine current, just as the British Isles were soaked by the Gulf Stream. His logic was identical to that of Mècre's and Courbet's: "sick men would in this brief period [the short crossing from China] be enabled to exchange the frightful climate of these places during the most unhealthy season for a climate as near as possible similar to that of one of the most favoured parts of England." Charles Alexander Gordon, *China from a Medical Point of View in 1860 and 1861 to which is added a chapter on Nagasaki as Sanitarium* (London: John Churchill, 1863), pp. 459, 463 (quote from 463).

40. ANOM, IAF 325, Ministry of Foreign Affairs, Paris, Minister Flourens to Ministry of the Colonies, December 1, 1897.

41. ANOM, IAF 325, Ambassador (Tokyo) to Ministry of Foreign Affairs, Paris, January 17, 1887.

42. ANOM, IAF 325, "Projet relatif à l'établissement d'un sanitarium sur la colline française de Yokohama."

43. For hydrotherapy, see Eric Jennings, *Curing the Colonizers: Hydrotherapy, Climatology, and French Colonial Spas* (Raleigh: Duke University Press, 2006). ANOM, INF 289, "Tableau A, dépenses occasionnées pour faire face aux obligations de contrat."

44. ANOM, INF 289, draft of letter to Gauthier.

45. ANOM, IAF 325, "Conseil supérieur de Santé de la Marine, séance du 12 janvier 1888."

46. Pierre Brocheux and Daniel Hémery, *Indochine, la colonisation ambiguë* (Paris: La Découverte, 2001), pp. 83–84.

47. ANOM, IAF 325, "Conseil supérieur de Santé de la Marine, séance du 12 janvier 1888."

48. A 1920 guidebook put Saigon fifteen days away from Yokohama by ship, and San Francisco twenty-two days away. Pierre Bouvard and M. Millet, *La Chasse au Lang Bian* (Bergerac: Imprimerie du Sud-Ouest, 1920), p. 6.

49. ANOM, IAF 325, "Conseil supérieur de Santé de la Marine, séance du 12 janvier 1888."

50. Ibid.

51. The date of 1887 comes from Fernand Bernard, "L'Indochine, erreurs et dangers," *La Revue de Paris* (February 1901), p. 756. Republished as a book: Capitaine Fernand Bernard, *Indo-Chine, erreurs et dangers: Un programme* (Paris: Charpentier, 1901). All other material on Baria is drawn from Kermorgant.

52. Kermorgant, p. 359.

53. On the international (British, French, Italian) race to confirm malaria's mosquito transmission, and on the thorny question of who reached the finish line first, see Jeanne Guillemin, "Choosing Scientific Patrimony: Sir Ronald Ross, Alphonse Laveran, and the Mosquito-Vector Hypothesis for Malaria," *Journal of the History of Medicine and Allied Sciences* 57, no. 4 (October 2002): pp. 385–409.

54. All information from this paragraph is from ANOM, AGEFOM, 238, dossier 304, Dalat, "Les origines de Dalat."

55. The most detailed and rigorous account of Yersin's life, and especially of his years in Indochina, remains Jacqueline Brossollet and Henri Mollaret, *Yersin: Un Pasteurien en Indochine* (first published by Fayard in 1985, reedited in 1993 by Belin).

56. Brossollet and Mollaret, pp. 141–44 (Belin edition). The letters to his mother are reproduced on p. 144.

57. AIP, Yersin letters to his mother. Letter of February 23, 1895.

58. Here Yersin contributed to a mountain of ethnographic collections, ethnography being a discipline that was well represented at the Museum, inasmuch as it had branched out of natural history. This realm too featured considerable international competition and mutual observation. See Alice Conklin, "Civil Society, Science and Empire in Late Republican France: The Foundation of Paris's Museum of Man," *Osiris* 17 (2002): p. 259.

59. AIP, Yersin letters to his mother. Letter of January 12, 1894.

60. Gerald Hickey, *Sons of the Mountains: Ethnohistory of the Vietnamese Central Highlands to 1954* (New Haven: Yale University Press, 1982), p. 255.

61. AIP, Yersin, carton 4, "Yersin, pays moï, correspondance."

62. AIP, Yersin carton 3, dossier 24.363, "Sept mois chez les Moïs de l'Indochine," p. 2.

63. AIP, Yersin carton 3, dossier 13651, "Yersin pays moï, deuxième expédition," entry for June 21, 1893, p. 117.

64. Ibid., entry for June 18, 1893, p. 113.

65. AIP, Yersin carton 3, dossier 10.677, "Yersin pays moï, deuxième expédition" and "De Nha-Trang à Tourane par les pays moïs."

66. Ibid.

67. Hickey, *Sons of the Mountains*, p. 246.

68. Alexandre Yersin, "De Nha-Trang à Tourane par les plateaux moïs," *Indochine, hebdomadaire illustré*, April 15, 1943, p. 3.

69. AIP, Yersin carton 3, dossier 10.677, "Yersin pays moï, deuxième expédition" and "De Nha-Trang à Tourane par les pays moïs."

70. Alexandre Yersin, "De Nha-Trang à Tourane par les plateaux moïs," *Indochine, hebdomadaire illustré*, April 15, 1943, p. 7.

71. AIP, Yersin letters to his mother. Letter of January 17, 1894.

72. ANOM, GGI 5967, Résident supérieur d'Annam to the Governor General, Hanoi, June 1, 1893.

73. AIP, Yersin letters to his mother. Letters from March 8, 1894 and April 6, 1894.

74. AIP, Yersin letters to his mother. Letter from October 10, 1897.

75. AIP, Yersin letters to his mother. Letter from December 11, 1897.

76. All information in this paragraph is drawn from ANOM, GGI 5969, Kermorgant, Paris, June 14, 1898.

77. ANOM, GGI 5969, Doumer to Ministry of the Colonies, April 18, 1898.

78. Mathieu Guérin, "Des casques blancs sur le plateau des herbes: La pacification des aborigènes des hautes terres du Sud-Indochinois, 1859–1940," PhD thesis, University of Paris VII, 2003, p. 240.

79. All primary material in this paragraph and the preceding one, with the exception of Montfort's hunting skill, is from ANOM, GGI 5969, Doumer to Ministry of the Colonies, April 18, 1898. On Montfort's abilities to shoot the Lang-Bian's elk half a kilometer away, or dove with a pistol, see Etienne Tardif, *La Naissance de Dalat, 1899–1900* (Vienne: Ternet-Martin, 1948), p. 114. On "Phu Lang sa," see Caroline Herbelin, "Dalat: modèle d'urbanisme colonial ou anecdote architecturale?" forthcoming in *Cahiers d'études vietnamiennes*, p. 16 (all page numbers from the draft kindly provided by Caroline Herbelin).

80. Paul Doumer, quoted in "Actes de la société de géographie, procès verbaux des séances, séance du 11 avril 1902," in *Bulletin de la Société de géographie* (1902), p. 387.

81. On Doumerian excess, see Gilles de Gantès, p. 307.

82. Fernand Bernard noted that there was one French administrator per 7,900 inhabitants in French Cochinchina versus one administrator per 76,000 inhabitants in Dutch colonial Java. Fernand Bernard, *Indo-Chine*, p. 43.

83. Most information in this paragraph comes from Brocheux and Hémery, pp. 79–89.

84. Joseph Buttinger, *Vietnam: a Dragon Embattled* (New York: Praeger, 1967), p. 35.

CHAPTER 2

1. "Sanatorium dans l'Annam central," *La quinzaine coloniale*, April 25, 1901, p. 246.

2. ANOM, GGI 5979, Captain Debay, "Etude sur les regions centrales du Massif annamitique," March 1899.

3. Capitaine Debay, "Un Sanatorium pour l'Annam Central," *Revue des Troupes coloniales* (1904), pp. 5–6. The stand-alone publication is available at BNF, 8-TE165–128.

4. ANOM, GGI 5964, Mission Debay, "Recherche d'un emplacement pour un Sanatorium en Annam."

5. Debay, "Un Sanatorium pour l'Annam Central," p. 15.

6. ANOM, GGI 5964, Mission Debay.

7. Debay, "Un Sanatorium pour l'Annam Central," pp. 5–6.

8. Sven Lindqvist, *Exterminate all the Brutes* (Granta, 1996), p. 170.

9. All information on Debay up to now is drawn from SHAT, 7YF 73393; ANF, LH 677/46 (19); and the *Annuaire de la Marine*.

10. SHAT, 7YF 73393, "Livret matricule d'homme de troupe."

11. SHAT, 7YF 73393, "Renseignements concernant le sous-lieutenant Debay," Sontay, April 17, 1891.

12. ANOM, GGI B/220/21, Hanoi to Hué, September 14, 1894, pp. 414–15.

13. ANOM, GGI 5960, "Le juge de la Paix à competence étendue de Tourane à Monsieur le Procureur general, chef du service judiciaire en Indochine à Hanoi," December 6, 1901. Another copy of the same report can be found in SHAT, 7YF 73393.

14. ANOM, GGI 5960.

15. Ibid.

16. SHAT, 7YF 73393, "Procès-verbal d'audition de témoins," case 13, Dinh-Dua.

17. SHAT, 7YF 73393, "Procès-verbal d'audition de témoins," case 33, Nguyen Van Tuan.

18. ANOM, GGI 5960, "Le juge de la Paix à competence étendue de Tourane à Monsieur le Procureur general, chef du service judiciaire en Indochine à Hanoi," December 6, 1901.

19. SHAT, 7YF 73393, "Procès-verbal d'audition de témoins," case 39, Bien Van Nhi.

20. SHAT, 7YF 73393, "Procès-verbal d'audition de témoins," case 18.

21. On this practice, and the obstacles it faced, including linguistic ones, see Hélène Blais, "Les enquêtes des cartographes en Algérie, ou les ambiguïtés des savoirs vernaculaires en situation coloniale," *Revue d'histoire moderne et contemporaine* 54:4 (2007), pp. 70–85.

22. SHAT, 7YF 73393, "Procès-verbal d'audition de témoins," case 34.

23. SHAT, 7YF 73393, "Procès-verbal d'audition de témoins," case 83/ 15.

24. SHAT, 7YF 73393, Debay to Général, commandant la subdivision de Marseille, Marseille, May 26, 1902.

25. Victor Adrien Debay, *La colonisation en Annam* (Paris: H. Charles-Lavauzelle, 1904), p. 19.

26. Ibid.

27. ANOM, GGI 5964, "Mission de recherche d'un emplacement de sanatorium pour l'Annam central." SHAT, 7YF 73393, Debay to Général, commandant la subdivision de Marseille, Marseille, May 26, 1902. On Decherf's fevers, see Debay, "Un Sanatorium pour l'Annam Central," *Revue des Troupes coloniales* (1904), p. 19. On his demise, see p. 23.

28. SHAT, 7YF 73393, Debay to Général, commandant la subdivision de Marseille, Marseille, May 26, 1902.

29. Ibid.

30. SHAT, 7YF 733393, "Ministère de la Guerre, Paris, February 24, 1902, note pour le Cabinet du Ministre"

31. ANOM, GGI 5960, M. Assaud, "Enquête sur les violences reprochées au Capitaine Debay," December 21, 1901.

32. SHAT, 7YF 733393, "Direction des troupes coloniales, Proposition de placer le Capitaine Debay de l'infanterie coloniale en non-activité par retrait d'emploi," Undated.

33. SHAT, 7YF 733393, "Demande de non-activité du Captaine Debay de l'infanterie coloniale pour violences graves," General Dodds, to the War Minister, December 26, 1901.

34. SHAT, 7YF 733393, Ministère de la Guerre, Paris February 24, 1902, "Note pour le Cabinet du Ministre," from Taupin, in the "Direction du Contentieux et de la Justice militaire."

35. SHAT, 7YF 733393, letter dated Paris, September 30, 1902.

36. SHAT, 7YF 733393, "Proposition de rappeler à l'activité le Capitaine Debay," Paris, January 28, 1904.

37. SHAT, 7YF 733393, Debay, "Travail d'avancement de 1908," Hanoi, February 1, 1908.

38. SHAT, 7YF 73393, Debay to Général, commandant la subdivision de Marseille, Marseille, May 26, 1902.

39. ANF, LH 677/46 (19).

40. http://www.adventuretours.vn/nationatiol_parks/ba_na-nuichua_nature_reserve/index.htm. Site last consulted on September 12, 2008.

41. See Chantal Ahounou's historical context in the preface to *A la recherche de Voulet: Sur les traces sanglantes de la mission Afrique centrale* (Paris: Cosmopole, 2001), pp. 147–54.

42. Raphaëlle Branche, *La Torture et la guerre d'Algérie* (Paris: Gallimard, 2001), pp. 28–31.

43. Sven Lindqvist, *Exterminate all the Brutes,* and Olivier Le Cour Grandmaison, *Coloniser, Exterminer: Sur la guerre et l'Etat colonial* (Paris: Fayard, 2005).

44. Isabel Hull, *Absolute Destruction: Military Culture and the Practice of War in Imperial Germany* (Cornell: Cornell University Press, 2004), p. 331.

45. On the nature of the violence wrought during the conquest and subsequent "pacification" of Algeria, and its justifications, see Benjamin Brower, *A Desert Named Peace* (New York: Columbia University Press, 2009), p. 89. On the comparison with the Philippines, see Robert Gerwarth and Stephan Malinowski, "L'Antichambre de l'Holocauste? A propos du débat sur les violences coloniales et la guerre d'extermination nazie," *Vingtième Siècle, Revue d'Histoire* 99 (2008): pp. 148–50.

46. Bogumil Jewsiewicki, *Mami Wata: la peinture urbaine au Congo* (Paris: Gallimard, 2003), pp. 92–5. Marie-Bénédicte Dembour, "La chicote comme symbole du colonialisme belge?" *Canadian Journal of African Studies* 26, no. 2 (1992): pp. 205–25.

47. Pierre Brocheux, "Le colonialisme français en Indochine," in *Livre noir du colonialisme: De l'extermination à la repentance,* ed. Marc Ferro (Paris: Robert Laffont, 2003), p. 357.

48. ANOM, Affaires politiques 3152, Governor Sarraut, April 30, 1917.

49. Primary sources on some of these smaller hill stations include: "Le thermalisme et le climatisme en Indochine," *Le Monde thermal* (April 1930); "Bana et Bach-Ma, stations d'altitude de l'Annam," *Le Monde colonial illustré* (September 1939); Dr. Serge Abbatucci, "Les stations climatiques en Indochine," *Outre-mer, revue générale de colonisation* (September 1930), p. 293; and "Stations climatiques de l'Indochine," *Bulletin de l'agence économique de l'Indochine* 3, no. 29 (May 1930). Relatively few of them have been the subject of historical investigation. Exceptions include interesting studies on Sapa by Jean Michaud, *Sapa français: Une brève histoire* (Sapa: Victoria, 1999) and Aline Demay, "Tourisme sanitaire au Tonkin: Le cas de Cha Pa," *Ultramarines* 25 (2007): pp. 42–48. Raymond Fife's recent thesis dealt with the small hill station of Bach-Ma, founded in the 1930s: "Bach Ma: History and Archaeology of a French colonial hill station in Central Vietnam 1930–1990," PhD thesis, University of New England, Australia, 2009. For an exposé of hill station vs. beach tourism, see Emmanuelle Peyvel, "Tourisme et colonialisme au Vietnam" in *Le Tourisme dans l'Empire français: Politiques, pratiques et imaginaires,* eds. Colette Zytnicki, Habib Kazdaghli, pp. 133–43 (Paris: Société française d'histoire d'outre-mer, 2009). Aline Demay and Erich de Wald's forthcoming dissertations on French colonial tourism in Indochina both promise to situate hill stations and beach resorts in broader contexts.

50. "Stations climatiques de l'Indochine," *Bulletin de l'agence économique de l'Indochine* 3, no. 29 (May 1930), p. 154. On Bana's catering to settlers and colonial officials from cen-

tral Vietnam, also see Emmanuelle Peyvel, "L'Emergence du Tourisme au Viêt Nam: Lieux, Pratiques et Imaginaires," PhD thesis, Université de Nice, 2009, p. 216.

CHAPTER 3

1. In 1911, Pennequin would hatch the concept of an Asian army for France. See "Le Général Pennequin," *Bulletin du Comité de Madagascar* (1899): pp. 150–51; and Mireille Le Van Ho, "Le Général Pennequin et le projet d'Armée jaune, 1911–1915," *Revue française d'histoire d'outre-mer* 279 (1988): pp. 148–49.

2. ANOM, GGI 66188.

3. Curtin, *Death by Migration*, pp. 135–36.

4. Kermorgant, "Sanatoria et camps de dissémination de nos colonies," p. 345.

5. See Nancy Stepan, "Biological Degeneration: Races and Proper Places" in *Degeneration: the Dark Side of Progress,* eds. J. Edward Chamberlin and Sander Gilman, pp. 98–104 (New York: Columbia University Press, 1985); Warwick Anderson, *The Cultivation of Whiteness: Science, Health and Racial Destiny in Australia* (Melbourne: University of Melbourne Press, 2002), pp. 75–95; Mary Stewart, " 'Let us begin with the Weather': Climate, Race, and Cultural Distinctiveness" in *Nature and Society in Historical Context,* eds. Mikulas Teich, Roy Porter, and Bo Gustafsson, pp. 240–56 (Cambridge: Cambridge University Press, 1997); Dane Kennedy, "The perils of the midday sun: climatic anxieties in the colonial tropics" in *Imperialism and the Natural World,* ed. John Mackenzie, pp. 118–40 (Manchester: University of Manchester Press, 1990); David Arnold, *Colonizing the Body: State Medicine and Epidemic Disease in Nineteenth-Century India* (Berkeley: University of California Press, 1993), pp. 28–43; David Livingstone, "Human Acclimatization: Perspectives on a Contested Field of Enquiry in Science, Medicine and Geography," *History of Science* 15 (1987): pp. 359–94; Warwick Anderson, "Climates of Opinion: Acclimatization in Nineteenth-century France and England," *Victorian Studies* 35 (1992): pp. 2–24; Michael Osborne, "Acclimatizing the World: A History of the Paradigmatic Colonial Science," *Osiris* 15 (2000): pp. 135–51.

6. Jennings, *Curing the Colonizers*, pp. 15–17, 35–39.

7. Anne-Marie Moulin, "Expatriés français sous les tropiques: Cent ans d'histoire de la santé," *Bulletin de la Société de pathologie exotique* 90, no. 4 (1997): pp. 224. The phrase "small acclimatization" was apparently coined by Alphonse Bertillon. See Jean Lémure, *Madagascar, l'expédition au point de vue médical et hygiénique: L'acclimatement et la colonisation* (Paris: Baillière et fils, 1896), pp. 82–83.

8. Kermorgant, "Sanatoria et camps de dissémination de nos colonies," p. 345.

9. ANOM, GGI 5969, Doumer, Saigon, July 23, 1897.

10. ANOM, GGI 5969, Rapports sur le projet d'établissement d'un sanatorium au Lang-Bian.

11. ANOM, GGI 5967, Rapports du Dr. Yersin.

12. Ibid.

13. Ibid.

14. Statistics drawn from LDPL, Dalat, DC 067, p. 313.

15. Dane Kennedy, *The Magic Mountains: Hill Stations of the British Raj* (Berkeley, University of California Press, 1996). On the hill stations of the Raj, also see Vikram Bhatt, *Resorts of the Raj: Hill Stations of India* (Ahmedabad: Mapin Publishing, 1997); Raja Bhasin,

Simla, the Summer Capital of British India (London: Penguin, 1992); Monika Bührlein, *Nuwara Eliya: Hill Station und Zentraler Ort im Hochland der Insel Ceylon* (Stuttgart: Franz Steiner, 1991); Barbara Crossette, *The Great Hill Stations of Asia* (Boulder: Westview Press, 1998); Pamela Kanwar, "The Changing Profile of the Summer Capital of British India: Simla, 1864–1947," *Modern Asian Studies* 18, no. 2 (1984): pp. 215–236; Judith Kenny, "Claiming the High Ground: Theories of Imperial Authority and the British Hill Station in India," *Political Geography* (November 1997): pp. 655–673; Judith Kenny, "Constructing an Imperial Hill Station: The Representation of British Authority in Ootacamund" (PhD thesis, Syracuse University, 1990); Nora Mitchell, *The Indian Hill-Station: Kodaikanal* (Chicago: University of Chicago Geography Department, 1972).

16. ANOM, GGI 66188, Pennequin report.

17. Ibid.

18. On *le cafard* or the "blues" in French colonial Indochina, see Michael Vann, "White City on the Red River: Race, Power and Culture in French Colonial Hanoi, 1872–1954," PhD thesis, University of California at Santa Cruz, 1999.

19. Dalat's role as a Europe-substitute is mentioned in Pierre Brocheux and Daniel Hémery, *Indochine, la colonisation ambiguë* (Paris: La Découverte, 2001), p. 182.

20. On Bernard's funding the French Resistance after 1940, see Henry Frenay, *La nuit finira* (Paris: Robert Laffont, 1973), pp. 75, 99. Frenay draws the following portrait of the now ageing man: "Colonel Bernard is a small man, slim, with a lively glance, a thin mustache yellowed by tobacco. His words and gestures are trenchant, his opinions fixed. He served many years in the colonial army, then settled in Indochina, where he must have made his fortune."

21. ANF, AB XIX 4283, Fernand Bernard to his parents, Lang-Bian Plateau, November 27, 1898 (note that when I consulted this in 2009, it was incorrectly located in file 2, comprised of letters from Bernard to his brother and son).

22. Ibid.

23. ANF, AB XIX 4283, Fernand Bernard to his parents, Kréan, December 5, 1898.

24. Ibid.

25. Philippe Devilliers, *Français et Annamites: Partenaires ou ennemis? 1856–1902* (Paris: Denoël, 1998), p. 463.

26. Fernand Bernard, "L'Indochine, erreurs et dangers," *La Revue de Paris* (February 1901), pp. 535–65, 727–60. In the book edition, the Lang-Bian is covered on pp. 170–91.

27. Ibid., book edition, p. 189, article version, p. 756.

28. Drs. Vassal and Tardif led vigorous counterattacks against Bernard. See Dr. Vassal, "L'Etat sanitaire de l'Indochine et le Lang-Bian," *La Quinzaine coloniale* (First semester 1907), p. 16; Dr. Etienne Tardif, *Un sanatorium en Annam: La mission du Lang-Bian* (Vienne: Ogeret-Martin, 1902), introduction. Also see Tardif, *La Naissance de Dalat, 1899–1900* (Vienne: Ternet-Martin, 1948), p. 39.

29. "Le sanatorium du Lang-Bian," *La Quinzaine coloniale,* March 10, 1906, p. 134.

30. Bernard, "L'Indochine, erreurs et dangers," article version, p. 757.

31. Tardif, *La Naissance de Dalat,* p. 23.

32. Tardif, *Un sanatorium en Annam,* p. 23. William B. Cohen has remarked on how infrequently French colonial doctors recommended quinine as a prophylaxis. See William B.

Cohen, "Malaria and French Imperialism," *The Journal of African History* 24 (1983): pp. 23–36.

33. Tardif, *Un sanatorium en Annam*, p. 23.

34. ANOM, GGI 5959, Guynet to Governor General, January 16, 1900; and Tardif, *Un sanatorium en Annam*, p. 63. Only in a subsequent work published a half century after the event did Tardif finally acknowledge that the sergeant had died of malaria.

35. Tardif, *La Naissance de Dalat*, pp. 227, 243.

36. Tardif, *Un sanatorium en Annam*, p. 63.

37. Tardif, *Un sanatorium en Annam*, p. 21. On the book's aim to rebut the sanatorium's critics, see its introduction.

38. Kennedy, *The Magic Mountains*, p. 19.

39. Kermorgant, "Sanatoria et camps de dissémination de nos colonies," p. 347.

40. Philip Curtin shows that in 1901, the prestigious French Academy of Medicine struck a malaria committee that advocated new, resolutely Rossian measures: mosquito prevention and isolation of the sick. But by the same token, it clung to old formulae: blacks were considered immune, tilling the earth could awaken the disease from a long slumber, and consequently blacks, rather than whites, should undertake agricultural tasks in the tropics. Similarly, a 1905 official report by Dr. Gilbert Sersiron on malaria in Algeria called for greater use of quinine and increased mosquito prevention, but also large-scale emigration of populations to the mountains in the hottest months, and the use of hill stations to cure malaria through altitude. Curtin, *Death by Migration*, p. 137; Dr. Gilbert Sersiron, *Rapport sur le paludisme en Algérie considéré comme maladie sociale* (Paris, Octave Douin, 1905), pp. 17–32.

41. Harish Naraindas, "Poisons, Putrescence and the Weather," in *Les sciences hors d'occident au xxème siècle*, vol. 4., *Médecines et santé, Medical Practices and Health* (Paris: ORSTOM, 1996), p. 33.

42. Wolfgang Eckart, "Creating Confidence: Heinrich Zeiss as a Traveller in the Soviet Union, 1921–1932," in *Doing Medicine Together: Germany and Russia Between the Wars*, ed. Susan Gross Solomon (University of Toronto Press, 2006), pp. 199–239; Wolfgang Eckart, "Generalarzt Ernst Rodenwaldt," in *Hitlers militärische Elite*, vol. 1 (Darmstadt: Gerd Ueberschär, 1998), pp. 210–22; Warwick Anderson, "Disease, Race and Empire," *The Bulletin of the History of Medicine* 70 (1996), p. 66.

43. David Livingstone, "Race, Space and Moral Climatology: Notes toward a Geneology," *Journal of Historical Geography* 28, no. 2 (2002): pp. 159–80.

44. Mark Philip Bradley, *Imagining Vietnam and America: The Making of Postcolonial Vietnam, 1919–1950* (Chapel Hill: University of North Carolina Press, 2000), pp. 51–55.

45. Monnais-Rousselot, p. 263. M. Borel, "Dalat et le paludisme," *Bulletin économique de l'Indochine* 187 (1927): p. 393.

46. ANOM, GGI 66188. The 800-meter bar had served as conventional wisdom for much of the late nineteenth century. Rochard, "Encyclopédie d'hygiène et de médecine publiques," vol. 1 (Paris: 1890), cited in Vassal, "L'Etat sanitaire de l'Indochine et le Lang-Bian," p. 18.

47. This suggests that Annick Guénel might be off the mark in her assessment that French doctors failed to undertake detailed studies of malarial transmission in Indochina. She states: "In the case of a disease as major as malaria was in Indochina, far-reaching research with a methodical inventory of the anopheline fauna was not carried out until 1925." Annick Guénel,

"The Creation of the First Overseas Pasteur Institute and the Beginning of Albert Calmette's Pastorian Career," *Medical History* 43 (1999): p. 24.

48. At age seventy, Schilling would conduct experiments on the effects of malaria on humans at Dachau. See Wolfgang Eckart and H. Vondra, "Malaria and World War II: German malaria experiments 1939–1945," *Parassitologia* 42, nos. 1–2 (2000): pp. 53–58. On the extent of Franco-German dialogue in the field of tropical medicine prior to 1914, see Deborah J. Neill, *Networks in Tropical Medicine*, forthcoming with Stanford University Press.

49. This portrait is based on biographical summaries from the Pasteur Institute Archives in Paris.

50. Dr. Vassal, "Rapport sur une mission au Lang-Bian au point du vue du paludisme," *Bulletin économique de l'Indochine* (October 1905), pp. 921–23 (quotation from p. 921).

51. Vassal, "L'Etat sanitaire de l'Indochine et le Lang-Bian," p. 15.

52. Luise White has shown how European medical practices surrounding blood extraction led to fears of European vampirism amongst many Africans. Luise White, *Speaking with Vampires: Rumor and History in Colonial Africa* (Berkeley: University of California Press, 2000).

53. Vassal, "Rapport sur une mission au Lang-Bian au point du vue du paludisme," pp. 922–23.

54. Ibid., p. 926.

55. Vassal, "L'Etat sanitaire de l'Indochine et le Lang-Bian," pp. 17–19.

56. All material from this paragraph is drawn from Dr. Vassal, 1914 report on the Lang-Bian, in AIP, fonds Paul Louis Simond (SIM 16) E.

57. Paul Doumer, *Situation de L'Indochine, 1897–1901* (Hanoi: Schneider, 1902), p. 113.

58. On this point, see ANOM, 5956, Thoaurd report, 1898.

59. ANOM, GGI 5959, Guynet report to Doumer, September 25, 1899.

60. On this curious obsession, see Crossette, p. 212.

61. Etienne Tardif, *La naissance de Dalat*, pp. 128, 144–47, 219.

62. ANOM, GGI 6963, "Note relative à l'emplacement d'un Sanatorium sur le Lang-Bian."

63. ANOM, RSA F1, Rapport politique du Haut-Donnaï, octobre à novembre 1900.

64. Quoted in Amaury Lorin, "Dalat, station d'altitude: Fondation ex nihilo de Paul Doumer, Gouverneur Général de l'Indochine (1898)," *Péninsule* 52 (2006): p. 229.

65. ANOM, GGI 66188, "Rapport du Dr. Haueur," Saigon, June 4, 1903.

66. AIP, Yersin to his mother, August 26, 1899. On connections and borrowings between French and Dutch orientalist schools, see Pierre Singaravélou, *L'Ecole française d'Extrême-Orient ou l'institution des marges: 1898–1956* (Paris: L'Harmattan, 1999), pp. 81–83.

67. ANF, AB XIX 4283, Bernard to his parents, Batavia, March 14, 1900.

68. Joseph Vassal, "Baguio, station d'altitude des Philippines," *Annales d'hygiène et de médecine coloniales* 11 (1908), pp. 502–511. For a recent comparison of Dalat and Baguio's respective development, see Robert Reed, "Constructing Highland Cities in Southeast Asia: Baguio (Philippines) and Dalat (Vietnam) as Scenes of Envrionmental Degradation," in *Southeast Asian Urban Environments,* eds. Carla Chifos and Ruth Yabes, pp. 183–273 (Tempe: Arizona State University Program for Southeast Asian Studies, 2000). Reed notes that the recurring hypothesis that Baguio was an American invention is erroneous (p. 195). On Baguio, also see Robert Reed, *City of Pines: The Origins of Baguio as a Colonial Hill Station and Regional Capital* (Berkeley: Center for South and Southeast Asian Studies, 1976).

69. ANOM, INF 290.

70. Ibid.

71. ANOM, GGI 54086, Consul de France à Singapour au Gouverneur Général de l'Indochine, October 10, 1923.

72. Dr. Dourne, "Le Sanatorium du Lang-Bian," *Annales d'hygiène et de médecine coloniales* 1913 (16), p. 220.

73. On the improvement of European mortality rates in the first decades of the twentieth century see de Gantès, p. 28.

74. Henry Edward Shortt, "The occurrence of malaria in a hill station," *Indian Journal of Medical Research* 11, no. 3 (January 1924): p. 771.

75. Ibid., p. 772.

76. VNA2, RSA 4091 (Bureau municipal d'hygiène de Dalat, 1925), now renumbered as VNA4, RSA 4113, Médecin chef du poste medical de Dalat à Monsieur le Gouverneur général.

77. VNA2, RSA 4091 (Bureau municipal d'hygiène de Dalat, 1925) now renumbered as VNA4, RSA 4113, "Commission municipale d'hygiène, Réunion du 16 janvier 1925." On the draining of the lake closest to the doctor's residence by prisoners, see VNA2, RSA 4087 (Décision du Gouverneur général concernant divers travaux à Dalat), now renumbered as VNA4 RSA 4109, "Application des décisions prises le 16 août 1924 par le Gouverneur général relatives aux travaux à exécuter à Dalat," Dalat, September 16, 1924.

78. Borel, "Dalat et le paludisme," *Bulletin économique de l'Indochine* 187 (1927), p. 394.

79. Ibid., p. 397.

80. Ibid., p. 397.

81. Ibid., pp. 393–99.

82. ANOM, GGI 49510.

83. Anonymous, "La salubrité de Dalat," *Bulletin économique de l'Indochine* 193 (March 1928), pp. 229–32.

84. M. Treillard, "Une modalité de la zoophilie anophélienne en Indochine méridionale: Neocellia fuliginosa à la station d'altitude de Dalat, Annam," *Bulletin de Pathologie exotique* 27 (1934): p. 755.

85. VNA2, RSA 3700, (Dalat, Lutte antipalustre, 1937–1938), now renumbered as VNA4, RSA 3721, Hué, October 9, 1937.

86. VNA2, RSA 4100, now renumbered as VNA4, RSA 4122, Commission municipale, session ordinaire, September 14, 1928.

87. Monnais-Rousselot, p. 204.

88. VNA 2, RSA 3700 (Dalat, Lutte antipalustre, 1937–1938), now renumbered as VNA4, RSA 3721, Hué, January 14, 1938.

89. VNA 2, RSA 3700, (Dalat, Lutte antipalustre, 1937–1938), now renumbered as VNA4, RSA 3721, Haut-Donnaï, January 21, 1938.

90. P. Carton, "Etude climatologique des stations d'altitude de l'Indochine en 1939," *Archives des Institut Pasteur d'Indochine* 8, no. 29 (April-October 1939), pp. 138–40.

91. P. Carton and Henry Morin, *De l'influence des facteurs climatiques sur la répartition de l'endémie palustre en Indochine* (Hanoi: Imprimerie d'Extrême-Orient, 1934), pp. 10–11.

92. P. Carton, "Etude climatologique des stations d'altitude de l'Indochine en 1939," pp. 167–68.

93. Marguerite Duras, *L'Amant de la Chine du Nord* (Paris: Gallimard, 1991), p. 52.

94. In *The Lover,* the leading character is described as "having become a young woman of this land, Indochina." See Julia Waters, "Cholen, la capitale chinoise de l'Indochine française: Reading Marguerite Duras' (Indo)Chinese novels," in *France and Indochina: Cultural Representations,* eds. Kathryn Robson and Jennifer Yee, p. 181 (Lanham: Lexington Books, 2005); as well as Julia Waters, *Duras and Indochina: Postcolonial Perspectives* (Liverpool: SFPS, 2006), pp. 82–83. Also see Laure Adler, *Marguerite Duras* (Paris: Gallimard, 1998), p. 61.

95. According to Jean Vallier, Lagonelle later died at a sanatorium in Pau in 1934. Jean Vallier, *C'était Marguerite Duras,* vol. 1 (Paris: Fayard, 2006), p. 384, footnote 43. The colonial archives indicate that the actual Hélène Lagonelle was born on December 17, 1913. They specify that Marie and Bernard-Martial Lagonelle, Hélène's parents, who had been appointed respectively teacher and principal at the Petit Lycée de Dalat in 1931 and 1928, took leaves of absence in 1931, 1932, and 1933 before returning on emergency leave to the metropole in April 1934. ANOM, GGI 49394 and ANOM, GGI 49393.

96. Marguerite Duras, *L'Amant* (Paris: Les Editions de Minuit, 1984), pp. 89–90.

97. Marguerite Duras, *L'Amant de la Chine du Nord,* p. 52.

98. Ibid., p. 53.

99. Silbermann, pp. 302–3.

100. ANOM, GGI 5965, "Rapport sur l'établissement d'un camp militaire sur le massif du Lang-Bian," 1903. The same question of prostitution is raised by Dr. Haueur in 1903, in ANOM, GGI 66188, "Rapport sur l'établissement d'un camp militaire dans le massif du Lang-Bian." Commission Beylié, comprenant le chef de bataillon Grimaud et le médecin major Haueur.

101. ANOM, 66188, "Rapports du Général Pennquin, le Médecin inspecteur Grall, le médecin principal Hénaff."

102. "Le sanatorium du Lang-Bian," *La quinzaine coloniale,* March 10, 1906, p. 135.

103. Voyron testimony, ANOM, GGI 66188, "Voyage du Gouverneur général au Lang-Bian."

104. ANOM, GGI 66188, "Note pour le Gouverneur Général par intérim," Hanoi, August 21, 1906, signed Leblond, Chef du bureau militaire.

105. ANOM, GGI 66188, Beau to Champoudry, July 4, 1904.

106. VNA2, RSA 2751 (Construction d'un sanatorium militaire à Dalat), now renumbered as VNA4, RSA 2762, Pasquier cited in a letter of December 1, 1930.

107. VNA2, RSA 2751 (Construction d'un sanatorium militaire à Dalat), now renumbered as VNA4, RSA 2762, Governor general, April 3, 1931.

108. VNA2, RSA 2751 (Construction d'un sanatorium militaire à Dalat), now renumbered as VNA4, RSA 2762, Gouverneur général au Gouvenreur de division, commandant supérieur des troupes du groupe de l'Indochine, December 1, 1930.

109. ANOM, GGI 66587.

110. ANOM, GGI 66587, Jean Decoux, head of naval forces in Indochina, to the Governor General, August 9, 1928.

111. ANOM, GGI 66587, Bongrain, Commander of the Navy in Indochina, Saigon, March 25, 1931.

112. VNA2, RSA 2751 (Construction d'un sanatorium militaire à Dalat), now renumbered as VNA4, RSA 2762, General Billotte, Hanoi, February 21, 1931.

113. "Séjours aux colonies," *L'Avenir du Tonkin,* January 20–21, 1902.

114. Georges Dioque, ed., *Félix Dioque: Un Colonial* (Gap: Société d'études des Hautes-Alpes, 2008), p. 184; and Dr. Dourne, p. 219.

115. VNA2, RSA 4069 (Lettre du Gouverneur général N 215 du 26/9/04 demandant la liste du personnel de l'administration de l'Annam pour prévoir des habitations au Lang Bian après l'achèvement du chemin de fer), now renumbered as VNA4, RSA 4090. The Cambodia reference is from National Archives of Cambodia, RSC 23761.

116. Circular of September 9, 1936, referring to the *arrêté* of January 10, 1916. *Bulletin administratif de l'Annam,* 1936, pp. 1196–97.

117. ANOM. AFFPOL 3152, Mission d'Inspection, 1916, 1917, Saurin report, March 20, 1917.

118. "Perles parlementaires," *L'Eveil économique de l'Indochine,* March 25, 1923, p. 7.

119. Cited in Dr. Gaide, *Les stations climatiques en Indochine* (Hanoi: IDEO, 1930), p. 6.

120. On this debate in another setting, see Stephen Frenkel and John Western, "Pretext or Prophylaxis? Racial Segregation and Malarial Mosquitoes in a British Tropical Colony: Sierra Leone," *Annals of the Association of American Geographers* 78, no. 2 (1988): pp. 211–28.

121. See for example Greg Mitman, "Hay Fever Holiday: Health, Leisure and Place in Gilded-age America," *Bulletin of the History of Medicine* 77 (Fall 2003), pp. 600–35.

122. Kennedy, *The Magic Mountains,* p. 37.

CHAPTER 4

1. ANOM, GGI 5972, rapport de M Odend'hal sur le fonctionnement du sanatorium de Dalat, October 25, 1901.

2. Mathieu Guérin and Arnoult Seveau, eds., "Manuscrit de Pierre Dru, extrait," *Outre-mers, revue d'histoire* 362–3 (2009): p. 170.

3. On the spikes, see Henri Maitre, *Les régions Moïs du Sud Indo-Chinois* (Paris: Plon, 1909), p. 182.

4. Paul Doumer, *Situation de l'Indochine, 1897–1901* (Hanoi: F.H. Schneider, 1902), pp. 112–14.

5. A useful recap of the decision to build transportation routes first, and the sanatorium second, can be found in ANOM, 1TP 165, dossier 4.

6. ANOM, GGI 5956, Thouard report on his mission undertaken between January 1 and July 1898. Report dated July 18, 1898.

7. ANOM, GGI 5956, Thoaurd to Yersin.

8. ANOM, GGI 5956, Thouard report.

9. ANOM, GGI 5956, Thouard report's conclusion.

10. ANOM, GGI 5954, Chesne to Doumer, Bien Hoa, July 30, 1898.

11. ANF, AB XIX 4283, Bernard to his parents, September 27, 1898.

12. ANOM, GGI 5954, Chesne to Doumer, Bien Hoa, July 30, 1898.

13. ANOM, GGI 5954, Oddéra report, Bien Hoa, September 23, 1898.

14. ANOM, GGI 5955, Yersin to Doumer, May 2, 1898.

15. P. Munier, "Dalat," *Indochine, hebdomadaire illustré,* March 13, 1941, p. 6.

16. ANOM, GGI 5955, Yersin to Doumer, May 2, 1898.

17. ANOM, GGI 5955, Garnier to Governor General, July 23, 1898.

18. Munier, p. 7.

19. François de Tessan, "Une station d'altitude en Indochine," *L'Illustration*, February 17, 1923, p. 156.

20. Doumer, *Situation de l'Indochine*, p. 113.

21. ANOM, GGI 5959, Guynet, Phan Rang, September 25, 1898.

22. A short description of Guynet can be found in Etienne Tardif, *La Naissance de Dalat*, p. 22.

23. ANOM, GGI 5959.

24. Ibid.

25. ANOM, GGI 5963, Capus report, March 30, 1900.

26. Ho Chi Minh, *Oeuvres choisies* (Paris: Maspéro, 1967), p. 63.

27. Jean Ajalbert, "Champoudry chez les Moïs" (1908) reprinted in both Jean Ajalbert, *Les Nuages sur l'Indochine* (Paris: Louis-Michaud, 1912), p. 198, and *Le Camly*, August 22, 1925, p. 1.

28. ANOM, GGI 5954, Oddéra report, September 23, 1898.

29. ANOM, GGI 2961, Mission Blim, "Note au sujet de l'établissement de deux postes en pays moï," Saigon, August 29, 1899.

30. ANOM, GGI 5962 in draft form, and GGI 2962 in printed form.

31. ANOM, RSA F1, Province du Haut-Donnaï, rapport politique, June–July 1900.

32. ANOM, RSA F1, Province du Haut-Donnaï, rapport politique, October–November 1901.

33. ANOM, RSA F1, Province du Haut-Donnaï, rapport politique, December 1900–January 1901.

34. ANOM, GGI 5972, Rapport de M Odend'hal sur le fonctionnement du sanatorium de Dalat, October 25, 1901.

35. Hickey, p. 315.

36. Although the rail line had crept nearer to Dalat throughout the 1920s, it only reached Dalat proper in 1932, and the train station only opened in 1939. André-Joseph Berjoan, "Dalat," *Indochine, hebdomadaire illustré*, January 28, 1943, p. 2. Also see David Del Testa, "Imperial Corridor: Association, Transportation and Power in French Colonial Indochina," *Science, Technology and Society* 4, no. 2 (1999): p. 344. On the direct inland road that put Dalat within 308 kilometers of Saigon, see "La vraie route vers Dalat," *Extrême-Asie: Revue illustrée indochinoise* 66 (July 1932): pp. 635–39.

37. Anonymous, "Une visite au Sanatorium du Langbian, par un pionnier," *Revue de Géographie* (February 1905): p. 41.

38. Léon Garnier's testimony, cited in François de Tessan, *Dans l'Asie qui s'éveille*, (Paris: Renaissance du Livre, 1923), p. 128. Gabrielle Vassal, *On and off Duty in Annam* (London: Heinemann, 1910), p. 206.

39. ANOM, GGI 5972, Rapport de M Odend'hal sur le fonctionnement du sanatorium de Dalat, October 25, 1901.

40. Gabrielle Eberhardt, "Le futur sanatorium de l'Annam: Le Langbiang," *Le Tour du monde* 14, no. 25 (June 20, 1908), p. 290.

41. Constantin, "Le Sanatorium du Langbian," *Revue indochinoise* 3 (1916): p. 319.

42. JOIF, March 21, 1917, p. 392.

43. ANOM, GGI 5955, Garnier report to Doumer, note number 399.

44. Tardif, *La Naissance de Dalat*, pp. 50, 86, 104, 189.

45. ANOM, GGI 5959, Guynet to Governor General, Phan Rang, May 23, 1899.

46. ANOM, GGI 5959, Guynet to Doumer, Phan Rang, January 16, 1900.

47. Tardif, *La Naissance de Dalat*, pp. 254–54.

48. Tardif, *Un Sanatorium en Annam*, pp. 74–75.

49. Cunhac would later serve as Lang-Bian province's résident. See André Baudrit, "La naissance de Dalat," *Indochine, hebdomadaire illustré* (February 10, 1944): p. 24. Cunhac was born in 1870 and began service in Indochina in 1899. The spelling of his first name varies: "Elie" or "Ely." See *Annuaire général de l'Indochine* (Hanoi: IEO, 1925): pp. 300, 368.

50. Tardif, *La Naissance de Dalat*, pp. 200–201.

51. ANOM, GGI 5972, Odend'hal report, October 25, 1901.

52. Cited in De Tessan, "Une station d'altitude en Indochine," p. 157.

53. ANOM, GGI 5968, Charléty contracts.

54. Peter Zinoman discusses the use of prisoner labor in road construction in Peter Zinoman, *The Colonial Bastille: A History of Imprisonment in Vietnam, 1862–1940* (Berkeley: University of California Press, 2001), p. 87.

55. Anonymous, "Une visite au Sanatorium du Langbian, par un pionnier," p. 41.

56. Marc Ferro relates a case in which colonial officials in Indochina described days of lost labor as "more serious" than the workers' eventual death of malaria. Marc Ferro, *Histoire des colonisations* (Paris: Le Seuil, 1994), p. 194.

57. On the history of the railroad in French colonial Indochina, see David Del Testa, "Paint the railroads red: Labor, nationalism and the railroads in French colonial Indochina, 1898–1945," PhD thesis, University of California at Davis, 2001.

58. ANOM, GGI 5967, rapports du Dr Yersin, 1898–1899, "Le sanatorium du Lang-Bian."

59. Doumer, *Situation de l'Indochine*, p. 113.

60. *La quinzaine coloniale*, May 10, 1903, p. 285.

61. Moulie testimony, ANOM, 66188, "Voyage du Gouverneur général au Lang-Bian."

62. Garnier testimony, ANOM, 66188, "Voyage du Gouverneur général au Lang-Bian."

63. "Le Chemin de fer du Lang-Bian," *L'Echo annamite*, March 17, 1923.

64. L. Constantin, "Le Sanatorium du Langbian," *La revue indochinoise* (1916), pp. 306–7. See also AIP, SIM 16, Sanatorium du Lang-Bian, Rapport de l'Inspecteur général des travaux publics, 1915, p. 2.

65. Ibid., and ANOM, Affaires Politiques 3152, Mission d'Inspection, 1916, 1917; and Le Brusq, p. 99. According to *Le petit provençal* (February 17, 1927), a 10-kilometer stretch of line had been inaugurated in January 1927, eight kilometers of which were tooth rack, over very steep terrain.

66. Léo Pages, "Inauguration de la Ligne à crémaillère du Lang-Bian," *Le petit provençal*, February 17, 1927.

67. Louis-Georges Pineau, "Le Plan d'aménagement et d'extension de Dalat," *Vie urbaine* 49 (1939), p. 38.

68. He was technically an *administrateur* before Dalat gained formal recognition as a town in 1926.

69. On Champoudry's time as a member of the Paris municipal council, see Nobuhito Nagaï, *Les conseillers municipaux de Paris sous la troisième République* (Paris: Publications de la Sorbonne, 2002), pp. 62, 167; and Yvan Combeau, *Paris et les élections municipales sous la troisème République* (Paris: L'Harmattan, 1998), p. 156.

70. Ajalbert, "Champoudry chez les Moïs" (1908) reprinted in both Ajalbert, *Les Nuages,* pp. 197–201, and in *Le Camly,* August 22, 1925, p. 2.

71. P. Duclaux, "Le Dalat de 1908," *Indochine, hebdomadaire illustré,* May 29, 1941, p. 5.

72. ANOM, GGI 5972, "Organisation administrative du sanatorium," Phan Rang, October 25, 1901.

73. Penny Edwards, "The Tyranny of Proximity: Power and Mobility in Colonial Cambodia, 1863–1954," *The Journal of Southeast Asian Studies* 37, no. 3 (October 2006): p. 422.

74. Ibid., p. 425.

75. P. Duclaux, "Le Dalat de 1908," *Indochine, hebdomadaire illustré,* May 29, 1941, p. 5.

76. Tardif attributes six daughters to Champoudry in *La Naissance de Dalat,* p. 225. Ajalbert, conversely, writes of only three daughters (Ajalbert, *Les Nuages sur l'Indochine,* p. 198).

77. Duclaux, and Jean Ajalbert, *Les Nuages sur l'Indochine,* p. 201.

78. ANOM, GGI 5977, telegrams dated December 26, 1901 and January 26, 1904.

79. Henri Maitre, *Mission H. Maitre: Indochine Sud-Centrale, Les Jungles Moï* (Paris: Emile Larose, 1912), pp. 299–301. Quote from p. 299.

80. Constantin, "Le Sanatorium du Langbian," *Revue indochinoise* 3 (1916): pp. 306, 318.

81. ANOM, GGI 5963, "Rapports et notes diverses," 1913. On the dismantling of the Sala, see "Quelques réflexions et souvenirs sur de vieilles planches," *Le Camly,* December 15, 1923, p. 1.

82. VNA2, RSA 4073, now renumbered as VNA4, RSA 4094, Ministry of the Colonies to Governor General of Indochina, August 17, 1917; and ANOM, Affaires Politiques 3152, Mission d'Inspection, 1916, 1917, Sanatoria: Lang-Bian, Kep, Tam-Dao, Chapa.

83. ANOM, Affaires Politiques 3152, Mission d'Inspection, 1916, 1917.

84. ANOM, Affaires Politiques 3152, Mission d'Inspection, 1916, 1917.

CHAPTER 5

Epigraph: ANOM, AGEFOM 238 dossier 304. "Dalat," *La Nouvelle dépêche* October 12, 1935.

1. Jean le Pichon, "Dalat, force, joie, santé," *Indochine, hebdomadaire illustré,* July 8, 1943.

2. Jean Ajalbert, "Champoudry chez les Moïs," in *Les Nuages sur l'Indochine,* p. 200, and *Le Camly,* September 5, 1925 p. 1.

3. De Tessan, "Une station d'altitude en Indochine," p. 157.

4. Libby Vann, "Discovering the Alps in Indochina: European Nature and the French Colonial Sanatorium of Dalat, 1893–1927," Paper presented to the department of anthropology, University of Virginia, April 7, 1997, p. 15. On the Vosges comparison, see Pierre Troude, "A Dalat et Kandal, premières découvertes," in *La France d'outre-mer, 1930–1960: Témoignages d'administrateurs et de magistrats,* ed. Jean Clauzel, p. 545 (Paris: Karthala, 2003). For the Pyrénées, see Andrée Viollis, *Indochine SOS* (first published by Gallimard in 1935, reedited in Paris: Les bons caractères, 2008), p. 66.

5. André Goineaud-Bérard, *Indo 46: C'était encore l'Indochine française* (Paris: Publibook, 2003), p. 64.

6. ANOM, GGI 24741.

7. Anonymous, "Fragment de journal d'un évadé," *France libre* 3, no. 15 (January 15, 1942): p. 220.

8. Of course, Indochina's other hill stations also fostered and triggered such nostalgia. Thus, Sapa (also spelled Chapa) was likened to both the Pyrénées and the Alps. Peyvel, "L'Emergence du Tourisme au Viêt Nam, pp. 220–1.

9. Michael Vann, "Of *le cafard* and other tropical threats," in *France and Indochina: Cultural Representations,* eds. Jennifer Yee and Kathryn Robson, p. 97 (Lanham: Lexington Books, 2005).

10. Cited in Dr. Gaide, *Les stations climatiques en Indochine,* (Paris: Exposition coloniale internationale, 1931), pp. 6–7.

11. Bernard Hue, *Littératures de la péninsule indochinoise* (Paris: Karthala, 1999), p. 115. Gabrielle Vassal, *On and off Duty,* p. 13.

12. Kermorgant and Reynaud, "Précautions hygiéniques à prendre pour les expéditions et les explorations aux pays chauds," *Annales d'hygiène et de médecine coloniales* (July–September 1900): pp. 388, 394.

13. The 1886 source (Division d'occupation d'Annam et du Tonkin, *Instructions médicales à l'usage des postes militaires dépourvus de médecins* Hanoi) is quoted in William Cohen, "Malaria and French Imperialism," p. 26. The 1900 opinion appears in Kermorgant and Reynaud, p. 349.

14. Paul d'Enjoy, "La voie ferrée de Bessac à Saigon," *Bulletin de la Société de Géographie* 17 (1896): pp. 392–398; Paul d'Enjoy, "Le baiser en Europe et en Chine," drawn from the *Bulletin de la Société d'Anthropologie,* 1897); Paul d'Enjoy, *Indochine française: étude pratique de la législation civile annamite* (Paris: Imprimerie de Roussel, 1894).

15. Paul d'Enjoy, *La santé aux colonies: Manuel d'hygiène et de prophylaxie climatologiques, médecine coloniale* (Paris: Société d'éditions scientifiques, 1901), pp. 92, 94, 96, 108, 111.

16. Mainstream medicine would only establish the direct connection between lung cancer and smoking several decades later. See David Cantor and Carsten Timmermann, "Lung Cancer," in *Tobacco in History and Culture: An Encyclopedia,* (Farmington Hills: Gale Publishing, 2004), pp. 320–325.

17. Erwan Bergot, *Sud lointain* (Paris: France loisirs, 1997), p. 36.

18. Edmond Nordemann, *Connaissances nécessaires aux personnes appelées à faire leur carrière en Indochine: Conférence faite à l'école coloniale le 8 mars 1910* (Paris: Imprimerie Chaix, 1910), pp. 8–10.

19. Tardif, *La naissance de Dalat,* p. 118.

20. Tardif, *La naissance de Dalat,* p. 132.

21. See Libby Vann, "Discovering the Alps in Indochina," p. 15.

22. *Petit guide illustré de Dalat* (1930), cover.

23. See René Poujade, *Cours martiales d'Indochine, 1940–1945: Les évasions de Résistants dans l'Indochine occupée par les Japonais* (Paris: La Bruyère, 1997), p. 31, on Jubelin's time at the Dalat Palace Hotel.

24. Anonymous, "Fragment de journal d'un évadé."

25. Dominique Mourey, *Mon Lycée en Annam* (Toulon: Presses du Midi, 2004), pp. 73–74.

26. Ibid., p. 59.

27. Gregg Mitman, p. 604, 635.

28. Janet Hoskins, "Postcards from the Edge of Empire: Images and Messages from French Indochina," *IIAS Newsletter* 44 (Summer 2007), pp. 16–17.

29. These postcards are part of the author's collection. Last names of senders and names of recipients have been withheld to maintain privacy.

30. Claudie Beaucarnot (Brugière) 1943 Indochina vacation diary, ANOM, 67 APOM, d. 2, fonds Biggi, now available online thanks to David Del Testa at: www.bucknell.edu/Beaucarnot/. This quote is drawn from the entry for July 8.

31. Mourey, p. 183.

32. ANOM, GGI 66188, "Rapports du Général Pennequin, le Médecin inspecteur Grall, le Médecin principal Hénaff."

33. On both canned goods and "eating French" in the colonies, see Ellen Furlough, "Une leçon des choses: Tourism, Empire, and the Nation in Interwar France," *French Historical Studies* 25, no. 3 (2002): p. 463; Erica Peters, "Negotiating Power through Everyday Practices in French Vietnam, 1880–1924," PhD thesis, University of Chicago, 2000, p. 140; Susanne Freidberg, "French beans for the masses: A modern historical geography of food in Burkina Faso," *Journal of Historical Geography* 29, no. 3 (2003): pp. 445–63; and Deborah Neill, "Finding the Ideal Diet: Nutrition, Culture and Dietary Practices in France and Equatorial Africa, 1890s-1920s," *Food and Foodways* 17 (2009): pp. 1–28. On French colonial doctors expressing reservations about the healthfulness of canned goods, see Eric Jennings, *Curing the Colonizers*, pp. 59–60. On manichean representations of colonial food, see Eric Jennings, "L'Affaire Dreyfus et l'univers colonial français," in "Zola l'homme récit, actes du colloque de Toronto," Numéro hors-série, *Les cahiers naturalistes* 49 (June 2003): pp. 43–45.

34. Pierre Nicolas, *Notes sur la vie française en Cochinchine* (Paris: Flammarion, 1900), pp. 33–34.

35. Georges Dioque, ed. *Félix Dioque, Un Colonial: Six ans en Guinée ... Quarante ans en Indochine* (Gap: Société d'études des hautes alpes, 2008), p. 133.

36. ANOM, GGI 54021, le Nestour to "Monsieur le Directeur de l'Agriculture ... Hanoi." The settler in question opens his letter by noting with satisfaction the successes of the Lang-Bian farm.

37. Vte d'André, "L'élevage au Lang-Bian," *Bulletin économique de l'Indochine* (May-June 1905): p. 558. D'André, "Etude sur le Lang-Bian (Annam)," *Revue coloniale* (November-December 1903): p. 261.

38. ANOM, AGEFOM 858, d. 2324, Station Dankia.

39. ANOM, GGI 5978, Mission d'André. A.F.M d'André was born in 1862 and began his service in Indochina in 1899. *Annuaire général de l'Indochine* (Hanoi: F.H. Schneider, 1904), p.557.

40. ANOM, GGI 24728, Domerc (Dankia) to Governor General, July 17, 1899.

41. Gabrielle Vassal, *On and off Duty*, p. 236.

42. ANOM, GGI 24741, Garnier, September 23, 1898.

43. "Expériences de culture au Lang-Bian," *La quinzaine coloniale*, July 25, 1901, p. 439.

44. ANOM, GGI 5966, Rapport Roux, July 24, 1903.

45. AIP, SIM 16, Sanatorium du Lang-Bian, Rapport de l'Inspecteur général des travaux publics, p. 19.

46. Joseph Vassal, "Le Lang-Bian," in *Revue indochinoise* 53 (March 1907), p. 17.

47. Gabrielle Vassal, *On and off Duty*, p. 235.

48. Financial results proved less rosy. Already in 1903, Roux reported that the farm should focus on livestock only, so as to turn a profit. In 1907, with costs far outpacing profits, the entire farm had to be sold. It was henceforth in private hands. P. Munier, "Dalat," *Indochine, hebdomadaire illustré* (March 13, 1941), p. 7; and ANOM, GGI 5966, "Rapport Roux."

49. D'André, "Etude sur le Lang-Bian," *Revue coloniale* (November-December 1903), p. 262.

50. Anonymous, "Le transport des légumes de Dalat à Saigon par chemin de fer," *L'Eveil économique de l'Indochine,* September 27, 1931, pp. 5–6.

51. Ad reading: "Maison Légumes frais Dalat: grand arrivage quotidien," *La Presse indochinoise,* July 3, 1936.

52. MEP, E. Soullard, "Un voyage à Dalat et à Djiring." *Bulletin de la Société des Missions Etrangères,* 1930, p. 357.

53. Pierre Bouvard, M. Millet, *La Chasse au Lang-Bian* (Bergerac: Imprimerie du Sud-Ouest, 1920), p. 42. (NB: The volume is bilingual, French English, but the English translation is poor. I have substituted my own.)

54. Beaucarnot diary, entry for July 8.

55. ANOM, Affaires politiques 3152, Saurin report, March 20, 1917.

56. Le Chemineau, "Le Langbian," *Revue indochinoise,* 1916, p. 1. Cited in Mathieu Guérin, "Des casques blancs sur le plateau des herbes: La pacification des aborigènes des hautes terres du Sud-Indochinois, 1859–1940," PhD thesis, University of Paris VII, 2003, p. 277.

57. Guides Madrolle, *De Saigon à Tourane* (Paris Hachette, 1926), p. 78.

58. Anonymous, *Petit guide illustré de Dalat* (Dalat: 1930), p. 33; "Physionomie de Dalat en 1937," *L'Asie nouvelle illustrée* 56 (1937): p. 13.

59. Madeleine Jacomme, *Vers les mimosas de Dalat* (Longueuil, Québec: Editions Philémon, 2003), p. 57.

60. On the introduction of French sporting movements and philosophies (especially Hébertisme) to Indochina, see Agathe Larcher-Goscha, "Volonté de puissance coloniale et puissance de volonté nationaliste: Aux origines de la création de l'école d'éducation physique d'Hanoi, 1913–1922," in *Sports et loisirs dans les colonies,* ed. Evelyne Combeau-Mari, pp. 35–48 (Paris: SEDES, 2004).

61. Orwell wrote: "In any town in India the European Club is the spiritual citadel, the real seat of the British power, the Nirvana for which native officials and millionaires pine in vain." George Orwell, *Burmese Days* (Harmondsworth: Penguin, 1985), p. 17.

62. ANOM, AGEFOM 858, d. 2324, Cercle de Dalat.

63. "Physionomie de Dalat en 1937," *L'Asie nouvelle illustrée* 56 (1937), p. 13.

64. Office central du Tourisme indochinois, *Dalat* (Hanoi: 1943); NLV M16095, p. 8.

65. Iphigénie-Catherine Shellshear, *Far from the Tamarind Tree: A Childhood Account of Indochine* (Double-Bay, Australia: Longueville Media, 2003), p. 35.

66. Beaucarnot diary, p. 40 (entry for July 28).

67. Mourey, pp, 183, 250.

68. André Angladette, "La vie quotidienne en Indochine de 1939 à 1946," *Mondes et cultures: Comptes rendus trimestriels des séances de l'Académie des sciences d'outre-mer* 39, no. 3 (June 1979), p. 469.

69. Beaucarnot, p. 44, entry for August 9.

70. *Télé-Havas: Annuaire officiel des abonnés au telephone, Cochinchine, Sud-Annam* (1949). Retreived at CUKL, HE 8390.5A51.

71. Shellshear, p. 33.

72. The April 26, 1924 issue of *Le Camly* (p. 1) relates that hotels are "once again" full for the Easter holiday. The article adds that Europeans in Dalat opened their homes to accommodate the fifty or so visitors who could not find hotel rooms.

73. "Les fêtes de Pâques à Dalat: Programme," *La presse indochinoise,* April 17, 1935; and "Les fêtes de Pâques à Dalat," *La presse indochinoise,* April 24, 1935.

74. Bouvard and Millet, p. 54.

75. Not all of Indochina's hill stations presented hunting opportunities. Describing the hill station of Sapa (Chapa) in 1935, E. de Rozario remarked: "Chapa's fauna is less rich than its flora. No tigers, nor panthers, nor bears . . . " E. de Rozario, "Chapa, station d'altitude," *Cahiers de la Société de Géographie de Hanoi* 28 (1935): p. 21.

76. John McKenzie, *The Empire of Nature: Hunting, Conservation and British Imperialism* (Manchester University Press, 1988).

77. De Tessan would serve as deputy for the Seine-et-Marne starting in 1928. Tied to the French foreign office in the 1930s, he published a book in 1936 warning of the dangers of Hitler and his ideology. In this same era, he took under his wing a young Maurce Papon. François de Tessan would die at Buchenwald in 1944. Dictionnaire des parlementaires français (Paris: La documentation française, 1988), T. 1, p. 79; and www.assemblee-nationale.fr/sycomore/fiche.asp?num_dept=6999. The information on Papon, who would later be tried for his role of the deportation of Jews in Bordeaux, was kindly provided to me by Marc Olivier Baruch.

78. De Tessan, "Une station d'altitude en Indochine," p. 158.

79. McKenzie, *The Empire of Nature,* pp. 178–79.

80. William Ellis, *Three visits to Madagascar during the years 1853, 1854, 1856* (London John Murray, 1858), p. 317.

81. De Tessan, *Dans l'Asie qui s'éveille,* p. 136.

82. Henry C. Flower, Jr., "On the trail of the Lord Tiger," *Asia: the American Magazine of the Orient* (October 1920): pp. 893–97. Quotation from p. 894.

83. Archibald Harrison, *Indochina, a Sportsman's Opportunity* (Plymouth: Mayflower Press, 1933), pp. 42, 95. Harrison's account dates from 1917, and was published posthumously. Further north in Tonkin, the reward was set even higher in 1916: forty piastres per tiger and fifteen per panther. JOIF, December 9, 1916, p. 1904.

84. ANOM, GGI B/21/136, Sarraut to the Minister of the Colonies, Hanoi, April 9, 1917.

85. JOIF, 1917, pp. 318–19. On the zones, also see Mathieu Guérin, "Des casques blancs sur le plateau des herbes," p. 277.

86. Caroline Ford, "Nature, Culture and Conservation in France and her Colonies," *Past and Present* 183 (May 2004): p. 176.

87. ANOM, GGI 66801. On the West African, North African, and Malagasy contexts, see Caroline Ford, p. 196.

88. ANOM, GGI 66801.

89. ANOM, GGI 66801.

90. ANOM, AGEFOM 254, dossier 378.

91. Admittedly a second list did limit hunting of other species according to season. Thus, local municipalities could add date restrictions on the hunting of gaur or male elephants, for example. Decrees of December 14, 1931, JOIF, January 2, 1931, pp. 5–6.

92. Gabrielle Vassal, p. 190.

93. Ibid., p. 214.

94. Ibid., p. 213. The story is recounted by Pierre Dru in his unpublished memoir, with the added detail that the tiger deeply wounded Canivey's leg. "Manuscrit de Pierre Dru," p. 179.

95. Gabrielle Vassal, p. 245.

96. This is likely Henri-Louis Agostini, listed in the 1904 *Annuaire* to Indochina as belonging to Indochina's forestry department.

97. Gabrielle Vassal, pp. 244–58.

98. Mary Procida, "Good Sports and Right Sorts: Guns, Gender and Imperialism in British India," *The Journal of British Studies* 40, no. 4 (October 2001): p. 455.

99. Callum Mackenzie, "Sadly neglected: Hunting and Gendered Identities," *The International Journal of the History of Sport* 22, no. 3 (July 2005): pp. 548–49.

100. Mary Procida, p. 462.

101. Karen Wonders, "Hunting Narratives of the Age of Empire: A gender Reading of their Iconography," *Environment and History* 11, no. 3 (2005): p. 279.

102. Mary Procida, pp. 474–77.

103. "Le Capitaine Lavit et sa femme à l'affût," *Le petit journal: Supplément illustré*, July 25, 1909, p. 234.

104. McKenzie, p. 195.

105. Nguyen-Phan-Long, "Remerciements aux deux tigres tués à Dalat par M. Valude," *L'Echo annamite*, March 8, 1923. In addition to the Daudet reference, Nguyen-Pham-Long might have considered the ridicule of the boastful and awkward king in Ruy Blas, who famously and pitifully wrote: "There is much wind and I have killed six wolves." Victor Hugo, "Ruy Blas," Act II, scene III.

106. Joseph Buttinger, *Vietnam: A Dragon Embattled* (New York: Praeger, 1967), p. 246.

107. ANOM, GGI 24741, Garnier (from the Lang-Bian) September 23, 1898.

108. De Tessan, "Une station d'altitude en Indochine," p. 157.

109. Postcard, author's collection.

110. International Conference on Ennui—Nineteenth and Twentieth centuries (Historical approaches). Held at the University of Paris I (Sorbonne), November 29 and 30, 2007.

111. On *le cafard* in French colonies, see Michael Vann, "Of *le cafard*"; David Slavin, *Colonial cinema and imperial France: White blind spots, male fantasies, settler myths* (Johns Hopkins University Press: Baltimore, 2001), pp. 169–170.

112. ANOM, GGI 5954.

113. ANOM, GGI 5976, Grall report, 1904.

114. ANOM, GGI 5963, "Sanatorium du Langbian, Rapports et notes diverses, Dalat."

115. ANOM, GGI 5977, Correspondence concerning Champoudry in December 1901.

116. ANOM, GGI 15543, "Relèvement des tarifs du SCAL, rapport du Chef du trafic et mouvement," January 11, 1920.

117. *Cordée, Revue mensuelle des jeunes de Dalat* 3 (January 1, 1944): p. 37.

118. *Cordée, Revue mensuelle des jeunes de Dalat* 7 (June 1944): p. 39.

CHAPTER 6

1. Oscar Salemink, *The Ethnography of Vietnam's Central Highlanders* (Honolulu: University of Hawai'i Press, 2003), p. 31.

2. Libby Vann has argued that these purported fears were used by the French to claim the Lang-Bian for themselves. She writes: "Th[e] notion that Lang Bian was a European environment appears to have been strengthened by the notion that lowland Vietnamese and the highland Montagnards considered it a dangerous region. The name given to Lang Bian by the highland peoples, French colonials pointed out, meant: "disinherited or cursed." Libby Vann, p. 13.

3. ANOM, GGI 66188.

4. ANOM, GGI 5973, Rapport Outrey.

5. On some of the complexities of montagnard-French-Vietnamese relations (albeit for Northern Vietnam), see Jean Michaud, "The Montagnards and the State in Northern Vietnam from 1802 to 1975: a Historical Overview," *Ethnohistory* 47, no. 2 (Spring 2000): pp. 345–49.

6. Frédéric Thomas, "L'Invention des 'Hauts Plateaux' en Indochine," *Ethnologie française* 34 (2004): p. 644.

7. Hickey, *Sons of the Mountains*, p. 292. Vietnamese emperors had already practiced this strategy in the sixteenth and seventeenth centuries. See Nguyen The Anh, "La frontière sino-vietnamienne du xième au xviième siècle," in *Les frontières du Vietnam*, ed. P. B. Lafont, p. 68 (Paris: L'Harmattan, 1989).

8. Alison Bashford, "Is White Australia Possible? Race, Colonialism and Tropical Medicine," *Ethnic and Racial Studies*, 23:2 (2000), p. 250.

9. AIP, Yersin 4, 24.365, "Exploration et souvenirs du Dr. Yersin."

10. Dr. Abbatucci, "Climatologie dans l'Indo-Chine," *Revue d'hygiène et de médecine préventive* 56 (1934): p. 53. Also in Serge Abbatucci, "Les stations climatiques en Indochine," *Outre-mer, revue générale de colonisation* (September 1930): p. 295.

11. Garnier, cited in François de Tessan, *Dans l'Asie qui s'éveille*, pp. 126–7.

12. "Champoudry chez les Moïs," *Le Camly*, September 5, 1925, p. 1.

13. Joseph Vassal, "Le Lang-Bian," in *Revue indochinoise* 53 (March 1907): p. 18.

14. CAOM, GGI 5956, Wolf report.

15. Introduction by Le Quoc Hung, in *Dalat ville d'altitude*, eds. Truong Tro and Vuong Lan, p. 7 (Ho Chi Minh City, 1993).

16. Truong Phuc An, ed., *Dalat Tram Nam [A Hundred Years of History of Dalat]* (Dalat: Tourist office, 1993), p. 44.

17. Quoted in Kennedy, *The Magic Mountains* p. 69.

18. Dana Hale, "French Images of Race on Product Trademarks during the Third Republic," in *The Color of Liberty: Histories of Race in France*, eds. Sue Peabody and Tyler Stovall, p. 141 (Raleigh: Duke University Press, 2003).

19. Lucien Roussel, *La chasse en Indochine*, (Paris: Librairie Plon, 1913), p. 66.

20. Duc de Montpensier, *En Indochine: Mes chasses, mes voyages* (Paris: Pierre Lafite et Compagnie, 1912), pp. 38–39, 158, 160.

21. Gabrielle Vassal, *On and off Duty*, p. 215.

22. Ibid., pp. 221–2.

23. Iphigénie-Catherine Shellshear, *Far from the Tamarind Tree: A Childhood Account of Indochine*, Double-Bay: Longueville Media, 2003. p. 41. Mourey, p. 159.

24. Maitre, *Les régions moïs*, pp. 53–54.

25. Salemink, pp. 69, 71.

26. Maitre, *Les régions Moïs*, p. 330.

27. "Types moïs," *La presse indochinoise*, August 17, 1935.

28. D. Antomarchi, "Le Bi Duê, Recueil des coutumes rhadées," *Indochine, hebdomadaire illustré*, February 20, 1941, p. 7.

29. "Carnet d'un Moï," *L'Union française*, January 3, 1948, p. 1.

30. "Carnet d'un Moï," *L'Union française*, February 7, 1948, p. 1.

31. The analogy with the American West had been elaborated long before. Roland Dorgelès' famous 1929 *On the Mandarin Road* frequently compared Indochinese highland minorities to American Indians, and the author himself to Fenimore Cooper. Roland Dorgelès, *Sur la Route mandarine* (Paris: Albin Michel, 1929), pp. 256, 262, 263.

32. Bernard Cohn, *Colonialism and its Forms of Knowledge: The British in India* (Princeton: Princeton University Press, 1996), p. 53.

33. Johannes Fabian, *Language and Colonial Power* (Berkeley: University of California Press, 1986), pp. 76, 114.

34. Jean Michaud, *"Incidental" Ethnographers: French Catholic Missions on the Tonkin-Yunnan Frontier* (Leiden: Brill, 2007), p. 183.

35. ANOM, GGI 23843.

36. Oddéra, "Vocabulaire Français/ Cho-Ma," CAOM GGI 5962.

37. RP Jean Cassaigne, *Petit manuel de conversation courante en langue Moï, à l'usage des planteurs, chasseurs, touristes, région Djiring-Dalat* (Saigon: Imprimerie de la Mission, 1930).

38. Gilbert Bochet, *Eléments de conversation franco-koho: Us et coutumes des montagnards de la Province du Haut-Donnaï* (Dalat: Service géographique de l'Indochine, 1951), pp. 36, 78.

39. Roussel, p. 11.

40. Ibid., p. 102.

41. J. C. Demariaux, *La grande chasse au Darlac indochinois* (Paris: Pyeronnet, 1949), 17.

42. AIP, SIM 16, fonds Paul Louis Simond, Vassal's 1914 report, p. 2.

43. IFA, fonds Pineau, "Aménagement et extension de Dalat, Rapport."

44. Beaucarnot recalls minorities shopping at a particular Chinese merchant in Dalat. See Beaucarnot, entry for July 7.

45. Georges Condominas, *Nous avons mangé la forêt: Chronique d'un village mnong gar, hauts plateaux du Viet-Nam* (Paris: Mercure de France, 1974), pp. 22, 53, 86, 255.

46. Jules Canivey, "Notice sur les moeurs et coutumes des Moï de la region de Dalat" *Revue d'ethnographie et de sociologie* (1913): p. 1.

47. James Scott, "Stilled to Silence at 500 Metres: Making Sense of Historical Change in Southeast Asia," *IIAS Newsletter* 49 (Fall 2008), pp. 12–13.

48. Hickey, p. 304.

49. On the administration's preference for ethnic Vietnamese over highland minority labor, see Steve Déry, *La colonisation agricole au Viêt Nam : Contribution à l'étude de la construction d'un État moderne; du bouleversement à l'intégration des Plateaux centraux* (Québec: Les Presses de l'Université du Québec, 2004), p. 72.

50. VNA2, RSA 4087, Divers travaux à Dalat, now renumbered as VNA4, RSA 4109.

51. ANOM, HCI 440.

52. Hickey, *Sons of the Mountains*, pp. 317, 333.

53. Haut-Commissariat de France pour l'Indochine, *Lycée Yersin, Dalat* (Dalat: Imprimerie Verdun, 1948).

54. Claude Perrens, "Lettre de Dalat," *Indochine, hebdomadaire illustré*, July 8, 1943, p. 14.

55. ANOM, RSA F1.

56. Hickey, *Sons of the Mountains*, p. 285.

57. Hickey, *Sons of the Mountains*, p. 294.

58. ANOM, GGI 49507, Résident supérieur d'Annam to the Governor General, April 13, 1916.

59. Christopher Goscha, *Vietnam or Indochina? Contesting Concepts of Space in Vietnamese Nationalism, 1887–1954* (Copenhagen: NIAS Press, 1995), pp. 25–29.

60. Hickey, *Sons of the Mountains*, p. 297.

61. Maitre, p. 61.

62. Salemink, p. 68.

63. Salemink, p. 140.

64. ANOM, INF 1240. Governor Brévié to the Direction des Affaires politiques, Ministère des Colonies Paris, Dalat, July 21, 1939, p. 3.

65. On the ongoing, problematic colonial meanings of the term "montagnard," see Hjorloifur Jonsson, "French Natural in the Vietnamese Highlands: Nostalgia and Erasure in Montagnard Identity" in *Of Vietnam: Identities in Dialogue,* eds. Jane Bradley Winston and Leakthina Chau-Pech Ollier, pp. 52–65 (New York: Palgrave, 2001). In particular, Jonsson points out that the term "montagnard" appears not to apply to minority populations in Northern Vietnam, and derived new connotations from the U.S.-Vietnam war, during which time emerged the portrait of a sympathetic, pro-American "yard," for short.

66. ANOM, Conspol 233, Saigon, July 26, 1946, Suppression du terme Moï du vocabulaire officiel.

67. Salemink, p. 149.

68. Hickey, *Sons of the Mountains*, p. 303.

69. Salemink, pp. 83–85. *Le Camly*, March 15, 1924.

70. Claude Perrens, "Lettre de Dalat," *Indochine, hebdomadaire illustré*, July 8, 1943, p. 14.

71. CUKL, "Pénétration du pays moï, Cabinet, 1937–1938," vol. 1, Emile Erard to Résident, Dalat.

72. CUKL, "Pénétration du pays moï, Cabinet, 1937–1938," vol. 1, Procès-verbal de la Conférence mixte interprovinciale pour les régions moïs, 1936.

73. CUKL, "Pénétration du pays moï, Cabinet, 1937–1938," vol. 2, Questions Moïs, 1937–1938, Cabinet. Procès-verbal de la Conférence inter-pays pour les regions Moï, 1937.

74. All materials up to this point in this paragraph are based on ANOM, INF 1239.

75. ANOM, INF 1240, Catroux, Hanoi, December 8, 1939.

76. ANOM, INF 1240.

77. ANOM, Conspol 233, M le Gall, Inspecteur primaire à M. de Raymond, inspecteur des Colonies. November 18, 1945.

78. ANOM, Conspol 233, Moutet to d'Argenlieu, Paris, March 13, 1946, Création d'un territoire autonome moï.

79. ANOM, Conspol 233, Extrait: Note quotidienne d'Information # 73, Renseignements provenant des services de sûreté.

CHAPTER 7

Epiraph: "Physionomie de Dalat en 1937," *L'Asie nouvelle illustrée* 56 (1937): p. 11.

1. Over the past fifteen years, much fine work has been devoted to urban planning and architecture in French colonial Indochina. See Gwendolyn Wright, *The Politics of Design in French Colonial Architecture* (Chicago: University of Chicago Press, 1991), chapter 4; Arnauld Le Brusq, *Le Vietnam à travers l'architecture coloniale* (Paris: Editions de l'Amateur, 1999); Panivong Norindr, *Phantasmatic Indochina: French Colonial Ideology in Architecture, Film and Literature* (Durham: Duke University Press, 1996); Philippe Papin, *Histoire de Hanoi* (Paris: Fayard, 2001); Pierre Clément et al., *Hanoi, le cycle des métamorphoses* (Paris: Ipraus, 2001); To Anh Dang, "La villa en ville: La transformation morphologique de l'architecture des villas coloniales françaises à Hanoi," Master's thesis, Hanoi University and the Ecole d'Architecture de Toulouse, 2004; Christian Pédelahore de Loddis, "Hanoi, miroir de l'architecture indochinoise," in *Architectures françaises outre-mer,* eds. Maurice Culot and J.-M. Thiveaud (IFA: Mardaga, 1992).

2. Quoted in Anthony King, "Writing Colonial Space: A review article," *Comparative Studies in Society and History* 37, no. 3 (July 1995), p. 541. Some of these studies include: Gwendolyn Wright, *Politics of Design,* Zeynep Çelik, *Urban Forms and Colonial Confrontations: Algiers under French Rule* (Berkeley: University of California Press, 1997), Thomas Metcalf, *An Imperial Vision: Indian Architecture and Britain's Raj* (Berkeley: University of California Press, 1989).

3. Gwendolyn Wright, p. 3; Zeynep Çelik, pp. 70–71.

4. Odile Goerg has made use of local records to undertake a study of this sort on French West Africa: Odile Goerg, "Conakry: un modèle de ville coloniale française? Règlements fonciers et urbanisme de 1885 aux années 1920," *Cahiers d'Etudes africaines* 25, no. 3 (1985): pp. 309–35.

5. ANOM, GGI 66188, Rapport de décembre 1900.

6. IFA, L. G. Pineau Collection. Pineau, "Aménagement et extension de Dalat, Rapport," p. 6.

7. The figures of 750 villas (1944) and of 2,537 summer visitors (September 1942 alone) are drawn from *Cordée, Revue mensuelle des jeunes de Dalat* 3 (January 1, 1944): p. 37.

8. Jacques Lagisquet's brother Joseph and father Charles were both architects as well. Dioque, p. 353.

9. ANOM, GGI 66188, Rapport à M. le Gouverneur Général par Paul Champoudry, Administrateur de Dalat (June 1905).

10. All quotations in this paragraph are drawn from Ernest Hébrard, "Dalat le nouveau plan, dispositions générales," *L'Eveil Economique* (Indochine), October 21, 1923.

11. "Relations Saigon-Dalat," *La tribune indochinoise*, March 26, 1937, p. 4.

12. ANOM, 86 APOM 100. Itinerary for Mr Boudet, May 31, 1940, arrival June 1.

13. Louis-Georges Pineau, *Dalat, Capitale administrative de l'Indochine* (Hanoi: Imprimerie d'Extrême-Orient, 1937), p. 35, and A. Berjoan, "Dalat," *Indochine, hebdomadaire illustré*, January 28, 1943, p. ii.

14. Berjoan, p. iii.

15. In 1932, Dalat's mayor wrote to Pineau that the construction of new public buildings, including city hall, would have to be delayed indefinitely because the "budgetary crisis had hit Dalat especially hard." IFA, L. G. Pineau Collection, Mayor to Pineau, October 29, 1932.

16. CIAM, Pineau correspondence 1930, "Note concernant le compte-rendu de la commission du 20 mai 1930."

17. David Peyceré, "Louis-Georges Pineau et ses archives à l'Institut français d'Architecture," in Pierre Clément et al., *Hanoi, le cycle des métamorphoses* pp. 94–96.

18. Pineau, *Dalat, Capitale administrative de l'Indochine*, pp. 19–20.

19. ANOM, GGI 66188, Rapport à M. le Gouverneur Général par Paul Champoudry, Administrateur de Dalat (June 1905).

20. ANOM, GGI 46409, Rapport O'Neil (étude préliminaire sur le développement de la Station de Dalat), October 28, 1919, p. 2.

21. Ibid., p. 5. IFA, L. G. Pineau Collection. Pineau, "Aménagement et extension de Dalat, Rapport," p. 1.

22. IFA, L. G. Pineau Collection. Pineau, "Aménagement et extension de Dalat, Rapport," pp. 12–13.

23. ANOM, GGI 64225, Rapport politique, Annam, 4ème trimestre 1920.

24. ANOM, GGI 46409, Rapport O'Neil, October 28, 1919, p. 8.

25. "Notre station d'altitude," *Le Courrier de Saigon*, May 30, 1932, p. 1.

26. VNA2, RSA 4081, Travaux à Dalat: village annamite, marché, terrain Combeau, logement ingénieurs, 1923–1925, now renumbered as VNA4, RSA 4102, Garnier to Résident supérieur d'Annam, March 25, 1924.

27. Ibid.

28. Gwendolyn Wright notes the vehement local criticisms voiced against Hébrard's Dalat plan. His only praise on this project, she notes, appears to have come from the metropole. Wright, p. 232.

29. VNA2, RSA 4090 (Procès verbaux du comité de salubrité publique de Dalat, 1925), now renumbered as VNA4, RSA 4112.

30. Dalat's committee of public salubrity had voted for its removal in August 1923. "Village annamite," *Le Camly*, August 23, 1923, p. 1.

31. VNA2, RSA 4080, Plans de lotissement de Dalat, 1923–1925, now renumbered as VNA4, RSA 4101, Hébrard to Garnier, April 9, 1925.

32. VNA2, RSA 4081, Travaux à Dalat: village annamite, marché, terrain Combeau, lo-

gement ingénieurs, 1923–1925, now renumbered as VNA4, RSA 4102, Garnier to Hébrard, April 28, 1925.

33. VNA2, RSA 4090, Procès verbaux du comité de salubrité publique de Dalat, 1925, now renumbered as VNA4, RSA 4112, August 29 session.

34. VNA2, RSA 4090, Procès verbaux du comité de salubrité publique de Dalat, 1925, now renumbered as VNA4, RSA 4112, June 2 session.

35. VNA2, RSA 4096, Réunions de la commission municipale de Dalat, 1926, now renumbered as VNA4, RSA 4118, November 25 session.

36. VNA2, RSA 4096, (Réunion de la commission municipale de Dalat, 1926), now renumbered as VNA4, RSA 4118, November 27 session.

37. Ibid.

38. ANOM, GGI 46409, Rapport O'Neil, October 28, 1919, p. 5.

39. Michael Vann shows a very similar phenomenon at work in colonial Hanoi, where large properties were likewise synonymous with white power. Vann, "White City on the Red River," p. 102.

40. VNA2, RSA 4096, Réunion de la commission municipale de Dalat, 1926, now renumbered as VNA4, RSA 4118, November 27 session.

41. "Fausses nouvelles," Le Camly, March 22, 1924, p. 2.

42. "Village annamite," Le Camly, August 23, 1923, p. 1.

43. VNA2, RSA 4105, Réunions de la commission municipale de Dalat, 1935, now renumbered as VNA4, RSA 4126, May 25, 1935 session.

44. Anonymous, Petit guide illustré de Dalat, p. 13.

45. Arnauld Le Brusq, p. 108.

46. The same trend can be detected at Cambodia's main hill station, Bokor. There, Penny Edwards has shown, the resort "found a loyal clientele among the upper echelons of the Cambodian Elite." Penny Edwards, "Cambodge: The Cultivation of a Nation, 1860–1945," PhD thesis, Monash University (Australia), 1999, chapter 4.

47. "Vo Dinh Dung," in Souverains et Notabilités d'Indochine (Hanoi, Editions du Gouvernement Général de L'Indochine, 1943), p. 23.

48. Information derived from a cadastral map of Dalat circa 1937, author's collection.

49. Xuan Phuong, Ao Dai: Du Couvent des Oiseaux à la jungle du Viêt-Minh (Paris: Plon, 2001), p. 14.

50. VNA2, RSA 4080, Plans de lotissement de Dalat, 1923–1925, now renumbered as VNA4, RSA 4101, Garnier to l'architecte en chef des bâtiments civils de l'Indochine, March 17, 1925.

51. VNA2, RSA 3078, Concession de terrains Bourgery, Grand Lycée, Lê Duong, à Dalat, 1934, now renumbered as VNA4, RSA 3098, "Terrain Le Duong, 1933–4."

52. "Notre station d'altitude," Le Courrier de Saigon, May 30, 1932, p. 1.

53. IFA, L. G. Pineau Collection, Mayor to Pineau, October 29, 1932.

54. CIAM, Pineau file, 1932, Pineau to Giedion.

55. SHM, 171 GG2, Decoux papers, carton 3, Dalat, September 14, 1943.

56. ANOM, GGI, 66188.

57. Gwendolyn Wright, p. 233.

58. Hébrard, "Dalat le nouveau plan, dispositions générales," *L'Eveil Economique* (Indochine), October 21, 1923.

59. Ibid.

60. VNA2, RSA 4090, "Procès verbaux du comité de salubrité public de Dalat, 1925," now renumbered as VNA4, RSA 4112, August 30, 1925 session.

61. Le Brusq, p. 108.

62. Pineau, *Dalat, Capitale administrative de l'Indochine*, pp. 32–33.

63. Xuan Phuong, p. 14.

64. P. Munier, "Dalat," *Indochine, hebdomadaire illustré*, March 13, 1941, p. 7.

65. Kennedy, p. 105.

66. SHG, 2007 ZM1/000231 (formerly 04425), Lietuenant Bruez, bordereau d'envoi, December 11, 1950.

67. Le Brusq, p. 102.

68. Paul Rabinow, *French Modern: Forms and Norms of the Social Environment* (Boston: MIT Press, 1989), p. 202.

69. Shanny Peer, *France on Display: Peasants, Provincials and Folklore in the 1937 Paris World's Fair* (Albany: SUNY Press, 1998), p. 53.

70. Ibid., pp. 53, 72.

71. Ibid., pp. 64, 78.

72. Paul Veysseyre, private papers.

73. Claude Perrens, "Lettre de Dalat," *Indochine, hebdomadaire illustré*, May 27, 1943, p. 18.

74. Suzanne Coussillan, letter to the editor, *Le Monde*, January 25, 1992, p. 24.

75. This is reflected in Pineau's correspondence from the 1930s. CIAM, Pineau papers.

76. "A vendre: Trois belles villas sises à Dalat," NLV, M8364.

77. On the Vichy regime in Indochina, see Eric Jennings, *Vichy in the Tropics: Pétain's National Revolution in Madagascar, Guadeloupe and Indochina, 1940–1944.* (Stanford: Stanford University Press, 2001).

78. "Les stations de repos," in "Architecture moderne en Indochine," special issue, *Indochine, hebdomadaire illustré*, August 19, 1943, p. xxi.

79. "Dalat, Cité-Jardin Amiral Decoux" flyer.

80. "Dalat, Cité-Jardin Amiral Decoux" flyer.

81. SHM, 171 GG2, Decoux papers, carton 3, Dalat, January 8, 1943.

82. On attempts to elaborate a Vichyite social system, see Jean-Philippe Hesse and Jean-Pierre Le Crom eds., *La protection sociale sous le régime de Vichy* (Rennes: Presses Universitaires de Rennes, 2001).

83. "Architecture moderne en Indochine," special issue, *Indochine, hebdomadaire illustré*, August 19, 1943, pp. xxvi-xxvii.

84. CIAM, Pineau correspondence 1930, Pineau to Giedion, Paris, June 29, 1930.

85. All quotes from *Technika Chronica*, CIAM Fourth Congress, pp. 1187–88 (CIAM).

86. CIAM, Dalat maps, 42/04/7/22/1–6.

87. Of course, as Michael Vann has shown, French colonial planners were also trying to introduce such features in Indochina's capital. Vann, pp. 91–107, p. 100 on buffer zones.

88. IFA, L. G. Pineau Collection. Pineau, "Aménagement et extension de Dalat, Rapport," p. 7.

89. Pineau, *Dalat, Capitale administrative de l'Indochine*, p. 31.

90. Le Brusq, p. 233.

91. A. D., "Architecture coloniale," *Extrême-Asie*, June 30, 1930, p. 295–96.

92. A. D., "Dalat, un criminel attentat," first published in *L'Impartial*, reproduced in *La Volonté Indochinoise* 1937, exact issue unknown. Found in IFA, L. G. Pineau Collection.

93. Louis-Georges Pineau, "Le Plan d'aménagement et d'extension de Dalat," *La Vie urbaine* 49 (1939): p. 38.

94. VNA2, RSA 4105, Séance de la commission municipale, May 25, 1935, now renumbered as VNA4, RSA 4126.

95. ANOM, TP 261 dossier 15 la gare.

96. Le Brusq, p. 103.

97. VNA2, RSA 4104, "Commission municipale de Dalat," now renumbered as VNA4, RSA 4125, "Réponse au voeu émis par M. Acouturier à la séance du 8 septembre 1934 de la commission municipale au sujet de la construction d'une gare à Dalat."

98. VNA2, RSA 4109, "Réunions de la commission municipale de Dalat, 1936–7," now renumbered as VNA4, RSA 4130, "Gare de Dalat."

99. "Architecture moderne en Indochine," special issue, *Indochine, hebdomadaire illustré*, August 19, 1943, p. xxii.

100. Shellshear, p. 32.

101. Papin, p. 245. To Anh Dang, p. 61.

102. Truong Tro, ed. *Dalat, ville d'altitude*, p. 140.

CHAPTER 8

1. Robert Reed, "From Highland Hamlet to Regional Capital: Reflections on the Colonial Origins, Urban Transformation and Environmental Impact of Dalat," in *The Challenges of Highland Development in Vietnam*, eds., Terry Rambo, Robert Reed, Le Trong Cuc et al., p. 51 (Hawaii: East-West Center Program on Environment, 1995).

2. On French colonial tourism, see *Revue tourisme* 15 (May 2006), dedicated to colonial-era tourism in North Africa; as well as Alison Murray, "Le tourisme Citroën au Sahara, 1924–1925," *Vingtième Siècle, Revue d'Histoire* 68 (October–December 2000): pp. 95–107; Daniel Sherman, "Paradis à vendre: tourisme et imitation en Polynésie française: 1958–1971," *Terrain* 44 (March 2005): pp. 39–56; and Ellen Furlough, "Une leçon des choses," pp. 441–73.

3. ANOM, GGI 5966; ANOM, GGI 66188, Rapport du Dr Haueur, Saigon, June 4, 1903.

4. Françoise Ged argues that luxury hotels in general evolved over time from sites of escapism and exoticism into comforting spaces where fatigued travelers could find reminders of home. Françoise Ged, "Urbanité, modernité et permanence du grand hôtel shanghaïen" in *Les grands hôtels en Asie: Modernité, dynamiques urbaines et sociabilité*, ed. Thierry Sanjuan, p. 130 (Paris: Sorbonne, 2003).

5. On rigidity, stratification, and seclusion in French colonial society, see Charles Meyer, *Les Français en Indochine*, p. 78.

6. IFA, fonds Pineau, "Croquis de Dalat, 1906."

7. ANOM, AFFPOL 3152, Note de l'Inspecteur général des Colonies Phérivong, au sujet du Sanatorium du Langbian, May 10, 1917.

8. "Visite de M. Long à Dalat," *L'Echo annamite,* July 24, 1920, p. 2.

9. ANOM, GGI 46407, Governor of Indochina to Minister of the Colonies, August 8, 1923.

10. Mourey, *Mon Lycée en Annam,* p. 89. Henry de Lachevrotière, "Va-t-on délaisser Dalat?" *L'Impartial* (Saigon), April 12, 1923, p. 1.

11. "Le tourisme en Indochine," *Le Moniteur d'Indochine,* February 24, 1923.

12. "Terrible accident à Dalat," *Le Camly,* September 6, 1924, p. 1. On the lawsuit, see ANOM, GGI 37997.

13. "Fermeture de l'hôtel," *Le Camly,* June 6, 1925, p. 1.

14. VNA1, GGI 5034, Cahier des Charges pour l'exploitation des hôtels du groupe de Dalat, p. 9.

15. Desanti had managed Dalat's first hotel, known officially as the "Langbian hôtel de Dalat," (and unofficially as the Hôtel Desanti) which closed in May 1925, shortly after the opening of the Lang-Bian Palace. It would later reopen as a cheaper alternative to the Palace. See "Quelques réflexions et souvenirs sur de vieilles planches," *Le Camly,* December 15, 1923, p. 1, and "Fermeture de l'hôtel," *Le Camly,* June 6, 1925, p. 1.

16. See ANOM, GGI 38218 for all information regarding Passiot and his lawsuit.

17. VNA2, RSA 4090, "Procès verbaux du comité de salubrité public de Dalat, 1925," now renumbered as VNA4, RSA 4112; and VNA2, RSA 4085, "Questions diverses concernant la voirie, la police et l'architecture à Dalat," now renumbered as VNA4, RSA 4107.

18. VNA2, RSA 4087, now renumbered as VNA4, RSA 4109, Décision du 16/08/24 du Gouvernement Général concernant divers travaux à Dalat, Procès verbal de la Commission de contrôle du Langbian Palace.

19. Letter to the editor, congratulating the Lang-Bian Palace on its facilities, *Le Camly,* December 29, 1923, p. 1.

20. Shellshear, *Far from the Tamarind Tree,* p. 35. Note that Shellshear was mistaken on Feraudy "having had the hotel built."

21. Cornell University Library, Wason Pamphlets, Indochina 51, *Les Hôtels en Indochine;* and *Petit guide illustré de Dalat* (1930), p. 13.

22. Bruno Duron, "The Dalat Palace: A Hotel of the Past, Today," pp. 47–48. In this unpublished manuscript, Bruno Duron, commissioned to trace the history of the Palace Hotel by American tycoon Larry Hillblom, provides a compendium of useful sources relating to the history of the hotel.

23. VNA1, GGI 5034, "Cahier des charges pour l'exploitation des hôtels du groupe de Dalat," p. 14.

24. Ibid., p. 9.

25. Morgan Sportès, *Tonkinoise* (Paris: Le Seuil, 1995), p. 197.

26. Wright, p. 231.

27. On the Vichy period in Indochina, see Jennings, *Vichy in the Tropics,* pp. 130–98. The hotel's Vichy-era renovations are shown in *Indochine, hebdomadaire illustré,* February 11, 1943.

28. See Le Brusq, pp. 101–10.

29. SHM, Decoux papers, 171 GG2, carton 3, entry for July 1, 1942.

30. Claude Perrens, "Lettre de Dalat," *Indochine, hebdomadaire illustré*, May 27, 1943, p. 18.

31. On the changes to the Saigon theater, see *Indochine, hebdomadaire illustré*, September 23, 1943; on the alterations to the palace of the governor general of Cochinchina, see *Indochine, hebdomadaire illustré*, January 27, 1944.

32. Verney, p. 708f288.

33. De Tessan, "Une station d''altitude en Indochine," p. 158.

34. Ibid.

35. Original postcard, author's collection. Last names withheld to protect privacy. The ennui suffered by French women in Indochina was recounted in—amongst other sources—George Groslier's colonial novel, *Le Retour à l'argile*. One of its main characters, Raymonde, complains constantly of boredom while her husband cheats on her with a Cambodian mistress. See George Groslier, *Le Retour à l'argile* (Pondichéry: Kailash Editions, original edition 1928, republished 1996), p. 102.

36. "Humour dalatois: Inversions vestimentaires ou du danger de la baignade aux environs de Dalat (histoire vécue)," *Indochine, hebdomadaire illustré*, July 13, 1944.

37. Michael Vann, "White City on the Red River," pp. 550–553.

38. *Le Guide du Routard, Vietnam* (Paris: Hachette, 1999), p. 309.

39. ANOM, SPCE 94.

40. Nicolas Fiévé, "Pouvoir politique, modernité architecturale et paysage urbain dans le Japon de l'ère Meiji: L'hôtel impérial de Tokyo," in *Les grands hôtels en Asie*, ed. Thierry Sanjuan, p. 22.

41. Duron, "The Dalat Palace," p. 105.

42. Bruce Lockhart, "Monarchy and Decolonization in Indochina," paper delivered at the International Workshop on "Decolonization and Transformation in Southeast Asia," Singapore, February 19, 2001, p. 17.

43. VNA2, RSA 4090, Procès verbaux du comité de salubrité public de Dalat, 1925, now renumbered as VNA4, RSA 4112.

44. Reprinted in *Extrême-Asie*, December 1933, p. 370.

45. ANOM, RSA L5, "Articles de presse concernant le tourisme."

46. Cornell University Library, Wason Pamphlets, Indochina 51, *Les Hôtels en Indochine*.

47. ANOM, RSA L4, Governor General to Governor of Cochinchina, June 29, 1929.

48. Ibid.

49. Pierre Brocheux and Daniel Hémery, *Indochine, la colonisation ambiguë*, pp. 260–63.

50. Duron, "The Dalat Palace," p. 97.

51. VNA1, GGI 5014, Résident Supérieur d'Annam to Gouverneur Général d'Indochine, May 14, 1928.

52. ANOM, GGI 59875, Inspecteur des finances to Gouverneur Général, December 8, 1931.

53. ANOM, GGI 59875, Feraudy to Mayor of Dalat, August 2, 1931.

54. All luxury hotels suffered during this time, including the legendary Raffles in Singapore. See Ilsa Sharp, *There Is Only One Raffles: The Story of a Grand Hotel* (London: Souvenir Press, 1981), p. 44.

55. ANOM, GGI 59875, Résident Mayor, letter of September 6, 1931.

56. Duron, "The Dalat Palace," p. 105.

57. "The Lang-Bian Hotel was reserved for our big-wigs," writes Gilbert David in *Chroniques secrètes de l'Indochine* (Paris: L'Harmattan, 1994), p. 149. Although serious concerns have emerged over this book's claims regarding political events and conspiracies, and over its very legitimacy, this particular description rings true. For a list of the many doubts relating to this book, see Jean Deuve, review of *Chroniques secrètes de l'Indochine*, by Gilbert David, *Guerres mondiales et conflits contemporains* 220 (2005): pp. 152–56.

58. Long before any historian, Vietnamese and French contemporaries alike recognized this phenomenon. They did so with remarkable frequency and constancy. In his famous *Procès de la colonisation française*, Ho Chi Minh wrote: "In the colonies, if one has white skin, one belongs to the aristocracy: one is of a superior race. In order to maintain his social status, even the European customs officer has at least one servant, a 'boy' who, quite often, is a maid of all work." Ho Chi Minh, *Selected Works*, vol. 2 (Hanoi: Foreign Language Publishing, 1961), p. 53. In 1926, the journalist Léon Werth wrote that the entire colonial hierarchy "from governors to gendarmes" morphed into "potentates" in Indochina. Léon Werth, *Cochinchine* (Paris: Vivianne Hamy, 1997, first published 1926), p. 42. Likewise a character in George Groslier's 1928 colonial novel *Le retour à l'argile* argued: "The conquered populations who surround (the French functionary) in servitude only inflate the vanity of colonial society and put it on a pedestal: a warrant officer or a customs agent becomes a high lord surrounded by a thousand coolies." Groslier, p. 133.

59. LDPL, DC 253, "Dalat, Le nouveau plan: dispositions générales," *L'Eveil économique*, no date.

60. ANOM, AGEFOM 858, d. 2324.

61. Duron, "The Dalat Palace," p. 126.

62. Ibid.

63. Peters, "Negotiating Power," pp. 207–64.

64. Duron, "The Dalat Palace," pp. 128–30.

65. ANOM, GGI 59875, Feraudy to Governor General, July 4, 1931.

66. ANOM, GGI 59873, Mr. Courtinat to the mayor of Dalat, January 21, 1932.

67. VNA1, GGI 5034, "Cahier des charges pour l'exploitation des hôtels du groupe de Dalat," p. 1.

68. Duron, "The Dalat Palace," p. 6.

69. Ibid., p. 67.

70. All of the information in this paragraph comes from the report by Paul Veysseyre, architect: "Effondrement de la descente à couvert du Lang-Bian Palace, le samedi 6 mars 1943; rapport d'expert," Paul Veysseyre, private papers.

71. See Adam Schwarz, "Beaches and Sand Traps," *Far-Eastern Economic Review* 159 (February 29, 1996), p. 41.

72. Robert Templer, *Shadows and Wind: A View of Modern Vietnam* (London: Penguin, 1998), p. 9. A much harsher criticism has been articulated by Penny Edwards on colonial nostalgia surrounding the hotel at Dalat's "sister hill station" of Bokor, in Cambodia. Edwards argues: "In eclipsing the carnage of Bokor's construction with the glitter of hotel ballrooms, Muller falls prey to the 'Indo-Chic' syndrome recently identified by the literary critic

Panivong Norindr. . . . Excised from their historical context, these totems of lost empire invent new memories. Colonialism is remade as a romantic interlude where a happy time was had by all—except, of course, for the victims of bad service at the Bokor Palace Hotel." Penny Edwards, "Tango dancing in the blood of Bokor," *Phnom Penh Post*, March 27–April 9, 1998.

73. Crossette, p. 214.

74. Roger Cohen, "Indochina Dreaming," *The New York Times*, June 1, 2009.

75. On the Indochic phenomenon, see Norindr, *Phantasmatic Indochina*.

76. Derek Maitland and Jill Goeler, eds., *Traveler's Companion: Vietnam, Laos and Cambodia* (Connecticut: Globe Pequot Press, 1999), p. 40.

CHAPTER 9

1. Jean Rouget, *Indochine, les dernières moussons: Un regard sur les rapports France-Vietnam* (Panazol: Charles Lavauzelle, 2004), p. 36.

2. Dane Kennedy, p. 175.

3. ANOM, GGI 22212.

4. Paul Vidal de la Blache, *Principes de Géographie humaine* (Paris: Armand Colin, 1922), p. 110.

5. Dr. Abbatucci, "Climatologie dans l'Indo-Chine," *Revue d'hygiène et de médecine preventive* 56 (1934): p. 43.

6. In fairness this was an updated second edition of a 1940 work. Pierre Gourou, *La Terre et l'homme en Extrême-Orient* (Paris: Flammarion, 1972), pp. 29, 38. Gavin Bowd and Daniel Clayton, "Tropicality, Orientalism and French Colonialism in Indochina: The Work of Pierre Gourou," *French Historical Studies* 28, no. 2 (Spring 2005): p. 316, show that Gourou cannot be deemed a climatic determinist.

7. Roger Trinquier, *Les Maquis d'Indochine: Les Missions spéciales du service Action* (Paris: Albatros, 1976), p. 109.

8. Wynn Wilcox, "Transnationalism and Multiethnicity in the Early Nguyen Anh Gia Long Period," in *Viêt Nam: Borderless Histories,* eds. Nhung Tuyet Tran and Anthony Reid, eds., pp. 197–99, 208 (Madison: University of Wisconsin Press, 2006).

9. Andrew Hardy, *Red Hills: Migrants and the State in the Highlands of Vietnam* (Honolulu: University of Hawai'i Press, 2003), pp. 7, 46, 70–73.

10. Nguyen The Anh, "La frontière sino-vietnamienne du xième au xviième siècle," in *Les Frontières du Vietnam,* ed. P. B. Lafont, pp. 67–69 (Paris: L'Harmattan, 1989).

11. Charles Fourniau, Trinh Van Thao, Gilles de Gantès, Philippe le Failler, Jean-Marie Mancini, and Gilles Raffi, *Le Contact colonial franco-vietnamien: Le premier demi-siècle, 1858–1911* (Aix-en-Provence: Presses universitaires de Provence, 1999), p. 96.

12. My thanks to David Biggs, at the University of California at Riverside, for most of these points.

13. Steve Déry, pp. 23, 52.

14. Hardy, p. 70.

15. Joseph Vassal, "Le Lang-Bian," *La Revue indochinoise* 53 (March 1907), p. 18.

16. AIP, SIM 16, fonds Paul Louis Simond, Vassal's 1914 report, pp. 1–2.

17. AIP, SIM 16, fonds Paul Louis Simond, Vassal's 1914 report, p. 3.

18. Hardy, pp. 100–5.

19. Joseph Vassal, "Le Lang-Bian," *La Revue indochinoise* 53 (March 1907), p. 18.

20. IFA, Pineau Report. For the higher figure, see "La Station d'altitude de Dalat," *L'Echo annamite*, December 4, 1925.

21. IFA, Pineau Report.

22. SHG, 2007 ZMI 000447, July 20, 1932.

23. IFA, Pineau Report.

24. "La Station d'altitude de Dalat," *L'Echo annamite*, December 4, 1925.

25. Xuân Son, "Spring Days in Da Lat," *Công Luân Báo* (6476), February 25, 1934.

26. *Télé-Havas: Annuaire officiel des abonnés au telephone, Cochinchine, Sud-Annam*, 1945–1949, CUKL, HE 8390.5A51.

27. Gerald Hickey, *Sons of the Mountains*, p. 367.

28. Nguyễn Nhân Bằng, "Ap Hà Dông," *Sudia* (1971), pp. 93–110.

29. ANOM, 9 APOM 1.

30. Liên Đoàn Lao Động Tỉnh Lâm Đồng, *Lịch Sử Phong Trào Công Nhân Và Công Đoàn Tỉnh Lâm Đồng, 1929–1999 [History of the Workers' Movement and Unions of Lam Dong Province]*, (Hà Nội: Nhà Xuất Bản Lao Động, 1999), chapter 1, evokes the growing presence of ethnic Vietnamese teachers, health care workers, tax, electricity, and postal officials in Dalat.

31. Kennedy, p. 187.

32. "Dalat, vol de 1600 Piastres," *L'Echo annamite*, March 23, 1925, p. 3.

33. *Lịch Sử Phong Trào Công Nhân Và Công Đoàn Tỉnh Lâm Đồng*, p. 17.

34. ANOM, 9 APOM 1, 1957, Report by Georges Azambre.

35. ANOM, 86 APOM 100, Association des planteurs de café du Haut Donnaï to Résidents en Annam et au Haut Donnaï, Djiring, April 18, 1940.

36. ANOM, 86 APOM 100.

37. For two recent analyses of the wretched conditions on Indochinese rubber plantations, see Stephen Harp, "Marketing in the Metropole: Colonial Rubber Plantations and French Consumerism in the Early Twentieth Century," in *Views from the Margins: Creating Identities in Modern France*, eds. Sarah Curtis and Kevin Callahan, pp. 84–107 (Lincoln: Nebraska University Press, 2008); and Sébastien Verney, "Le nécessaire compromis colonial: Le cas de la Plantation Michelin de Dau Tieng de 1932 à 1937," in *Les Administrations coloniales, xixème-xxème siècles: Esquisse d'une histoire comparée*, ed. Samia El Mechat (Rennes: Presses Universitaires de Rennes, 2009).

38. ANOM, 86 APOM 100.

39. ANOM, GGI 64227, Rapport Politique Annam, 4ème trimestre 1922.

40. SHG, 2007 ZM 1/ 000447 (formerly 04641), August 16, 1928 letter to the Résident-Maire of Dalat.

41. SHG, 2007 ZM 1/ 000447 (formerly 04641), November 15, 1928, Letter to the Résident-Maire of Dalat.

42. *Lịch Sử Phong Trào Công Nhân Và Công Đoàn Tỉnh Lâm Đồng*, pp. 23–25. On the challenges of producing written Communist propaganda in the late 1920s and early 1930s, see Shawn McHale, *Print and Power: Confucianism, Communism and Buddhism in the Making of Modern Vietnam* (Honolulu: University of Hawai'i Press, 2004), p. 115.

43. ANOM, GGI 65458, Sûreté Annam, 1937.

44. ANOM, GGI 65459, Sûreté Annam, 1938, "Note sur l'activité révolutionnaire en Annam au cours du mois d'août 1938."

45. ANOM, GGI 65460, Notice sur les intrigues politiques de tendance subversive dans les milieux indigènes et étrangers de l'Annam pendant le mois d'août 1939.

46. *Lịch Sử Phong Trào Công Nhân Và Công Đoàn Tỉnh Lâm Đồng*, p. 30.

47. ANOM, GGI 65460, Activités politiques constatées en Annam au cours du mois de juin 1939, Grèves des marchandes au marché de Dalat.

48. ANOM GGI 65458, Note sur l'activité révolutionnaire en Annam au cours de mois de juillet 1937.

49. On the French colonial police's tendency to view all dissent in Indochina as Communist, see Arthur J. Dommen, *The Indochinese Experience of the French and the Americans* (Bloomington: Indiana University Press, 2001), p. 40.

50. Ban Tuyên Giáo tỉnh ủy Lâm Đồng [Propaganda Commitee of Lam Dong province], *Cách mạng tháng 8 năm 1945 ở Lâm Đồng [The August 1945 Revolution in Lam-Dong Province]* (Dalat, 1995), p. 10.

51. Ibid., p. 13.

52. ANOM, CAOM GGI 65462, Sûreté Annam 1941.

53. *Cách mạng tháng 8 năm 1945 ở Lâm Đồng*, p. 14.

54. Xuan Phuong, *Ao Dai*, pp. 13–16, 17, 19, 31.

55. Truong Nhu Tang, *Journal of a Viet Cong* (New York: Harcourt Brace, 1985), p. 107.

56. "Dalat, residence d'été préférée de la Cour d'Annam," *La Dépêche coloniale*, September 26, 1936.

57. *Souverains et notabilités d'Indochine* (Hanoi: IDEO, 1943); and "L'Annam sans Empereur," *France illustration*, June 14, 1947, p. 629.

58. ANOM, INF 2664, Rapports politiques Annam, 1933–1934, p. 19. "Dalat, résidence d'été préférée de la Cour d'Annam," *La Dépêche coloniale*, September 26, 1936.

59. Bruce M. Lockhart, *The End of the Vietnamese Monarchy* (New Haven: Council on Southeast Asian Studies, 1993), p. 92.

60. "La gracieuse personnalité de l'Impératrice d'Annam," *La Dépêche coloniale*, April 7, 1934.

61. Lockhart, pp. 87–89.

62. "Le Roman d'amour de Mariette Nguyen Honhao," *Paris-soir*, June 21, 1939.

63. *Souverains et Notabilités d'Indochine*, pp. 3–4.

64. David Marr, *Vietnamese Tradition on Trial* (Berkeley: University of California Press, 1981), pp. 136–189; Arthur J. Dommen, p. 34. On the gender dimension, also see Judith Henchy, "Vietnamese New Women and the Fashioning of Modernity," in *France and Indochina: Cultural Represenations,* eds. Jennifer Yee and Kathryn Robson, pp. 121–38 (Lanham: Lexington books, 2005); Bui Tran Phuong, "Việt Nam 1918–1945, genre et modernité: Emergence de nouvelles perceptions et expérimentations," PhD thesis, University Lyon II, 2008.

65. Peter Zinoman, preface to Vu Trong Phung, *Dumb Luck* (Ann Arbor: University of Michigan Press, 2002), p. 2.

66. Ibid., p. 10.

67. "Nos stations d'altitude et balnéaires," *La Tribune indigène*, October 13, 1923. On

the wage imbalance, see Alexander Woodside, "The Development of Social Organizations in Vietnamese Cities in the Late Colonial Period," *Pacific Affairs* 44, no. 1 (Spring 1971): p. 47.

68. As late as 1947, R. Tollard still maintained that "the Annamese are naturally less sapped by the climate . . . they have obviously no reason to take leaves in France." R. T., *La France et le Peuple annamite vont-ils être trahis et ruinés?* (self-published, 1947), p. 18.

69. "Peut-on développer le Tamdao?" *Eveil économique de l'Indochine*, September 20, 1924, p. 3.

70. "Dalat et les Annamites," *L'Echo annamite*, December 31, 1925.

71. "Summer Vacations," *Vê Sinh Báo* 41 (June 1929).

72. Christopher Goscha, "Récits de voyage viêtnamiens et prise de conscience indochinoise, 1920–1945," in *Récits de voyages des Asiatiques: Genres, mentalités, conceptions de l'espace*, ed. Claudine Salman, pp. 253–79 (Paris: EFEO, 1996).

73. Nguyen Tien Lang, *Indochine la douce* (Hanoi: Nam-Ky, 1936), p. 139.

74. Bat Long, *Du-Lich Trung Ky [Travelling in Annam]* (Hué: Tiêng Dân, 1930), pp. 17–18.

75. De Tessan, *Dans l'Asie qui s'éveille*, p. 15.

76. http://www.jean-michel-truong.net/bio/pages/truong-ngoc-hau.html, last consulted April 17, 2009.

77. Also see David Del Testa, "Automobiles and Anomie in Colonial Indochina," in *France and Indochina: Cultural Representations*, eds. Kathryn Robson and Jennifer Yee, pp. 63–78 (Lanham: Lexington Books, 2005).

78. David Marr, *Vietnamese Tradition on Trial*, p. 62.

79. Hue-Tam Ho Tai, "The Politics of Compromise: The Constitutionalist Party and Electoral Reforms of 1922 in French Indochina," *Modern Asian Studies* 18, no. 3 (1984), p. 382. Emmanuelle Saada, *Les Enfants de la Colonie: Les Métis de l'Empire français entre sujétion et citoyenneté* (Paris: La Découverte, 2007), p. 130.

80. Cited in Yerri Urban, "Race et nationalité dans le droit colonial français, 1865–1955," PhD thesis in public law, Université de Bourgogne, 2009, p. 467.

81. Phan Thua Luong, "Nghi Mat Va Tam Be" ["In our country, where should we go for summer vacation?"], *Khoa-Hoc Tap-Chí [Scientific Journal]*, June 15, 1934.

82. Ibid.

83. "Ve viec cat nha nghi mat o Da-lat" ["About the construction of a vacation house in Dalat"], *Tân Tiên Báo [Evolué Journal]*, January 30, 1936.

84. VNA2, RSA 4109, "Réunion de la Commission municipale de Dalat, 1936–7," now renumbered as VNA4, RSA 4130, "Création de maisons de repos pour les fonctionnaires Annamites de Cochinchine."

85. Nguyen Trung Thu, "Cho'i Xuan Dalat" ["Spring Vacation in Dalat: Memoir of a Tennis Player"] *Tân Tiên Báo*, February 20, 1938.

86. Nguyen Trung Thu, "Cho'i Xuan Dalat" ("Spring Vacation in Dalat: Memoir of a Tennis Player"] *Tân Tiên Báo*, March 5, 1938.

87. Nguyen Tien Lang, "Le premier monument historique annamite à Dalat," *Indochine hebdomadaire illustré*, October 9, 1941, p. 9.

88. Nguyen Trung Thu, "Cho'i Xuan Dalat" ("Spring Vacation in Dalat: Memoir of a Tennis Player"] *Tân Tiên Báo*, March 12 and 27, 1938.

89. Hoài Thanh—Hoài Chân, *Thi Nhân Viet Nam [Vietnamese poets]* (Hanoi: Hoi Nha Van, 2000). Poem translated by Thuy Linh Nguyen.

90. Ibid.

CHAPTER 10

1. *Petit guide illustré de Dalat* (1930), p. 13.

2. Kennedy, *The Magic Mountains,* pp. 117–46.

3. Doumer, *Situation de l'Indo-Chine 1897–1901,* pp. 113–14.

4. "Le Sanatorium du Lang-Bian," *Annales d'hygiène publique et de médecine légale* 4 no. 6 (1906); p. 444.

5. ANOM, GGI 66188, Missions au Lang-Bian, Annam.

6. Take, for example, the description of Dalat by former Lycée Yersin student Dominique Mourey: "Dalat's bucolic setting, a town conceived in the country as Alphonse Allais would have liked, its vivifying climate, all conferred upon Dalat an obvious schooling vocation." Mourey, p. 65.

7. VNA2, RSA 2751, Pasquier cited in a letter of December 1, 1930.

8. ANOM, AGEFOM 858, d 2324, Projet de lycée à Dalat, p. 2.

9. On the history of education in colonial Indochina, see Trinh Van Tao, *L'école française en Indochine* (Paris: Karthala, 1995); Gail Paradise Kelly, *French Colonial Education: Essays on Vietnam and West Africa* (New York: AMS Press, 2000); and Pascale Bezançon, *Une colonisation éducatrice? L'expérience indochinoise, 1860–1945* (Paris: L'Harmattan, 2002).

10. "Une bonne nouvelle," *Le Camly,* December 22, 1923, p. 1. VNA2, RSA 4089, "Affectation des immeubles de Dalat, répartition des logements," now renumbered as VNA4, RSA 4111.

11. Haut-Commissariat de France pour l'Indochine, *Lycée Yersin, Dalat,* p. 3.

12. VNA2, RSA 4109, "Réunion de la commission municipale de Dalat, 1936–7," now renumbered as VNA4, RSA 4130.

13. Justin Godart, *Rapport de Mission en Indochine, 1937* (Paris: L'Harmattan, 1994), p. 153.

14. Shellshear remembers the Couvent des Oiseaux as "the bastion of new honey-coloured bricks, housing a wealth of culture where I would spend most of my time for the next six years. It was here that I was to gain some of the richest experiences of my childhood." Shellshear, p. 40. Mourey, *Mon Lycée en Annam.* Xuan Phuong, *Ao Dai.* Jacomme, *Vers les mimosas de Dalat.*

15. Kelly, p. 81. Hue-Tam Ho Tai, *Radicalism and the Origins of the Vietnamese Revolution* (Cambridge: Harvard University Press, 1992), p. 33.

16. Direction de l'Instruction publique, *Le Petit Lycée de Dalat* (Hanoi: Imprimerie d'Extrême-Orient, 1930), p. 7.

17. Ibid., p. 10.

18. Bezançon, pp. 263, 304.

19. Direction de l'Instruction publique, *Le Petit Lycée de Dalat,* p. 28.

20. Trinh Van Thao, p. 105.

21. Direction de l'Instruction publique, *Le Petit Lycée de Dalat,* p. 13.

22. Mourey, p.113.

23. Direction de l'Instruction publique, *Le Petit Lycée de Dalat*, p. 15.

24. Ibid., p. 17.

25. Ibid., p. 19.

26. On the slippages between moral and hygienic school discipline, see Luc Boltanski, *Prime éducation et morale de classe* (Paris: Mouton, 1969), pp. 110–11.

27. Erica Peters, "Negotiating Power through Everyday Practices," pp. 164–66, 185–91.

28. "Mort aux vaches!" *L'Impartial,* June 17, 1935, p. 1.

29. Boltanski, p. 102.

30. Martin Thomas, *The French Empire between the Wars: Imperialism, Politics and Society* (Manchester: Manchester University Press, 2005), p. 171.

31. Micheline Lessard, "We Know . . . the Duties We Must Fulfill: Modern 'Mothers and Fathers' of the Vietnamese Nation," *French Colonial History* 3 (2003): pp. 122–23.

32. "Les Annamites et le Lycée de Dalat," *La Presse indochinoise,* July 15, 1934.

33. Herman Lebovics, *True France: The Wars over Cultural Identity, 1900–1945* (Ithaca: Cornell University Press, 1992), p. 117.

34. "Rentrée des classes au Lycée Yersin à Dalat," *La Presse indochinoise,* August 11, 1936.

35. VNA2, RSA 4109, Rapport de la séance du 5 décembre 1936 de la commission municipale de Dalat.

36. On the Popular Front, see Gilles de Gantès and Panivong Norindr's chapters in *The French Colonial Empire and the Popular Front,* eds. Tony Chafer and Amanda Sackur, pp. 109–30, 230–48 (London: MacMillan, 1999). On challenges to racial determinism in this period, see Nancy Stepan, p. 114 as well as Elazar Barkan, *The Retreat of Scientific Racism: Changing Concepts of Race in Britain and the United States Between the Wars* (Cambridge: Cambridge University Press, 1992). On the results of the Guernut inquiry in this same context, see Owen White, *Children of the French Empire: Miscegenation and Colonial Society in French West Africa, 1895–1960* (Oxford: Oxford University Press, 1999), pp. 119, 121. For the counterpoint, that distilled biological racism endured in official French colonial thought throughout the 1930s, see Clifford Rosenberg, "Albert Sarraut and Republican Racial Thought," *French Politics, Culture and Society* 20, no. 3 (Fall 2002): pp. 97–114.

37. VNA2, RSA 4109, Rapport de la séance du 5 décembre 1936 de la commission municipale de Dalat.

38. Mourey, pp. 65, 153, 220.

39. Mourey, pp. 86, 220.

40. Jacomme, p. 58.

41. On another such logic of exception, in a different colonial context, see Jean-Hervé Jézéquel, "Grammaire de la distinction coloniale. L'organisation des cadres de l'enseignement en Afrique occidentale française," *Genèses* 69 (2007): pp. 4–25.

42. Godart, *Rapport de Mission,* pp. 57, 153.

43. Xuan Phuong, pp. 13, 14, 34.

44. Ibid., p. 34.

45. ACND, Vietnam 2, "enfants Annamites du pensionnat."

46. ANOM, 90F 37, Dalat 1949.

47. ANOM, 90F 41, Dalat 1950. Note that because the baccalaureate was held over the

final two years of high school, some of these names repeat over the two years. But this does not alter the ratio of Vietnamese to French students.

48. Mourey, p. 319.

49. *La Quinzaine coloniale*, January 25, 1897, p. 37.

50. Gaston Mery, "Féminisme," *La Libre parole*, October 20, 1898.

51. Gilles de Gantès, "Coloniaux, Gouverneurs et Ministres," p. 43.

52. Marie-Paule Ha, "La Femme française aux colonies: Promoting Colonial Female Emigration at the Turn of the Century," *French Colonial History* 6 (2005): p. 217.

53. Marie-Paule Ha, "French Women and the Empire," in *France and Indochina*, eds. Robson and Yee, pp. 112–13.

54. Clothilde Chivas-Baron, *La Femme française aux colonies* (Paris: Larose, 1929), p. 115.

55. Ibid., pp. 188–89.

56. S. Guay, "Enfants du samedi," in "Le coin des Saïgonnaises," *La Presse indochinoise* May 5–6, 1934.

57. Jacomme, p. 56.

58. Mourey, pp. 51–52.

59. Owen White, *Children of the French Empire*; Emmanuelle Saada, *Les Enfants de la Colonie*.

60. The secular-religious alliance on Eurasian issues is reflected in the FOEFI's 1949 statutes. These stipulate that the foundation's administrative council should include representatives from different charitable organizations, from the clergy, and from the colonial administration. ANOM, HCI 665, "FOEFI, Statuts."

61. On state-church clashes and points of convergence in French colonial Indochina, see J. P. Daughton, *An Empire Divided: Religion, Republicanism and the Making of French Colonialism* (Oxford: Oxford University Press, 2006).

62. ANOM, AGEFOM, 252, dossier 376, "Condition légale des enfants métis non-reconnus."

63. ANOM, RSA F1, April 1900, Report from Upper-Donnaï.

64. Saada, p. 92.

65. Saada, p. 234.

66. David Pomfret, "Raising Eurasia: Race, Class and Age in French and British Colonies," *Comparative Studies in Society and History* 51, no. 2 (2009): pp. 335, 340.

67. ANOM, RSTNF 4857 for 1937 and 1938. ANOM, HCI 802, Exercice 1953, assemblée générale ordinaire des 13, 14 et 15 sept 1954, p. 17, for 1953.

68. ANOM, Commission Guernut 97, Annam, Dalat, "Enquête numéro 4 sur le problème des métis," May 17, 1938.

69. Christina Firpo, "The durability of the empire: Race, empire and 'abandoned' children in colonial Vietnam, 1870—1956," PhD thesis, University of California at Los Angeles, 2007, chapter 5.

70. ANOM, HCI 665.

71. ANOM, HCI 715.

72. ANOM, HCI 665.

73. ANOM, HCI 715, Saigon, 7 mai 1949, Rebouillat, Affaires sociales, à Monsieur le Haut-Commissaire, au sujet de la Fondation eurasienne.

74. Kim Lefèvre, *Métisse blanche* (Paris: Bernard Barrault, 1989), pp. 267–305. Quotations from pp. 267, 283.

75. See Alison Blunt, "Home, Identity and Nationality for Anglo-Indians in British India, 1919–1947," *History Workshop Journal* 54 (2002), pp. 49–72.

76. ANOM, Conspol 233, Fiche au sujet de la division politique et administrative de l'Indochine, Paris, December 20, 1945.

77. ANOM, HCI 802, "Recrutement Eurasien, Ecole des Enfants de Troupe de Dalat," Fiche à l'attention du Général de Brigade, Directeur du Cabinet Militaire, Saigon, September 11, 1951, p. 2.

78. "A Dalat, l'Ecole d'Enfants de Troupe," *Indochine, hebdomadaire illustré* 57 (October 2, 1941): pp. 9–10; and ANOM, HCI 493, Ecole des enfants de troupe de Dalat, 1949–1953.

79. ANOM, RSTNF 6282, Rapport annuel Tonkin 1941, "Ecole d'enfants de troupe eurasiens de Dalat."

80. "A Dalat, l'Ecole d'Enfants de Troupe," *Indochine, hebdomadaire illustré* 57 (October 2, 1941): pp. 9–10; and ANOM, HCI 493, Ecole des enfants de troupe de Dalat, 1949–1953.

81. ANOM, HCI 493, Ecole des enfants de troupe de Dalat, 1949–1953.

82. http://aet.d.club.fr/Savani.htm. Accessed on September 26, 2008.

83. ANOM, HCI 493, Ecole des enfants de troupe de Dalat, 1949–1953.

84. Saada, p. 226.

85. Saada notes that during debates over decrees to make métis French citizens, "it is remarkable that not a single voice was raised to underline the incongruity of race as a criterion of French citizenship." Saada, p. 210.

86. ANOM, HCI 665, Service juridique pour le Haut Commissaire, Saigon, July 15, 1948.

87. ANOM, HCI 665, "Note pour M le Général d'Armée Blaizot," Saigon, October 13, 1948, "Dénomination des personnes nées de parents français et asiatiques."

88. White, p. 140; Saada, p. 218.

89. ANOM, HCI 493, Ecole des enfants de troupe de Dalat, 1949–1953, article 7 of "dispositions générales."

90. ANOM, HCI 493.

91. In 1956, the school moved to Autun, in metropolitan France: http://aet.d.club.fr/divers_central.htm. Accessed on September 30, 2008.

92. ANOM, HCI 493, Ecole des enfants de troupe de Dalat, Instruction générale numéro 2029 (tampon: 7 août 1952): Sur l'organisation, le fonctionnement et l'administration de l'Ecole des enfants de troupe de Dalat signed General Salan.

93. "A Dalat, l'Ecole d'Enfants de Troupe," *Indochine, hebdomadaire illustré* 57 (October 2, 1941), p. 10.

94. ANOM, HCI 802, "Recrutement Eurasien Ecole des Enfants de Troupe de Dalat," Fiche à l'attention du Général de Brigade, Directeur du Cabinet Militaire, Saigon September 11, 1951, pp. 2–3.

CHAPTER 11

1. D'Anthouard, pp. 14–16, 23, 48–50 on embezzlement and the "relaxing of morals"; pp. 62–63 on nostalgia, temptation, depression, and homesickness.

2. Ibid., pp. 64–65 and *Hommes et destins*, vol. 8 (Paris: Académie des Sciences d'outre-mer, 1988), p. 1.

3. Daughton, pp. 90–100.

4. D'Anthouard, pp. 26–28.

5. Ibid., p. 50.

6. Ibid., p. 50 and *Hommes et destins*, p. 1. To be sure, not all Catholics took the Commune to be necessary diabolical, despite its separation of church and state. Sarah Curtis shows how Filles de la Charité sisters identified poverty, rather than inherent radicalism, as the root cause of revolt. Sarah Curtis, "Charitable Ladies: Gender, Class and Religion in Mid-Nineteenth Century Paris," *Past and Present* 177 (2002): pp. 151–52.

7. On a similar displacement, from metropolitan French "pagans" and Protestants onto Canadian natives and Turks in the seventeenth century, see Dominique Deslandres, *Croire et faire croire: Les missions françaises au xviième siècle* (Paris: Fayard, 2003), pp. 56–57.

8. Andrée Viollis, *Indochine SOS*, p. 66.

9. Christophe Bataille, *Annam* (Paris: Arléa, 1993), pp. 69, 78.

10. VNA2, RSA 4109, "Réunion de la commission municipale de Dalat, 1936–7," now renumbered as VNA4, RSA 4130, "Demande de la Compagnie des Filles de la Charité de Saint-Vincent de Paul."

11. ACND, box 3, "Un prêtre originaire de Lorraine: Le Père Céleste Nicolas, Missionnaire 1880–1961."

12. ARSAB, Vietnam, carton 6, dossier "Studentat," "Situation religieuse de Dalat."

13. This is one of the arguments advanced by Charles Keith in "Catholic Vietnam: Church, Colonialism and Revolution, 1887–1945," PhD thesis, Yale University, 2008.

14. ACND, "Nos Missions," 1933–1935, "Votre terrain."

15. ACND, "Nos Missions," 1933–1935, "Notre-Dame du Lang-Bian." The original reads: "*Sur la brousse immense, c'est l'aridité. La Sainte Présence vient tout féconder. Sur la brousse immense, c'est l'isolement, mais voici de France la Vierge et l'Enfant.*"

16. ACND, "Nos Missions," 1933–1935, "Dans le transindochinois."

17. ACND, "Nos Missions," 1933–1935, "Dîner annamite."

18. ACND, "Circulaires," April 15, 1936.

19. ACND, "Circulaires," March 30, 1937.

20. Daughton, p. 53.

21. ACND, "Nos Missions," 1933–1935, "Au premier Noël du Lang-Bian."

22. ANOM, GGI 65464, Rapport de Sûreté, Annam, 1926–1927, pp. 23–24.

23. ARSAB, Vietnam, carton 6, "Lettres Dalat," Constantin Aiutti, January 17, 1927.

24. ARSAB, Vietnam, carton 6, "Lettres Dalat," Constantin Aiutti to Father Pintal, March 3, 1927.

25. Anonymous, *Les Nôtres au Vietnam, Mission accomplie*, (Sainte-Anne de Beaupré: Les Rédomptaristes, 1982).

26. ARSAB, Vietnam, carton 6, "Lettres Dalat," Father Galipeau, October 1946.

27. Mathieu Guérin, *Paysans de la forêt à l'époque coloniale: La pacification des aborigènes des hautes terres du Cambodge, 1863–1940* (Rennes: Presses Universitaires de Rennes, 2008), p. 173.

28. Jean Michaud, *"Incidental" Ethnographers*, p. 118.

29. Oscar Salemink, pp. 43–46.

30. Quoted in Luc Garcia, *Quand les missionnaires rencontraient les Vietnamiens, 1920–1960* (Paris: Karthala, 2008), p. 64.

31. ACND, "Nos Missions," 1935–1937, "Moïs et lépreux."

32. Jean Michaud, *"Incidental" Ethnographers*, pp. 133–39.

33. ACND, "Circulaires," June 12, 1936.

34. Ibid.

35. MEP, Lettres communes 91, December 31, 1956, pp. 49–50.

36. MEP, Père Céleste Nicolas, dossier 2798, Letter dated April 5, 1927, sent from Nicolas in Dalat.

37. MEP, Père Céleste Nicolas, dossier 2798, Letter dated September 7, 1938, sent from Nicolas in Dalat.

38. MEP, Lettres communes 62, December 1922, p. 100.

39. MEP, Lettres communes 91, December 31, 1956, pp. 49–50.

40. F. Parrel, "Dalat et ses Montagnards," *Bulletin des missions étrangères de Paris* (1952): pp. 162–68.

41. MEP, Lettres communes 88, December 31, 1953, p. 56.

42. MEP, Lettres communes 92, December 31, 1957, p. 55.

43. MEP, Lettres communes 94, December 31, 1959, p. 70.

44. *Les Nôtres au Vietnam*, p. 10.

45. *Les Nôtres au Vietnam*, pp. 31–32.

46. Fernand Parrel, "Au Village Saint-Jean de Dalat," *Missionnaires d'Asie* (1949): pp. 56–59.

47. Ibid.

48. Daughton, pp. 38, 229.

49. ACND, "Nos Missions," 1933–1935, "Un fameux concours."

50. ACND, "Nos Missions," 1935–1937, "Dans la boîte aux lettres de Dalat."

51. ACND, "Nos Missions," 1935–1937, "Tableau d'honneur."

52. On missionary pedagogical texts, see Daughton, p. 232.

53. Daughton, pp. 73–83 and Salemink, pp. 53–54.

54. Daughton, pp. 113–16.

55. Ibid., pp. 237–42.

56. Charles Keith, pp. 258, 268, and Garcia, pp. 84–87.

57. ACND, "Nos Missions," 1933–1935, "Les difficultés dans la joie."

58. ACND, "A la porte du Monastère."

59. ACND, "Circulaires," "Le mot du lundi, Dalat," date uncertain. "1936?" is scribbled in pencil.

60. F. Parrel, "Dalat et ses Montagnards," *Bulletin des missions étrangères de Paris* (1952): pp. 162–68.

61. The French colonial authorities' hounding of Protestant pastors in the late 1920s would actually draw protests from the Ligue des Droits de l'Homme. See Charles Keith, "Catholic Vietnam," p. 275. On the parallelism between the treatment of Protestants and practitioners of Cao Daï, see the same thesis, p. 277.

62. ANOM, GGI 65464, Security report for Annam, 1926–1927, pp. 23–24.

63. ANOM, GGI 65457, Security report for Annam, 1936.

64. ANOM, GGI 65458, Security report for Annam, 1937.

65. ANOM, HCI 507, "Les Missions protestantes américaines en Indochine."

66. ANOM, HCI 507, "Synode de la Christian and Missionary Alliance."

67. ANOM, Conspol 208.

68. ANOM, GGI 65460, "Activités politiques constatées en Annam," 1939.

69. ANOM, HCI 507, Notice sur l'activité du clergé catholique annamite, Saigon, December 20, 1945.

CHAPTER 12

1. A. Berjoan, "Dalat," *Indochine, hebdomadaire illustré*, January 28, 1943, p. iii.

2. Governor Jean Decoux hatched a plan to double the number of rooms in the hotel. SHM, 171 GG2, box 3, entry for July 27, 1942.

3. ANOM, GGI 66587, Decoux, August 9, 1928.

4. This is the interpretation of novelist cum historian Erwan Bergot in *Sud lointain*, p. 595.

5. David Marr, *Vietnam 1945* (Berkeley: University of California, Press, 1995), pp. 18–19.

6. Ibid., p. 25; and Ralph B. Smith, "The Japanese Period in Indochina and the Coup of 9 March 1945," *Journal of Southeast Asian Studies* 9 no. 2 (September 1978): p. 268.

7. Claude de Boisanger, *On pouvait éviter la guerre d'Indochine* (Paris: Maisonneuve, 1977), p. 47.

8. René Poujade, *Cours martiales d'Indochine, 1940–1945: Les évasions de Résistants dans l'Indochine occupée par les Japonais* (Paris: La Bruyère, 1997), p. 31.

9. SHM, TTD 816, "Dossier Santé," Saigon, July 8, 1940, "Utilisation des centres de repos de Dalat et du Cap Saint-Jacques."

10. In addition to the decree of August 6, 1940, see the decree of September 5, 1941 on special leave authorizations in the colonies.

11. PHARO, 320, folder on "Stations climatiques coloniales," Decoux to Ministry of the Colonies (Vichy), May 19, 1941.

12. AMB, carton 10, "Doubles de télégrammes," circulaire 174-P/I, Hanoi, May 26, 1941.

13. Ibid.

14. *Journal officiel de l'Indochine française*, June 27, 1942, p. 1786, and August 26, 1942, p. 2330.

15. PHARO, 320, folder on "Stations climatiques coloniales," Decoux to Ministry of the Colonies (Vichy), May 19, 1941.

16. "Les trente villas de la Cité Amiral-Jean-Decoux à Dalat, abritent cent trente enfants," *Indochine, hebdomadaire illustré*, August 26, 1943. ANOM, ICM 999, "Hanoi, le 4 septembre 1942, Decoux to Messieurs les Chefs d'administration locale"; and BNF, 16 V pièce 355, "Dalat, Cité-jardin Amiral Decoux."

17. "Colonie de vacances à Dalat," *L'Echo annamite*, June 12, 1943, p. 2.

18. SHM, 171 GG2, box 3, entry for February 2, 1942. On the new establishments for girls, also see Sébastien Verney's PhD thesis, University of Saint-Etienne, chapter 3. Jean le Pichon, "Dalat, force, joie, santé," *Indochine, hebdomadaire illustré*, July 8, 1943.

19. "La journée du Gouverneur général à Dalat," *Tribune indochinoise*, May 29, 1942, p. 4.

20. SHM, 171 GG2, box 3, entry for September 14, 1943.

21. "L'effort français en Indochine: Dalat," *Indochine, hebdomadaire illustré*, January 28, 1943, pp. iv, v.

22. Shellshear, p. 42.

23. SHM, 171 GG2, box 3, Dalat, June 16, 1943.

24. *Cordée, Revue mensuelle des jeunes de Dalat* 6 (May 1944): p. 40.

25. *Cordée, Revue mensuelle des jeunes de Dalat* 8 (August 1944): p. 52.

26. Rouget, p. 41.

27. Mourey, p. 203.

28. *Cordée, Revue mensuelle des jeunes de Dalat* 1 (November 1, 1943): p. 11.

29. Sébastien Verney, "La Révolution nationale, matrice d'une construction identitaire dans un contexte colonial," PhD thesis, University of St Etienne, 2010, p. 677.

30. Mourey, p. 117.

31. SHM, 171 GG2, box 3, Dalat, May 14, 1944: "*Ensuite eut lieu, dans le décor admirable du stade [de Dalat], l'hommage de la Jeunesse d'Empire à Jeanne d'Arc et aux soeurs Trung, suivi d'une brillante manifestation sportive*." On the celebration of the Trung sisters under Vichy, see Jennings, *Vichy in the Tropics*, pp. 154, 217–218. On the cloning of metropolitan youth leagues, see Marcel Gaultier, *La Tragédie indochinoise* (Paris: Editions Henrys, 1947), p. 127.

32. *Cordée, Revue mensuelle des jeunes de Dalat* 3 (January 1944): p. 30.

33. *Cordée, Revue mensuelle des jeunes de Dalat* 1 (November 1943): p. 30.

34. Ibid.

35. *Cordée, Revue mensuelle des jeunes de Dalat* 2 (December 1943): preface.

36. SHM, 171 GG 2, box 3, Dalat, January 6, 1943.

37. SHM, 171 GG 2, box 3, Dalat, May 30, 1942.

38. SHG, 2007 ZM 1/ 000447 (formerly 04641), Gendarmerie Dalat to Monsieur le Colonel Commandant la 11ème RIC à Saigon, December 10, 1942.

39. Mourey, pp. 135, 175, 189. Jean-Marie Abadie was already teaching in Dalat in 1935. He was born in 1900. *Annuaire administratif de l'Indochine 1935* (Hanoi, Imprimerie d'Extrême-Orient, 1935): p. 62.

40. Shellshear, p. 49.

41. AMB, Decoux papers, carton 10, doubles de télégrammes. Dalat May 28 and Hanoi June 16, 1942, "Travaux importants en cours d'exécution."

42. Jean Decoux himself set the tone after the war, categorically denying that Indochina had been "occupied": Decoux, *A la barre de l'Indochine: Histoire de mon Gouvernement Général, 1940–1945* (Paris: Plon, 1959). On the flimsiness of his argument, which has to do with the fact that on average only twenty-five thousand Japanese troops had allegedly been present in Indochina between 1941 and 1945, see Julien Legrand, *L'Indochine à l'heure japonaise* (Cannes: Imprimerie Aegitna, 1963), pp. 201–2. Philippe Franchini cites a February 1945 letter from René Pleven to Governor Decoux, in which the former proved incredulous to Decoux's argument that Japan never "occupied" Indochina. Franchini prefers the term "cohabitation," although he recognizes that Decoux himself used the word "collaboration" to denote his relationship with Japan. Philippe Franchini, *Les Mensonges de la Guerre d'Indochine* (Paris, CIDE, 2003), pp. 43–45.

43. Martin Thomas makes the important point that Decoux's approach to collaboration

with Japan changed over time. Decoux actually dove headlong into quixotic economic collaboration plans in 1944, with Indochina's economy in peril, and links with the metropole all but severed. Martin Thomas, *The French Empire at War, 1940–1945* (Manchester: Manchester University Press, 1998), pp. 203–4.

44. J. Legrand, p. 71.

45. On "collaboration" see René Poujade, *L'Indochine dans la sphere de coprospérité japonaise de 1940 à 1945* (Paris: L'Harmattan, 2007), pp. 29, 38, 60, 61, 71, 76. On his reservations on the exact matching of these terms with the French context, see p. 54. Poujade uses instead the word "collusion" on p. 54 and evokes Vichy as a "de facto ally of Japan" on p. 62. On p. 94 Poujade makes the point that veterans' organizations, overwhelmingly interested in the Indochina war of 1946–1954, still speak of a mere "Japanese presence" in Indochina between 1940 and 1945.

46. Ibid., pp. 131–36.

47. ANOM, ICM 999, dossier "Dalat."

48. Marr, *Vietnam 1945*, p. 314. For the argument that Mordant was prepared to mount an attack against the Japanese as early as 1944, see Gaultier, p. 112. On Mordant's "impossible position," torn between loyalty to Decoux and his Resistance contacts, see Martin Thomas, "Free France, the British Government and the Future of French Indo-China, 1940–1945," *Journal of Southeast Asian Studies* 28, no. 1 (March 1997): p. 152.

49. Général Eugène Mordant, *Au service de la France en Indochine* (Saigon: IFOM, 1950), pp. 37, 38, 43, 79, 80.

50. SHG, 2007 ZM 1/ 000447 (formerly 04641), Adjudant Faucher, Gendarmerie Dalat to Monsieur le Général commandant la subdivision de Saigon, June 11, 1942.

51. SHG, 2007 ZM 1/ 000447 (formerly 04641), Gendarmerie Dalat to Monsieur le Général commandant la subdivision de Saigon, December 6, 1942.

52. ANOM, INF 1146, Vichy, Ministry of the Colonies to Foreign Minister, Prisonniers militaires et internés civils américains, September 10, 1942,.

53. ANOM, INF 1146, Vichy to U.S. Embassy, October 24, 1942. Britain and Vichy had no direct diplomatic relations.

54. ANOM, INF 1102, Bulletin de renseignements 323 EO, September 14, 1944, p. 4.

55. Thus, Information Minister Jacques Soustelle declared on August 17, 1945: "It is with pride that we think of Indochina's resistance. We salute the heroes of Tonkin who fell after having fought at uneven strength, and those who, after long and exhausting marches through the jungle, were able to reorganize in friendly Chinese territory." The latter was a reference to the famous Alessandri column. *Le Courrier* (Geneva), August 17, 1945.

56. "Le dernier carré pétainiste s'effondre en Indochine," *Franc-Tireur*, March 12, 1945.

57. Franchini, p. 43. Simon Kitson, *The Hunt for Nazi Spies: Fighting Espionage in Vichy France* (Chicago: University of Chicago Press, 2008).

58. On the topic of the Japanese *coup de force*, see Marr, *Vietnam 1945*.

59. These events have been well chronicled. See, amongst others, *Documents pour servir à l'histoire de la guerre 1939–1945: Conditions d'internement des Français en Indochine. Les crimes japonais après le 9 mars 1945* (Saigon: Imprimerie française d'Outre-mer, 1948).

60. Ralph B. Smith, pp. 284–85.

61. In all of Cochinchina, only one French fonctionnaire, a veterinary inspector, remained

in his post beyond April 2, 1945. Still, as Sébastien Verney has noted, some settlers were allowed to remain on their lands. And the Japanese seem to have worried about too great a symbolic rupture in some cases, showing a displeasure for wholesale street name changes, for example. See Sébastien Verney, "La Révolution nationale," pp. 819, 826.

62. Mourey, p. 247; Shellshear, p. 63.

63. PHARO, 194, "Rapport d'inspection du service de santé dans les provinces Moïs de Lang-Bian et du Haut-Donnaï," February 26–March 12, 1946.

64. Marr, *Vietnam 1945*, pp. 214–15.

65. Ban Tuyên Giáo tỉnh ủy Lâm Đồng [Propaganda Committee of Lam Dong Province], *Cách mạng tháng 8 năm 1945 ở Lâm Đồng [The August 1945 Revolution in Lam-Dong Province]* (Dalat, 1995), p. 17.

66. ANOM, Conspol 207, "Bureau français de liaison, Dalat."

67. Louis Salles, "Tornade jaune: six mois dans l'oeil du typhoon: Souvenirs de Louis Salles, ancien Proviseur du Lycée Yersin, membre du Bureau français de liaison, Dalat, 1945," pp. 12–13. Shellshear, pp. 61, 67.

68. Salles, "Tornade jaune," p. 16. On non-French Europeans at Bellevue, see Shellshear, pp. 68–71, 86–92.

69. ACND, Vietnam 2, "Annales, Dalat les Oiseaux," entry for April 1, 1945; and ACND, Vietnam 3, Note from Father Nicolas, as well as a copy of the placard.

70. ANOM, INF 1102, Admiral d'Argenlieu, Saigon, January 29, 1947, to Secrétaire général du Comité interministériel de l'Indochine pour le Ministre de la France d'Outre-mer.

71. "Les Français d'Indochine durent vivre dans des quartiers réservés," *Nouvelles du Matin*, October 1, 1945. Even René Poujade makes the case that proportionately more French people were interned by the Japanese in Indochina than by the Nazis in France. He also calls the practice of massing of French civilans in spécial areas "a kind of ghetto." Poujade, *l'Indochine dans la sphere de coprospérité japonaise*, p. 131.

72. Ralph B. Smith, p. 292.

73. *Lịch Sử Phong Trào Công Nhân Và Công Đoàn Tỉnh Lâm Đồng*, p. 41.

74. ACND, Vietnam 3, "Cité vaticane."

75. Much the same occurred at the famous Raffles hotel in Singapore in 1942. Sharp, p. 56.

76. Marius Borel, Souvenirs d'un vieux colonialiste (Borel: Rodez, 1963), p. 282.

77. Julien Legrand argues that in all seven cities with remaining "French perimeters" the Japanese allowed Vietnamese to harass and humiliate the French. The example he gives seems rather dubious, however: Legrand mentions the fact that Europeans were no longer allowed to ride in rickshaws *(pousses)*—symbols par excellence of colonial domination. Legrand, p. 284.

78. *Lịch Sử Phong Trào Công Nhân Và Công Đoàn Tỉnh Lâm Đồng*, p. 43.

79. Mourey, p. 262.

80. Bernard Fall, *Street Without Joy* (Harrisburg: Stackpole, 1964), p. 25.

81. ANOM, INF, 1247, Notice technique: Le Viet-Minh: l'action de la Chine et du Japon dans sa formation et son accession au pouvoir, p. 30. This French report seems to have missed Phan Ke Toai's connections with some Viet-Minh members prior to the August Revolution. This issue is raised by Marr, *Vietnam 1945*, p. 391, and by Bao Dai in *Le Dragon d'Annam* (Paris: Plon, 1980), p. 113.

82. *Cách mạng tháng 8 năm 1945 ở Lâm Đồng,* p. 27.

83. *Lịch Sử Phong Trào Công Nhân Và Công Đoàn Tỉnh Lâm Đồng,* p. 46.

84. *Cách mạng tháng 8 năm 1945 ở Lâm Đồng,* p. 27.

85. ACND, Vietnam 3, "De 1939 à 1945: Les évènements d'Extrême-Orient," p. 4.

86. Marr, *Vietnam 1945,* p. 515.

87. Fernand Merle, *Un Voyage au long cours: Les aventures d'un médecin outre-mer* (Paris: Albin Michel, 1984), p. 76.

88. Journal de Mme X, in Marius Borel, entry for August 18, 1945.

89. ANOM, Conspol 207, Bureau français de liaison, Dalat; and Salles, "Tornade jaune," p. 20.

90. Salles, pp. 24–26. Mourey, p. 263.

91. *Cách mạng tháng 8 năm 1945 ở Lâm Đồng,* p. 28.

92. Even in Dalat, on November 6, 1945, the Allies dropped flyers urging Japanese deserters to the Viet-Minh to surrender at once. ACND, Vietnam 3, flyer in Japanese and Vietnamese. On Japanese elements in the Viet-Minh, and their motivations for joining (some had little choice), see Christopher Goscha, "Alliés tardifs: Les apports techniques des déserteurs japonais au Viet-Minh durant les premières années de la guerre franco-vietnamienne," *Guerres mondiales et conflits contemporains* 202 (2001): pp. 81–109.

93. Marr, *Vietnam 1945,* p. 438.

94. ANOM, INF, 1247, Notice technique: Le Viet-Minh: L'action de la Chine et du Japon dans sa formation et son accession au pouvoir, p. 52.

95. *Cách mạng tháng 8 năm 1945 ở Lâm Đồng,* p. 31.

96. ACND, carton 3, "L'occupation japonaise," Letter from Marie Jeanne d'Arc, October 16, 1945. Also see Journal de Mme X, in Marius Borel, entry for October 5, 1945.

97. *Cách mạng tháng 8 năm 1945 ở Lâm Đồng,* p. 36.

98. Mourey, pp. 268–80.

99. "La situation à Dalat," *Le Journal de Saigon,* November 19, 1945.

100. ACND, Vietnam 3, "Evènements d'Extrême-Orient et la vie des deux maisons de l'Indochine," entry for August 26, 1945. The Japanese, however, took no chances, and posted two soldiers on guard outside the Couvent des Oiseaux on September 8, 1945. ACND, Vietnam 2, "Annales, Dalat, les Oiseaux," entry for September 8, 1945. ANOM, AGEFOM 272, d. 452, *Bulletin hebdomadaire d'information du Ministère des Colonies,* October 22, 1945.

101. "La situation à Dalat," *Le Journal de Saigon,* November 19, 1945.

102. Mourey, pp. 280–94.

103. Journal de Mme X, in Marius Borel, entry for November 16, 1945.

104. *Lịch Sử Phong Trào Công Nhân Và Công Đoàn Tỉnh Lâm Đồng,* p. 57.

105. ACND, Vietnam 3, "Evènements d'Extrême-Orient et la vie des deux maisons de l'Indochine," entry for November 5, 1945.

106. "La situation à Dalat," *Le Journal de Saigon,* November 19, 1945.

107. MAE, Etats Associés, section 2, carton 49, dossier "Activités militaires en Indochine, Dec 45–Dec 46, December 23, 1946.

108. *Lịch Sử Phong Trào Công Nhân Và Công Đoàn Tỉnh Lâm Đồng,* pp. 59–60; and ACND, Vietnam 2, "Annales Dalat les Oiseaux," entries for January 28 and 29, 1946.

109. Shellshear, p. 104.

110. ACND, Vietnam 3, Congrégation Notre-Dame, December 8, 1946.

111. In September 1945, when he was finally able to communicate again with the outside world, a Québecois missionary wrote to his parents of the terrible suffering he had witnessed in Tonkin over the previous year: "The cost of living reached incredible heights. Rice that used to cost eight or ten piastres for a hundred pounds went up to five hundred piastres. . . . Famine struck. To add to the miseries, this last winter was unbelievably cold. I never suffered from the cold in Canada the way I did here last winter. Hundreds of thousands of people had nothing to wear. Because of the cold and privations, typhus set in: the cold, hunger, and typhus killed two million people in Tonkin alone. Entire villages have been wiped off the map. Roads were covered with the dead and dying. There were groups of beggars, living skeletons." ARSAB, Missionnaire Gérard Gagnon to his parents, boîte Gagnon, SU 1, Hanoi, September 20, 1945. For historical analyses of the famine, see David Marr, *Vietnam 1945*. Marr notes on p. 104 that the precise number of famine victims remains unknown. He puts forward the figure of a million deaths based on his research. On this topic, also see Bui Minh Dung, "Japan's role in the Vietnamese Starvation of 1944–1945," *Modern Asian Studies* 29 no. 3 (July 1995): pp. 573–618.

112. ACND, Vietnam 2, "Annales Dalat les Oiseaux," entry for June 17, 1945.

113. ACND, Vietnam 3, "Protection Mariale."

114. "La situation à Dalat," *Le Journal de Saigon*, November 19, 1945.

115. PHARO, 168 and 194. On typhus also see ANOM, INF 1415, "Rapports sur la situation sanitaire," August 1946 report, p. 1.

116. ANOM, INF 1102.

117. PHARO, 168.

118. SHG, 2007 ZM 1/ 000447 (formerly 04641), Rapport, Dalat, November 10, 1948.

119. ANOM, Conspol 207, Bureau français de Liaison, Dalat.

120. Poujade, *L'Indochine dans la sphere de coprospérité japonaise*, p. 156, makes the point that Leclerc and d'Argenlieu had more pressing tasks on their hands, and were sidetracked by these recriminations.

121. "A Dalat, le bureau français de liaison reçoit du Haut Commissaire un témoignage de satisfaction mérité," *Le Journal de Saigon*, September 25, 1946.

122. ANOM, Conspol 207, Bureau français de Liaison, Dalat.

123. ANOM, Conspol 207, Association "Vérité."

124. "Départ des rapatriés français," *L'Avenir: Quotidien de l'Union française* (Saigon), June 3, 1946, p. 2.

CHAPTER 13

1. There are, to be sure, interesting accounts of how the capitals of Indochina's constituent parts came to be selected. See for instance Pierre-Lucien Lamant's contribution on the emergence of Phnom Penh as a capital in the 1860s. Lamant, "La Création d'une capitale par le pouvoir colonial: Phnom Penh," in *Péninsule indochinoise, Etudes urbaines*, ed. Pierre-Bernard Lafont, pp. 59–102 (Paris: L'Harmattan, 1991).

2. "La capitale de l'Indochine," *La Quinzaine coloniale*, December 25, 1907, pp. 1101–02.

3. Goscha, *Vietnam or Indochina? Contesting Concepts of Space in Vietnamese Nationalism, 1887–1954* (Copenhagen: NIAS Press, 1995).

4. See Hickey, *Sons of the Mountains*, p. xix.

5. Thongchai Winichakul has made this point with respect to French "patronage" over Cambodia. See Thongchai Winichakul, *Siam Mapped: A History of the Geo-Body of a Nation* (Honolulu: University of Hawai'i Press, 1994), p. 93.

6. Salemink, p. 65.

7. ANOM, GGI 64225, Rapport Politique Annam, 1920.

8. Although the treaty of 1884 was much harsher than that of 1874, it nonetheless stipulated that the French Résident "would avoid meddling in the internal affairs and administration of the provinces. Indigenous officials of all rank will continue to govern and administer under [Vietnamese] control, but they can be revoked upon request by French authorities" (article 7). Article 16 stated that "his majesty the king of Annam will continue, as in the past, to guide the internal administration of his states, except for the restrictions contained in the present convention." Treaty reproduced in Devillers, pp. 482–84.

9. Tran Chanh Thanh would later join the Viet-Minh, before leaving them for South Vietnam in 1952. Thereafter, he would become South Vietnam's minister for youth and information. J. A. C. Grant, "The Viet Nam Constitution of 1956," *The American Political Science Review* 52, no. 2 (June 1958): pp. 458, footnote 34.

10. Tran Chanh Thanh, "Statut politique et juridique des plateaux Moïs," *Revue indochinoise, juridique et économique* 17 (1942): pp. 118–32.

11. Goscha, *Vietnam or Indochina*, p. 41.

12. A. Baudrit, "La naissance de Dalat," *Indochine, hebdomadaire illustré* 180 (February 10, 1944), p. 24.

13. ANOM, GGI 49507, Résident supérieur d'Annam to members of the Conseil de Protectorat, November 1915.

14. ANOM, GGI 64225, Rapport Politique Annam, 1920; and Tran Chanh Thanh, p. 122.

15. Notwithstanding Tran Chanh Thanh's assertion of the contrary in ibid., p. 122. Tran Chanh Thanh asserts that the 1920 reform "still placed Dalat in the Annamese imperial domain." While technically accurate, the autonomy of the new French enclave is ignored by Tran Chanh Thanh, whose political agenda is clear: to claim Hué's sovereignty over the minority areas.

16. VNA2, RSA 4078, "Minutes des arrêtés, décisions du Gouverneur sur le développement et l'organisation du sanatorium de Dalat, 1923," now renumbered as VNA4, RSA 4099; and "La station d'altitude de Dalat," *L'Echo annamite*, December 5, 1925, p. 1.

17. A. Baudrit, "La naissance de Dalat," *Indochine, hebdomadaire illustré* 180 (February 10, 1944), p. 24.

18. Louis-Georges Pineau, "Dalat, Capitale administrative de l'Indochine," *Revue indochinoise, juridique et économique* 11 (1937): pp. 18–19.

19. Caroline Herbelin, "Dalat: Modèle d'urbanisme colonial ou anecdote architecturale?" forthcoming in *Cahiers d'études vietnamiennes*, p. 9. All page numbers are from the draft kindly provided by Caroline Herbelin.

20. "Le Haut commissariat du Pacifique," *Eveil économique de l'Indochine*, July 22, 1923, p. 5.

21. "Editorial," *Le Camly*, December 5, 1925, p. 1.

22. VNA2, RSA 4100 now renumbered as VNA4, RSA 4122, Commission municipale, session ordinaire du 14 septembre 1928. .

23. P. B., "Dalat, capitale administrative de l'Indochine," *L'Alerte*, July 10, 1937.

24. See Panivong Norindr, "The Popular Front's Colonial Policies in Indochina: Reassessing the Popular Front's 'Colonisation Altruiste'" in *French Colonial Empire and the Popular Front: Hope and Disillusion*, eds. Tony Chafer and Amanda Sackur, pp. 230–48 (London: St. Martin's Press, 1999). On the limits of the Popular Front's colonial reforms in general, see William B. Cohen, "The Colonial Policy of the Popular Front," *French Historical Studies* 7, no. 2 (Spring 1972): pp. 368–93. On prisoner releases, and for the argument that they originated more from political pressure within Vietnam than from Parisian munificence, see Zinoman, *The Colonial Bastille*, p. 267.

25. Pineau, "Dalat, Capitale administrative de l'Indochine," p. 8.

26. Pineau, "Dalat, Capitale administrative de l'Indochine," p. 1.

27. Ibid., pp. 1, 2, 8.

28. Ibid., p. 20.

29. Salemink, pp. 140, 143.

30. Goscha, *Vietnam or Indochina*, pp. 79–83.

31. "Dalat, capitale administrative de l'Indochine," *L'Avenir du Tonkin*, May 25, 1937.

32. Decoux, pp. 461, 462, footnote to p. 462.

33. Georges Pineau, "Le Plan d'aménagement et d'extension de Dalat," *Vie urbaine* 49 (1939): p. 49.

34. Salemink, p. 145; Goscha, *Vietnam or Indochina*, pp. 74, 88, 102.

35. Stein Tønnesson, *The Vietnamese Revolution of 1945* (London: Sage, 1991), p. 315.

36. MAE, Etats Associés, section 2, 49, "Occupation des Plateaux Moïs," General Juin to d'Argenlieu, December 28, 1945.

37. ANOM, INF 1240.

38. MAE, Etats Associés, section 2, 49, "Occupation des Plateaux Moïs," De Langlade (signed Moutet) to Haut-Commissaire, Saigon, March 11, 1946.

39. MAE, Etats Associés, section 2, 49, "Occupation des Plateaux Moïs," Various correspondence, including telegram from d'Argenlieu to Paris, June 25, 1946.

40. See for instance, Marr, p. 548.

41. Stein Tønnesson, *Vietnam, 1946: How the War Began* (Berkeley: University of California Press, 2010), pp. 30, 36.

42. See Daniel Hémery, "Asie du Sud-Est, 1945: Vers un nouvel impérialisme colonial? Le projet indochinois de la France au lendemain de la Seconde Guerre mondiale" in *Décolonisations européennes: Actes du colloque international "Décolonisations comparées,"* ed. Marc Michel, pp. 68, 71 (Aix-en-Provence: Publications de l'Université de Provence, 1995).

43. Ibid.

44. ANOM, HCI 451, Gassier report; and ANOM, Conspol 215.

45. ANOM, Indochine Haut Commissariat, Conseiller politique, 145, dossier "Projets de constitution fédérale."

46. See Martin Shipway, *The Road to War: France and Vietnam, 1944–1947* (New York: Berghahn, 1996), pp. 179, 182. Pierre Brocheux, *Ho Chi Minh, a Biography* (Cambridge: Cambridge University Press, 2007), p. 117.

47. Stein Tønnesson, *Vietnam, 1946*, p. 71.

48. March 6, 1946, preliminary convention, reproduced in Philippe Devillers, *Histoire*

du Viet-Nam de 1940 à 1952 (Paris: Editions du Seuil, 1952), p. 225. Thierry d'Argenlieu, *Chronique d'Indochine* (Paris: Albin Michel, 1985), p. 199. Jean Sainteny notes d'Argenlieu's strong preference for Dalat in his *Histoire d'une paix manqué: Indochine, 1945–1947* (Paris: Amiot-Dumont, 1953), p. 195.

49. Philippe Devillers, *Paris, Saigon, Hanoi, les archives de la guerre 1944–1947* (Paris: Gallimard, 1988), p. 169.

50. DDF, 1946, 232, March 29, 1946, p. 521.

51. Devillers, *Paris, Saigon, Hanoi*, p. 170, and Tønnesson, *Vietnam 1946*, p. 67.

52. Vo Nguyen Giap, *Unforgettable Days* (Hanoi: Foreign Languages Publishing, 1975), p. 223.

53. ANOM, Conspol 215, "Rapport à M. Rotel, Commissaire fédéral aux questions juridiques," Saigon, May 21, 1946, p. 2.

54. D'Argenlieu, *Chronique*, p. 246.

55. Raoul Salan, *Mémoires, Fin d'un empire*, vol. 1 (Paris: Presses de la Cité, 1970), p. 370.

56. ANOM, Montguillot papers, 56PA 6, Captured Viet-Minh document.

57. MAE, Etats Associés, section 2, 52, 1ère conférence de Dalat, telegram from d'Argenlieu to Paris, April 23, 1946.

58. MAE, Etats Associés, section 2, 52, 1ère conférence de Dalat, d'Argenlieu memorandum, April 26, 1946. During Dalat 1, the French delegate Bousquet stated pointedly: "I would like the Government of Vietnam not to take on Germany's attitude (vis-à-vis Grossdeutschland)." To which General Giap quipped: "France too." ANOM, Conspol 210, Commission politique, compte-rendu de la séance du 11 mai 1946.

59. Giap recalls d'Argenlieu "boast[ing] that he knew a lot about us." The reports on each participant were indeed quite detailed. Giap, *Unforgettable Days*, p. 247.

60. ANOM, 56PA 6, "Note sur les minorités ethniques," Dalat, May 8, 1946.

61. ANOM, Conspol 210, Commission politique, séance du 11 mai 1946.

62. ANOM, 39PA 1, "Archives de l'Inspecteur Gayet," "Note de la délégation vietnamienne sur le problème de la fédération."

63. ANOM, Conspol 103, "Négociations franco-vietnamiennes," April 12, 1946. The French team actually drafted a note on the Soviet federal model. ANOM Conspol 103, Dalat, April 18, 1946, HCI, "Note sur l'organisation des services fédéraux." Raoul Salan scoffed at the study of U.S. and Soviet models as unimaginative. See Salan, p. 373.

64. ANOM, Conspol 210, "Documentation générale."

65. Philippe Franchini quotes Nguyên Tuong Tam of the Vietnamese delegation as saying: "We have agreed on one single point, that we can agree on nothing!" Franchini, p. 183.

66. MAE, Etats Associés, section 2, 52, 1ère conférence de Dalat, summary dated June 7, 1946.

67. "Les délégués Annamites sont arrives à Dalat," *Le Journal de Saigon*, April 18, 1946, p. 1.

68. Devillers, *Histoire du Viet-Nam*, p. 263.

69. Giap, *Unforgettable Days*, p. 248.

70. The French delegation was composed, he wrote, of "French monopoly capitalists" and a "defrocked priest [with] small wily eyes under a wrinkled forehead"—the latter a jibe at the admiral in person. Ibid., p. 245 for monopoly capitalists, p. 247 for the defrocked priest, p. 246 for his love of Dalat.

71. Ibid., pp. 246, 250.

72. MAE, Etats Associés, section 2, 52, 1ère conférence de Dalat, summary dated June 7, 1946.

73. Shipway, pp. 211–12; William Duiker, *Ho Chi Minh* (New York: Hyperion, 2000), p. 375.

74. ANOM, 56PA 6, "Séance privée du 25 juillet après-midi."

75. ANOM, 56PA 6, carnet 29, délégation française, séance privée du 25 juillet 1946.

76. *"La fédération indochinoise, dans l'esprit du colonel Xuan, pourrait être comparée à un organisme de gestion d'affaires, pourvu d'un Conseil d'Administration dont le Haut-Commissaire de France serait le Président."* ANOM, 56PA 6, "Deuxième conférence de Dalat," Compte-rendu schématique de la séance de la commission politique du 3 août 1946.

77. *Conférence préparatoire de Dalat sur le statut de la Fédération indochinoise dans l'Union française* (Saigon: Direction fédérale de l'Information, 1946), p. 55.

78. Ma Krong is described in the conference proceedings as "Chief of the Darlac Rhadés, of the Western M'nongs, elephant hunter, President of the Darlac Customary court" (Ibid., p. 5). A highlander leader of Lao-Mnong origins, Ma Krong had indeed been a major figure in the elephant hunting trade in and around Ban Don. He became an ally of Léopold Sabatier, and eventually served as judge in Ban Me Thuot in the 1920s. By the time of the 1946 conference, he served as president of Darlac's customary tribunal. See Salemink, pp. 83, 148. *Conférence préparatoire de Dalat*, p. 5.

79. *Conférence préparatoire de Dalat*, p. 72. The French words read "all people who wear belts," but I am deferring here to the logical translation of Oscar Salemink, p. 148.

80. *Conférence préparatoire de Dalat*, p. 73.

81. See Salemink, p. 149.

82. *Conférence préparatoire de Dalat*, p. 14, as well as DDF, August 9, 1946, 89, Saigon August 9, 1946, p. 225.

83. *Conférence préparatoire de Dalat*, p. 14.

84. ANOM, 56PA 6, "Compte-rendu de la commission militaire réunie le 6 août sous la présidence du Colonel Xuan."

85. Salemink, p. 148.

86. Thongchai Winichakul, p. 129.

87. These are some of the markers of the "multiple sovereignty" that characterized pre-modern Southeast Asian according to Thongchai Winichakul, *Siam Mapped*, pp. 88–89.

88. Jennings, *Curing the Colonizers*, pp. 149–52.

89. Benedict Anderson, *Imagined Communities: Reflections on the Origin and Spread of Nationalism* (New York: Verso, 1991), p. 132.

CHAPTER 14

1. Lucien Bodard, *La Guerre d'Indochine, l'enlisement* (Paris: Gallimard, 1963), pp. 238–39.

2. Ibid., p. 240.

3. ANOM, AGEFOM 258, d. 397, Agence France Presse release, April 28, 1949.

4. Bao Dai, *Le Dragon d'Annam* (Paris: Plon, 1980), p. 225.

5. See Todd Shepard, *The Invention of Decolonization: The Algerian War and the Remaking of France* (Ithaca: Cornell University Press, 2006), p. 109.

6. ANOM, HCI 440.

7. Bao Dai, p. 377.

8. Bao Dai's order, May 21, 1951, Dalat, Texas Tech Vietnam Project, http://www.vietnam.ttu.edu/resources/digital.php. Accessed September 3, 2010.

9. Bao Dai, p. 248.

10. ANOM, HCI 440.

11. Ibid.

12. Ibid.

13. Ibid.

14. Salemink, p. 171.

15. ANOM, HCI 440.

16. SHG, 2007 ZM 1/ 000231 (formerly 04425), Rapport du 13 novembre 1950.

17. ANOM, 9 APOM, Azambre papers, "Monographie de Dalat."

18. ANOM, HCI 451, Report on Nguyen Dê.

19. André Gribius, *Une Vie d'Officier* (Paris: Editions France-Empire, 1971), pp. 204–5.

20. Nguyen Thieu Nguyen, "Dalat ville de rêve," *Indochine, sud-est asiatique* 30 (July 1954): p. 40.

21. Bodard, p. 239.

22. ANOM, 9 APOM, Azambre papers, "Monographie de Dalat"; and Luc Boulet, *Chroniques indochinoises* (Paris: Houtland Editions, 1997), pp. 149–50.

23. SHG, 2007 ZM 1/ 000231 (formerly 04425), "Urgent, note de service, 24 novembre 1950."

24. Bao Dai, p. 264.

25. SHG, 2007 ZM 1/ 000236 (formerly 04430), Rapport Delorme, July 13, 1952.

26. So noted a French gendarmerie report in 1951. SHG, 2007 ZM 1/ 000235 (formerly 04429), Rapport du Lieutenant Bruez, February 12, 1951, p. 2.

27. Spencer C. Tucker, *Vietnam* (London: UCL Press, 1999), p. 53.

28. Nguyen Khac Vien, *Histoire du Viet Nam* (Paris: Editions sociales, 1974), pp. 212–16.

29. Gribius, p. 200.

30. ANOM, INF 1244, Evènements militaires en Indochine, semaine du 21 au 28 septembre 1947.

31. MEP, Lettres communes, 84, December 31, 1949.

32. ANOM, HCI 440.

33. Gilbert Bodinier, *La Guerre d'Indochine, 1947, textes et documents* (Vincennes: Service Historique de l'Armée de Terre, 1989), pp. 34, 275.

34. Christopher Andrew and Jeremy Noakes, *Intelligence and International Relations, 1900–1945,* (University of Exeter Press, 1987), pp. 2 and 82.

35. Roger Faligot and Pascal Krop, *La Piscine: Les services secrets français, 1944–1984* (Paris: Editions du Seuil, 1985), pp. 116–17.

36. SHG, 2007 ZM 1/ 000447 (formerly 04641), Rapport, Dalat, April 1, 1948.

37. Philippe Gras, *L'Armée de l'air en Indochine, 1945–1954: Mission impossible* (Paris: L'Harmattan, 2001), p. 187.

38. Raoul Salan, *Mémoires: Fin d'un empire*, vol. 2, p. 137.

39. Gras, p. 188; Salan, pp. 137–38.

40. "L'Attaque du convoi de Dalat, récit d'un rescapé," *L'Union française* (Saigon), March 3, 1948, p. 1.

41. SHG, 2007 ZM 1/ 000447 (formerly 04641), Rapport, Dalat, April 1, 1948.

42. SHG, 2007 ZM 1/ 000235 (formerly 04429), Rapport du Lieutenant Bruez, October 9, 1950.

43. ANOM, SPCE 94, "Relevé chronologique des principaux évènements qui ont précédé et succédé à l'assassinat à Dalat de Victor Haasz, le 11 mai 1951."

44. SHG, 2007 ZM 1/ 000235 (formerly 04429), Rapport du Lieutenant Bruez, April 5, 1951.

45. Ibid. and ANOM, SPCE 94, "Relevé chronologique des principaux évènements qui ont précédé et succédé à l'assassinat à Dalat de Victor Haasz, le 11 mai 1951."

46. SHG, 2007 ZM 1/ 000235 (formerly 04429).

47. ANOM, SPCE 94, "Relevé chronologique des principaux évènements qui ont précédé et succédé à l'assassinat à Dalat de Victor Haasz, le 11 mai 1951."

48. ANOM, SPCE 94, Viet-Minh document found at Dalat on June 1, 1951, "This week's gift offered to Ho Chi Minh," p. 2.

49. ANOM, SPCE 94, Franpresse, Saigon, May 22, 1951.

50. ANOM, SPCE 94, BQR du SVN, "Presse locale autorisée," May 22, 1951.

51. ANOM, SPCE 94, Revue de presse du Service de Sécurité du Haut-Commissariat au Cambodge, June 7, 1951.

52. ANOM, SPCE 94, "Propos relatifs aux évènements de Dalat," Letter from R. Fauchois to Marcel Fauchois, sent on May 23, 1951, intercepted on May 25, 1951.

53. ANOM, SPCE 94, Extrait du Bulletin des écoutes, VM N 1267, June 21, 1951.

54. ANOM, SPCE 94, Extrait de la note de Fransecur, Sud Vietnam, 99234 S/RG, June 8, 1951.

55. ANOM, SPCE 94, "Opinion et commentaires sur la situation à Dalat," Le Xuan letter to Tran Van Chuong, Paris, sent on May 15, 1951, intercepted on May 18, 1951.

56. ANOM, SPCE 94, Letter from R. Fauchois to Marcel Fauchois, dated May 23, 1951, intercepted on May 25, 1951.

57. Ibid.

58. ANOM, SPCE 94, "La Voix du Nam-Bo," September 20, 1951.

59. ANOM, SPCE 94, Extrait du Bulletin des Ecoutes, VM N 1234, May 19, 1951.

60. Ibid.

61. ANOM, SPCE 94, Extrait du Bulletin des Ecoutes, VM N 1238, May 23, 1951, "L'Histoire flétrit toujours les buveurs de sang."

62. ANOM, SPCE 94, Extrait du Bulletin des Ecoutes, VM N 1233, May 18, 1951.

63. *L'Humanité,* May 16, 1951.

64. ANOM, SPCE 94, "A l'Assemblée nationale, protestation indignée de René Arthaud au nom du groupe communiste contre l'abominable massacre des vingt otages vietnamiens."

65. Pierre Thibault, "L'Affaire de Dalat," *France-Soir,* May 18, 1951.

66. ANOM, SPCE 94, Head of security of the PMSI to his Majesty's delegate to the PM, June 12, 1951.

67. SHG, 2007 ZM 1/ 000235 (formerly 04429), Rapport Bruez, July 2, 1951.

68. SHG, 2007 ZM 1/ 000235 (formerly 04429), Rapport Bruez, October 15, 1951.

69. ANOM, SPCE 94, Chef de Sécurité du Haut-Commissariat pour les PMS, to Monsieur le Directeur des Services de Sécurité du Haut-Commissariat, Dalat, June 1, 1951.

70. ANOM, SPCE 94, "Opinion et commentaires sur la situation à Dalat," Le Xuan letter to Tran Van Chuong, Paris, sent on May 15, 1951, intercepted on May 18, 1951.

71. ANOM, SPCE 94, "Note pour Monsieur le Ministre d'Etat chargé des relations avec les Etats Associés," Saigon, October 22, 1952.

72. ANOM, SPCE 94, Letter from Mr X to Nguyen Van Phoi, Saigon, sent on May 28, 1951, intercepted on June 2, 1951.

73. ANOM, SPCE 94, "Propos relatifs aux évènements de Dalat (Monsieur Adam, C.E.E.), letter sent June 5, 1951, intercepted on June 7, 1951.

74. ANOM, SPCE 94, Letter from P.M Legras, Dalat to Madame Roger de Cordemoy, Tours, sent on May 24, 1951, intercepted on May 25, 1951.

75. SHG, 2007 ZM 1/ 000235 (formerly 04429), Rapport Bruez, July 2, 1951.

76. ANOM, SPCE 94, "République du Vietnam, informations," May 20, 1951.

77. ANOM, SPCE 94, "Nous sommes là où se trouve l'ennemi," (traduction), October 16, 1951.

78. ANOM, SPCE 94, Viet-Minh pamphlet found at Dalat on June 1, 1951.

79. ANOM, Agefom 258, dossier 397, "Une conférence pour la sécurité de Dalat."

80. "Echos et confidences," L'Echo du Vietnam, July 5, 1951.

81. Ibid.

82. ANOM, SPCE 94, "Le directeur régional des services de police et de sûreté nationale des PMS à Monsieur le Directeur général des services de police et de sûreté nationale du Vietnam à Saigon," Dalat, March 7, 1952.

83. Ibid.

84. SHG, 2007 ZM 1/ 000236 (formerly 04430), Rapport Delorme, January 13, 1953.

85. William S. Turley, The Second Indochina War (Boulder: Westview Press, 1986), p. 71.

86. SHG, 2007 ZM 1/ 000448, Rapport de l'Adjudant Maurel, December 13, 1951.

87. ANOM, 9 APOM, Azambre papers, "Monographie de Dalat."

88. SHG, 2007 ZM 1/ 000236 (formerly 04430), Rapport Bordes, April 10, 1954.

89. SHG, 2007 ZM 1/ 000236 (formerly 04430), Rapport Bordes, October 12, 1954.

90. Turley, p. 11.

91. Ibid., p. 12.

92. Gerald Cannon Hickey, Free in the Forest: Ethnohistory of the Vietnamese Central Highlands, 1954–1976 (New Haven: Yale University Press, 1982), pp. 9–10, 17.

93. ARSAB, carton 6, "Studentat," Paroisse CSSR, 20/2/1958, VN B8 envoi 7.

94. MEP, Lettres communes 94, December 31, 1959, pp. 69–70.

95. ARSAB, carton 6, "Studentat," Paroisse.

96. Hickey, Free in the Forest and Po Dharma, Du FLM au FURLO (Paris: Les Indes savantes, 2006), pp. 26–27.

97. ANOM, 9 APOM, Azambre papers.

98. USNA, COPROR/SR/4, Vietnam Subject Files, 1955–1962, lot file 66D193, General Records of the Department of State, RG 59, Report dated April 20, 1962, p. 3.

99. Marshall S. Carter, Acting Director, CIA, Memorandum for the Secretary of Defense,

July 13, 1962, in *The Pentagon Papers* (Gravel Edition, Boston: Beacon Press, 1971), vol. 2, document 117, pp. 684–89.

100. Ambassador Noltin, Telegram to the Secretary of State, August 7, 1962, reproduced in *Foreign Relations of the United States, 1961–1963*, vol. 2, Vietnam 1962, document 260.

101. USNA, COPROR/SR/25 Vietnam Subject Files, 1955–1962, lot file 66D193, General Records of the Department of State, RG 59, Report dated September 9, 1962, p. 3.

102. USNA, Vietnam Subject Files, 1955–1962, Lot File 66D193, General Records of the Department of State, RG 59, Joint USIS/CAS Message, telegram Saigon 1731, dated August 21, 1962.

103. Tucker, p. 101, 104.

104. Hickey, *Free in the Forest*, p. 168.

105. Pham Dinh Tieu, "Le Climat de Dalat: Contribution à l'étude d'un climat d'altitude au Vietnam," PhD thesis, Université Louis Pasteur, Strasbourg, September 1976, p. 329.

106. "Dalat, Viet-Nam," National Tourist Office, Texas Tech Vietnam Project, http://www.vietnam.ttu.edu/resources/digital.php.

107. USNA, 1968, Tet Offensive, II Corps Tactical Zone, Combat Operations, After Action Report, Dalat; Records of the Office of the Command Historian; Records of Headquarters U.S. Army Vietnam (USARV); General Records of the U.S. Forces in Southeast Asia, 1950–1975, RG 472.

108. Hickey, *Free in the Forest*, p. 184.

109. USNA, 1968 Tet Offensive, II Corps Tactical Zone, Combat Operations, After Action Report, Dalat; Records of the Office of the Command Historian; Records of Headquarters U.S. Army Vietnam (USARV); General Records of the U.S. Forces in Southeast Asia, 1950–1975, RG 472.

110. Anonymous, *An Outline History of the Viet Nam Worker's Party, 1930–1975* (Hanoi: Foreign Language Publishing House, 1976), p. 112.

111. Turley, p. 167.

112. Pham Dinh Tieu, "Le Climat de Dalat," pp. 16–20.

113. Turley, pp. 173–78.

114. General Van Tien Dung, *Our Great Spring Victory: An Account of the Liberation of South Vietnam* (New York: Monthly Review Press, 1977), p. 118.

115. Xuan Phuong, *Ao Dai*, pp. 224–25.

116. General Van Tien Dung, p. 117.

117. Truong Nhu Tang, pp. 284–85.

118. Ann Laura Stoler, "Colonial Aphasia: Race and disabled histories in France," paper delivered at the University of Toronto, September 4, 2009.

EPILOGUE

1. Crossette, *The Great Hill Stations of Asia*, p. 207.

2. Graham Huggan, *The Postcolonial Exotic: Marketing the Margins* (London: Routledge, 2001), p. 179.

3. James Sullivan, "French Twist," *DestinAsian* (April-May 2007): pp. 79 121. On the con-

stant use of the term "kitsch" to describe the "Crazy House," see Claudia Bell and John Lyall, "Tourist Performers at the Crazy House, Dalat, Vietnam," *Continuum: Journal of Media and Cultural Studies* 19, no. 2 (2005): pp. 285–97.

4. Bradley Winterton, "Falling in Love with Dalat," *Taipei Times*, February 21, 2008, p. 13.

5. Pip Morgan, "Hot Spot: Vietnam's Love Capital," *Time Asia* 162, no. 2, July 14, 2003.

6. http://iamayardsale.blogspot.com/2006/02/what-happened-in-dalat.html. Last accessed October 28, 2009.

7. Françoise Huguier, "Voyage au coeur de ma mémoire," in "Vietnam Spécial anniversaire, 1875–2005," special issue, *Géo* 83 (2005): pp. 88–91.

8. Mong Binh, "A Nostalgic return to the Alma Mater," *The Saigon Times Daily*, July 7, 2004, p. 6.

9. Samantha Coomber, "Paradise by the Dashboard Light," *En-Route Magazine* (Air Canada), January 2008.

10. Jean-Luc Coatelem, *Suite indochinoise* (Paris: La Table Ronde, 1993, reedited 2008), p. 95, cited by Peyvel, "L'Emergence du Tourisme au Việt Nam," p. 311.

11. Franc Nichele, "Un joli parfum d'Indochine," *Désirs de Voyages: Art de Vivre et Adresses secrètes* 6 (March-April 2008): pp. 45–50. On renaming in 1954, see Truong Phuc An, *Secrets of the Fower City of Dalat* (Ho Chi Minh City: Lam Dong Book Distribution Company, 2000), p. 140.

12. "Vietnam's Dalat to get new airport," *The Globe and Mail*, March 2, 2002, p. T8.

13. "Da Lat, a Park City," *Vietnam Review* 510 (June 2001): p. 33.

14. Truong Phuc An, *Secrets of the Fower City of Dalat*, p. 218.

15. "Dalat Love Festival to Mark Several Vietnam Records," *Vietnam News Brief Service*, October 14, 2005.

16. Thanh Phuong, "Dalat starts birthday bash with ethnic festival," *The Saigon Daily Times*, April 22, 2003.

17. "Vietnam highland town reveals plans for ethnic beauty contest," Vietnam travel news, http://tftravel.vn/lang_en/tintuc/id-292/Vietnam-highland-town-reveals-plans-for-ethnic-beauty-contest.html . Accessed on October 28, 2009.

18. Truong Phuc An, *Dalat Tram Nam*, p. 40.

19. Ibid., p. 212.

20. Huggan, p. 58.

SELECT BIBLIOGRAPHY

PRIMARY SOURCES

Journals and Newspapers Frequently Cited

Individual articles from these reviews are not listed in the bibliography, but they are in the backnotes.

Annales d'hygiène et de médecine coloniales
Annuaire général de l'Indochine
Archives des Institut Pasteur d'Indochine
L'Asie nouvelle illustrée
Bulletin administratif de l'Annam
Bulletin de la Société de géographie
Bulletin de la Société des Missions Etrangères (Bulletin des Missions Etrangères)
Bulletin économique de l'Indochine (Bulletin de l'agence économique de l'Indochine)
Le Cam-Ly (Dalat)
Công Luân Báo
Cordée, Revue mensuelle des jeunes de Dalat
La Dépêche coloniale
L'Echo annamite
L'Eveil économique de l'Indochine
Extrême-Asie: Revue illustrée indochinoise
L'Impartial (Saigon)
Indochine, hebdomadaire illustré
Le Journal de Saigon
Le Journal officiel de l'Indochine française
Khoa-Hoc Tap-Chí [Scientific Journal]

La Presse indochinoise
La Quinzaine coloniale
La Revue coloniale
La Revue de Géographie
La Revue indochinoise
Tân Tiên Báo [Evolué Journal]
Technika Chronica
La Tribune indigène
La Tribune indochinoise
L'Union française
Vê Sinh Báo

Other Printed Primary Sources

Abbatucci, Serge. "Climatologie dans l'Indo-Chine." *Revue d'hygiène et de médecine preventive* 56 (1934): 43–60.

———. "Les stations climatiques en Indochine." *Outre-mer, revue générale de colonisation* (September 1930): 292–300.

Ajalbert, Jean. *Les Nuages sur l'Indochine*. Paris: Louis-Michaud, 1912.

Anonymous. *Conférence préparatoire de Dalat sur le statut de la Fédération indochinoise dans l'Union française*. Saigon: Direction fédérale de l'Information, 1946.

———. *Dalat, Cité-jardin Amiral Decoux*. BNF 16 V pièce 355.

———. *Documents pour servir à l'histoire de la guerre 1939–1945: Conditions d'internement des Français en Indochine. Les crimes japonais après le 9 mars 1945*. Saigon: Imprimerie française d'Outre-mer, 1948.

———. "Le Général Pennequin: Gouverneur intérimaire de Madagascar." *Bulletin du Comité de Madagascar* 1899: 150–52.

———. *Guides Madrolle, De Saigon à Tourane*. Paris: Hachette, 1926.

———. *Petit guide illustré de Dalat*. Dalat: 1930.

———. "Le Sanatorium du Lang-Bian." *Annales d'hygiène publique et de médecine légale* 4, no. 6 (1906): 444.

———. *Souverains et Notabilités d'Indochine*. Hanoi: Editions du Gouvernement Général de L'Indochine, 1943.

———. "Le thermalisme et le climatisme en Indochine." *Le Monde thermal* (April 1930).

d'Anthouard (de Wasservas), Albert. *Mes souvenirs: Cochinchine, 1881–1885*. Brioude: Watel, 1927.

d'Argenlieu, Thierry. *Chronique d'Indochine*. Paris: Albin Michel, 1985.

Armand, Adolphe. *Médecine et hygiène des pays chauds*. Paris: Challamel ainé, 1853.

Bao Dai. *Le Dragon d'Annam*. Paris: Plon, 1980.

Bat Long. *Du-Lich Trung Ky [Travelling in Annam]*. Hué: Tiêng Dân, 1930.

Bernard, Fernand. *Indo-Chine, erreurs et dangers: Un programme*. Paris: Charpentier, 1901.

Bernard, François-Eugène. "De l'influence du climat de la Cochinchine sur les maladies des Européens." PhD thesis in medicine, University of Montpellier, 1867.

de la Blache, Paul Vidal. *Principes de Géographie humaine*. Paris: Armand Colin, 1922.

Bochet, Gilbert. *Eléments de conversation franco-koho: Us et coutumes des montagnards de la Province du Haut-Donnaï*. Dalat: Service géographique de l'Indochine, 1951.

Bodard, Lucien. *La Guerre d'Indochine, l'enlisement*. Paris: Gallimard, 1963.

Bodinier, Gilbert. *La Guerre d'Indochine, 1947, textes et documents*. Vincennes: Service Historique de l'Armée de Terre, 1989.

de Boisanger, Claude. *On pouvait éviter la guerre d'Indochine*. Paris: Maisonneuve, 1977.

Bonnafy, Dr. "Statistique médicale de la Cochinchine, 1861–1888." *Archives de médecine navale* 67 (mars 1897): 161–96.

Borel, Marius. *Souvenirs d'un vieux colonialiste*. Borel: Rodez, 1963.

Bouvard, Pierre, and M. Millet. *La Chasse au Lang Bian*. Bergerac: Imprimerie du Sud-Ouest, 1920.

Canivey, Jules. "Notice sur les moeurs et coutumes des Moï de la region de Dalat." *Revue d'ethnographie et de sociologie* (1913): 1–30.

Carton, P., and Henry Morin. *De l'influence des facteurs climatiques sur la répartition de l'endémie palustre en Indochine*. Hanoi: Imprimerie d'Extrême-Orient, 1934.

Cassaigne, Jean. *Petit manuel de conversation courante en langue Moï, à l'usage des planteurs, chasseurs, touristes, région Djiring-Dalat*. Saigon: Imprimerie de la Mission, 1930.

Chivas-Baron, Clothilde. *La Femme française aux colonies*. Paris: Larose, 1929.

Clauzel, Jean, ed. *La France d'outre-mer, 1930–1960: Témoignages d'administrateurs et de magistrats*. Paris: Karthala, 2003.

Condominas, Georges. *Nous avons mangé la forêt: Chronique d'un village mnong gar, hauts plateaux du Viet-Nam*. Paris: Mercure de France, 1974.

Danguy des Déserts, Auguste-Pascal-Marie. "Considérations sur l'hygiène de l'Européen en Cochinchine." Medical thesis, University of Paris, 1876.

Debay, Victor A. *La colonisation en Annam*. Paris: H. Charles-Lavauzelle, 1904.

———. "Un Sanatorium pour l'Annam Central." *Revue des Troupes coloniales* (1904): 1–43.

Decoux, Jean. *A la barre de l'Indochine: Histoire de mon Gouvernement Général, 1940–1945*. Paris: Plon, 1959.

Demariaux, J. C. *La grande chasse au Darlac indochinois*. Paris: Peyronnet, 1949.

Dioque, Georges, ed. *Félix Dioque, Un Colonial: Six ans en Guinée . . . Quarante ans en Indochine*. Gap: Société d'études des Hautes Alpes, 2008.

Direction de l'Instruction publique. *Le Petit Lycée de Dalat*. Hanoi: Imprimerie d'Extrême-Orient, 1930.

Doumer, Paul. *Situation de L'Indochine, 1897–1901*. Hanoi: Schneider, 1902.

Eberhardt, Gabrielle. "Le futur sanatorium de l'Annam: Le Langbiang." *Le Tour du monde* 14, no. 25 (June 20, 1908): 289–300.

d'Enjoy, Paul. *Indochine française: Etude pratique de la législation civile annamite*. Paris: Imprimerie de Roussel, 1894.

———. *La santé aux colonies: Manuel d'hygiène et de prophylaxie climatologiques, médecine coloniale*. Paris: Société d'éditions scientifiques, 1901.

Flower, Henry C., Jr. "On the trail of the Lord Tiger." *Asia: The American Magazine of the Orient* (October 1920): 893–97.

Frenay, Henry. *La nuit finira*. Paris: Robert Laffont, 1973.

Gaide, Dr. *Les stations climatiques en Indochine*. Hanoi: IDEO, 1930.

Gaffarel, Paul. *Les colonies françaises*. Paris: Felix Alcan, 1888.

Glérende, Yves. "Bana et Bach-Ma, stations d'altitude de l'Annam." *Le Monde colonial illustré* (September 1939): 216–17.

Godart, Justin. *Rapport de Mission en Indochine, 1937*. Paris: L'Harmattan, 1994.

Goineaud-Bérard, André. *Indo 46: C'était encore l'Indochine française*. Paris: Publibook, 2003.

Gourou, Pierre. *La Terre et l'homme en Extrême-Orient*. Paris: Flammarion, 1972.

Gribius, André. *Une Vie d'Officier*. Paris: Editions France-Empire, 1971.

Guérin, Mathieu, and Arnoult Seveau, eds. "Manuscrit de Pierre Dru, extrait." *Outre-mers, revue d'histoire* 362, no. 3 (2009): 167–87.

Harrison, Archibald. *Indochina, a Sportsman's Opportunity*. Plymouth: Mayflower Press, 1933.

Haut-Commissariat de France pour l'Indochine. *Lycée Yersin, Dalat*. Dalat: Imprimerie Verdun, 1948.

Ho Chi Minh. *Oeuvres choisies*. Paris: Maspéro, 1967.

———. *Selected Works*. Hanoi: Foreign Language Publishing, 1961.

Jacomme, Madeleine. *Vers les mimosas de Dalat*. Longueuil, Québec: Editions Philémon, 2003.

Lefèvre, Kim. *Métisse blanche*. Paris: Bernard Barrault, 1989.

Lémure, Jean. *Madagascar, l'expédition au point de vue médical et hygiénique: L'acclimatement et la colonisation*. Paris: Baillière et fils, 1896.

Léon, A. *Souvenirs d'un médecin de la marine 1853–1867*. Paris: L. Battaille and co., 1896.

Maitre, Henri. *Mission H. Maitre: Indochine Sud-Centrale, Les Jungles Moï*. Paris: Emile Larose, 1912.

———. *Les régions Moïs du Sud Indo-Chinois*. Paris: Plon, 1909.

Merle, Fernand. *Un Voyage au long cours: Les aventures d'un médecin outre-mer*. Paris: Albin Michel, 1984.

Montpensier, Duc de. *En Indochine: Mes chasses, mes voyages*. Paris: Pierre Lafite et Compagnie, 1912.

Mordant, Général Eugène. *Au service de la France en Indochine*. Saigon: IFOM, 1950.

Mourey, Dominique. *Mon Lycée en Annam*. Toulon: Presses du Midi, 2004.

Nicolas, Pierre. *Notes sur la vie française en Cochinchine*. Paris: Flammarion, 1900.

Nordemann, Edmond. *Connaissances nécessaires aux personnes appelées à faire leur carrière en Indochine: Conférence faite à l'école coloniale le 8 mars 1910*. Paris: Imprimerie Chaix, 1910.

Office central du Tourisme indochinois. *Dalat*. Hanoi: 1943.

Palud, Lazare-Gabriel-Marie. "Un Transport-hôpital au point de vue hygiénique et thérapeutique." Thèse pour le doctorat en médecine. Bordeaux, 1886.

Parrel, Fernand. "Au Village Saint-Jean de Dalat." *Missionnaires d'Asie* (1949): 56–59.

Pineau, Louis-Georges. *Dalat, Capitale administrative de l'Indochine*. Hanoi: Imprimerie d'Extrême-Orient, 1937.

———. "Le Plan d'aménagement et d'extension de Dalat." *La Vie urbaine* 49 (1939).

du Puy-Montbun, Déodat. *L'Honneur de la guerre*. Paris: Albin Michel, 2002.

Rouget, Jean. *Indochine, les dernières moussons: Un regard sur les rapports France-Vietnam*. Panazol: Charles Lavauzelle, 2004.

Roussel, Lucien. *La chasse en Indochine*. Paris, Librairie Plon, 1913.

Salan, Raoul. *Mémoires, Fin d'un empire*. Paris: Presses de la Cité, 1970.

Salles, Louis. "Tornade jaune: six mois dans l'oeil du typhoon: Souvenirs de Louis Salles, ancien Proviseur du Lycée Yersin, membre du Bureau français de liaison, Dalat, 1945." Unpublished manuscript in author's collection.

Sersiron, Gilbert. *Rapport sur le paludisme en Algérie considéré comme maladie sociale*. Paris: Octave Douin, 1905.

Shellshear, Iphigénie-Catherine. *Far from the Tamarind Tree: A Childhood Account of Indochine*. Double-Bay, Australia: Longueville Media, 2003.

Shortt, Henry Edward. "The occurrence of malaria in a hill station." *Indian Journal of Medical Research* 11, no. 3 (January 1924): 771–89.

Silbermann, Léon [Le soldat Silbermann]. *Cinq ans à la Légion étrangère, Dix ans dans l'infanterie de marine, Souvenirs de campagne*. Paris: Plon, 1910.

Tardif, Etienne. *La Naissance de Dalat, 1899–1900*. Vienne: Ternet-Martin, 1948.

———. *Un Sanatorium en Annam: La mission du Lang-Bian*. Vienne: Ogeret-Martin, 1902.

de Tessan, François. *Dans l'Asie qui s'éveille*. Paris: La Renaissance du Livre, 1923.

———. "Une station d'altitude en Indochine." *L'Illustration* (February 17, 1923).

Tran Chanh Thanh. "Statut politique et juridique des plateaux Moïs." *Revue indochinoise, juridique et économique* 17 (1942): 118–32.

Treillard, M. "Une modalité de la zoophilie anophélienne en Indochine méridionale: Neocellia fuliginosa à la station d'altitude de Dalat, Annam." *Bulletin de Pathologie exotique* 27 (1934).

Treille, Georges. *Hygiène coloniale*. Paris: Masson et Cie., 1899.

Trinquier, Roger. *Les Maquis d'Indochine: Les Missions spéciales du service Action*. Paris: Albatros, 1976.

Van Tien Dung. *Our Great Spring Victory: An Account of the Liberation of South Vietnam*. New York: Monthly Review Press, 1977.

Vassal, Gabrielle. *On and Off Duty in Annam*. London: Heinemann, 1910.

Viollis, Andrée. *Indochine SOS*. Paris: Les bons caractères, 2008.

Vo Nguyen Giap. *Unforgettable Days*. Hanoi: Foreign Language Publishing, 1975.

Werth, Léon. *Cochinchine*. Paris: Vivianne Hamy, 1997.

SECONDARY SOURCES

Adler, Laure. *Marguerite Duras*. Paris: Gallimard, 1998.

Ahounou, Chantal, ed. *A la recherche de Voulet: Sur les traces sanglantes de la mission Afrique centrale*. Paris: Cosmopole, 2001.

Aiken, Robert. *Imperial Belvederes: The Hill Stations of Malaya*. Kuala Lumpur: Oxford University Press, 1994.

Anderson, Benedict. *Imagined Communities: Reflections on the Origin and Spread of Nationalism*. New York: Verso, 1991.

Anderson, Warwick. "Climates of Opinion: Acclimatization in Nineteenth-century France and England." *Victorian Studies* 35 (1992): 2–24.

———. *The Cultivation of Whiteness: Science, Health and Racial Destiny in Australia*. Melbourne: University of Melbourne Press, 2002.

———. "Disease, Race and Empire." *The Bulletin of the History of Medicine* 70 (1996): 62–67.

Angladette, André. "La vie quotidienne en Indochine de 1939 à 1946." *Mondes et cultures: Comptes rendus trimestriels des séances de l'Académie des sciences d'outre-mer* 39, no. 3 (June 1979): 467–98.

Anonymous. *Hommes et destins.* Paris: Académie des sciences d'outre-mer, 1988.

———. *Les Nôtres au Vietnam, Mission accomplie.* Sainte-Anne de Beaupré: Les Rédomptaristes, 1982.

Arnold, David. *Colonizing the Body: State Medicine and Epidemic Disease in Nineteenth-Century India.* Berkeley: University of California Press, 1993.

Ban Tuyên Giáo tỉnh ủy Lâm Đồng [Propaganda Commitee of Lam Dong Province], *Cách mạng tháng 8 năm 1945 ở Lâm Đồng [The August 1945 Revolution in Lam-Dong Province].* Dalat: Tháng, 1995.

Bashford, Alison. "Is White Australia Possible? Race, Colonialism and Tropical Medicine," *Ethnic and Racial Studies* 23:2 (2000), 248–71.

Bezançon, Pascale. *Une colonisation éducatrice? L'expérience indochinoise, 1860–1945.* Paris: L'Harmattan, 2002.

Bhasin, Raja. *Simla, the Summer Capital of British India.* London: Penguin, 1992.

Bhatt, Vikram. *Resorts of the Raj: Hill Stations of India.* Ahmedabad: Mapin Publishing, 1997.

Blais, Hélène. Les enquêtes des cartographes en Algérie, ou les ambiguïtés des savoirs vernaculaires en situation coloniale," *Revue d'histoire moderne et contemporaine* 54:4 (2007), 70–85.

Blunt, Alison. "Home, Identity and Nationality for Anglo-Indians in British India, 1919–1947," *History Workshop Journal* 54 (2002), 49–72.

Boltanski, Luc. *Prime éducation et morale de classe.* Paris: Mouton, 1969.

Bowd, Gavin, and Daniel Clayton. "Tropicality, Orientalism and French Colonialism in Indochina: the Work of Pierre Gourou." *French Historical Studies* 28, no. 2 (Spring 2005): 297–327.

Bradley, Mark Philip. *Imagining Vietnam and America: The Making of Postcolonial Vietnam, 1919–1950.* Chapel Hill: University of North Carolina Press, 2000.

Bradley Winston, Jane, and Leakthina Chau-Pech Ollier. *Of Vietnam: Identities in Dialogue.* New York: Palgrave, 2001.

Branche, Raphaëlle. *La Torture et la guerre d'Algérie.* Paris: Gallimard, 2001.

Brocheux, Pierre. "Le colonialisme français en Indochine." In *Livre noir du colonialisme: De l'extermination à la repentance,* ed. Marc Ferro, 351–72. Paris: Robert Laffont, 2003.

———. *Ho Chi Minh, a Biography.* Cambridge: Cambridge University Press, 2007.

Brocheux, Pierre, and Daniel Hémery. *Indochine, la colonisation ambiguë.* Paris: La Découverte, 2001.

Brossollet, Jacqueline, and Henri Mollaret. *Yersin: Un Pasteurien en Indochine.* First published by Fayard in 1985, reedited in 1993 by Belin.

Brower, Benjamin. *A Desert Named Peace: The Violence of France's Empire in the Algerian Sahara, 1844–1902.* New York: Columbia University Press, 2009.

Bührlein, Monika. *Nuwara Eliya: Hill Station und Zentraler Ort im Hochland der Insel Ceylon.* Stuttgart: Franz Steiner, 1991.

Bui Minh Dung. "Japan's role in the Vietnamese Starvation of 1944–1945." *Modern Asian Studies* 29, no. 3 (July 1995): 573–618.

Buttinger, Joseph. *Vietnam: A Dragon Embattled.* New York: Praeger, 1967.

Çelik, Zeynep. *Urban Forms and Colonial Confrontations: Algiers under French Rule.* Berkeley: University of California Press, 1997.

Chafer, Tony, and Amanda Sackur. *French Colonial Empire and the Popular Front: Hope and Disillusion.* London: St. Martin's Press, 1999.

Clément, Pierre et al. *Hanoi, le cycle des metamorphoses.* Paris: Ipraus, 2001.

Cohen, Roger. "Indochina Dreaming." *New York Times,* June 1, 2009.

Cohen, William B. "The Colonial Policy of the Popular Front." *French Historical Studies* 7, no. 2 (Spring 1972): 368–93.

———. "Malaria and French Imperialism." *The Journal of African History* 24 (1983): 23–36.

Cohn, Bernard. *Colonialism and its Forms of Knowledge: The British in India.* Princeton: Princeton University Press, 1996.

Combeau, Yvan. *Paris et les élections municipales sous la 3ème République.* Paris: L'Harmattan, 1998.

Conklin, Alice. "Civil Society, Science and Empire in Late Republican France: The Foundation of Paris's Museum of Man." *Osiris* 17 (2002): 255–90.

———. *A Mission to Civilize: The Republican Idea of Empire in France and West Africa, 1895–1930.* Stanford: Stanford University Press, 1997.

Crossette, Barbara. *The Great Hill Stations of Asia.* Boulder: Westview Press, 1998.

Curtin, Philip. *Death by Migration: Europe's Encounters with the Tropical World in the Nineteenth Century.* Cambridge: Cambridge University Press, 1989.

Curtis, Sarah. "Charitable Ladies: Gender, Class and Religion in Mid-Nineteenth Century Paris." *Past and Present* 177 (2002): 121–56.

Daughton, J. P. *An Empire Divided: Religion, Republicanism and the Making of French Colonialism.* Oxford: Oxford University Press, 2006.

David, Gilbert. *Chroniques secrètes de l'Indochine.* Paris: L'Harmattan, 1994.

Del Testa, David. "Imperial Corridor: Association, Transportation and Power in French Colonial Indochina." *Science, Technology and Society* 4, no. 2 (1999): 319–54.

———. "Paint the railroads red: Labor, nationalism and the railroads in French colonial Indochina, 1898–1945." PhD thesis, University of California at Davis, 2001.

Demay, Aline. "Tourisme sanitaire au Tonkin: Le cas de Cha Pa." *Ultramarines* 25 (2007): 42–48.

Dembour, Marie-Bénédicte. "La chicote comme symbole du colonialisme belge?" *Canadian Journal of African Studies* 26, no. 2 (1992): 205–25.

Déry, Steve. *La colonisation agricole au Viêt Nam: Contribution à l'étude de la construction d'un État moderne; du bouleversement à l'intégration des Plateaux centraux.* Québec: Les Presses de l'Université du Québec, 2004.

Deslandres, Dominique. *Croire et faire croire: Les missions françaises au xviième siècle.* Paris: Fayard, 2003.

Deuve, Jean. Review of *Chroniques secrètes de l'Indochine,* by Gilbert David. *Guerres mondiales et conflits contemporains* 220 (2005): 152–56.

Devillers, Philippe. *Français et Annamites: Partenaires ou ennemis? 1856–1902.* Paris: Denoël, 1998.

———. *Histoire du Viet-Nam de 1940 à 1952.* Paris: Editions du Seuil, 1952.

———. *Paris, Saigon, Hanoi, les archives de la guerre 1944–1947.* Paris: Gallimard, 1988.

Dommen, Arthur J. *The Indochinese Experience of the French and the Americans.* Bloomington: Indiana University Press, 2001.

Duiker, William. *Ho Chi Minh.* New York: Hyperion, 2000.

Duron, Bruno. "The Dalat Palace: A Hotel of the Past, Today." Unpublished manuscript.

Eckart, Wolfgang. "Creating Confidence: Heinrich Zeiss as a Traveller in the Soviet Union, 1921–1932." In *Doing Medicine Together: Germany and Russia Between the Wars,* edited by Susan Gross Solomon. University of Toronto Press, 2006, 199–239.

Eckart, Wolfgang, and H. Vondra. "Malaria and World War II: German malaria experiments 1939–1945." *Parassitologia* 42, nos. 1–2 (June 2000): 53–58.

Edwards, Kathryn. "Le Mal Jaune: The Memory of the Indochina War in France, 1954–2006," PhD thesis, University of Toronto, 2010.

Edwards, Penny. "Tango dancing in the blood of Bokor." *Phnom Penh Post,* March 27–April 9, 1998.

———. "The Tyranny of Proximity: Power and Mobility in Colonial Cambodia, 1863–1954." *The Journal of Southeast Asian Studies* 37, no. 3 (October 2006): 421–43.

Fabian, Johannes. *Language and Colonial Power.* Berkeley: University of California Press, 1986.

Faligot, Roger, and Pascal Krop. *La Piscine: Les services secrets français, 1944–1984.* Paris: Editions du Seuil, 1985.

Fall, Bernard. *Street Without Joy.* Harrisburg: Stackpole, 1964.

Ferro, Marc. *Histoire des colonisations.* Paris: Le Seuil, 1994.

Fife, Raymond. "Bach Ma: History and Archaeology of a French colonial hill station in Central Vietnam 1930–1990," PhD thesis, University of New England, Australia, 2009.

Firpo, Christina. "The durability of the empire: Race, empire and 'abandoned' children in colonial Vietnam, 1870—1956." PhD thesis, University of California at Los Angeles, 2007.

Ford, Caroline. "Nature, Culture, and Conservation in France and her Colonies." *Past and Present* 183 (May 2004): 173–98.

Fourniau, Charles. *Vietnam: Domination coloniale et résistance nationale, 1858–1914.* Paris: Les Indes savantes, 2002.

Fourniau, Charles, Trinh Van Thao, Gilles de Gantès, Philippe le Failler, Jean-Marie Mancini, and Gilles Raffi. *Le Contact colonial franco-vietnamien: Le premier demi-siècle, 1858–1911.* Aix-en-Provence: Presses universitaires de Provence, 1999.

Franchini, Philippe. *Les Mensonges de la Guerre d'Indochine.* Paris: CIDE, 2003.

Freidberg, Susanne. "French beans for the masses: A modern historical geography of food in Burkina Faso." *Journal of Historical Geography* 29, no. 3 (2003): 445–63.

Frenkel, Stephen, and John Western. "Pretext or Prophylaxis? Racial Segregation and Malarial Mosquitoes in a British Tropical Colony: Sierra Leone." *Annals of the Association of American Geographers* 78, no. 2 (1988): 211–28.

Furlough, Ellen. "Une leçon des choses: Tourism, Empire, and the Nation in Interwar France." *French Historical Studies* 25, no. 3 (2002): 441–73.

de Gantès, Gilles. "Coloniaux, Gouverneurs et Ministres: l'Influence des Français du Vietnam sur l'Evolution du pays à l'époque coloniale, 1902–1914." PhD thesis, University of Paris VII, 1994.

Garcia, Luc. *Quand les missionnaires rencontraient les Vietnamiens, 1920–1960.* Paris: Karthala, 2008.

Gaultier, Marcel. *La Tragédie indochinoise.* Paris: Editions Henrys, 1947.

Gerwarth, Robert, and Stephan Malinowski. "L'Antichambre de l'Holocauste? A propos du débat sur les violences coloniales et la guerre d'extermination nazie." *Vingtième Siècle, Revue d'Histoire* 99 (2008): 143–59.

Goerg, Odile. "Conakry: un modèle de ville coloniale française? Règlements fonciers et urbanisme de 1885 aux années 1920." *Cahiers d'Etudes africaines* 25, no. 3 (1985): 309–35.

Goscha, Christopher. "Alliés tardifs: Les apports techniques des déserteurs japonais au Viet-Minh durant les premières années de la guerre franco-vietnamienne." *Guerres mondiales et conflits contemporains* 202 (2001): 81–109.

———. "Récits de voyage viêtnamiens et prise de conscience indochinoise, 1920–1945." In *Récits de voyages des Asiatiques: Genres, mentalités, conceptions de l'espace,* edited by Claudine Salman, 253–79. Paris: EFEO, 1996.

———. *Vietnam or Indochina? Contesting Concepts of Space in Vietnamese Nationalism, 1887–1954.* Copenhagen: NIAS Press, 1995.

Gras, Philippe. *L'Armée de l'air en Indochine, 1945–1954: Mission impossible.* Paris: L'Harmattan, 2001.

Guénel, Annick. "The Creation of the First Overseas Pasteur Institute and the Beginning of Albert Calmette's Pastorian Career." *Medical History* 43 (1999): 1–25.

Guérin, Mathieu. "Des casques blancs sur le plateau des herbes: La pacification des aborigènes des hautes terres du Sud-Indochinois, 1859–1940." PhD thesis, University of Paris VII, 2003.

———. *Paysans de la forêt à l'époque coloniale: La pacification des aborigènes des hautes terres du Cambodge, 1863–1940.* Rennes: Presses Universitaires de Rennes, 2008.

Guillemin, Jeanne. "Choosing Scientific Patrimony: Sir Ronald Ross, Alphonse Laveran, and the Mosquito-Vector Hypothesis for Malaria." *Journal of the History of Medicine and Allied Sciences* 57, no. 4 (October 2002): 385–409.

Ha, Marie-Paule. "La Femme française aux colonies: Promoting Colonial Female Emigration at the Turn of the Century." *French Colonial History* 6 (2005): 205–24.

Hardy, Andrew. *Red Hills: Migrants and the State in the Highlands of Vietnam.* Honolulu: University of Hawai'i Press, 2003.

Harp, Stephen. "Marketing in the Metropole: Colonial Rubber Plantations and French Consumerism in the Early Twentieth Century." In *Views from the Margins: Creating Identities in Modern France,* edited by Sarah Curtis and Kevin Callahan, 84–107. Lincoln: Nebraska University Press, 2008.

Hémery, Daniel. "Asie du Sud-Est, 1945: Vers un nouvel impérialisme colonial? Le projet indochinois de la France au lendemain de la Seconde Guerre mondiale." In *Décolonisations européennes: Actes du colloque international "Décolonisations comparées,"* edited by Marc Michel. Aix-en-Provence: Publications de l'Université de Provence, 1995.

Herbelin, Caroline. "Dalat: modèle d'urbanisme colonial ou anecdote architecturale?" Forthcoming in *Cahiers d'études vietnamiennes.* All page numbers from the draft kindly provided by Caroline Herbelin.

Hickey, Gerald C. *Free in the Forest: Ethnohistory of the Vietnamese Central Highlands, 1954–1976.* New Haven: Yale University Press, 1982.

————. *Sons of the Mountains: Ethnohistory of the Vietnamese Central Highlands to 1954.* New Haven: Yale University Press, 1982.

Hoskins, Janet. "Postcards from the Edge of Empire: Images and Messages from French Indochina," *IIAS Newsletter* 44 (Summer 2007), 16–7.

Hue, Bernard. *Littératures de la péninsule indochinoise.* Paris: Karthala, 1999.

Hue-Tam Ho Tai. "The Politics of Compromise: The Constitutionalist Party and Electoral Reforms of 1922 in French Indochina." *Modern Asian Studies* 18, no. 3 (1984): 371–91.

————. *Radicalism and the Origins of the Vietnamese Revolution.* Cambridge: Harvard University Press, 1992.

Hull, Isabel. *Absolute Destruction: Military Culture and the Practice of War in Imperial Germany.* Cornell: Cornell University Press, 2004.

Jennings, Eric. "L'Affaire Dreyfus et l'univers colonial français." Numéro hors-série, "Zola l'homme récit, actes du colloque de Toronto," *Les cahiers naturalistes* 49 (June 2003): 39–50.

————. *Curing the Colonizers: Hydrotherapy, Climatology, and French Colonial Spas.* Raleigh: Duke University Press, 2006.

————. *Vichy in the Tropics: Pétain's National Revolution in Madagascar, Guadeloupe and Indochina, 1940–1944.* Stanford: Stanford University Press, 2001.

Jewsiewicki, Bogumil. *Mami Wata: la peinture urbaine au Congo.* Paris: Gallimard, 2003.

Jézéquel, Jean-Hervé. "Grammaire de la distinction coloniale. L'organisation des cadres de l'enseignement en Afrique occidentale française." *Genèses* 69 (2007): 4–25.

Kanwar, Pamela. "The Changing Profile of the Summer Capital of British India: Simla, 1864–1947." *Modern Asian Studies* 18, no. 2 (1984): 215–36.

Keith, Charles. "Catholic Vietnam: Church, Colonialism and Revolution, 1887–1945." PhD thesis, Yale University, 2008.

Kelly, Gail Paradise. *French Colonial Education: Essays on Vietnam and West Africa.* New York: AMS Press, 2000.

Kennedy, Dane. *The Magic Mountains: Hill Stations of the British Raj.* Berkeley, University of California Press, 1996.

————. "The Perils of the Midday Sun: Climatic Anxieties in the Colonial Tropics." In *Imperialism and the Natural World,* edited by John Mackenzie, 118–40. Manchester: University of Manchester Press, 1990.

Kenny, Judith. "Claiming the High Ground: Theories of Imperial Authority and the British Hill Station in India." *Political Geography* 16, no. 8 (1997): 655–73.

————. "Constructing an Imperial Hill Station: The Representation of British Authority in Ootacamund." PhD thesis, Syracuse University, 1990.

Kitson, Simon. *The Hunt for Nazi Spies: Fighting Espionage in Vichy France.* Chicago: University of Chicago Press, 2008.

Lafont, Pierre-Bernard. ed. *Péninsule indochinoise, Etudes urbaines.* Paris: L'Harmattan, 1991.

Larcher-Goscha, Agathe. "Volonté de puissance coloniale et puissance de volonté nationaliste: Aux origines de la création de l'école d'éducation physique d'Hanoi, 1913–1922." In *Sports et loisirs dans les colonies,* edited by Evelyne Combeau-Mari, 35–48. Paris: SEDES, 2004.

Lebovics, Herman. *True France: The Wars over Cultural Identity, 1900–1945.* Ithaca: Cornell University Press, 1992.

Le Brusq, Arnauld. *Le Vietnam à travers l'architecture coloniale.* Paris: Editions de l'Amateur, 1999.

Le Cour Grandmaison, Olivier. *Coloniser, Exterminer: Sur la guerre et l'Etat colonial.* Paris: Fayard, 2005.

Legrand, Julien. *L'Indochine à l'heure japonaise.* Cannes: Imprimerie Aegitna, 1963.

Lessard, Micheline. "We Know . . . the Duties We Must Fulfil: Modern 'Mothers and Fathers' of the Vietnamese Nation." *French Colonial History* 3 (2003): 119–41.

Le Van Ho, Mireille. "Le Général Pennequin et le projet d'Armée jaune, 1911–1915." *Revue française d'histoire d'outre-mer* 75, no. 279 (1988): 145–67.

Lindqvist, Sven. *Exterminate all the Brutes.* London: Granta, 1996.

Livingstone, David. "Human Acclimatization: Perspectives on a Contested Field of Enquiry in Science, Medicine and Geography." *History of Science* 15 (1987): 359–94.

———. "Race, Space and Moral Climatology: Notes toward a Geneology." *Journal of Historical Geography* 28, no. 2 (2002): 159–80.

Lorin, Amaury. "Dalat, station d'altitude: Fondation ex nihilo de Paul Doumer, Gouverneur Général de l'Indochine (1898)." *Péninsule* 52 (2006): 225–34.

Mackenzie, Callum. "Sadly neglected: Hunting and Gendered Identities." *The International Journal of the History of Sport* 22, no. 3 (July 2005): 545–62.

Marr, David. *Vietnam 1945.* Berkeley: University of California Press, 1995.

———. *Vietnamese Tradition on Trial.* Berkeley: University of California Press, 1981.

McHale, Shawn. *Print and Power: Confucianism, Communism and Buddhism in the Making of Modern Vietnam.* Honolulu: University of Hawai'i Press, 2004.

McKenzie, John. *The Empire of Nature: Hunting, Conservation and British Imperialism.* Manchester University Press, 1988.

Metcalf, Thomas. *An Imperial Vision: Indian Architecture and Britain's Raj.* Berkeley: University of California Press, 1989.

Meyer, Charles. *Les Français en Indochine, 1860–1910.* Paris: Hachette, 1995.

Michaud, Jean. *"Incidental" Ethnographers: French Catholic Missions on the Tonkin-Yunnan Frontier.* Leiden: Brill, 2007.

———. "The Montagnards and the State in Northern Vietnam from 1802 to 1975: A Historical Overview." *Ethnohistory* 47, no. 2 (Spring 2000): 333–68.

———. *Sapa français: Une brève histoire.* Sapa: Victoria, 1999.

Mitchell, Nora. *The Indian Hill-Station: Kodaikanal.* Chicago: University of Chicago Geography Department, 1972.

Mitman, Greg. "Hay Fever Holiday: Health, Leisure and Place in Gilded-age America." *Bulletin of the History of Medicine* 77, no. 3 (Fall 2003): 600–35.

Monnais-Rousselot, Laurence. *Médecine et colonisation: L'aventure indochinoise, 1860–1939.* Paris: CNRS Editions, 1999.

Moulin, Anne-Marie. "Expatriés français sous les tropiques: Cent ans d'histoire de la santé." *Bulletin de la Société de pathologie exotique* 90, no. 4 (1997): 268–72.

Murray, Alison. "Le tourisme Citroën au Sahara, 1924–1925." *Vingtième Siècle, Revue d'Histoire* 68 (October–December 2000): 95–107.

Nagaï, Nobuhito. *Les conseillers municipaux de Paris sous la 3ème République.* Paris: Publications de la Sorbonne, 2002.

Naraindas, Harish. "Poisons, Putrescence and the Weather." In *Les sciences hors d'occident au xxème siècle*. Vol. 4, *Médecines et santé, Medical Practices and Health* Paris: ORSTOM, 1996: 31–55.

Neill, Deborah. "Finding the Ideal Diet: Nutrition, Culture and Dietary Practices in France and Equatorial Africa, 1890s-1920s." *Food and Foodways* 17 (2009): 1–28.

———. *Networks in Tropical Medicine*, forthcoming with Stanford University Press.

Nguyen The Anh. "La frontière sino-vietnamienne du xième au xviième siècle." In *Les frontières du Vietnam*, edited by P. B. Lafont. Paris: L'Harmattan, 1989.

Nhung Tuyet Tran, and Anthony Reid, eds. *Viêt Nam: Borderless Histories*. Madison: University of Wisconsin Press, 2006.

Norindr, Panivong. *Phantasmatic Indochina: French Colonial Ideology in Architecture, Film and Literature*. Durham: Duke University Press, 1996.

Osborne, Michael. "Acclimatizing the World: A History of the Paradigmatic Colonial Science." *Osiris* 15 (2000): 135–51.

Papin, Philippe. *Histoire de Hanoi*. Paris: Fayard, 2001.

Peabody, Sue, and Tyler Stovall, eds. *The Color of Liberty: Histories of Race in France*. Raleigh: Duke University Press, 2003.

Pédelahore de Loddis, Christian. "Hanoi, miroir de l'architecture indochinoise." In *Architectures françaises outre-mer*. Wavre: Mardaga/IFA, 1992.

Peer, Shanny. *France on Display: Peasants, Provincials and Folklore in the 1937 Paris World's Fair*. Albany: SUNY Press, 1998.

Peters, Erica. "Negotiating Power through Everyday Practices in French Vietnam, 1880–1924." PhD thesis, University of Chicago, 2000.

Peyvel, Emmanuelle. "L'Emergence du Tourisme au Viêt Nam: Lieux, Pratiques et Imaginaires," PhD thesis, Université de Nice, 2009.

Pomfret, David. "Raising Eurasia: Race, Class and Age in French and British Colonies." *Comparative Studies in Society and History* 51, no. 2 (2009): 314–43.

Poujade, René. *Cours martiales d'Indochine, 1940–1945: Les evasions de Résistants dans l'Indochine occupée par les Japonais*. Paris: La Bruyère, 1997.

———. *l'Indochine dans la sphere de coprospérité japonaise de 1940 à 1945*. Paris: L'Harmattan, 2007.

Procida, Mary. "Good Sports and Right Sorts: Guns, Gender and Imperialism in British India." *The Journal of British Studies* 40, no. 4 (October 2001): 454–88.

Rabinow, Paul. *French Modern: Forms and Norms of the Social Environment*. Boston: MIT Press, 1989.

Reed, Robert. *City of Pines: The Origins of Baguio as a Colonial Hill Station and Regional Capital*. Berkeley: Center for South and Southeast Asian Studies, 1976.

———. "Constructing Highland Cities in Southeast Asia: Baguio (Philippines) and Dalat (Vietnam) as Scenes of Envrionmental Degradation." In *Southeast Asian Urban Environments*, edited by Carla Chifos and Ruth Yabes, 183–273. Tempe: Arizona State University Program for Southeast Asian Studies, 2000.

———. "From Highland Hamlet to Regional Capital: Reflections on the Colonial Origins, Urban Transformation and Environmental Impact of Dalat." In *The Challenges of High-*

land Development in Vietnam, edited by Terry Rambo, Robert Reed, Le Trong Cuc et al., 39–62. Hawaii: East-West Center Program on Environment, 1995.

Robson, Kathryn, and Jennifer Yee. *France and Indochina: Cultural Representations.* Lanham: Lexington Books, 2005.

Rosenberg, Clifford. "Albert Sarraut and Republican Racial Thought." *French Politics, Culture and Society* 20, no. 3 (Fall 2002): 97–114.

Saada, Emmanuelle. *Les Enfants de la Colonie: Les Métis de l'Empire français entre sujétion et citoyenneté.* Paris: La Découverte, 2007.

Salemink, Oscar. *The Ethnography of Vietnam's Central Highlanders.* Honolulu: University of Hawai&ʻi Press, 2003.

Sanjuan, Thierry, ed. *Les grands hôtels en Asie: Modernité, dynamiques urbaines et sociabilité.* Paris: Editions de la Sorbonne, 2003.

Scott, James. "Stilled to Silence at 500 Metres: Making Sense of Historical Change in Southeast Asia." *IIAS Newsletter* 49 (Fall 2008): 12–13.

Sharp, Ilsa. *There Is Only One Raffles: The Story of a Grand Hotel.* London: Souvenir Press, 1981.

Shepard, Todd. *The Invention of Decolonization: The Algerian War and the Remaking of France.* Ithaca: Cornell University Press, 2006.

Sherman, Daniel. "Paradis à vendre: tourisme et imitation en Polynésie française: 1958–1971." *Terrain* 44 (March 2005): 39–56.

Shipway, Martin. *The Road to War: France and Vietnam, 1944–1947.* New York: Berghahn, 1996.

Singaravélou, Pierre. *L'Ecole française d'Extrême-Orient ou l'institution des marges: 1898–1956.* Paris: L'Harmattan, 1999.

Slavin, David. *Colonial Cinema and Imperial France: White Blind Spots, Male Fantasies, Settler Myths.* Johns Hopkins University Press: Baltimore, 2001.

Smith, Ralph B. "The Japanese Period in Indochina and the Coup of 9 March 1945." *Journal of Southeast Asian Studies* 9, no. 2 (September 1978): 268–301.

Stepan, Nancy. "Biological Degeneration: Races and Proper Places." In *Degeneration: The Dark Side of Progress,* edited by J. Edward Chamberlin and Sander Gilman, 97–120. New York: Columbia University Press, 1985.

Stewart, Mary. " 'Let us begin with the Weather': Climate, Race, and Cultural Distinctiveness." In *Nature and Society in Historical Context,* edited by Mikulas Teich, Roy Porter, and Bo Gustafsson, 240–56. Cambridge: Cambridge University Press, 1997.

Templer, Robert. *Shadows and Wind: A View of Modern Vietnam.* London: Penguin, 1998.

Thomas, Frédéric. "L'Invention des 'Hauts Plateaux' en Indochine." *Ethnologie française* 34, no. 4 (2004): 639–49.

Thomas, Martin. "Free France, the British Government and the Future of French Indo-China, 1940–1945." *Journal of Southeast Asian Studies* 28, no. 1 (March 1997): 137–60.

———. *The French Empire at War, 1940–1945.* Manchester: Manchester University Press, 1998.

———. *The French Empire between the Wars: Imperialism, Politics and Society.* Manchester: Manchester University Press, 2005.

To Anh Dang. "La villa en ville: La transformation morphologique de l'architecture des villas coloniales françaises à Hanoi." Master's thesis, Hanoi University and the Ecole d'Architecture de Toulouse, 2004.

Tønnesson, Stein. *Vietnam, 1946: How the War Began.* Berkeley: University of California Press, 2010.

——. *The Vietnamese Revolution of 1945.* London: Sage, 1991.

Trinh Van Tao. *L'école française en Indochine.* Paris: Karthala, 1995.

Truong Nhu Tang. *Journal of a Viet Cong.* London: Jonathan Cape, 1986.

Truong Phuc An, ed. *Dalat Tram Nam [A Hundred Years of History of Dalat].* Dalat: Tourist office, 1993.

Truong Tro and Vuong Lan, eds. *Dalat ville d'altitude.* Ho Chi Minh City, 1993.

Tucker, Spencer C. *Vietnam.* London: UCL Press, 1999.

Turley, William S. *The Second Indochina War.* Boulder: Westview Press, 1986.

Urban, Yerri. "Race et nationalité dans le droit colonial français, 1865–1955." PhD thesis in public law, Université de Bourgogne, 2009.

Vallier, Jean. *C'était Marguerite Duras.* Paris: Fayard, 2006.

Vann, Libby. "Discovering the Alps in Indochina: European Nature and the French Colonial Sanatorium of Dalat, 1893–1927." Paper presented to the department of anthropology, University of Virginia, April 7, 1997.

Vann, Michael. "White City on the Red River: Race, Power and Culture in French Colonial Hanoi, 1872–1954." PhD thesis, University of California at Santa Cruz, 1999.

Verney, Sébastien. "Le nécessaire compromis colonial: le cas de la Plantation Michelin de Dau Tieng de 1932 à 1937." In *Les Administrations coloniales, xixème-xxème siècles: Esquisse d'une histoire comparée,* edited by Samia El Mechat. Rennes: Presses Universitaires de Rennes, 2009.

——. "La Révolution nationale, matrice d'une construction identitaire dans un contexte colonial," PhD thesis, University of St Etienne, 2010.

Waters, Julia. *Duras and Indochina: Postcolonial Perspectives.* Liverpool: SFPS, 2006.

White, Owen. *Children of the French Empire: Miscegenation and Colonial Society in French West Africa, 1895–1960.* Oxford: Oxford University Press, 1999.

Winichakul, Thongchai. *Siam Mapped: A History of the Geo-Body of a Nation.* Honolulu: University of Hawai'i Press, 1994.

Wonders, Karen. "Hunting Narratives of the Age of Empire: A Gender Reading of Their Iconography." *Environment and History* 11, no. 3 (2005): 269–91.

Woodside, Alexander. "The Development of Social Organizations in Vietnamese Cities in the Late Colonial Period." *Pacific Affairs* 44, no. 1 (Spring 1971): 39–64.

Wright, Gwendolyn. *The Politics of Design in French Colonial Architecture.* Chicago: University of Chicago Press, 1991.

Xuan Phuong. *Ao Dai: Du Couvent des Oiseaux à la jungle du Viêt-Minh.* Paris: Plon, 2001.

Zinoman, Peter. *The Colonial Bastille: A History of Imprisonment in Vietnam, 1862–1940.* Berkeley: University of California Press, 2001.

Zytnicki, Colette, and Habib Kazdaghli, eds. *Le Tourisme dans l'Empire français: Politiques, pratiques et imaginaires.* Paris: Société française d'histoire d'outre-mer, 2009.

FICTION

Bataille, Christophe. *Annam*. Paris: Arléa, 1993.

Bergot, Erwan. *Sud lointain*. Paris: France loisirs, 1997.

Duras, Marguerite. *L'Amant*. Paris: Les Editions de Minuit, 1984.

———. *L'Amant de la Chine du Nord*. Paris: Gallimard, 1991.

Groslier, Georges. *Le Retour à l'argile*. Pondichéry: Kailash Editions, original edition 1928, republished 1996.

Nguyen Tien Lang. *Indochine la douce*. Hanoi: Nam-Ky, 1936.

Orwell, George. *Burmese Days*. Harmondsworth: Penguin, 1985.

Sportès, Morgan. *Tonkinoise*. Paris: Le Seuil, 1995.

INDEX

TEXT

10/12.5 Minion Pro

DISPLAY

Minion Pro

COMPOSITOR:

Integrated Composition Systems

PRINTER AND BINDER

Sheridan Books, Inc.